PARABLES FOR PREACHERS

Parables for Preachers
The Gospel of Luke
Year C

Barbara E. Reid, O.P.

A Liturgical Press Book

 THE LITURGICAL PRESS
Collegeville, Minnesota

www.litpress.org

Cover design by Greg Becker

Year B: 0-8146-2551-7
Year C: 0-8146-2552-5

1	2	3	4	5	6	7	8

Library of Congress Cataloging-in-Publication Data

Reid, Barbara E.
    Parables for preachers / Barbara E. Reid.
      p. c.m.
    Includes bibliographical references.
    Contents: — [2] Year B. The Gospel of Mark.
    ISBN 0-8146-2551-7 (v. 2 : alk. paper)
    1. Jesus Christ—Parables—Homiletical use. 2. Bible. N.T.
Mark—Criticism, interpretation, etc. 3. Bible. N.T. Mark—
Homiletical use. 4. Lectionary preaching—Catholic Church.
BT375.2.R45 1999
226.8'06—dc21   99-28090
                                               CIP

In gratitude to those preachers,
especially my Dominican sisters,
whose telling of the gospel story
has fed and converted me.

Contents

Lukan Parables in the Lectionary

Lukan parables are assigned for the gospel reading on seventeen Sundays of Year C. All but one are repeated in the weekday Lectionary. The parable of the prodigal son is proclaimed on two Sundays. Eight parables of Luke that do not appear in the Sunday Lectionary are assigned for weekday reading. The Lukan version of the parable of the vineyard and the tenants (20:9-19) is omitted from the Lectionary.

SUNDAY AND WEEKDAY LECTIONARIES:

Luke 13:1-9	Third Sunday of Lent
	Saturday of the Twenty-ninth Week of Ordinary Time
Luke 15:1-3, 11-32	Fourth Sunday of Lent
	Saturday of the Second Week of Lent
Luke 4:21-30	Fourth Sunday of Ordinary Time
	Monday of the Twenty-second Week of Ordinary Time (Luke 4:16-30)
Luke 6:39-45	Eighth Sunday of Ordinary Time
	Friday of the Twenty-third Week of Ordinary Time (Luke 6:39-42)
Luke 7:36–8:3	Eleventh Sunday of Ordinary Time
	Thursday of the Twenty-fourth Week of Ordinary Time (Luke 7:36-50)
Luke 10:25-37	Fifteenth Sunday of Ordinary Time

Luke 18:1-8	Twenty-ninth Sunday of Ordinary Time
	Saturday of the Thirty-second Week of Ordinary Time
Luke 18:9-14	Thirtieth Sunday of Ordinary Time

WEEKDAY LECTIONARY:

The following Lukan parables appear only in the weekday lectionary:

Luke 5:33-39	Friday of the Twenty-second Week of Ordinary Time
Luke 6:43-49	Saturday of the Twenty-third Week of Ordinary Time
Luke 7:31-35	Wednesday of the Twenty-fourth Week of Ordinary Time
Luke 8:4-15	Saturday of the Twenty-fourth Week of Ordinary Time
Luke 13:18-21	Tuesday of the Thirtieth Week of Ordinary Time
Luke 14:15-24	Tuesday of the Thirty-first Week of Ordinary Time
Luke 19:11-28	Wednesday of the Thirty-third Week of Ordinary Time
Luke 21:29-33	Friday of the Thirty-fourth Week of Ordinary Time

Abbreviations

AB	Anchor Bible
ABD	*Anchor Bible Dictionary,* ed. David N. Freedman
ABRL	Anchor Bible Reference Library
ANEP	*Ancient Near East in Pictures,* ed. J. B. Pritchard
AsSeign	*Assemblées du Seigneur*
B.C.E.	Before the Christian Era
BDF	F. Blass, A. Debrunner, and R. W. Funk, *A Greek Grammar of the NT*
Bib	*Biblica*
BibInt	*Biblical Interpretation*
BibRev	*Bible Review*
BibSac	*Bibliotheca Sacra*
BR	*Biblical Research*
BTB	*Biblical Theology Bulletin*
BullBibRes	*Bulletin for Biblical Research*
C.E.	Christian Era
CBQ	*Catholic Biblical Quarterly*
CBQMS	CBQ Monograph Series
CPDBT	*Collegeville Pastoral Dictionary of Biblical Theology*
CurTM	*Currents in Theology and Mission*
EB	Études Bibliques
EspVie	*Esprit et Vie*
ETL	*Ephemerides theologicae lovanienses*

ExpTim	*Expository Times*
GNS	Good News Studies Series
HeyJ	*Heythrop Journal*
HTS	Harvard Theological Studies
IBS	*Irish Biblical Studies*
ICC	International Critical Commentary
Int	*Interpretation*
JBL	*Journal of Biblical Literature*
JEvThSoc	*Journal of the Evangelical Theological Society*
JR	*Journal of Religion*
JSJ	*Journal for the Study of Judaism*
JSNT	*Journal for the Study of the New Testament*
JSNTSup	JSNT Supplement Series
JSOT	*Journal for the Study of the Old Testament*
JTS	*Journal of Theological Studies*
LXX	Septuagint (Greek Translation of the Hebrew OT)
MillStud	*Milltown Studies*
NAB	*New American Bible*
NIGTC	New International Greek Testament Commentary
NJB	*New Jerusalem Bible*
NJBC	*New Jerome Biblical Commentary,* ed. R. E. Brown et al.
NovT	*Novum Testamentum*
NRSV	*New Revised Standard Version*
NT	New Testament
NTMS	New Testament Message Series
NTS	*New Testament Studies*
OBT	Overtures to Biblical Theology
OT	Old Testament
RB	*Revue Biblique*

REB	*Revised English Bible*
RevExp	*Review & Expositor*
RSR	*Religious Studies Review*
SBEC	Studies in the Bible and Early Christianity Series
SBL	Society of Biblical Literature
SBLDS	Society of Biblical Literature Dissertation Series
SBLEJL	Society of Biblical Literature Early Judaism and Its Literature
SBLMS	Society of Biblical Literature Monograph Series
ScEs	*Science et Esprit*
SJT	*Scottish Journal of Theology*
SNTSMS	Society for New Testament Studies Monograph Series
SNTW	Studies of the New Testament and Its World
TBT	*The Bible Today*
USQR	*Union Seminary Quarterly Review*
WUNT	Wissenschaftliche Untersuchungen zum Neuen Testament
ZNW	*Zeitschrift für die neutestamentliche Wissenschaft*

Introduction

A disciple once complained,
  "You tell us stories,
  but you never reveal their meaning to us."
Said the master,
  "How would you like it if someone
  offered you fruit and masticated it
  before giving it to you?"[1]

In the Synoptic Gospels, Jesus rarely explains his parables.[2] They are meant to be wrestled with by each generation of hearers who allow themselves to be disturbed and challenged by Jesus' subversive stories. Yet Sunday after Sunday preachers are asked to open up the meaning of parables to their congregations. How can a preacher avoid offering pre-masticated fruit? How can the one who opens up the Scriptures do so in a way that enhances the savory offerings therein without ruining the power of the story? How can a preacher offer fresh fare when the same parable appears time after time in the Lectionary?

The first aim of this book is to aid preachers by bringing together current biblical research on the parables, in the hope that it will open new vistas of meaning for them and will spark their own creativity. Second, the book offers an understanding of how parables communicate, and invites the preacher to try out parabolic techniques of preaching. The Synoptic Gospels show Jesus preaching primarily by means of parables, spoken and lived. A greater understanding of the dynamics and meaning of

---

[1] Anthony de Mello, *The Song of the Bird* (Garden City, N.Y.: Doubleday, 1984) 1.

[2] The exceptions are the seed parable explained in Luke 8:11-15 and pars., the parable of the weeds explained in Matthew 13:36-43, and the explanation of defilement from within in Mark 7:17-23. Most scholars believe these to be creations of the early church and not from the lips of Jesus.

1

Jesus' parables in their original context can aid preachers today in creating the same effect in modern believers in a new context. This book is intended not only for preachers, but for all who are interested in a deeper understanding of the parables, particularly teachers, catechists, liturgy planners, and members of groups for homily preparation, Bible study, or faith sharing.

PARABLES IN THE LECTIONARY

The term "parable" covers a wide range of figurative speech: similitudes, extended metaphors, symbolic expressions, exemplary and true-to-life stories. Included in this volume are all passages in the Gospel of Luke in which the term *parabolē* ("parable") occurs[3] with the exception of the parable of the vineyard and the tenants (20:9-19), which does not appear in the Lectionary.[4] Also included are similes with variations of the phrase *homoios estin*, "[such] is like . . ." (6:47, 48, 49; 7:31, 32; 12:36; 13:18, 19, 21) and *houtōs*, "in the same way" (14:33) or "so should it be with you" (17:10). Included as well are Lukan stories such as The Two Debtors (7:40-42), The Good Samaritan (10:25-37), The Friend at Midnight (11:5-8), The Dishonest Steward (16:1-13), The Rich Man and Lazarus (16:19-31), and The Great Feast (14:15-24) that are clearly parabolic, though the term is not used of them in the gospel itself. There are other sayings and stories that could well be considered parabolic not included in this study. In one sense, the whole gospel can be regarded as a parable. As John R. Donahue puts it, the parables "offer a Gospel in miniature and at the same time give shape, direction, and meaning to the Gospels in which they are found. To study the parables of the Gospels is to study the gospel in parable."[5]

---

[3] The term *parabolē* occurs eighteen times in the Gospel of Luke: 4:23; 5:36; 6:39; 8:4, 9, 10, 11; 12:16, 41; 13:6; 14:7; 15:3; 18:1, 9; 19:11; 20:9, 19; 21:29. It occurs sixteen times in Matthew, twelve times in Mark, and twice in Hebrews.

[4] The Markan version (Mark 12:1-12) is assigned to Monday of the Ninth Week of Ordinary Time. See Barbara E. Reid, *Parables for Preachers: Year B* (Collegeville: The Liturgical Press, 1999) 111–20. The Matthean account (Matt 21:33-43) appears on the Twenty-seventh Sunday of Ordinary Time in Year A and on Friday of the Second Week of Lent.

[5] John R. Donahue, *The Gospel in Parable* (Philadelphia: Fortress, 1988) ix.

Other volumes in this series treat the parables of Matthew (Lectionary Cycle A) and Mark (Lectionary Cycle B). Parables are noticeably absent from the Gospel of John. The fourth evangelist never uses the term *parabolē*, nor does he preserve any of Jesus' stories in the same parabolic form as do the Synoptic writers. Nonetheless symbolic speech abounds in the Fourth Gospel. The closest thing to a parable is found in chapter 10, where Jesus speaks of himself as the Good Shepherd and the gate for the sheep. And in John 10:6 Jesus' disciples have the same difficulty in understanding this "figure of speech" *(paroimia)* as they do with the parables in Mark 4:10-12 and pars. The term *paroimia* occurs two more times in the Gospel of John (16:25, 29), where Jesus assures the disciples that a time will come when he will no longer speak in "figures" but plainly. This comes on the heels of the comparison of the disciples' anguish at Jesus' departure with that of a woman in labor. As she forgets her pain after her child is born, so will the disciples' grief turn into joy (16:21-24).

In chapter 1 we explore the dynamics of Jesus' parables. Understanding how a parable "works" is the first step. In chapter 2 is a sketch of contemporary trends in biblical interpretation of the parables. Next is an overview of the Gospel of Luke, its author, historical context, and major theological themes. The remaining chapters examine each of the parables of the Gospel of Luke in the order in which they appear in the Lectionary for Year C. We will first treat the parables that appear in both the Sunday Lectionary and the weekday Lectionary, followed by those that appear only in the weekday Lectionary. The concluding chapter and bibliography point toward further areas of study.

CHAPTER ONE

Preaching Parabolically

TO PREACH AS JESUS DID[1]

Jesus was not the first to preach in parables. There is a long tradition of such storytelling in the ancient world, not only by religious figures, but by rhetoricians, politicians, prophets, and philosophers as well. In the Hebrew Scriptures there are several examples of parables. In 2 Samuel 12:1-12, for example, the prophet Nathan tells King David a parable about a rich man who took a poor man's lone ewe lamb and made it into a meal for a visitor. The song of the vineyard in Isaiah 5:1-7 and the sayings about plowing and threshing in Isaiah 28:23-29 present agricultural metaphors not unlike those used by Jesus in his parables. The Jewish rabbis also spoke in parables.[2]

One result of parabolic preaching is that the storyteller allows the listener to back away from a sensitive topic and enter into a make-believe (but true-to-life) situation, where one can see more clearly what is right. Nathan successfully brought David to repentance for taking Uriah's wife when the king angrily pronounced sentence on the rich man of the parable. In the Synoptic Gospels we see Jesus using the same technique, for example, when addressing Simon the Pharisee in Luke 7:40-48; or

---

[1] An earlier version of this chapter, entitled "Preaching Justice Parabolically," appeared in *Emmanuel* 102/6 (1996) 342–47.

[2] On rabbinic connections with Jesus' parables see Philip L. Culbertson, *A Word Fitly Spoken* (Albany: State University of New York Press, 1995); Brad H. Young, *Jesus and His Jewish Parables: Rediscovering the Roots of Jesus' Teaching* (New York: Paulist Press, 1989); *The Parables: Jewish Tradition and Christian Interpretation* (Peabody, Mass.: Hendrickson, 1998).

when driving home his point to the Pharisees and scribes in Luke 15:1-32. Contemporary preachers can become more skilled in using the same dynamics of storytelling as did Jesus, and thus engage their listeners more effectively with the gospel message.

ENCOUNTER WITH THE HOLY

Before attempting to emulate Jesus' way of preaching, a preacher must know Jesus and his message first-hand. An effective preacher speaks from his or her personal and ongoing encounter with Christ in study, in prayer, in other people, and in all creation. Just as Jesus' constant communion with God[3] shaped his preaching, so must this be the foundation for the contemporary preacher. It is evident when a person speaks of the Holy, whether they speak from their own experience or merely pass on what they have heard or studied. Intimate experience of the Divine in prayer is what energizes, sustains, and transforms the preacher. The inability to bring about deeply unitive experiences of prayer by one's own efforts keeps the preacher aware that these are gifts. So, too, is the ministry of preaching. It is God's word that a preacher speaks.

It is the joy of having experienced oneself as the object of God's love and delight that impels the contemplative preacher to share this message. There is the ever-present danger that the other demands of ministry erode the minister's time for prayer. Another pitfall is to let a striving for prayerfulness at all times take the place of specific time set aside for contemplative prayer. One who allows this to happen runs the risk of preaching a hollow word.

THE FAMILIAR RADICALLY TWISTED

In his parables, Jesus always begins with the familiar. The images and situations he paints in his stories are from the fabric of daily life of his audience. He tells how God is encountered in sowing and reaping (Luke 8:4-15), in baking bread (Luke 13:20-

---

[3] The Gospel of Luke has the most references to Jesus' habitual prayer: Luke 3:21; 6:12; 9:18, 28; 11:1; 22:32, 41; 23:46.

21), in searching for what is lost (Luke 15:1-32). In this way he captures peoples' attention and draws them along with him to the end of the story. In the same manner, an effective preacher today transforms the gospel images and situations into ones that relate to the everyday world of those gathered. For example, the majority of the assembly will quickly tune out when the homily begins, "When I was in the seminary . . . ." Or if the gospel presumes rural, pre-industrial experiences when the gathered community is composed of urban professionals, the homilist will need to recontextualize the message for the contemporary situation.

In Jesus' parables no sphere of life is outside God's realm: the political, social, economic, ecclesial, and theological are all intertwined, as in the parables of the rich man and Lazarus (Luke 16:19-31); the rich fool (Luke 12:16-21); the dishonest steward (Luke 16:1-8), the parable of the great banquet (Luke 14:15-24), the Pharisee and the tax collector (Luke 18:9-14), the widow and the judge (Luke 18:1-8). Jesus' preaching brought a vision of all life as locus for the sacred; nothing is outside the realm of the holy. Likewise, a preacher today will help the assembly to see that holiness is not found by separating oneself from "the world," but is encountered in all reality. S/he will lead people to see God in the midst of the contradictions and the chaos, in the crucifying and dying, not only in the peacefulness and the rising to new life.

Jesus' parables do not stay on the level of the familiar. Always there is a catch. They are not pleasant stories that entertain or that confirm the status quo. They are startling and confusing, usually having an unexpected twist that leaves the hearers pondering what the story means and what it demands. As John Dominic Crossan puts it, "You can usually recognize a parable because your immediate reaction will be self-contradictory: 'I don't know what you mean by that story but I'm certain I don't like it.'"[4]

Jesus' parables are invitations to see the realm of God as God sees it and to act as Jesus acted. Such a vision demands

---

[4] John Dominic Crossan, *The Dark Interval: Towards a Theology of Story* (Niles, Ill.: Argus Communications, 1975) 56.

profound changes in the way the hearer thinks about God and the realm of God, both as it can be in the here and now and in its future fullness. By shattering the structures of our accepted world, parables remove our defenses and make us vulnerable to God.[5] Preachers should be suspicious of interpretations that reinforce life as it is.[6] The gospel is always about change.[7] An effective preacher studies the text so as to understand what it originally meant and then tries to repeat that unsettling dynamic in their own preaching.

THE RIDDLE OF INTERPRETATION

The difficulty with Jesus' parables is that they are open-ended; Jesus rarely interpreted these stories for his disciples. For example, at the end of the story of the father with two difficult sons (Luke 15:11-32), does the elder brother go in to the party after the father pleads with him? Or does he remain outside, angry and resentful? There lies the challenge. Jesus does not give the answer, but leaves it up to the hearer to determine the rest of the story. Over the ages each community of Christians has had to work out its responses to the challenges of Jesus' teaching; this task is no less incumbent upon believers today. Just as Jesus does not give the interpretation of his parables, neither do effective preachers provide pat answers.

Because they are told in figurative language, the parables are capable of conveying distinct messages to different people in diverse circumstances.[8] For instance, to a person in need of forgiveness, the parable in Luke 15:11-32 is the story of a lost son or daughter who is invited to let him or herself be found by God and be lavished with love that cannot be earned. For a person in authority, the same story may serve as a call to emulate

[5] Ibid., 122.

[6] This is the function of myth rather than parable. See Crossan, *The Dark Interval*, 47–62.

[7] See M. J. Gillingham ("The Parables as Attitude Change," *ExpTim* 109 [1998] 297–300) who explores the dynamics of cognitive dissonance in Jesus' parables.

[8] See Mary Ann Tolbert, *Perspectives on the Parables: An Approach to Multiple Interpretations* (Philadelphia: Fortress, 1979).

the character of the father who searches out ones who have embarked on a destructive path and runs to meet them and bring them back, at great personal cost. For persons who try always to be faithful to following God's ways, the story invites them to let go of joyless resentment and slavish attitudes in their service of God. The point of the story depends on one's point of entry and the character with whom one identifies. A preacher cannot be content with one stock interpretation, but must continually plumb the depths of the text for other possible meanings. On each occasion s/he must discern which of the many possible messages is the word that now needs be spoken.

BREVITY

The parables of Jesus are short and to the point. Some are only one line long. Like the Argentinian poet Jorge Luis Borges who laughed at those who wanted "to go on for five hundred pages developing an idea whose perfect oral expression is possible in a few minutes,"[9] Jesus knew the art of pithy expression. The brevity of the parables makes them easy to remember and enhances their ability to communicate forcefully. Likewise, when a preacher can convey his or her message briefly, there is a better chance that the word will be remembered and its transforming potential will be more fully released.

STANCE WITH THE MARGINAL

While multiple interpretations are possible, the preacher always tells the story slant, inviting the hearers to take a particular position in the narrative. Jesus often did this in telling his parables. And the stance to which he invites his hearers is with the marginal. For example, when addressing Pharisees and scribes that complained against him welcoming sinners and eating with them (Luke 15:1-2), Jesus asks them, "What man among you having a hundred sheep and losing one of them would not leave the ninety-nine in the desert and go after

---

[9] John Dominic Crossan (*Cliffs of Fall: Paradox and Polyvalence in the Parables of Jesus* [New York: Seabury, 1980] 3) relays this quote from the Prologue of Jorge Luis Borges, *Ficciones* (New York: Grove, 1962).

the lost one until he finds it?" (Luke 15:4).[10] Jesus has deliberately asked them to take the stance of the shepherd.

To understand the twist in this, it is important to know that although "shepherd" was used as an image for God (e.g., Psalm 23), and as a metaphor for religious leaders (e.g., Ezekiel 34), real shepherds in Jesus' day were disdained as dishonest and thieving. Jesus asked the Pharisees and scribes, religious leaders who thought themselves upright, to consider themselves as despised shepherds. The power of the story lies in the invitation to identify with people who are marginalized and to take their part. If that were not shocking enough, in the next parable (Luke 15:8-10), Jesus asks them to put themselves in the place of a woman who invests enormous energy to seek out a lost coin. The challenge to the religious leaders was not only to emulate shepherds and women who expend themselves greatly to bring back the lost, but also to be able to see a despised shepherd or an "inferior" woman as embodying God in the same way they imagined of themselves.

Jesus' parables proclaim that God is not neutral. Rather, God is always on the side of those who are poorest and most oppressed. Because of the inequities that exist, God must take their part in order to balance the scales.[11] One of the most crucial tasks of the preacher today, particularly in gatherings of those who are comfortable financially and socially, is to take up the perspective of those who are marginalized and invite the congregation to do the same. The point is not to make people feel guilty, but rather to move them to see from the perspective of those most disadvantaged and to ask then, what would love require of me? If one is not poor, then Christian discipleship demands solidarity with the poor, service to the needs of the least, and readiness to suffer persecution that follows from these actions.

[10] All biblical quotations are taken from *New American Bible* with revised New Testament, 1986, unless otherwise noted.

[11] See, e.g., Clodovis Boff and Jorge Pixley (*The Bible, the Church, and the Poor* [Theology and Liberation Series; Maryknoll, N.Y.: Orbis, 1989]) who demonstrate how in every section of the Bible, God's concern is always for the poor.

A COMMUNAL ENDEAVOR

One of the more difficult aspects of preaching, especially in contemporary American culture, is to present gospel living as a communal endeavor, not a pursuit of individual salvation.[12] From its inception, the people of God is a community bound together by the covenant. But there is a further twist in the vision of community that Jesus' parables present. In the story of The Great Feast (Luke 14:15-24), for example, the people of God encompasses all—particularly the most despised and outcast. Or, consider Jesus' parable of the workers in the vineyard (Matt 20:1-16) for an entirely unsettling vision of a just community. The configuration is not that of each one pulling his or her own weight with appropriate compensation. Rather, the believing community is one in which each member has the means by which to subsist for the day, no matter what his or her contribution to the group.

A LIVED PARABLE

The ultimate aim of preaching is that the word be acted upon. The desired effect is that people's hearts be moved to praise of God that finds further expression in transformative action. Such a word gives hope and courage to those oppressed. It declares that injustice is not God's desire and emboldens impoverished communities to act together for change. For those who are privileged, the preached word moves them not only to love and to stand with the wronged, but to act in solidarity with them to dismantle unjust structures.

The power of Jesus' preaching came from his very life being a parable.[13] His paradoxical choice of death to bring life, of self-emptying to bring fullness for all, of humiliation and suffering to bring dignity and joy to the oppressed, proclaimed a radically

---

[12] See further Edward J. Van Merrienboer, "Preaching the Social Gospel," *In the Company of Preachers,* ed. R. Siegfried and E. Ruane (Collegeville: The Liturgical Press, 1993) 176–90.

[13] See Crossan, *The Dark Interval,* 123–28, on "The Parabler Becomes Parable," and John R. Donahue, "Jesus as the Parable of God in the Gospel of Mark," *Int* 32 (1978) 369–86.

different way to God. It was a life that issued an invitation to conversion and left people struggling to understand its meaning and demands. Effective preachers give such a parabolic witness in our day. No preaching takes root unless the life of the preacher is a living witness.[14] This witness, like the parables, prompts all whose lives are touched by the preacher to ask, "What does this mean?" "What am I to do?" "What does this ask of me?" If the life of a preacher does not present a paradox, then the power of the gospel s/he preaches is weakened.

Effective preachers are aware that they preach what their own lives proclaim imperfectly. The word takes root, though, when the preacher visibly joins in the struggle with the gathered community, together seeking to conform their lives ever more to that of Christ. Together they seek contemplative intimacy with God, engage in serious study of the word, both in the biblical text, and in their lived reality.

Such a preacher must be willing to be consumed by a passion for the gospel and its all-encompassing demands, willing even to risk rejection and opposition. The prophet Jeremiah, who tried to hold in the word, says it became "like fire burning in my heart" (Jer 20:9) and he could not resist speaking it forth. With such passion for the gospel, a preacher becomes a sign of hope, not a prophet of doom. In parabolically proclaiming the vision of Jesus, it is not naive optimism that the preacher declares, nor a depressing guilt trip, but a word that galvanizes the community to conversion of heart and transformative action that is undergirded by profound love for all God's people.

---

[14] Pope Paul VI underscored this in his address to members of the *Consilium de Laicis* on October 2, 1974, when he said, "Modern man [sic] listens more willingly to witnesses than to teachers, and if he [sic] does listen to teachers, it is because they are witnesses" (*Evangelii Nuntiandi*, §21, p. 41).

CHAPTER TWO

Interpreting Parables

SPOILING THE PUNCHLINE

Having to interpret a parable is like having to explain a joke when someone misses the punchline. Yet, because of our familiarity with the parables, our lack of understanding of their rhetoric and of how Jesus' first audience would have reacted to his stories, we can miss the punchline of a parable. A critical step in the preparation for preaching a parable is serious biblical study that attempts to retrieve, as far as possible, what the story meant in its original telling. The preacher then attempts to re-effect such a dynamic in the contemporary context. Preaching that simply explains the original meaning to the assembly is instructional, but does not achieve its purpose.

DIFFICULTIES IN UNDERSTANDING THE PARABLES

In the Gospels, the disciples question Jesus about the parables because they do not understand (Luke 8:9-10 and pars.). The parables are far from simple stories that make Jesus' teaching easy to grasp. Although Jesus used familiar imagery, the stories remained enigmatic and confusing.[1] They are no less challenging to contemporary interpreters. Three factors contribute to our difficulty in understanding: the nature of the parables, the nature of the Gospels, and the nature of our sources of knowledge about the ancient world.

---

[1] Andrew Parker (*Painfully Clear: The Parables of Jesus* [Biblical Seminar 37; Sheffield: Sheffield Academic Press, 1996]) argues that Jesus' parables were not meant to be enigmatic. They were painfully clear and confrontational.

THE NATURE OF THE PARABLES

Parables, by their very nature, are puzzling. They are figurative speech, symbolic language, with more than one level of meaning.[2] The term "parable" (*parabolē* in Greek; *māshāl* in Hebrew) has a wide range of meanings. It can refer to a proverb, such as "physician, cure yourself" (Luke 4:23). A wisdom saying or a riddle, such as, "Nothing that enters one from outside can defile that person; but the things that come out from within are what defile" (Mark 7:15) is dubbed a parable (Mark 7:17). A similitude, or a slightly developed comparison can be called a parable, as the lesson (*parabolē*) of the fig tree (Mark 13:28-29). The author of Hebrews twice uses the term in the sense of "symbol" (Heb 9:9; 11:19).

Gospel commentators often divide the parables of Jesus into three categories: similitude, parable, and exemplary story.[3] Similitudes are concise narratives that make a comparison between an aspect of God's realm and a typical or recurrent event in real life (e.g., seed growing in Mark 4:26-29; or losing a coin in Luke 15:8-10). Parables are usually longer and more detailed. They tell a story about a one-time fictitious, but true-to-life event, such as that of a widow who confronts an unjust judge (Luke 18:1-8) or a steward who faces dismissal (Luke 16:1-8). An exemplary story (e.g., the Good Samaritan in Luke 10:29-37) presents a specific example that illustrates a general principle. It differs from a similitude and a parable in that its comparison is between two things that are similar, not dissimilar.

Whichever form a parable takes, it is not an entertaining story that confirms the status quo. Its purpose is to persuade the hearer to adopt a particular view of God and life in God's realm. Its aim is to convert the hearer. Parables turn the world upside down by challenging presumptions, reversing expectations, and proposing a different view of life with God. Their open endings make it necessary for the hearers of every age to grapple with their implications.

[2] See John Dominic Crossan, *Cliffs of Fall: Paradox and Polyvalence in the Parables of Jesus* (New York: Seabury, 1980) 1–24, on Paradox and Metaphor; and 65–104 on Polyvalence and Play.

[3] E.g., M. Boucher, *The Parables* (NTM 7; Wilmington: Glazier, 1981) 19–23.

THE NATURE OF THE GOSPELS

Another difficulty in knowing Jesus' originally intended meaning of a parable has to do with the nature of the Gospels in which the parables are found. In the first place, the Gospels are written documents, whereas the parables were originally communicated orally. The shift from oral communication to written affects meaning. In addition, the literary context in which a gospel parable is placed may give it a different sense than it had in its original spoken context.

Moreover, the Gospels do not record the exact words of Jesus. The gospel parables are two stages removed from the stories told by the earthly Jesus. Jesus' parables were preached by his followers, and underwent modifications in the retelling. As they took written form, some thirty to fifty years after Jesus' death, the parables were reshaped by each evangelist to meet the needs of his particular community of faith. The intent of the gospel writers was not to preserve as accurately as possible the exact words of Jesus; rather, like modern preachers, they reinterpreted Jesus' stories for their new contexts. As a result, we find various versions of the same parable in different gospels. Similar parables are placed in different settings, directed to different audiences, with resultant different meanings.

Analysis of the history of the traditions also reveals that often in the retelling of Jesus' parables moralizing and/or allegorizing tendencies were introduced. Whereas his original stories began as paradoxical challenges, they were many times tamed into illustrations of moral actions. It is necessary to sift through the layers of the tradition so as to uncover as best we can, the originally upsetting contrasts Jesus' stories presented.

THE NATURE OF OUR SOURCES OF KNOWLEDGE ABOUT THE ANCIENT WORLD

A further difficulty in knowing what Jesus intended to say and how his first audiences understood the parables is that our sources of knowledge about the ancient world are partial and incomplete. New discoveries from archaeology and of previously unknown manuscripts continue to enlighten us about the world of Jesus. Similarly, new methods of biblical interpretation bring to light fresh possibilities of meaning. Knowledge of the historical, social, economic, political, religious, and cultural world of Palestine and the Hellenistic world of the first century allows us to draw probable conclusions about a parable's original meaning, but the business of interpretation never rests on certitude.

METHODS OF PARABLE INTERPRETATION

Allegorical Interpretation

The earliest approach to parable interpretation, the allegorical method,[4] is found in the Gospels themselves. This approach treats parables as allegories, that is, a series of metaphors in which each detail of the story is given a symbolic meaning. The first biblical example concerns the parable of the sower and the seed (Luke 8:1-8 and pars.). The allegorical explanation in Luke 8:11-15 and pars. is that the seed is the word and the different types of soil represent the various ways that people hear and respond to the word. The seed that falls on the path represents those whose hearing is quickly derailed by the devil; those on rocky ground have no root and quickly fall away when tribulation comes; for those sown among thorns the word is choked off by worldly anxiety and pleasure; those on rich soil hear and accept the word and bear abundant fruit. A similar allegorical interpretation of the parable of the weeds and the wheat (Matt 13:24-30) is found in Matthew 13:36-43.[5] Most scholars recognize these as interpretations of the early faith communities, and not from Jesus himself.

The allegorical approach was the preferred method of patristic and medieval biblical scholars. From the time of Origen (second century C.E.) until the rise of modern biblical criticism, this method held sway. A good example is the interpretation of the parable of the Good Samaritan (Luke 10:29-37) used by Augustine and others: the traveler is Adam, representing human-

---

[4] See Carolyn Osiek, "Literal Meaning and Allegory," *TBT* 29/5 (1991) 261–66; Barbara E. Reid, "Once Upon a Time . . . Parable and Allegory in the Gospels," *TBT* 29/5 (1991) 267–72.

[5] Another pre-critical approach is proof-texting, which was used to interpret this parable in medieval times as justification for the burning of heretics.

kind. He descends from Jerusalem, the lost paradise, to Jericho, that is, the world. The robbers are evil spirits that deprive him of virtue and immortality. That he is left half dead means that he is alive insofar as he can know God, but dead in that he is in the power of sin. The priest and Levite are the law and the prophets of Israel, unable to help. The Samaritan is Christ, outsider to the theological claims of Israel. His animal is the body of Christ, on which are borne the sins of humanity. The inn is the Church, where oil and wine, the sacraments, heal the traveler's wounds. The inn-keeper, representing the apostles, is authorized to continue caring for the wounded man until the return of the Samaritan, that is, until the second coming of Christ.[6]

ONE MAIN POINT

At the end of the nineteenth century the German biblical scholar Adolph Jülicher[7] revolutionized the study of parables by arguing that a parable has only one main point. With the dawn of historical critical methods, Jülicher further insisted that the point must be sought in the historical context of the teaching of Jesus.

Since that time there has been much debate over whether there was any allegorical dimension at all to the original parables of Jesus. Some scholars contend that all allegorical elements are the later interpretations by the evangelists or the early Christian communities from whom they received the parables. Other exegetes do not so rigidly distinguish between parable and allegory. They argue that the gospel parables are allegorical in nature if one understands allegory not as a series of metaphors, but as an extended metaphor in narrative form.

MORE OR LESS ALLEGORICAL

One difference from earlier allegorical interpretation is that critics today do not try to find symbolism behind as many details. In addition, they attempt to find meanings that would be

---

[6] See, e.g., Irenaeus, *Adversus haereses* III.17, 3.
[7] Adolph Jülicher, *Die Gleichnisreden Jesu* (2 vols.; Tübingen: Mohr [Siebeck] 1888, 1899).

intelligible in Jesus' day. One solution is to think of parables on a sliding scale of more or less allegorical.[8]

There is a further difficulty with Jülicher's insistence that there is *one* main point in a parable. With many interpretations possible, how can we know which is *the* main point originally intended? It may be that each main character (human or not) in a parable may reveal an important point.[9] For example, in the sower parable (Luke 8:1-8 and pars.) if the sower is the focus, the point is God's lavish generosity (through Jesus' preaching, teaching, and healing) in sowing the word on all kinds of soil, good and bad alike. If the focus is the seed, the message is that the word is effective. Despite early failure or unremarkable initial results, it will eventually bear fruit in abundance. If the soil is the focal point, as in the interpretation in Luke 8:11-15, then the emphasis is for believers to make sure to be fertile soil, cultivating themselves to be receptive and nurturing to the word. Finally, if the harvest is highlighted, then the point is that the reign of God far exceeds all expectation. The explosiveness and grand scale of the yield, "thirty, sixty, and a hundredfold," is beyond anything a typical farmer experienced.

The task of the preacher is to discern *which* of the many possible points is the main one that the assembly needs to hear at this place and time. A significant contribution by Jülicher for preachers is the insight that a parable communicates best when it is told with one main point, or punchline, not as a series of metaphors.

Parables of the Kingdom

Another significant contribution to modern parable interpretation was made by C. H. Dodd,[10] who argued that the parables be understood against the context of Jesus' eschatological

---

[8] Craig Blomberg, "Interpreting the Parables: Where Are We and Where Do We Go from Here?" *CBQ* 53 (1991) 50–78; *Interpreting the Parables* (Downers Grove, Ill.: InterVarsity Press, 1990) 29–69; and Kline Snodgrass, *The Parable of the Wicked Tenants* (Tübingen: Mohr [Siebeck] 1983) 13–26.

[9] Blomberg, *Interpreting,* 21, advances that most parables make three main points.

[10] Charles H. Dodd, *The Parables of the Kingdom* (London: Collins, 1961; first published by James Nisbet and Co., 1935).

proclamation. For him, all the parables convey the message that the kingdom of God is inaugurated and realized in Jesus. Scholars today question that a single lens, such as realized eschatology, is adequate to unfold all the rich dimensions of the parables.

HISTORICAL CRITICISM: GETTING TO THE ORIGINAL STORY

A very significant advance in parable interpretation came with the rise of historical critical methodology.[11] With the use of form and redaction criticism, in particular, historical critics investigate the kinds of alterations made in the transmission of the parables and attempt to recover the most primitive form. One of the most influential scholars in this century who employed this method in parables research was Joachim Jeremias.[12] He identified ten principles of transformation by which the early church adapted Jesus' parables to their own situation: 1) translation from Aramaic to Greek; 2) shift from a Palestinian to a Hellenistic environment; 3) embellishment of details; 4) remodeling along the lines of Old Testament and folk-story themes; 5) change of audience from interested crowds or opponents to disciples; 6) shift from a warning to the multitude about the gravity of the eschatological crisis to a hortatory use to direct the conduct of Christians; 7) metaphors assume greater Christological and ecclesial significance; 8) allegorization of details; 9) tendency toward collection and conflation; 10) placement in a secondary setting. Recognizing these tendencies in the transmission of the tradition and using his vast knowledge of first-century Palestine, Jeremias worked to uncover the original words and settings of the parables of Jesus.

This method is still extremely valuable in trying to determine what was the original form of Jesus' parables and in what

[11] See Edgar Krentz, *The Historical-Critical Method* (Guides to Biblical Scholarship; Philadelphia: Fortress, 1975).

[12] Joachim Jeremias *The Parables of Jesus* (8th ed.; New York: Scribner's, 1972). Similarly, Rudolph Bultmann, *History of the Synoptic Tradition* (rev. ed.; New York: Harper & Row, 1968); A. T. Cadoux, *The Parables of Jesus* (London: James Clarke, 1931).

historical context they were spoken. This is one important step in a preacher's preparation. But the task of the preacher goes beyond simply recounting what the story meant in Jesus' day.

SOCIAL SCIENCE APPROACH

Closely related to historical critical methods is the recently developed science of social study of the New Testament.[13] This area of study engages biblical scholars, experts in social science, classicists, and ancient historians, who collaborate to reconstruct not only the history, but also the economic, social, and political life of Greek and Roman civilizations of the first centuries before and after Christ. They use art, contemporary literature, inscriptions, coins, and archaeological finds to gain knowledge of the institutions, social dynamics, and horizons of consciousness of people who lived at the time of Jesus.

An example is Richard Rohrbaugh's reading of the parable of the talents/pounds (Matt 25:14-20; Luke 19:11-27).[14] Reading from the point of view of a peasant of a first-century Mediterranean agrarian society rather than with the assumptions of a capitalist from the West, the parable results as a warning to those who mistreat the poor, not to those who lack adventurous industry.

One caution about this method is that it is a modern construction, not devised specifically for biblical study. A question remains of how well it can be applied to ancient texts and societies. Nonetheless, this approach opens up fresh meanings and can offer satisfactory solutions for details that other methods leave as inexplicable. It can also advance new possibilities for action in the contemporary world that would lead to genuine social change.

---

[13] See Carolyn Osiek, *What Are They Saying About the Social Setting of the New Testament?* (2nd ed.; New York: Paulist, 1992); Bruce J. Malina and Richard L. Rohrbaugh, *Social Science Commentary on the Synoptic Gospels* (Minneapolis: Fortress, 1992); John J. Pilch, *The Cultural World of Jesus: Sunday by Sunday, Cycle C* (Collegeville: The Liturgical Press, 1997).

[14] Richard L. Rohrbaugh, "A Peasant Reading of the Parable of the Talents/ Pounds: A Text of Terror?" *BTB* 23 (1993) 32–39.

LITERARY APPROACHES

Another turning point in parable study came in the 1960s with the work of Amos Wilder and Robert Funk, who moved into methods of literary interpretation.[15] They explore the aesthetics of the language in the parables, their poetry, imagery, and symbolism. They analyze how metaphor moves from a literary figure to a theological and hermeneutical category, providing a key to a new understanding of the parables.

A related direction of literary study is narrative criticism.[16] This approach analyzes the plot, character development, point of view, and dramatic movement of the story apart from its historical context. Narrative criticism also attends to the response evoked by the text in the reader.

Rhetorical criticism has also become an important tool for analyzing parables as persuasive speech. This method studies how the type of argument, its arrangement, and its style of presentation bring about the desired effect.

Finally, semiotic or structuralist methods[17] have been applied to the parables, although most people find them too complicated and diffuse to be of help. The aim is to uncover the deep structures of meaning through analysis of the synchronic structure. Grids delineating the subject, object, sender, recipient, helper, and opponent are employed to this end.

Literary methods deal with the finished form of the text as we have it, not the process through which it has come. They recognize that meaning is constructed in the interaction between

---

[15] Robert Funk, *Language, Hermeneutic, and Word of God* (New York: Harper & Row, 1966); *Parables and Presence* (Philadelphia: Fortress, 1982); Amos Wilder, *The Language of the Gospel* (New York: Harper & Row, 1964); *Jesus' Parables and the War of Myths* (Philadelphia: Fortress, 1982). John Dominic Crossan (*In Parables: The Challenge of the Historical Jesus* [New York: Harper & Row, 1973]; *The Dark Interval* [Sonoma: Polebridge, 1988]) bridges two methods when he begins with tradition-critical considerations and then moves to a literary metaphorical approach.

[16] E.g., Dan O. Via, *The Parables: Their Literary and Existential Dimension* (Philadelphia: Fortress, 1967). See also Mark A. Powell, *What Is Narrative Criticism?* (Guides to Biblical Scholarship; Philadelphia: Fortress, 1990).

[17] See Daniel Patte, *What Is Structural Exegesis?* (Guides to Biblical Scholarship; Philadelphia: Fortress, 1976).

text and reader, quite apart from the original intention of the author. They can be very useful in showing the ongoing function of the parable in any context to invite participation in Jesus' understanding of God and the divine realm.

LIBERATION APPROACHES

A new approach to biblical interpretation was born in Latin America some three decades ago.[18] Its underlying principle is that reflection on experience precedes theoretical analysis. And it is the experience of people who are poor and oppressed that is the starting point. The second step is critical analysis of the social and political causes of oppression. In the process a correlation is sought between the present situation and biblical stories of deliverance and liberation. The final move is to strategize and act for liberation. This method relies on the faithful reflection of ordinary people of faith, not solely or even primarily on that of biblical scholars. It is a communal endeavor that seeks to embody God's word of justice and hope in this world, here and now.

With regard to parable interpretation, this method challenges approaches that would claim to discover universal messages in Jesus' stories, applied and reapplied from one generation to the next and from one social context to another. It asks questions like: "What if the parables of Jesus were neither theological nor moral stories but political and economic ones? What if the concern of the parables was not the reign of God but the reigning systems of oppression that dominated Palestine in the time of Jesus? What if the parables are exposing exploitation rather than revealing justification?"[19]

A drawback to this approach is that some find that the kind of study required of social and political structures as well as of biblical and ecclesial tradition is too much to ask of simple

---

[18] See Christopher Rowland and Mark Corner, *Liberating Exegesis: The Challenge of Liberation Theology to Biblical Studies* (Louisville: Westminster/John Knox, 1989); Clodovis Boff and Jorge Pixley, *The Bible, the Church, and the Poor* (Theology and Liberation Series; Maryknoll, N.Y.: Orbis, 1989); Carlos Mesters, *Defenseless Flower: A New Reading of the Bible* (Maryknoll, N.Y.: Orbis, 1989).

[19] William R. Herzog II, *Parables as Subversive Speech: Jesus as Pedagogue of the Oppressed* (Louisville: Westminster/John Knox, 1994) 7.

believers. For some there is more solace in an approach that provides sure doctrines, simple morality, literal, authoritative interpretations of the Bible, and an assurance of future reward for enduring present oppression and suffering.

An advantage to this method is that it can be used in tandem with historical, social science, and literary methods, while providing the lens through which to view the text. It is an invaluable tool for engaging Jesus' stories in a new context in a way that can challenge the unjust structures in our day and bring good news to those oppressed. The danger, of course, is that one who would preach this way risks rejection and persecution as did the first proclaimer of the parables.

FEMINIST APPROACHES

New methods of feminist biblical interpretation have developed in the last decades.[20] Arising from the experiences of women in which the Bible has been used to legitimate patriarchy and violence toward women, feminist methods advance the dignity and equality of all persons by challenging texts and interpretations that promote domination of any sort, particularly that of males over females. Feminist scholars see in Jesus' proclamation of the reign of God an alternate vision by which relationship patterns as well as social, political, economic, and ecclesial structures can be transformed.

Elisabeth Schüssler Fiorenza offers a four-fold procedure for a feminist liberationist method.[21] The first step is to apply to the text a *Hermeneutics of Suspicion*. The term "hermeneutics" refers to the study of the methodological principles of interpretation. A hermeneutics of suspicion recognizes that the biblical

---

[20] For surveys of various approaches to feminist hermeneutics see Elizabeth Johnson, "Feminist Hermeneutics," *Chicago Studies* 27 (1988) 123–35; Carolyn Osiek, "The Feminist and the Bible: Hermeneutical Alternatives," *Feminist Perspectives on Biblical Scholarship* (Chico, Calif.: Scholars Press, 1985) 93–105; Elisabeth Schüssler Fiorenza, *But She Said* (Boston: Beacon, 1992) 20–50.

[21] See her groundbreaking works *In Memory of Her; Bread Not Stone: The Challenge of Feminist Biblical Interpretation* (Boston: Beacon, 1984); and the recent two-volume work edited by her that provides a feminist introduction and commentary: *Searching the Scriptures* (2 vols.; New York: Crossroad, 1993, 1994). See also the ten strategies outlined in chapter one of her book *But She Said*, 20–50.

texts and their interpretations through the centuries have been written, for the most part, by men, for men, and about men, and that they serve the interests of patriarchy. One who reads with a hermeneutics of suspicion is wary that the text can be oppressive for women. This does not deny the inspiration of Scripture, but recognizes the limitations of the human authors who set forth God's word.

The second movement is a *Hermeneutics of Proclamation.* This aspect draws attention to the fact that the biblical writings do not tell us what Jesus really did and said, but rather records how the tradition was understood by the men who shaped it, both in the decades of early Christian preaching and in the formation of the written traditions. A hermeneutics of proclamation assesses the Bible's power to continue to shape the faith community and advocates that texts that promote sexism or patriarchy no longer be proclaimed in the worship assembly. Alternatively, if texts that are abusive toward women are proclaimed, it is in *memoria passionis,* and with the resolve that such will never again be promulgated as God's will.[22]

Third, a *Hermeneutics of Remembrance* reclaims the struggles of women of past decades and attempts to reconstruct their history. It is conscious that the canonical Scriptures relate only part of the experience of the early Church. It searches for clues and allusions that indicate the reality of women's experience about which the text is silent. Retrieving this subversive memory places women in the center of the biblical community and the theological endeavor, not as appendages to men's religious history. Thus women's history can be integrated into the mainstream of biblical history, both past and future.

Finally, a *Hermeneutics of Ritualization and Celebration* recognizes the importance of creative expression of the active part women play in the ongoing biblical story. It engages in literary originality in retelling the biblical stories from a feminist perspective. It calls for the artistic use of music, dance, and all the creative arts, to liberate the imagination from the confines of a patriarchal worldview. It celebrates a new vision of women and men equally created in God's image, equally redeemed by

[22] See Phyllis Trible, *Texts of Terror* (Philadelphia: Fortress, 1984).

Christ, equally called to be disciples, equally entrusted with the mission, and equally endowed with the Spirit. The parables lend themselves particularly to such creative retelling in contemporary modes.

LITURGICAL INTERPRETATION

The methods of interpretation outlined above come from the discipline of biblical studies and aim to unfold meanings of the text in the context of the Bible. When these texts are taken from the Bible and placed in a new context in the Lectionary, this is another factor that must be considered in the task of interpretation for liturgical preaching. Preaching from the parables must take into account the other readings juxtaposed with the gospel, including the responsorial psalm,[23] as well as the other liturgical texts (the prayers, acclamations, and hymns), and the theology of the liturgical season. In addition the preacher's interpretation of the text will be in dialogue with the human story of his or her particular congregation and that of the global family in current world events. While comments about the Lectionary and the liturgical context will be included in each chapter, the primary focus of this book is on interpretation of the text with biblical methods.[24]

CONCLUSION

No one method provides the definitive key. Each contributes significantly to our understanding of what the parables

[23] See Irene Nowell, *Sing a New Song: The Psalms in the Sunday Lectionary* (Collegeville: The Liturgical Press, 1993). On Paul's letters, see Raymond F. Collins, *Preaching the Epistles* (New York: Paulist, 1996).

[24] A commentary on the Lectionary using literary-liturgical interpretation of all four readings for Sundays and major feasts is: Dianne Bergant, *Preaching the New Lectionary* (Collegeville: The Liturgical Press) in three volumes. Cycle B appeared in 1999; Cycles C and A are forthcoming in 2000 and 2001. See also Fritz West, *Scripture and Memory: The Ecumenical Hermeneutic of the Three-Year Lectionaries* (Collegeville: The Liturgical Press [A Pueblo Book], 1997); Normand Bonneau, *The Sunday Lectionary: Ritual Word, Paschal Shape* (Collegeville: The Liturgical Press, 1998); Edward Foley, *Preaching Basics* (Chicago: Liturgy Training Publications, 1998).

meant, how they conveyed their meaning, and what they can mean for us today. It is important for a preacher to know what method a biblical commentator is using, so as to understand what results it will yield. Likewise, preachers themselves should consciously choose the hermeneutical model by which they construct their preaching.[25] Preachers should also be aware that not all parables function in the same way. The term "parable" is elastic, stretching to fit different types of figurative stories, which do not all behave the same way rhetorically.[26]

The next chapter gives an overview of the Gospel of Luke. Subsequent chapters deal with the parables in the order in which they appear in the Lectionary. Attention will be given to how various methods result in different meanings. The interpretations offered are not exhaustive; other interpretations are possible. One thing of which to be wary is the title attached to any given parable. There are no titles in the Greek manuscripts; these are added by translators and commentators for ease in reference. The danger is that these labels circumvent the preacher's exploration of other possible meanings. The task of the preacher is not complete after having studied the text. It remains for the preacher to pray and discern which approach conveys the needed message for the particular assembly gathered in a specific place and time and to replicate its dynamics for contemporary hearers.

---

[25] See Raymond Bailey, ed., *Hermeneutics for Preaching: Approaches to Contemporary Interpretations of Scripture* (Nashville: Broadman, 1992); Mary Margaret Pazdan, "Hermeneutics and Proclaiming the Sunday Readings," *In the Company of Preachers* (Collegeville: The Liturgical Press, 1993) 26–37.

[26] See the excellent pointers by Thomas G. Long, "Preaching on the Parables of Jesus," in *Preaching the Literary Forms of the Bible* (Philadelphia: Fortress, 1989) 87–106.

CHAPTER THREE

Overview of the Gospel of Luke

RETRIEVING THE CONTEXT

In his book *The Gates of the Forest* Elie Wiesel tells the story of "When the great Rabbi Israel Baal Shem-Tov saw misfortune threatening the Jews it was his custom to go into a certain part of the forest to meditate. There he would light a fire, say a special prayer, and the miracle would be accomplished and the misfortune averted.

"Later, when his disciple, the celebrated Magid of Mezritch, had occasion, for the same reason, to intercede with heaven, he would go to the same place in the forest and say: 'Master of the Universe, listen! I do not know how to light the fire, but I am still able to say the prayer.' And again the miracle would be accomplished.

"Still later, Rabbi Moshe-Leib of Sassov, in order to save his people once more, would go into the forest and say: 'I do not know how to light the fire, I do not know the prayer, but I know the place and this must be sufficient.' It was sufficient and the miracle was accomplished.

"Then it fell to Rabbi Israel of Rizhyn to overcome misfortune. Sitting in his armchair, his head in his hands, he spoke to God: 'I am unable to light the fire and I do not know the prayer; I cannot even find the place in the forest. All I can do is to tell the story, and this must be sufficient.' And it was sufficient."[1]

Wiesel's account illustrates the power of stories, even when the details of their original context are lost. This is the

[1] Elie Wiesel, *The Gates of the Forest,* trans. Frances Frenaye (New York: Holt, Rinehart and Winston, 1966) i–iii.

situation we face when trying to retrieve the original settings and meanings of Jesus' parables. The form in which they have come to us is now three stages removed from their first telling. Like Rabbi Israel of Rizhyn, all we have is the story. To understand the meaning of a parable, it would be most helpful if we could retrieve the contexts in which it was shaped and reshaped. To that end, we will sketch briefly the setting and situation of Luke's community as best can be determined from our current "armchairs."[2]

AN ORDERLY ACCOUNT

Each evangelist has a slightly different manner of presenting the gospel story, as is clear from their various introductions. Whereas Mark sets forth his account as *euangelion,* "good news," and Matthew begins with "the book *(biblos)* of the genealogy of Christ," and John focuses on "witness" *(martyria),* Luke calls his account "a narrative *(diēgēsis)* of the events that have been fulfilled among us" (1:1). He begins with a formal prologue (1:1-4), like other contemporary Greco-Roman writers.[3] Luke claims to have investigated everything carefully from the beginning (1:3), with the purpose of writing an orderly account in which he wants his hearer to "realize the certainty of the teachings you have received" (1:4).

THE BELOVED PHYSICIAN?

Like many ancient writers the third evangelist nowhere identifies himself,[4] though certain things can be said about him by what he writes. In his prologue he acknowledges that he was

[2] An earlier version of this chapter, "The Gospel of Luke and the Lectionary," appeared in *Liturgy* 90 (1994) 4–8.

[3] Comparisons have been made with the classical prefaces of Herodotus, Thucydides, and Polybius as well as with prefaces of Hellenistic writers such as Discorides Pedanius, Hippocrates, Aristeas, and Josephus. See Joseph A. Fitzmyer, *The Gospel According to Luke* (AB28; Garden City, N.Y.: Doubleday, 1981) 288–90.

[4] The ascription *euangelion kata Loukan,* "Gospel according to Luke," appears at the end of P[75], the oldest existing manuscript of the gospel, which dates to 175–225 C.E.

not an eyewitness to the events he recounts (1:2). His polished Greek and his use of Greco-Roman literary forms betray a good education. His avoidance of Semitic words[5] and his omission of traditions about Jewish customs and controversies with the Pharisees (cf. Mark 7) are probable indicators that Luke was a Gentile convert from paganism, not a Jewish Christian.[6]

From the end of the second century the third evangelist has been identified with "Luke, the beloved physician" in Colossians 4:14.[7] Some scholars find confirmation of this identification in the way Luke has expanded the descriptions of illnesses in his healing stories. He heightens the fever of Simon's mother-in-law (Luke 4:38; cf. Mark 1:30) and describes a man "full of leprosy" (Luke 5:12; cf. Mark 1:40). Some manuscripts of Luke 8:43 delete the derogatory remark about how much money the woman with the flow of blood had spent on doctors. However, closer study of Luke's supposed medical vocabulary shows that such is found in the works of other ancient Greek authors who were not physicians.[8]

POSSIBLE COMPANION OF PAUL

In addition to Colossians 4:14, a co-worker of Paul named Luke is mentioned in Philemon 24 and 2 Timothy 4:11. Also, sections of Paul's voyages in Acts (16:10-17; 20:5-15; 21:1-18;

[5] E.g., where Mark uses *rabbi* as an address to Jesus, Luke either changes it to *epistatēs* (Luke 9:33; cf. Mark 9:5) or to *kyrie* (Luke 18:41; cf. Mark 10:51) or omits the address altogether (Luke 22:47; cf. Mark 14:45).

[6] Some scholars hold, however, that Luke was a Jewish Christian because of his many quotations of the Old Testament and because of the ancient (fourth-century) tradition (Epiphanius, *Panarion*, 51.11.6) that he was one of the seventy-two disciples sent out by Jesus (Luke 10:1). However, Luke's familiarity with the Jewish Scriptures can be explained by his being a proselyte or a God-fearer, i.e., a Gentile who had become attracted to Judaism before becoming a Christian (R. E. Brown, *An Introduction to the New Testament* [ABRL; New York: Doubleday, 1997] 268). For more detailed discussion on the identity of the evangelist, see Fitzmyer, *Luke*, 35–53.

[7] The earliest references to Luke as a companion of Paul are found in the Muratorian Canon, dating to ca. 170–180 C.E. and in Irenaeus (*Adversus haereses* 3.1, 1 and 3.14, 2-3).

[8] See H. J. Cadbury, *The Style and Literary Method of Luke*, HTS 6/1 (Cambridge, Mass.: Harvard University Press, 1920).

27:1–28:16) are written in the first person plural, giving the impression that Luke accompanied the apostle on these journeys. There is considerable debate about whether the third evangelist actually knew Paul and whether he is the same person mentioned in these Pauline letters. Doubts arise because Luke's portrayal of Paul in Acts differs greatly from what Paul says about himself in his own letters. Furthermore, Luke seems to have little or no acquaintance with Paul's letters and with the major theological and pastoral concerns therein.[9] An explanation for the first person accounts in Acts is that they are a literary construction. Use of first-person narrative in recounting sea voyages was a common literary device in antiquity.[10]

On the other hand the differences between Acts and Paul may not be as great as they first appear. A possible solution is that the evangelist was, indeed, the Luke mentioned in the Pauline letters, but that he was only a "sometime companion" of the apostle.[11] The "we" passages, then, could be autobiographical, from a type of diary kept when the writer accompanied Paul. It is not impossible that the oldest tradition about the third evangelist is correct, but with each theory about authorship problems still remain.[12]

Recently the suggestion has been made, based on the abundance of stories about women in this gospel, that the third evangelist was a woman.[13] Whether or not this is so, the author

[9] A few scholars dissent, e.g., W. O. Walker, "Acts and the Pauline Corpus Reconsidered," *JSNT* 24 (1985) 3–23.

[10] See S. M. Praeder, "Acts 27:1–28:16: Sea Voyages in Ancient Literature and the Theology of Luke-Acts," *CBQ* 46 (1984) 683–706; Vernon K. Robbins, "By Land and Sea: The We-Passages and Ancient Sea Voyages," *Perspectives on Luke-Acts*, ed. C. H. Talbert (Danville, Va.: Association of Baptist Professors of Religion, 1978) 215–42. Fitzmyer, however ("The Authorship of Luke-Acts Reconsidered," *Luke the Theologian: Aspects of His Teaching* [New York/Mahwah: Paulist Press, 1989] 1–26), finds the parallels wanting.

[11] Fitzmyer, "Authorship," 1–26.

[12] See further Brown, *Introduction*, 322–27.

[13] E.g., E. Jane Via, "Women in the Gospel of Luke," in *Women in the World's Religions: Past and Present*, ed. Ursula King (New York: Paragon House, 1987) 49–50, nn. 37–40. See also Ross S. Kraemer, "Women's Authorship of Jewish and Christian Literature in the Greco-Roman Period," in *"Women Like This": New Perspectives on Jewish Women in the Greco-Roman World*, ed. Amy-Jill Levine, SBLEJL 1 (Atlanta: Scholars Press, 1991) 221–42.

clearly assumes a male persona in the prologue, where the verb referring to the writer's activity, *parēkolouthēkoti*, "investigating," (1:3) is a masculine participle. More likely is that some of the traditions that came to the evangelist were preserved and shaped in circles of women disciples.[14]

AN ANTIOCHENE

The oldest tradition about Luke, found in a second-century extratextual Prologue to the Gospel, is that he was a native of Syrian Antioch.[15] Such an identification coheres with portions of Acts (11:19–15:40; 18:22-23) that show knowledge of the early Christian community there. Luke's form of the eucharistic formula in Luke 22:19-20 is closest to 1 Corinthians 11:23-25, which may be due to Antiochene tradition. Luke seems not to be a Palestinian because of mistakes he makes in geography.[16] Other suggestions for Luke's place of origin include Pisidian Antioch, Philippi, and Cyrene (identifying the evangelist with Lucius of Cyrene of Acts 13:1).

AUDIENCE

Luke directs his writings to "most excellent Theophilus" (Luke 1:3; Acts 1:1). Theophilus is otherwise unknown; possibly he was Luke's patron. Luke 1:4 implies that Theophilus was a catechumen. His name, a common one among both Gentiles and Jews, means "beloved of God" or "lover of God." While it

---

[14] Dennis MacDonald ("Virgins, Widows, and Paul in Second Century Asia Minor," *SBL 1979 Seminar Papers* [Missoula: Scholars Press, 1979] 169–84) provides evidence for women ecclesiastical storytellers.

[15] This same tradition is found in Eusebius (*Hist. eccl.* 3.4, 6) and in Jerome (*De vir.ill.* 7). Fitzmyer (*Luke,* 45) holds that Luke was a native Syrian inhabitant of Antioch, a Gentile from a Semitic cultural background.

[16] E.g., at Luke 4:44 he says that Jesus is going through the synagogues of Judea when the surrounding material clearly locates Jesus in Galilee. Is Luke uncertain about Palestinian geography or is this a universalizing tendency by which he uses "Judea" to mean "the country of the Jews," as also in 1:5; 6:17; 17:17; 23:5? Another example of mistaken geography is 17:11, where Luke says Jesus was going through the region "between Samaria and Galilee" (*NRSV*), two regions that are actually contiguous.

is unlikely that the name is purely symbolic, it can also function to direct the good news to any reader.

A number of factors point to Luke's audience being Gentile Christians in a predominantly Gentile setting. Luke eliminates traditions about Jewish ritual purity (cf. Mark 7:1-23) and other details of Jewish law (cf. Matt 5:21-48). He substitutes Greek words for Hebrew or Aramaic expressions.[17] He changes the thatched roof of Mark 2:4, a detail reflecting Palestinian local color, to a tiled roof (Luke 5:19), more familiar to a Hellenistic audience.[18] His depictions of Jesus at banquets (Luke 14:1-24) bear resemblances to Hellenistic symposia. And his portrayal of Jesus' agony (22:39-46) is akin to accounts in Philo of victorious struggle against the passion grief.[19] Finally, Luke's quotations of the Scriptures are derived from the Septuagint, the Greek translation of the Hebrew Scriptures.

A minority opinion is that of Jacob Jervell, who holds that Luke writes for a predominantly Jewish Christian community.[20] Jervell reads Acts as portraying the mission to the Jews a great success (e.g., Acts 2:41; 4:4; 6:7) and the Gentile mission as conducted within the sphere of Jewish Christianity. The influx of Gentiles in the Christian community is a sign of the fulfillment of the restoration of Israel promised in the Hebrew Scriptures, not a signal of the rejection of or replacement of Israel.

Whichever group predominated, all scholars agree that Luke wrote for a mixed community of Jewish and Gentile Christians who struggled to define their identity in relation to Jews of the synagogue that did not come to believe in Jesus. A

---

[17] E.g., he avoids the title *rabbi* and *rabbouni* for Jesus and uses instead *kyrios*, "Lord" (Luke 18:41), or *epistatēs*, "teacher" (Luke 9:33). He replaces *Golgotha* (Mark 15:22) with *kranion* ("skull" in Luke 23:33). Simon the Cananean (*Kananaios* in Mark 3:18) becomes Simon the Zealot (*Zēlōtēs* in Luke 6:15).

[18] See further Fitzmyer, *Luke*, 57–59; Luke T. Johnson, "On Finding the Lukan Community: A Cautionary Essay," *SBL Seminar 1979 Papers*, vol. 1 (Missoula: Scholars Press, 1979) 87–100; Eugene LaVerdiere, *Luke*, NTMS 5 (Wilmington: Glazier, 1980) xiv–xv; Marion L. Soards, "The Historical and Cultural Setting of Luke-Acts," *New Views on Luke and Acts*, ed. Earl Richard (Collegeville: The Liturgical Press, 1990) 33–47.

[19] See J. Neyrey, *The Passion According to Luke: A Redaction Study of Luke's Soteriology*, Theological Inquiries (New York: Paulist, 1985) 49–68.

[20] Jacob Jervell, *Luke and the People of God* (Minneapolis: Augsburg, 1972).

related question in Lukan studies is Luke's treatment of the Jews, on which further comments are made below.

SETTING

If Luke's place of origin was Antioch of Syria, it is not certain that this was also the locale of the community for whom he writes. Ancient traditions locate both Matthew's and Luke's communities in Syrian Antioch. However, it is questionable whether two early Christian communities with such diverse theologies coexisted in the same city. Given Luke's focus on Paul's apostolic journeys in Acts, it is likely that Luke's communities sprang from the Pauline mission. It is entirely possible that the Lukan communities were not confined to one city, but spread over a region, i.e., a cluster of missionary communities radiating from a mother foundation, somewhere in Asia Minor or an area of Greece.[21]

SOURCES, DATING, AND COMPOSITION

Because more than half of Luke's material has a counterpart in the Gospel of Mark and is told in the same sequence, often with the same wording, most scholars hold that Luke used Mark as a primary source.[22] A second source is postulated, based on some 230 verses of sayings material that Luke shares

[21] Suggestions include Achaia, Antioch, Boetia, Caesarea, the Decapolis, Rome, and Syria. See further Brown, *Introduction*, 269–71; Robert J. Karris, "Missionary Communities: A New Paradigm for the Study of Luke-Acts," *CBQ* 41 (1979) 80–97.

[22] See J. A. Fitzmyer, "The Priority of Mark and the Q Source," *To Advance the Gospel: New Testament Studies* (New York: Crossroad, 1981) 3–40; Mark Allan Powell, *What Are They Saying about Luke?* (New York/Mahwah: Paulist, 1989) 16–41. A few scholars believe that Luke relied on Matthew as a source and that Mark is an abridgment of Luke and Matthew. This hypothesis was first proposed by the eighteenth-century scholar Johann Griesbach. William R. Farmer (*The Synoptic Problem: A Critical Analysis* [New York: Macmillan, 1964]) has spearheaded the revival of "The Two-Gospel Hypothesis" in recent decades. A separate group of scholars, led by M. D. Goulder (*Luke: A New Paradigm* [JSNTSup 20; Sheffield: JSOT, 1989) and John Drury (*Tradition and Design in Luke's Gospel: A Study of Early Christian Historiography* [London: Darton, Longman, and Todd, 1976]), also deny the existence of Q and hold for direct dependence of Luke on

with Matthew but are absent from Mark. The wording is often identical and the sayings occur in the same order in the two gospels, though not always in the same context. The hypothetical written source for these sayings is referred to as "Q" (from the German word *Quelle,* meaning "source").[23] Luke also used sources unique to him, which scholars refer to as "L." Finally, the evangelist himself played an important role in the composition of the gospel. He both preserved tradition from his sources and composed sections himself, shaping the material in a way that conveyed the good news in a manner that would address the particular pastoral concerns of his communities.

Presuming Luke's use of Mark, which dates to 68–70 c.e., and taking references to the destruction of the Temple in Luke (13:35; 19:43-44; 21:20; 23:28-31) as a *fait accompli,* the most likely date of composition of the Third Gospel is 85 c.e., give or take five years.

GENRE

There is still much debate about the literary genre of Luke and Acts. Scholars see similarities to Hellenistic biographies, monographs, histories, antiquities, apologies, historical novels, and accounts of philosophical succession. Both Lukan books are a mixture of popular first-century Greco-Roman literary types. In addition they are suffused with language, imagery, settings, and character types from the Septuagint. This points to an educated audience that is both highly Hellenized and well familiar with Jewish biblical tradition.[24]

Matthew. While such theories eliminate the need for "Q," they ultimately create more difficulties than they resolve.

[23] See John Kloppenborg, *The Formation of Q: Trajectories in Ancient Wisdom Collections* (Studies in Antiquity and Christianity. Philadelphia: Fortress, 1987); Richard Edwards, *A Theology of Q: Eschatology, Prophecy and Wisdom* (Philadelphia: Fortress, 1976).

[24] See David Aune, *The New Testament in Its Literary Environment* (Library of Early Christianity. Philadelphia: Westminster, 1987) 77–157; John A. Darr, *On Character Building: The Rhetoric of Characterization in Luke-Acts,* Literary Currents in Biblical Interpretation (Louisville: Westminster/John Knox, 1992) 27–28, 48–49; Mikeal C. Parsons and Richard I. Pervo, *Rethinking the Unity of Luke and*

STRUCTURE

Luke's Gospel begins with a formal prologue (1:1-4), followed by his infancy narratives (1:5–2:52). Then, following the basic outline of Mark, Luke relates Jesus' preparation for public ministry (3:1–4:13), the first part of which takes place in Galilee (4:14–9:50). Many traditions unique to Luke, including the bulk of the parables, are found in his travel section recounting the journey to Jerusalem (9:51–19:27). A teaching ministry in Jerusalem (19:28–21:38) precedes the passion narrative (22:1–23:56). The discovery of the empty tomb, resurrection appearances, and Jesus' ascension (24:1-53) conclude Luke's first volume.

SALVATION HISTORY

Luke displays a keen interest in relating the gospel events to the broader stage of history. He opens his account with the time marker, "In the days of Herod, King of Judea" (Luke 1:5). He situates Jesus' birth in the days when Quirinius was governor of Syria (Luke 2:1-2).[25] He dates Jesus' baptism and the beginning of his ministry to the fifteenth year of the reign of Tiberius Caesar, the governorship of Pontius Pilate, the tetrarchies of the sons of Herod the Great, and the high priesthood of Annas and Caiaphas (3:1-2). Luke's style bears certain similarities to that of other ancient historiographers. Luke's purpose, however, was not to record history, but to tell the gospel story in a highly incarnational way—one that made it very concrete, taking place in a recognizable place and time. Moreover, Luke's historical concern serves his theological purpose to show all that happened in the gospel as fulfillment of God's promises to Israel.

Luke sketches salvation history in stages, showing that the same faithful God of Israel is the God of Jesus and of the early church. Hans Conzelmann proposed a three-stage develop-

---

Acts (Minneapolis: Fortress, 1993) 20–44; Richard Pervo, *Profit with Delight: The Literary Genre of the Acts of the Apostles* (Philadelphia: Fortress, 1987); Charles H. Talbert, *Literary Patterns, Theological Themes and the Genre of Luke-Acts*, SBLMS 20 (Missoula: Scholars Press, 1974).

[25] See Fitzmyer, *Luke*, 15, 393, for analysis of the problems with this dating.

ment of salvation history in Luke: 1) the period of Israel, 2) the period of Jesus' ministry, and 3) the period since the ascension, in which the Church looks back to the period of Jesus and forward to the parousia.[26] He sees Luke 16:16, where Jesus declares, "The law and the prophets lasted until John; but from then on the kingdom of God is proclaimed," as a demarcation in the gospel of the first two periods. The beginning of the third period is implied with the addition of Acts of the Apostles as a sequel to the gospel. More recently, scholars see Luke as presenting a two-stage history of salvation: the Old Age, the time of Israel as preparation, prophecy, and promise, and the New Age, inaugurated by the Christ-event and awaiting the final consummation.[27] In either case, Luke has created a schema of salvation history in which he presents Christianity as the continuation and fulfillment of God's saving acts and promises to Israel.[28]

ESCHATOLOGY

By extending his account in Acts of the Apostles to narrate the ongoing story of Jesus' disciples, Luke shifts his emphasis away from an expectation of an imminent parousia to attention toward the practices of living the gospel day-to-day. Sayings from his sources that emphasize an imminent end are either modified or omitted.[29] In sayings unique to Luke the delay in the parousia is evident, as in Luke 19:11, where Luke says that Jesus proceeded to tell the parable of the talents "because he was near Jerusalem and they thought that the kingdom of God would appear there immediately." Luke shifts attention away from the imminent coming to the notion of the timeless presence of the reign of God already inaugurated with the coming of Jesus in another peculiarly Lukan saying, in which Jesus as-

[26] Hans Conzelmann, *The Theology of St. Luke,* trans. Geoffrey Buswell (Philadelphia: Fortress, 1961) 16–17.

[27] Earl Richard, "Luke: Author and Thinker," *New Views on Luke and Acts,* ed. Earl Richard (Collegeville: The Liturgical Press, 1990) 15–32.

[28] See further Robert O'Toole, *The Unity of Luke's Theology: An Analysis of Luke-Acts* (GNS 9; Wilmington: Glazier, 1984) 62–94.

[29] Compare Mark 1:15 and Luke 4:15-21; Mark 9:1 and Luke 9:27.

serts, "The coming of the kingdom of God cannot be observed, and no one will announce, 'Look, here it is,' or, 'There it is.' For behold, the kingdom of God is among you" (Luke 17:20). Luke also dulls the eschatological edge in his version of the apocalyptic discourse (compare Luke 21 with Mark 13).

Although the end time is not so imminent for Luke as for other Christian writers, he nonetheless incorporates parables and sayings that show the end is still to be expected and Christians must be vigilant for its sudden coming. The admonitions to be ready as servants who do not know when their master will return (12:38, 45) and the parable of the barren fig tree (13:8) warn against complacency in the face of the delay.

Standing in tension with sayings about the delay are others that affirm an imminent coming of the reign of God or of judgment. In Luke 10:9, 11 the seventy(-two) are to proclaim that the reign of God has drawn near (cf. Matt 10:14). The sayings added by Luke to the ending of the parable of the widow and the judge in Luke 18:7-8 assure that God will not delay. Another assertion of the nearness of the reign of God is found in the parable of the fig tree (Luke 21:31; cf. Mark 13:29).

The issue of Lukan eschatology is not clear-cut. Luke both preserves and adds sayings about an imminent end even while his consciousness of the delay is evident. Luke has, to some degree, shifted attention away from the imminent end to emphasize the necessity of daily attentiveness in the living out of the gospel.[30]

JEWS AND GENTILES

It is clear that Luke writes for a mixed community of Jewish and Gentile Christians who are yet struggling to define their identity in relation to those Jews who did not believe in Jesus. Having their roots in Judaism, how do these Christians understand themselves as an institution apart from Judaism? Who are the true people of God? Why have the people of the promise as a whole not accepted the gospel?

---

[30] See further Fitzmyer, *Luke*, 18–22, 231–35.

There is no agreement among scholars on how Luke answers these questions. In both the gospel and Acts there are both positive and negative portrayals of Jews.[31] On the positive side, in the gospel the first followers of Jesus and those who benefit from his healing and exorcisms are Jews. Acts relates the conversion of many Jews (e.g., 2:41; 4:4; 6:7). There are positive portrayals of Pharisees (Luke 13:31-35; 20:27-39; Acts 5:34-39) and Paul never ceases being one (Acts 23:6-10). On the other hand, there are condemnations of Pharisees and scribes (e.g., Luke 11:37-51; 15:1-2; 16:13-15), and accusations of Israel's hardheartedness (Acts 7:51-53; 28:23-31). The Jewish Sanhedrin delivers Jesus to Pilate and a crowd of Jews demands his crucifixion while Pilate three times declares him innocent (Luke 22:66–23:25; Acts 2:22-23). There is rejection and persecution of Christians by some Jews (e.g., 9:23; 12:3, 11; 13:45; 14:2-5). This ambiguous portrayal has been resolved various ways by different scholars.[32]

For some, Luke portrays Israel as having rejected God's plan of salvation. As a result, they are excluded from God's promises, which are now fulfilled for those who have accepted them, namely, Gentile Christians.[33] In this schema Gentile Christians are assured of the legitimacy of their faith and the Jewish people are understood as replaced or superseded by Christians as the people of God. For some scholars[34] Luke's polemic against the Jews not only serves purposes of self-definition for Gentile Christians, but also reflects a specific threat to the community in Luke's day. For them the problem is much like the one Paul faced in Galatia where he had to battle Jewish Christians who advocated full observance of the Mosaic Law. Luke's story of Jesus' controversies with the Pharisees is aimed at helping his

---

[31] For a fuller treatment of texts that portray the Jews both positively and negatively see Robert O'Toole, "Reflections on Luke's Treatment of Jews in Luke-Acts," *Bib* 74 (1993) 529–55.

[32] For a summary of various positions see Mark Allen Powell, *What Are They Saying about Luke?* 51–59; Joseph Tyson, ed., *Luke-Acts and the Jewish People: Eight Critical Perspectives* (Minneapolis: Augsburg, 1988).

[33] So, for example, Robert Maddox, *The Purpose of Luke-Acts* (SNTW; Edinburg: T. & T. Clark, 1985).

[34] E.g., Jack T. Sanders, *The Jews in Luke-Acts* (Philadelphia: Fortress, 1987).

community deal with the present conflicts with law-observant Christians.

A different interpretation is that Luke never portrays Israel as a whole as rejected by God or in any way replaced. Rather, Luke insists that to the Jews belong the promises made by God through their ancestors (Luke 1:72; Acts 2:39; 7:17; 13:23) and these promises are never revoked. However, these have taken on a new form with the coming of Jesus and the pouring out of the Spirit. The people of God in this new age consists of those Jews who have accepted the gospel as well as those Gentiles who have done so. Israel, then, for Luke, is a divided people: some reject God's plan, just as some have always been disobedient to God's design, while others who have believed in Jesus constitute the restored Israel. The latter include those Gentiles who are granted a share in the blessings of Israel through their acceptance of the gospel. Hope is held out for all peoples to become part of the restored Israel.[35]

A further question is how contemporary Christians in a post-Holocaust era who are increasingly aware of Christian anti-Semitism are to read Luke. When there are assertions in Luke that are anti-Jewish, preachers and teachers must clearly represent the historical situation of the early Christians as the backdrop for such. Distinctions must be made between Luke's statements which, made in a context of intra-Jewish conflicts, take on an entirely different character when they are made by Christians who are no longer Jewish and when they are applied to the Jewish people as a whole. Christians must clearly denounce all contemporary forms of Christian anti-Judaism as abhorrent.

---

[35] See Joseph A. Fitzmyer, "The Jewish People and the Mosaic Law in Luke-Acts," in *Luke the Theologian: Aspects of His Teaching* (New York/Mahwah: Paulist, 1989) 175–202; Jacob Jervell, *Luke and the People of God: A New Look at Luke-Acts* (Minneapolis: Augsburg, 1984); David Moessner, ed., *Luke and the Heritage of Israel: Luke's Narrative Claim upon Israel's Legacy* (Luke the Interpreter of Israel; Harrisburg, Penn.: Trinity Press International, 1999).

THEOLOGICAL EMPHASES[36]

Following is a brief sketch of some of the most prominent theological emphases in the Third Gospel. Many of them occur repeatedly in the Lukan parables.

Fulfillment of Scripture

It is notable how often Luke alludes to the Scriptures or quotes them directly from the Septuagint, the Greek translation of the Hebrew Scriptures. The expression *dei*, "it is necessary" and the verb *plēroō*, "to fulfill," occur frequently. At the conclusion of the gospel this theme comes to a head when the risen Christ asks the two disciples on the road to Emmaus, "Was it not necessary *(dei)* that the Messiah should suffer these things and enter into his glory?" (24:26). He then interprets for them everything that referred to him in the Scriptures. Luke is intent on showing everything that happens as part of God's plan for salvation, not in the sense of predestination or predetermination, but in order to underscore God's faithfulness. The God who acted mightily on behalf of Israel is the same faithful God who acts with salvific power for the restored people of God.

Prayer

From the opening chapters the Third Gospel is steeped in an atmosphere of prayer, as Zechariah, Simeon, Anna, Jesus' parents, and the twelve-year-old Jesus are all drawn to the Temple. Even in the private sphere of the home, prayer permeates the scene of the visitation, as Elizabeth and Mary bless one another and proclaim God's praise (1:39-55). Luke shows Jesus at prayer as a regular occurrence (5:16) and at critical turning points in his life: at his baptism (3:21), before his choice of the Twelve (6:12), before Peter's confession of him as the Messiah (9:18), at the transfiguration (9:28-29), before his arrest on the Mount of Olives (22:39-46), and on the cross (23:46). Jesus gives voice to a spontaneous prayer of thanks (10:21-23) and assures Peter that he has prayed for unfailing faith for him (22:32).

---

[36] An earlier version of this section appeared in *Liturgy 90* (Nov./Dec. 1994) 4–8.

Prayer is likewise an important practice for his disciples. Jesus instructs them on prayer (Luke 6:28; 10:2; 20:45-47; 21:36; 22:40, 46), sometimes in parabolic form (11:1-13; 18:1-14). In Acts, the early Christians are portrayed as constantly at prayer. By highlighting Jesus' intimate union with God, Luke invites believers to pattern their lives in like fashion.

Crossing Boundaries

It is notable how often in the Gospel of Luke Jesus associates with those who are marginal or outcast from Jewish society. He is frequently in the company of tax collectors (5:27-32; 19:1-10) who were despised as greedy, dishonest, and ritually unclean. He also welcomes sinners (5:8, 20; 7:36-50) and eats with them (5:30; 15:1-2). He touches those who are sick and ritually impure (4:40; 5:13; 8:40-56; 13:13; 22:51). He declares that his mission is to bring good news to the poor, release to the captives, recovery of sight to the blind, freedom to the oppressed (4:18). Yet he also dines with Pharisees (7:36; 14:1) and invites a rich official to join him (18:18-23). Luke presents a portrait of a Jesus who easily crosses all boundaries so as to include everyone in his invitation to salvation. Luke thus invites disciples of Jesus to emulate him in crossing boundary differences of race, economics, gender, social status, etc. in relating to one another and in the mission of evangelizing.

Rich and Poor

One particular barrier that receives much attention in Luke is the relationship of material possessions and discipleship. In his Sermon on the Plain Jesus pronounces the poor blessed (6:20). He insists that a person cannot serve both God and mammon (16:13). When the rich official is unable to leave everything to follow Jesus as do Peter, James, John (5:11), and Levi (5:28), Jesus remarks on how difficult it is for a rich person to enter the reign of God (18:25). A poor widow who puts into the treasury all she has to live on is favorably contrasted with the rich who give from their abundance (21:1-4). The parables of the rich fool (12:16-21) and of the rich man and Lazarus (16:19-23) illustrate the dire consequences of accumulating riches for oneself.

Yet there are also wealthy disciples. Joanna, the wife of Herod's steward, along with Mary Magdalene, Susanna, and other Galilean women use their financial resources to support the mission of Jesus and the Twelve (8:1-3). Salvation comes to the house of the rich tax collector Zacchaeus, who gives (only!) half of his possessions to the poor (19:1-10). Well-to-do believers in Acts include an Ethiopian eunuch who was a court official in charge of the entire treasury of the queen of the Ethiopians (8:27), Mary, whose house was a gathering place of the disciples in Jerusalem (12:12), prominent women in Thessalonica (17:4), influential Greek men and women in Beroea (17:12), Prisca and Aquila who hosted Paul in Corinth (18:1-11) and who traveled with him to Ephesus to establish a new mission base there (18:18-28). In Acts, disciples are not poor but rather share everything in common (2:42-47; 4:32-34).

In Luke-Acts there is no one model of how a disciple is to dispose of material possessions. Some leave them all to follow Jesus; others retain them but place them at the disposal of the community. The ideal is that no one is wanting (Acts 2:45; 4:34, 35). Luke continues to confront contemporary Christians with very difficult questions about how one can retain possessions and still be a disciple. He presents the demands of justice most clearly and makes no bones that in an unequal world God sides with the poor.

Women[37]

It is often remarked that Luke has more stories about women than any of the other gospels. Only in Luke do we find the stories of Elizabeth (1:5-7, 24-25, 39-45, 57-66); Mary (1:26-56; 2:1-52; Acts 1:14); Anna (2:36-38); the widow of Nain (7:11-17); the woman who showed extravagant love (7:36-50); the ministry of Mary Magdalene, Joanna, Susanna, and the other Galilean women (8:1-3); Martha and Mary (10:38-42); the woman who utters a blessing (11:27-28); the woman bent double (13:10-17); the parable of the woman who searches for a lost coin (15:8-10); the parable of the widow demanding justice

---

[37] See further Barbara E. Reid, *Choosing the Better Part? Women in the Gospel of Luke* (Collegeville: The Liturgical Press, 1996).

(18:1-8); and the women of Jerusalem lamenting Jesus on the way of the cross (23:26-32).

In addition to these are the stories shared with Mark and Matthew featuring Simon's mother-in-law (4:38-39), Jairus' daughter and the woman with a hemorrhage (8:40-56), a woman baking bread (13:20-21), a widow who gives her all (Luke 21:1-4), the Galilean women who witness Jesus' death and burial (23:44-49, 50-56) and who discover the empty tomb (24:1-12).

It is this abundance of stories involving women that has led many to believe that the Third Gospel is the most apt for promoting equality of women and men disciples.[38] But recent feminist interpreters have noted that Luke's portrait of women is ambiguous at best, and dangerous at worst.[39] These scholars have noted the limited roles assigned to women in Luke and Acts. Outside of the infancy narratives, where Elizabeth, Mary, and Anna are portrayed as prophetic women, no woman disciple speaks except to be corrected by Jesus. Mary Magdalene's proclamation of the resurrection is dismissed as "nonsense" (24:11). Women are healed by Jesus and engage in charitable works, but are portrayed as having "chosen the better part" (10:42) when they remain silent and passive. Luke shows only the men being empowered to speak and act and bear responsibility within the Jesus movement. This becomes even more evident in the Acts of the Apostles, Luke's second volume. It seems that Luke,

[38] Alfred Plummer remarks, "the Third Gospel is in an especial sense the Gospel for *women* . . . all through this Gospel they are allowed a prominent place, and many types of womanhood are placed before us" (*The Gospel According to S. Luke* [5th ed.; ICC. Edinburgh: T. & T. Clark, 1981] xlii–xliii). In a similar vein, Robert O'Toole lists the passages he believes Luke has designed as parallel pairs of stories of men and women, that "suggest an equality. Men and women receive the same salvific benefits. God, Christ, and the disciples act in their lives in similar fashion. Women and men have similar experiences and fulfill similar functions. They believe and proclaim the gospel message" (*The Unity of Luke's Theology*, 118–26). See also Robert J. Karris, "Women and Discipleship in Luke," *CBQ* 56 (1994) 1–20.

[39] Mary Rose D'Angelo, "Women in Luke-Acts: A Redactional View," *JBL* 109/3 [1990] 441–61; Reid, *Choosing the Better Part?*; Jane Schaberg, "Luke," *The Women's Bible Commentary*, ed. Carol A. Newsom and Sharon H. Ringe (rev. ed.; Louisville: Westminster/John Knox, 1998) 363–80; Elisabeth Schüssler Fiorenza, *In Memory of Her* (New York: Crossroad, 1983); Turid Karlsen Seim, *The Double Message: Patterns of Gender in Luke-Acts* (Nashville: Abingdon, 1994).

rather than being the great advocate for women, is more intent on restricting and controlling them.

While gender is more clearly a category in Luke than in any other gospel, it is not entirely clear what Luke is saying. Plainly there are women disciples in Luke and Acts who are said to receive the word, believe, are baptized, follow Jesus, and host house churches. But their role is presented as different from that of the men. There are no narratives of women called, commissioned, enduring persecution, or ministering by the power of the Spirit, as there are of men.[40] Women in Luke and Acts do not exercise ministries of preaching, healing, exorcising, and forgiving, as do the male disciples. There is a double message. Luke preserves strong traditions about women and gives them certain positive functions. But their roles are not the same as those of the men. Luke's women are primarily shown in the private sphere of the household, but in the public sphere the ministries of praying, prophesying, teaching, healing, and leading are all exercised by men. Feminist methods of interpretation aid believers today in reflecting on these stories in a liberative manner for a culture vastly different from Luke's.

The Spirit

The action of the Spirit in Jesus and his disciples is another theme that is particularly emphasized by Luke. Every character in the opening chapters is filled with the Spirit: Elizabeth (1:41), Zechariah (1:67), John (1:15), Mary (1:35), and Simeon (2:25-27). Jesus, throughout his ministry, acts in the power of the Spirit (4:1,14,18; 10:21). He speaks to his disciples of the promised Spirit (11:13; 12:12; 24:49), who becomes their guiding force throughout Acts. It is the Spirit that enables disciples to act with boldness in the spreading of the gospel.

Meals

It seems that in Luke Jesus is always eating. At times he is the host, as when he provides food for five thousand people who come to hear him teach (9:10-17). He gives his very self as

---

[40] For more detailed analysis see Reid, *Choosing the Better Part?*, 21–54.

food for God's hungry creation (22:14-20). At other times he is a guest (5:30; 7:36; 10:38; 14:1; 19:7), though many of these meals must have ended with indigestion! In the dinner conversation Jesus frequently poses a challenge to the host and other guests that could convert them to a different vision of God's reign. Often this comes in the form of a parable.

Journey

One of the distinct features of the Third Gospel is the long journey narrative that spans ten chapters: 9:51–19:44. Much of the material is uniquely Lukan; some is Luke's redaction of Mark 8:22–10:52; some is from Q. It begins with Jesus resolutely setting his face to go to Jerusalem (9:51), with the consciousness that this is the place of *exodos*, as discussed with Moses and Elijah at the transfiguration (9:31). The word *exodos* has a double connotation and both meanings are intended. Jesus' *exodos*, his death, will be the means of the new coming out from bondage for his people. In Luke 13:33-34 Jesus is further aware that no prophet is killed outside of Jerusalem. The journey is one with a deliberate goal that is both sobering and liberating. It is in this journey section that the majority of the parables are found, along with other teachings of Jesus.[41] A central metaphor in Luke is that one comes to understand Jesus in the course of journeying with him. This is poignantly depicted in the resurrection appearance to the two disciples on the road to Emmaus (24:13-35). The metaphor of "the Way" is continued in Acts of the Apostles, where it becomes a designation for the Jesus movement (Acts 9:2; 18:25, 26; 19:9, 23; 22:4; 24:14, 22).

With this understanding of the evangelist and his concerns, we turn now to the Lukan parables in the order in which they appear in the Lectionary.

---

[41] See Kenneth E. Bailey, *Poet and Peasant: A Literary-Cultural Approach to the Parables in Luke* (Grand Rapids: Eerdmans, 1976) 79–85, for a detailed analysis of the literary structure of this section. See also David P. Moessner, *Lord of the Banquet: The Literary and Theological Significance of the Lukan Travel Narrative* (Minneapolis: Fortress, 1989).

CHAPTER FOUR

A Fruitless Fig
(Luke 13:1-9)

Third Sunday of Lent
Saturday of the Twenty-ninth Week of Ordinary Time

[1] *Some people told Jesus about the Galileans*
 whose blood Pilate had mingled with the blood of their sacrifices.
[2] *Jesus said to them in reply,*
 "Do you think that because these Galileans suffered in this way
 they were greater sinners than all other Galileans?
[3] *By no means!*
 But I tell you, if you do not repent,
 you will all perish as they did!
[4] *Or those eighteen people who were killed*
 when the tower at Siloam fell on them—
 do you think they were more guilty
 than everyone else who lived in Jerusalem?
[5] *By no means!*
 But I tell you, if you do not repent,
 you will all perish as they did!"

[6] *And he told them this parable:*
 "There once was a person who had a fig tree planted in his orchard,
 and when he came in search of fruit on it but found none,
 [7] *he said to the gardener,*
 'For three years now I have come in search of fruit on this fig tree
 but have found none.
 So cut it down.
 Why should it exhaust the soil?'
[8] *He said to him in reply,*
 'Sir, leave it for this year also,

and I shall cultivate the ground around it and fertilize it;
⁹ *it may bear fruit in the future.*
If not you can cut it down.'"

LUKAN LITERARY CONTEXT AND STRUCTURE

The central section of Luke's Gospel from 9:51–18:14 is commonly called the travel narrative. Inspired by Mark 10:1-52, it contains much material unique to Luke, including this parable of the fruitless fig and the recounting of the untimely deaths of some Galileans and Judeans. Jesus has resolutely set his face toward Jerusalem (9:51) and throughout this section he instructs his followers more fully, preparing them to be his witnesses. Only Luke has such an extended travel account at this point of the gospel. The majority of Luke's parables are found in this central section.

These beginning verses of chapter 13 follow on a section of the gospel that stressed the need for vigilance on the part of servants for the return of the master (12:35-49) and astuteness in recognizing and interpreting the signs of the present in view of the future (12:54-56). Immediately preceding the passage in today's Lectionary selection is a saying on the necessity of reconciliation with an opponent (12:57-59). Themes of impending crisis, preparedness, and setting relations aright lead into today's gospel.

Connections with what follows (the healing of the woman bent double in 13:10-17) are more difficult to discern. In fact, many commentators on Luke regard the travel narrative, and chapters 13 and 14 in particular, a loose collection of disparate sayings.[1] Robert J. Shirock[2] has shown, however, that there is a chiastic structure in Luke 13:1-35 in which the whole section explicates the deteriorating relationship between Jesus and his opponents as the consummation of his earthly ministry looms. The chapter can be arranged thus:

---

[1] E.g., I. Howard Marshall, *Commentary on Luke* (Grand Rapids: Eerdmans, 1978) 556, 562.

[2] Robert J. Shirock, "The Growth of the Kingdom in Light of Israel's Rejection of Jesus: Structure and Theology in Luke 13:1-35," *NovT* 35 (1993) 15–29.

A   13:1-9
  B   13:10-17
     C   13:18, 19
     C'   13:20, 21
  B'   13:22-30
A'   13:31-35

There are strong links between Luke 13:1-9 (a call to repentance) and 13:31-35 (the report of Herod's desire to kill Jesus and Jesus' lament over Jerusalem). Both sections begin with reports of hostility by a civil ruler. Both focus on imminent death. In the first it is Israel who is in danger of perishing; in the last it is Jesus. In both there is lament over frustration of divine intent: the owner over a fruitless fig tree; Jesus over an unwilling brood. Both refer to Jerusalem and both make use of the number three.

In the parable in the first section the owner is persuaded to leave *(aphes)* the tree one more year and the parable concludes on a note of uncertainty and hope. In the final section there is a note of certainty as Jesus' death and Jerusalem's abandonment *(aphietai)* is sure. Jesus the prophet pronounces both warnings of disaster and expressions of hope in the effort to bring his hearers to repentance. At the center of the chiasm are the parables of the mustard seed and the leaven that speak of the certainty of the growth of God's reign and its permeating influence.

TRADITION HISTORY

There are two sections to the unit that comprises Luke 13:1-9. Verses 1-5 relate two different episodes of tragic deaths. The first (vv. 1-3) concerns some Galileans who were slaughtered by Pilate while they were offering sacrifice. While there are a number of episodes of Pilate's cruelty toward Jews recounted by Josephus,[3] none of the known events matches this

---

[3] In one incident in 35 c.e. Pilate sent cavalry and infantry into a crowd of Samaritans in a village near Mount Gerizim. They killed some and dispersed the rest (*Ant.* 18.4,1 §86–87). Another time Pilate took money from the Temple treasury to pay for a new aqueduct for Jerusalem. Jews who demonstrated in protest outside Pilate's palace were beaten by his soldiers (*J.W.* 2.9, 4 §175–177).

one. Evidently Pilate had his soldiers kill some Galileans who had come to Jerusalem to offer sacrifice, possibly Passover lambs. Sacrifices *(thysiai)* were offered only in the Temple in Jerusalem. Presumably these Galileans had come to the holy city on pilgrimage for the feast, as Luke says Jesus' parents did each year (2:41).

Likewise, nothing more is known historically of the second incident (vv. 4-5) in which eighteen Jerusalemites were killed by a tower that collapsed in Siloam. Josephus relates that the ancient wall of Jerusalem turned from the east toward the south "above the fountain of Siloam" (*J.W.* 5.4, 2 §145). Although Josephus does not mention a tower, such would be presumed at a strategic turn in the wall. It is interesting that the pool of Siloam figures in John 9, the story of the healing of a man born blind, where the question is also raised about the connection between calamity and sin.

Joined to the narration of these two tragedies is the parable of the fruitless fig. While there are certain verbal links between this parable and the story of the cursing of the fig tree in Mark 11:12-14 (// Matt 21:18-19), there is no real connection between the two. The Markan episode of Jesus cursing the fig tree (11:12-14) and its subsequent withering (11:20-25) frames and interprets Jesus' prophetic action in the Temple (11:15-29), symbolizing its destruction. Luke omits this in his parallel material in chapter 19. It is important that the preacher keep separate these two gospel traditions about Jesus and fig trees.[4]

SIN AND SUFFERING

The two examples of untimely deaths raise a perennial human concern: Why do bad things happen to good people? Is there a connection between suffering and sin? A number of biblical passages make that connection. The Deuteronomist promises that if Israel keeps the commands of God, blessing and prosperity result (Deut 28:1). But if Israel is disobedient, then

---

[4] J. Duncan M. Derrett ("Figtrees in the New Testament," *HeyJ* 14 [1973] 249–65) studies all the passages in the New Testament that mention fig trees and asserts that they all concern Jesus' conception of the end time.

they incur curses and punishment (Deut 28:15). The thinking that suffering or death is a punishment for sin is also evident in Job 4:7-8; Proverbs 10:24-25; Ezekiel 18:26-28; John 9:1-3. In John 9:3 Jesus clearly pronounces that there is no link between suffering and sin. When calamity or death strikes a person it has nothing to do with their righteousness or lack of it. In the Lukan text of today's gospel Jesus does not give an answer to why people suffer, but he does clearly dissociates untimely death from sin and guilt. Those who died at the hands of Pilate and in the disaster at Siloam were no more culpable than any other.

TIMELY REPENTANCE

What Jesus' reply does emphasize is the unexpectedness of the end time and the necessity of repentance in light of that. It is not so much a threat to his hearers that if they do not repent they will suffer similarly, as it is a reminder that if they have not perished it is not because of their uprightness. The parable brings home the point that a crisis moment will come in which there will be a reckoning. There is not unlimited time. If one has procrastinated in responding in action to Jesus' invitation to discipleship, the gospel brings a sober reminder that there will be a reckoning and there must be visible fruit.

FRUITFUL FIGS AND FORBEARANCE

The parable in 13:6-9 conjures up familiar biblical images.[5] In several texts in the First Testament the combination of fruitful figs and productive vineyards symbolizes prosperity that comes as God's blessing (Mic 4:4; Joel 2:22). Fig trees were frequently planted in vineyards. In Micah 7:1 the prophet speaks of his frustrated search for figs and grapes at summer harvest time as a way of depicting God's disappointment over Israel's faithfulness. In Isaiah 5:1-7 the vinedresser similarly looks in

[5] See the insightfully poetic treatment of the intertextuality of this parable with the image of the rooted tree in Psalm 1 by Barbara Green, *Like a Tree Planted* (Collegeville: The Liturgical Press, 1997) 24–36. For a compendium of various scholarly interpretations of Luke 13:6-9 see Charles W. Hedrick, "Prolegomena to Reading Parables: Luke 13:6-9 as a Test Case," *RevExp* 94 (1997) 179–97.

vain for fruit from the well-tended vine.[6] While there is no explicit identification made of the owner of the vineyard and the gardener in Luke 13:6-9, the parable likewise evokes divine disappointment in the fruitlessness of Jesus' followers. The owner has waited three years.[7] Three is a number that signals completeness. He has given the tree a full measure of time to produce, but it has failed. This is echoed in 13:32 where Jesus asserts, "I cast out demons and I perform healings today and tomorrow, and on the third day I accomplish my purpose."

As the vintner in Isaiah 5, so in the Lukan parable the owner of the fruitless fig tree decides to destroy it. A tree that does not bear fruit is not a neutral thing: it is counterproductive by its wasting of the soil. But unlike Isaiah 5 there is an intervention by the gardener, who advocates forbearance and mercy for one more year in the hope of possible repentance. The point here is not a contrast between God's action of judgment in the First Testament and merciful forbearance in the New Age. In both, God is gracious and loving; in both there is the sober presentation of dire consequences for lack of responsiveness to divine mercy.

PREACHING POSSIBILITIES

The main point of the gospel is not speculation on a connection between suffering and sin or why bad things happen to good people. The verses that precede the parable are meant to evoke the realization that the end can come for anyone unexpectedly, whether one is righteous or not. All sin and all will die. The crucial issue is that fruitfulness be evident at the time of reckoning.

Luke underscores the necessity of repentance before it is too late.[8] While *metanoeō*, "to repent," and *metanoia*, "repent-

---

[6] A similar imagery appears in Jeremiah 12:10 and Song of Songs 8:12.

[7] Kenneth E. Bailey (*Through Peasant Eyes: More Lucan Parables, Their Culture and Style* [Grand Rapids: Eerdmans, 1980] 82) suggests that in actual fact the tree has gone nine years without producing fruit. Ordinarily a fig would need three years to grow before being capable of producing. Then the first three years of produce would be dedicated to God. Now as the owner finally expects to enjoy the fruit himself, the tree yields none.

[8] See above, pp. 36–37, on Lukan eschatology.

ance" are favorite words of the Third Evangelist, it is important to note that the ways in which he depicts repentance (for example, in Luke 15)[9] is that God begins the process and is the one who effects reconciliation. Repentance does not consist in turning oneself around by one's own efforts. The fig only bears fruit as a response to God's gracious offer of mercy and forbearance. It is God who cultivates and fertilizes the fig tree, enabling its fruitfulness. This same theme is echoed in the responsorial psalm, "The Lord is kind and merciful" (Ps 103:8a). The preacher will, therefore, want to avoid the pitfall of presenting this parable as a call to greater productivity and self-reliance as a means to effect salvation. Such feeds into a culture of overwork and productivity as a measure of success. While the invitation of grace offered by Jesus is free and unearned, the parable does insist that a fruitful response is required. A gratuitous extension of time and extra attention of the gardener may be given, but ultimately a yield is expected.

This theme in the gospel is also echoed in the second reading (2 Cor 10:1-6, 10-12). There Paul is warning the Corinthians not to be overly confident about the privileges that they have. He draws a parallel between Christian baptism and the Israelites' passing through the sea at the Exodus. Just as the latter had miraculous gifts of manna and water from God, so Christians have baptism and Eucharist. Despite these gifts from God, the Israelites still sinned. So Paul warns the Corinthians against complacency. God's gracious gifts are intended to lead to transformation of heart that becomes visible in action.

Reflecting on this gospel during the Lenten season, and taking into account its placement in the Lukan travel narrative where Jesus is relentlessly headed toward Jerusalem, there is a clear pointer forward to the death of Jesus. The linking of Pilate with the vicious execution of some Galileans offering sacrifice prepares the hearer of Luke's Gospel for Pilate's role in crucifying Jesus. In chapter 13 the victims' sinfulness or guilt is not the cause of their death. So, too, at his death the Lukan Jesus is pronounced not guilty three times by Pilate (23:4, 14, 22), by Herod (23:15), by one of the criminals hanged with him (23:41), and

---

[9] See below, chaps. 5 and 15.

by the centurion who witnesses his death (23:47). The brutal crucifixion of Jesus who did not deserve to die helps Christians understand the truth about the death of innocent victims and gives them courage to unmask the lies promoted by perpetrators of violence. One could make a connection with the first reading (Exod 3:1-8a, 13-15), where God is revealed to Moses as one who does not delight in the suffering of the innocent, but hears the cries of the afflicted Israelites and comes to rescue them from their oppressors.

Continuing in this vein, the story of the undeserved slaughter of the Galileans gives Christians courage to denounce officially sanctioned terrorism or exemplary violence used by political authorities to exercise control over captive peoples. When the link between sin and suffering is broken, the incident of the falling tower emboldens believers to question whether such "accidents" occur because of construction shortcuts taken when profit is more prized than human life. In such situations there is need both for preparedness for those whose days are foreshortened, and for repentance by those who cause their untimely death. Christian fruitfulness would be visibly measured by the ways in which Jesus' followers unmask the lies of perpetrators of violence and open a space for their repentance.[10]

---

[10] Sharon Ringe, *Luke,* Westminster Bible Companion (Louisville: Westminster/John Knox, 1995) 184.

CHAPTER FIVE

Lost and Found
(Luke 15:1-3, 11-32)

Fourth Sunday of Lent
Saturday of the Second Week of Lent

[1] *Tax collectors and sinners were all drawing near to listen to Jesus,*
  [2] *but the Pharisees and scribes began to complain, saying,*
  "This man welcomes sinners and eats with them."
[3] *So to them Jesus addressed this parable.*

[11] *"A man had two sons,* [12] *and the younger son said to his father,*
  'Father, give me the share of your estate that should come to me.'
  So the father divided the property between them.
[13] *After a few days, the younger son collected all his belongings*
  and set off to a distant country
  where he squandered his inheritance on a life of dissipation.
[14] *When he had freely spent everything,*
  a severe famine struck that country,
  and he found himself in dire need.
[15] *So he hired himself out to one of the local citizens*
  who sent him to his farm to tend the swine.
[16] *And he longed to eat his fill of the pods on which the swine fed,*
  but nobody gave him any.
[17] *Coming to his senses he thought,*
  'How many of my father's hired workers
  have more than enough food to eat,
  but here am I, dying from hunger.
[18] *I shall get up and go to my father and I shall say to him,*
  "Father, I have sinned against heaven and against you.
[19] *I no longer deserve to be called your son;*
  treat me as you would treat one of your hired workers."'

²⁰ *So he got up and went back to his father.*
   While he was still a long way off,
      his father caught sight of him, and was filled with compassion.
   He ran to his son, embraced him and kissed him.
²¹ *His son said to him,*
      'Father, I have sinned against heaven and against you;
      I no longer deserve to be called your son.'
²² *But his father ordered his servants,*
      'Quickly bring the finest robe and put it on him;
      put a ring on his finger and sandals on his feet.
²³ *Take the fattened calf and slaughter it.*
   Then let us celebrate with a feast,
         ²⁴ *because this son of mine was dead, and has come to life again;*
      he was lost, and has been found.'
   Then the celebration began.
²⁵ *Now the older son had been out in the field*
      and, on his way back, as he neared the house,
      he heard the sound of music and dancing.
²⁶ *He called one of the servants and asked what this might mean.*
²⁷ *The servant said to him,*
      'Your brother has returned
      and your father has slaughtered the fattened calf
      because he has him back safe and sound.'
²⁸ *He became angry,*
      and when he refused to enter the house,
      his father came out and pleaded with him.
²⁹ *He said to his father in reply,*
      'Look, all these years I served you
      and not once did I disobey your orders;
      yet you never gave me even a young goat to feast on with my friends.
³⁰ *But when your son returns*
      who swallowed up your property with prostitutes,
      for him you slaughter the fattened calf.'
³¹ *He said to him,*
      'My son, you are here with me always;
      everything I have is yours.
³² *But now we must celebrate and rejoice,*
      because your brother was dead and has come to life again;
      he was lost and has been found.'"

A FAMILIAR STORY[1]

This is one of the best known and most loved parables of Jesus. It presents a vignette of first-century family conflicts and their unexpected resolutions that still offers contemporary Christians patterns of restoring ruptured family and community relationships.

Like all gospel parables, it begins with a familiar situation. What family does not know conflicting desires between parents and children and jealous rivalry among siblings? What community has not experienced that some members faithfully labor for the good of the whole, while others go their merry way, only to end in ruin and in need of rescue? The parable presents a startling picture of how the path to reconciliation begins.

LUKAN LITERARY CONTEXT AND STRUCTURE

This is the third in a trilogy of parables that tells how God searches out the lost.[2] The introductory verses of the chapter (15:1-3) make these parables a response to the complaint of Pharisees and scribes that Jesus welcomes sinners and eats with them. In the first parable (15:4-7) Jesus asks these religious leaders to put themselves in the shoes of a shepherd who has lost one of the hundred sheep in his care. The parable underscores both the importance of each sheep and the costly love that is required of a pastor to search out a lost one. A second parable with identical contours uses a different image (15:8-10). Now it is a woman who searches for a precious coin of her daily earnings, indispensable for the subsistence of her family. Like the shepherd, she, too, expends great energy in searching out the lost. Both stories speak of the costly love on the part of God who is willing to expend any effort to bring back the precious lost one. As the third parable in the series, Luke 15:11-32 makes

---

[1] See also Barbara Reid, "Lost: Two Rebellious Sons—Who Will Find? (Luke 15:11-32)," in *The Family Handbook*, ed. Herbert Anderson, Don S. Browning, Ian S. Evison, Mary Steward Van Leeuwen (The Family, Religion, and Culture; Louisville: Westminster/John Knox, 1998) 238–41.

[2] See below, chap. 15, for commentary on the parables of the lost sheep and lost coin.

the same point. God's boundless efforts to seek out the lost can also be likened to those of a father who pays a great price to get back his lost sons.

Much of the surprising twist of this parable is lost on contemporary hearers both because of our familiarity with the story and because of our lack of understanding of the cultural dynamics of first-century Palestinian family life. In the commentary that follows, insights from recent social science studies will be used to interpret the narrative details from a first-century perspective.[3]

SIBLING RIVALRY

The stage is set with an introduction of the three main characters: a father and two sons. This calls to mind a number of biblical stories that feature two sons: Cain and Abel (Gen 4:1-16), Ishmael and Isaac (Gen 21:9-21), Jacob and Esau (Gen 25:19-34; 27:1-45). In each case there is conflict between the brothers and each is resolved with the younger triumphing over the elder. The expectation of a similar outcome is set by the opening line of this story as well.

One element lacking in Luke 15, however, is that there is no mention of a mother or daughters in the household. In Genesis 21 and 27 Sarah and Rebekah play a critical role in advocating for their youngest sons. The absence of women is noticeable in the parable in Luke 15:11-32.

AFFRONT TO THE FATHER

The story opens with the younger son deciding to leave home and asking his father for his share of the estate. There are a number of unsettling details in this scenario. First, one of the

---

[3] The following is based primarily on the interpretations of Richard L. Rohrbaugh, "A Dysfunctional Family and Its Neighbors (Luke 15:11b-32)," in *Jesus and His Parables: Interpreting the Parables of Jesus Today*, ed. V. George Shillington (Edinburgh: T. & T. Clark, 1997) 141–64; and Kenneth E. Bailey, *Poet and Peasant: A Literary-Cultural Approach to the Parables in Luke* (Grand Rapids: Eerdmans, 1976) 158–206. See also Barbara Green, *Like a Tree Planted* (Collegeville: The Liturgical Press, 1997) 37–53.

prime values in Palestinian village culture is family solidarity. Loyalty to kin is crucial for survival. Moreover, this was a dyadic culture, in which individuals understood themselves only in relation to their family, kin, village, and religious community.[4] So, to leave the family was an unconventional break from prevailing social values. Nonetheless, it was not entirely unusual for a son to leave home and try to make his own way in the wider world. One should not imagine, however, that he was off trying to "find himself," as individualistic self-definition was not in the consciousness of this culture.

A second startling detail is that the son demands his inheritance before his father's demise. This kind of request was tantamount to wishing his father dead and would have been heard as a shocking insult in the original telling. What is even more startling is that the father agrees! Sirach 33:19-23 advises against acquiescence to such a request:

> "Listen to me, O leaders of the multitude;
> O rulers of the assembly, give ear!
> Let neither son nor wife, neither brother nor friend,
> have power over you as long as you live.
> While breath of life is still in you,
> let no man have dominion over you.
> Give not to another your wealth,
> lest then you have to plead with him;
> Far better that your children plead with you
> than that you should look to their generosity.
> Keep control over all your affairs;
> let no one tarnish your glory."

A patriarch who relinquishes his power and authority over his family is one who lets go his honor and status as well. A father might, however, be moved to do such a thing for the sake of forestalling conflict among his sons after his death.[5] One final detail that calls attention is that the older son does not object or mediate in any way when the father divides the property

---

[4] See Bruce J. Malina, *The New Testament World: Insights from Cultural Anthropology* (rev. ed.; Louisville: Westminster/John Knox, 1993) 63–89.

[5] J.D.M. Derrett, "Law in the New Testament: the Parable of the Prodigal Son (Luke 15:11-32)," *NTS* 14 (1967) 56–74.

between the two sons (v. 12).[6] He, too, seems to go along with the shameful arrangement.

INHERITANCE LOST

The younger son then sets off for a distant land, presumably having converted his inheritance into cash. The parents' worst fears are realized as he squanders all he had on "dissolute living" (v. 13). The horror of the son's destitution is multiplied by the shame of having lost a portion of the land belonging to the family. Attachment to the land is intense for a people who claim it as God's promise, and who have at times been exiled from it (see the passion for the land, for example, in Psalms 126, 137). Relatives go to great lengths to retain all of the ancestral land. Leviticus 25:25 advises, "When one of your countrymen is reduced to poverty and has to sell some of his property, his closest relative, who has the right to redeem it, may go and buy back what his kinsman has sold."

The situation of the younger son is exacerbated by a severe famine that breaks out (v. 14). Having little recourse, he seeks out a patron, who sends him to his fields to feed the pigs (v. 15). To Jewish ears, this adds insult to injury, as the son now debases himself further by living with Gentiles who keep unclean animals. But the son's plight worsens still more. As his hunger mounts he would be happy even to fill up on the pigs' fodder. But no one offers him even this (v. 16).

A SURVIVAL PLAN

Being a resourceful young man, the son devises a plan to save himself (vv. 17-19). He remembers how well paid are his father's workers; they always have more than enough food to eat (v. 17). There is no need for him to die of hunger. He decides to go home and ask his father to make him one of his hired hands (v. 19). There is no repentance on the part of this young man. His soliloquy, "Father, I have sinned against heaven and against you" (v. 18) is reminiscent of the words of Pharaoh to

---

[6] According to Deuteronomy 21:17 the eldest son receives a double portion of what is given to the other sons.

Moses, "I have sinned against the LORD, your God, and against you" (Exod 10:16). Though Pharaoh's words sound repentant, he was simply at his wit's end with the plagues. He had endured water turned to blood, infestations of frogs, gnats, and flies, diseased livestock, boils, and now thunder and hail. In desperation he mouths admission of sin; in truth he does not repent. Likewise, the young son in Luke 15:18 is rehearsing a strategy by which he may emerge alive from his dire plight and eat again. He knows he has lost his rights as "son," and so devises a way in which he can be a hired servant to his father.

BEING FOUND

The next scene in the parable has a startling twist that leaves the hearer quite puzzled as to its meaning. It shows the father watching and waiting for his errant son's return, and his being filled with compassion at the sight of him. In a first-century Mediterranean family, this is most unexpected behavior on the part of a patriarch who has been so grievously shamed by his son. A more expected reaction would have been for the father to rend his garments and declare the son disowned. Instead, he is longing for his return and at the first sight of his approach, he runs to meet him—a most undignified action for a patriarch. Putting his arms around the boy, and kissing him (v. 20), the father shields him from any other repercussions from kin and neighbors who would be equally resentful of the shame his scandalous behavior has brought upon them. The son has not only betrayed his kin, but has broken village solidarity as well. Not only has he incurred the anger of the other villagers, but he has discovered how essential are community attachments and social conformity for survival.

As the son begins his rehearsed speech, the father silences him, not permitting him even to propose his plan to work for food (v. 21). Instead, the father calls for the best robe, a ring, and sandals to be put on him (v. 22). These are all symbols of distinction and authority.[7] Not only that, the fatted calf is killed for

---

[7] See Genesis 41:42 where Pharaoh bestows these same symbols on Joseph. Perhaps Luke means to evoke Isaiah 61:10, where the prophet extols God who clothes him with a "robe of salvation."

a great feast (vv. 23-24). The feast is not only for the sake of the son, but is a gesture of reconciliation with the villagers. By accepting the invitation they signal their willingness to forgive offenses incurred and agree to reintegrate this son and his family into their community networks.

COSTLY LOVE

What brings about the possibility of reconciliation is not the determination of the younger son to turn his life around. Rather, it is the watchfulness of the father and his running to meet the son that brings him back into the family embrace. The son had determined only to return as hired hand, as a strategy for survival. The father is the one who absorbs the shame and hurt, who bears the cost of the ruptured relations with family and villagers, and who nonetheless pays the great price to get his son back. It is his initiative and his doing that makes it possible for the young man to return to the family as son, not as servant. According to this parable, reconciliation does not come from firm determination of the lost one to return and make amends, but depends on his willingness to accept the costly love of the father who has spared nothing to win him back. The resulting joy of the father is expressed in extravagant terms: "this son of mine was dead, and has come to life again" (v. 24).

But this seemingly happy ending is not the conclusion of the story. There is more.

ANOTHER LOST SON

From the start of the story, it is told that the man had two sons (v. 11). The dramatic reconciliation of the father with the younger son ends on a joyous note. But what of the elder son? He, too, is lost, but in an entirely different way. He has remained in the father's house, but is no more at peace with him than was his younger brother. When he hears all the celebration over the return of his brother, he becomes enraged and refuses to go into the house (vv. 25-28). Again, the father does something most unusual for a first-century patriarch. He leaves the party and goes out to the elder son (who should have been helping him host the celebration) and pleads with him to join in (v. 28).

The jealousy and resentment that fester in this son are evident in his insulting explosion, "Look, all these years I served you and not once did I disobey your orders; yet you never gave me even a young goat to feast on with my friends. But when your son returns who swallowed up your property with prostitutes, for him you slaughter the fattened calf" (vv. 29-30). His outburst reveals that, not unlike his brother, who concocts a plan to become the father's hired hand, he, too, thinks of himself as a slave to his father. He dissociates himself from his brother by calling him "that son of yours." And he further interprets his brother's "dissolute living" (v. 13) as "devouring your property with prostitutes" (v. 30). This son is just as lost as the younger one in his inability to accept and celebrate his father's graciousness.

HUMILIATED AGAIN

The father has not only been shamed by the younger son, with his untimely demand for his inheritance and its subsequent loss, but the elder has behaved in a disgraceful manner to his father as well. He has not objected to the early distribution of the inheritance. He has not acted appropriately in helping to host the banquet and welcome the guests. He has kept himself outside the embrace of the father with his joyless resentment and his slavish service. The father absorbs the shame from his elder son, as he had with the younger. As with the younger son, the father goes out to the elder and meets him in his lostness. He pleads with him (v. 28), a most shameful scene from the perspective of a patriarchal world, where a father rules over his sons and commands their obedience. A father never entreats his sons to do what is obligatory.

THE OFFER

The father begins his reply to the elder sibling with "my son." This address underscores the son's slavish attitude and invites him to move from the self-imposed stance of slave into the embrace of the father as son. As the father continues, "you are here with me always; everything I have is yours" (v. 30), it is clear that it is the son who has chosen to place himself outside the circle of sonship with all its attendant benefits. The free offer of the father has been constant and always accessible.

It is clear from the last verse that there are wider ramifications than simply the relationship of a son to a father. If the elder son responds positively to the father's plea, it also entails restoring the relationship with his brother. As the father speaks of "your brother" (v. 30) it underscores how the elder son must also move from regarding him as "this son of yours" (v. 30, *NRSV*). Moreover, he must be willing to celebrate not only the new life offered to himself, but also that of the other who has been found as well.

And there the parable ends. Will the elder son also be able to accept the costly love of the father? Will he be able to let go of his joyless resentment and slavish attitude that keep him from reconciled oneness with the other family members? As usual in gospel parables, the story is open-ended. It is up to the listener to finish it.

PREACHING POSSIBILITIES

What one hears in this parable is partly dependent on which of the three characters is the one with which the hearer stands. For those who feel lost or alienated it is the younger son who draws attention. While most Christians may not identify with the desperate plight of the younger son as he hits rock bottom, many are still drawn to him, aware that there is always some aspect of their life in which there is alienation and need of reconciliation. From this stance, the parable offers an image of God as one who is watching, waiting, and always willing to run to meet the one who has turned away from God's family and to enfold such a one again in the divine embrace. Not even the worst imaginable offense is an irrevocable obstacle to that constant love of God.

Most who hear the story in church, however, are more like the elder son, trying to do what is right, week after week. The literary structure of the parable places the stress on this second half of the story, and more clearly invites the hearer to identify with this character. For this reason, the preacher would do well not to choose the short form of the gospel, but to proclaim the parable in its entirety. While the literary stress falls on the elder son, he is portrayed less sympathetically, and so may be less inviting to the hearer. Nonetheless, it may be from this angle that the parable most needs to be heard in contemporary congregations.

From the stance of this character the parable invites hearers to consider whether their discipleship has deteriorated into slavish service marked by joyless resentment, especially toward those who seem to be benefiting undeservedly from all that God offers. The parable invites such to recognize the free offer of God to all, a lavish benevolence constantly offered by the one who is willing to pay the high cost to gather in all the children, none of whom have earned the right to this inheritance. All are sons and daughters through the lavish gift of God; none are slaves. To accept the love of a God who acts like this is not only to restore right relation with God, but also to bring one into reconciled love with all people as brothers and sisters in God's family.

In the context of Luke's community they may have heard this story as addressed to the painful issue of incorporating the Gentiles into the people of God. Jewish Christians may have seen themselves as the elder brothers, who had been faithfully keeping all God's commands. This parable may have helped them address the question of how could the Gentiles, newcomers to the promise, now be enjoying all the same inheritance? Preachers today may find possibilities in this parable for addressing attitudes of entitlement or privilege in their communities that can block receptivity to newcomers. Whether the preacher focuses on the younger son or the elder, both parts of the story insist that God's love is not earned; we are God's sons and daughters, not slaves. The first step in reconciliation is to accept such free and costly love.

This parable does not, however, tell the rest of the story of what comes after the initial acceptance and celebratory welcome home. Other gospel stories (e.g., Luke 7:36-50; Matt 18:23-35; 22:11-14) speak of a response in kind that is expected from one who accepts unmerited love. In families and in communities costly love is offered freely, but the price for one who accepts it is to replicate such reconciling love in their own actions.

For anyone in authority, whether parent or pastoral leader, this parable speaks of the necessity of that one being willing to expend great effort, even being willing to endure humiliation in order to bring back those who are alienated. It asks a parent who has been deeply hurt by a son or daughter to relinquish their own pain and extend an offer of forgiving love. The restoration of right relation does not depend on wayward ones making their own way back, but rather, on the godly person's willingness to reach out to such a one.

THE MISSING MOTHER

There is one glaring omission in the story of the father and the two sons—is there no mother nor daughter in this family? A story recounted by a minister to street children in Saõ Paolo, Brazil brings home the point. She tells of a time she introduced this parable to youngsters unfamiliar with Bible stories. When she got to the part where the younger son decided to return home, she stopped and asked the children if the boy would be able to go home. They debated about it, and finally one of the boys asked, "Is there a mother in the house?" When she asked if that would make a difference, he said, "Yes, because if there is a mother, she will let him come home. She will pester the father, saying, 'You *will* let him in the house if he comes back, won't you? After all, he's our baby.'"

This young man, much like the first hearers of the gospel, lives in a patriarchal society, where the behavior of the father in Luke 15:11-32 seems very feminine—not at all typical of a macho father who sees as an important part of his role the imposition of obedience and discipline so as to maintain his honor and that of his family. Yet "feminizing" the father does not put female figures into this parable. And herein lies a danger in this story. In a Church that uses the term "Father" more than any other to address God, and that rarely, if ever, uses female images or terminology for God, patriarchy reigns not only on earth, but is also divinized. When our foundational stories about God exclude female images, then believers are left with the message that being male is more God-like.

In a society and Church where family structures and relationship patterns are changing, what is needed is not only a father figure with feminine qualities, but female images that express equally well what the father image says of God. When the story of the diligent woman householder in Luke 15:8-10 is read in tandem with that of the father reaching out to his lost sons in Luke 15:11-32, we have such.

LECTIONARY CONTEXT

This emphasis on the free, undeserved, gratuity of God's love is also a theme in other readings paired with this parable in the Lectionary. On the fourth Sunday of Lent Paul's second letter to the Corinthians (5:17-21) clearly casts reconciliation as Christ's work, not something accomplished through the efforts of the lost. His phrasing is notable: "be reconciled to God"—not "reconcile yourself to God." Moreover, Paul insists that this work is now entrusted to those who follow Christ. The responsorial psalm for this Sunday (Psalm 34) is a thanksgiving for God's deliverance and invites people to both taste and see the goodness of God. Savoring God's goodness ties the banquet imagery of the parable with the first reading from Joshua (5:9a, 10-12) which depicts the Israelites' first celebration of Passover in the promised land. "Everything I have is yours" (Luke 15:31) is concretely demonstrated in the beneficent provision of manna for the hungry Israelites to the produce they feast on in the new land, to a banquet for the starving younger son, to the eucharistic feast now at hand.

When this parable is joined with Micah 7:14-15, 18-20 on Saturday of the Second Week of Lent, the message of God's astounding forgiveness is salient. The prophet speaks of God who delights in clemency and compassion, who casts all our sins into the depths of the sea. The psalm response from Psalm 103 sings of God who is kind and merciful, never dealing with us according to our sins, but with pardon and healing.

CHAPTER SIX

The Unacceptable Prophet
(Luke 4:21-30)

Fourth Sunday of Ordinary Time

Monday of the Twenty-second Week of Ordinary Time
(Luke 4:16-30)

Jesus began speaking in the synagogue, saying:
  [21] *"Today this scripture passage is fulfilled in your hearing."*
[22] *And all spoke highly of him*
  and were amazed at the gracious words that came from his mouth.
  They also asked, "Isn't this the son of Joseph?"
[23] *He said to them, "Surely you will quote me this proverb,*
  'Physician, cure yourself,' and say,
  'Do here in your native place
  the things that we heard were done in Capernaum.'"
[24] *And he said, "Amen, I say to you,*
  no prophet is accepted in his own native place.
[25] *Indeed, I tell you,*
  there were many widows in Israel in the days of Elijah
  when the sky was closed for three and a half years
  and a severe famine spread over the entire land.
[26] *It was to none of these that Elijah was sent,*
  but only to a widow in Zarephath in the land of Sidon.
[27] *Again, there were many lepers in Israel*
  during the time of Elisha the prophet;
  yet not one of them was cleansed, but only Naaman the Syrian."
[28] *When the people in the synagogue heard this,*
  they were all filled with fury.
[29] *They rose up, drove him out of the town,*
  and led him to the brow of the hill

on which their town had been built,
to hurl him down headlong.
[30] *But Jesus passed through the midst of them and went away.*

LUKAN LITERARY CONTEXT

This scene is the second half of the episode that opens Jesus' Galilean ministry in the Third Gospel. It comes on the heels of the temptation in the desert, after which Jesus returns to Galilee in the power of the Spirit. He begins teaching in the synagogues for which he wins universal praise. He comes to his own home town synagogue on the sabbath and reads from the scroll of Isaiah about God's anointing of the prophet to bring good news to those who are poor, liberty to people held captive, recovery of sight to people who are blind, and freedom to all those oppressed.

Today's gospel begins with Jesus handing back the scroll, as he declares this Scripture fulfilled in the present moment. It is his inaugural declaration of his mission. As the gospel progresses, Jesus is portrayed doing exactly these things he has proclaimed. Luke has moved this scene forward from his Markan source, which locates it toward the end of the Galilean ministry (Mark 6:1-6), as also Matthew (13:53-58). In turn, Luke delays the call of the first disciples until 5:1-11, after Jesus has already performed a number of healings.

FULFILLMENT OF SCRIPTURE TODAY

One of the salient themes of the Third Gospel is that all that occurs in the life of Jesus and his disciples is a fulfillment of what is spoken in the Scriptures.[1] Everything occurs according to God's plan, not in the sense of divine predetermination or predestination, but rather, to show the continuity of God's salvific action, first with saving deeds toward Israel, and now for the new people of God in the Christ event. The same faithful

---

[1] One of the final scenes of the gospel shows the resurrected Jesus interpreting for the two disciples on the road to Emmaus everything that referred to him in the Scriptures, beginning with Moses and all the prophets (Luke 24:27).

God of the Israelites is the same faithful God of Jesus and of his followers in the present.[2]

The statement that the Scripture is fulfilled "in your hearing" also introduces another major Lukan theme: discipleship begins by hearing the word of God and then obeying it.[3] Whoever hears and obeys the word is family to Jesus (8:21) and blessed (11:28).

DIVIDED RESPONSES

This is the first of many episodes in the gospel in which Jesus' deeds and words provoke a divided response. The prophecy of Simeon in Luke 2:34-35 prepares for a story in which Jesus will be a sign of contradiction, leading to both the rise and downfall of many in Israel. Usually the scenario is that some who see Jesus' deeds of power and hear his gracious words respond positively and become disciples, while others who see and hear the same things, react with hostility, even to the point of plotting his death. In this scene in the Nazareth synagogue, however, the audience is united in their response: first positive affirmation followed by murderous fury.

AMAZING GRACE

The hometown folks are initially amazed at Jesus' gracious words. The verb *thaumazein*, "to wonder, to marvel, to amaze," is one of Luke's favorite words. Amazement typifies the response of all the people when Zechariah confirms Elizabeth's naming of John (1:63). And when the shepherds relay the message of Jesus' birth, all who hear it are amazed (2:18). This is also Mary and Joseph's reaction to what Simeon tells them about their son (2:33). The disciples are awed and amazed at Jesus' calming of the sea (8:25). Similarly, when Jesus drives out demons all are astonished (9:43; 11:14). Even those who try to trap him end up amazed at his words (20:26). The response of

---

[2] See above, pp. 36–37, on Luke's shift away from eschatological fulfillment to emphasis on the present day.

[3] Luke 6:27, 47; 7:22; 8:8, 10, 15; 9:35; 10:23-24; 11:21, 28, 31; 14:35.

Peter to the empty tomb (24:12) and of the disciples to the appearance of the risen Christ is amazement (24:41).

In the Nazareth synagogue the object of amazement is Jesus' gracious words *(logois tēs charitos)*, literally his "words of grace" or "favorable words." The word *charis*, "grace," or "favor," has already been sounded several times in the gospel. From a mother who was full of grace *(charis,* 1:28, 30), comes a son upon whom is the grace of God (2:40) and who continues to advance in wisdom and age and grace before God (2:52).[4] As he first speaks of God's favor (4:22) the response is affirmative. Some of Israel's great heroes were said to find favor with God: Noah (Gen 6:8), Moses (Exod 33:12-17), Gideon (Judg 6:17), and Samuel (1 Sam 2:26). However, being favored by God carries a heavy price. Those favored by God are called to a life of service on behalf of God's people, loving service even to the death.

REJECTED PROPHET

In that Jesus' ministry provokes both conversion and deadly antagonism, he is like every other prophet that has preceded him. Luke here introduces his theme of Jesus as rejected prophet.[5] Very few prophets besides Jesus appear in the Third Gospel. Zechariah prophesies as he speaks his canticle (1:67). Gabriel announces that John the Baptist "will be called prophet of the Most High" (1:76; see also 3:2; 20:6). Anna is the last prophet (2:36) mentioned before Jesus assumes this role. Luke casts Jesus as the promised "prophet like Moses" of Deuteronomy 18:15 (Luke 9:28-36).[6] He also emulates the prophets Elijah[7] and Elisha in his miracle working. He is preeminently "a

---

[4] The query, "Isn't this the son of Joseph?" (v. 22), is probably meant to evoke pleasant surprise at the talents of the local son. Luke 3:23 explains that it was common perception that Joseph was the father of Jesus while the annunciation scene (1:26-38) makes it clear that Jesus is Mary's son through the power of the holy Spirit.

[5] Luke 4:24, 39; 13:33; 24:19-20; Acts 7:52.

[6] This theme continues in Acts 3:22-23; 7:37. See Robert O'Toole, "The Parallels Between Jesus and Moses," *BTB* 20 (1990) 22–29.

[7] There is a double Elijah theme in Luke. While Luke 7:27 casts John the Baptist as a new Elijah in his role as precursor of the coming one (so also Luke 1:17, 76), elsewhere the third evangelist suppresses the identification of John

prophet mighty in deed and word" (24:19), who will suffer the fate of all the prophets who have gone before him: death in Jerusalem (Luke 13:33-34).

HEAL YOURSELF

While most English translations convey v. 23 as a "proverb," in the Greek the word is *parabolē*, "parable." This same "parable" is found in various forms in Greek and Jewish literature. Euripedes has, "A physician for others, but himself teeming with sores," (*Frag.* 1086). And a later rabbinic tractate preserves the proverb, "Physician, heal your own lameness" (*Genesis Rabbah* 23 [15c]). The point of such sayings is that those who would work at improving others do best to first examine themselves. This is more akin to the admonition of Jesus in Luke 6:41-42, that it is better to remove the beam from one's own eye before trying to take out the splinter from that of another.

In the second half of v. 23, however, this is not the meaning attached to the parable. What Jesus anticipates the townspeople will ask for is mighty deeds such as he did elsewhere. This is a different twist from the Markan story, where Jesus could perform no mighty deeds in Nazareth because of their lack of faith (Mark 6:6).

In the narrative, Luke has not yet portrayed Jesus ministering in Capernaum. The very next scene, however, brings Jesus to the synagogue in Capernaum where his cure of a man

with Elijah in favor of portraying Jesus as the new Elijah in the role of eschatological prophet and miracle worker. Luke retains allusions to Elijah in reference to Jesus from his Markan source in Luke 3:16; 8:22-25; 9:8, 10-17, 19, 22:33, 39. Twice Luke adds details to a Markan story to highlight the parallel with Elijah: Luke 4:2; 5:12. Many of the parallels between Jesus and Elijah are peculiarly Lukan: 4:16-30; 6:12; 7:11-17; 9:51, 54, 61-62; 12:49; 17:16; 19:1; 24:49; Acts 1:9. The Lukan Jesus rejects, however, the role of fiery reformer in 9:54, where James and John want him to call down fire from heaven as did Elijah. Another difference between Jesus and Elijah is found in Luke 9:61-62, where potential followers of Jesus are not allowed to look back after putting the hand to the plow (cf. 1 Kgs 19:20). See further Raymond E. Brown, "Jesus and Elisha," *Perspective* 12 (1971) 84–104; Joseph A. Fitzmyer, *The Gospel According to Luke* (AB28; Garden City, N.Y.: Doubleday, 1981) 213–15; J.A.T. Robinson, "Elijah, John and Jesus: An Essay in Detection," *NTS* 4 (1957-58) 263–81; R. Swaeles, "Jésus, nouvel Elie, dans saint Luc," *AsSeign* 69 (1964) 41–66.

possessed by a demon and his authoritative word command amazement (4:32, 36). Capernaum is also the locale of the healing of the slave of a centurion (7:1-10). But later in the gospel it is also excoriated for its lack of repentance (10:15).

The point at issue in the parable is clarified by the examples in the subsequent verses. If there is any thought that the inhabitants of Nazareth are curious, or perhaps jealous, or even possibly open to what Jesus has to offer, he immediately rejects the thought of doing any deeds for them as futile. Another popular proverb seals the indictment: the prophet Jesus will never be accepted by his own. There is a word play between v. 19 where Jesus proclaims a year acceptable *(dektos)* to the Lord and v. 24, where he declares no prophet is acceptable *(dektos)* to his own.

Parallels to this proverb are known from the Oxyrhynchus Papyri and from the *Gospel of Thomas*.[8] In the former "Jesus says, 'A prophet is not acceptable in his own homeland; and a physician does not work cures on those who know him'" (1:29-35). The latter has the saying: "No prophet is accepted in his own town; a physician does not heal those who know him" *(Gos.Thom. §31)*. It is clear that these extracanonical versions of the proverb are dependent on the Lukan form.[9] It is interesting that these versions put a different cast on the saying about the physician. Here they do not convey a critique of the healer to

[8] The Oxyrhynchus Papyri consist of four fragmentary texts of sayings of Jesus found in rubbish mounds at Oxyrhynchus, a city that flourished during Roman times in Middle Egypt, about 125 miles south of Cairo. The texts date from the first through the ninth centuries and were found in a series of excavations, beginning in 1897. The *Gospel of Thomas* is a Coptic translation of a lost Greek original collection of 114 sayings of Jesus. It is part of the Coptic Gnostic Library of Nag Hammadi, Egypt, which was buried in the fourth century and unearthed in 1945. This apocryphal gospel was probably composed at the end of the first century. The three Oxyrhynchus fragments that have sayings of Jesus derive from a Greek version of *Gos.Thom.*

[9] Mark's version says a prophet is "without honor" *(atimos,* 6:4), which Matthew follows (13:54) and elaborates on the rejection of the prophet by his own relatives. Luke has changed *atimos* to *dektos* to create the word play with v. 19 and omits the critique of Jesus' family, since, unlike Mark ((3:31-35; 6:4) he depicts them as open to Jesus' word (Luke 1:45; 8:21; Acts 1:14). So, too, the Oxyrhynchus form uses *dektos*. See Joseph A. Fitzmyer, *Essays on the Semitic Background of the New Testament* (Sources for Biblical Study 5; Atlanta: Scholars Press, 1974) 401–02; *Luke,* 527–28.

attend first to his own deficiencies, but rather are aligned with the meaning of the companion proverb: neither healers nor prophets find a good reception among their own.

OUTSIDERS

It is Jesus' reference to God's gracious acts toward those outside Israel that provokes fury from the people of Nazareth. Jesus recalls the story from 1 Kings 17:7-24 in which a widow[10] from Sidon whose son is raised back to life by Elijah shares her meager supplies with him and is blessed with a jar of flour and of oil that never run dry. The second reference is to the leper Naaman from Syria, whom Elijah healed, recounted in 2 Kings 5:1-19. Jesus further interprets that it was not that these prophets could find no one in need of such healing in Israel. God sent Elijah and Elisha to offer favor to outsiders even when there was work for them to do within Israel.

These verses are from Luke's hand and may be aimed at helping his community in their struggle for self-understanding as a group of predominantly Gentile Christians. Luke shows that God's current graciousness to Gentiles was already foreshadowed in the deeds of the prophets of old. In the new age the Lukan Jesus is portrayed as healing in the same manner as Elijah and Elisha. He, too, feeds hungry people (9:10-17), raises the only son of a widow (7:11-17), and heals people with leprosy (5:23-16), including a "foreign" Samaritan leper (17:11-19). His healing touch extends to a centurion's servant (7:1-10) and he attempts to minister in Samaria (9:51-56). This depiction of Jesus is played out further in Luke's second volume that shows the Christian mission spreading from Judea to Samaria to the ends of the earth (Acts 1:8). The restored people of God includes any who respond affirmatively to the prophet Jesus, both Jews and Gentiles.

---

[10] Luke makes more mention of widows than any other evangelist (Luke 2:36-38; 4:25-26; 7:11-17; 18:1-8; 20:47; 21:1-4; Acts 6:1-6; 9:36-43). While some of them serve as examples of God's care for the poor, a number of them are shown as ministering. The number of such stories in Luke may reflect the growing number and importance of widows in the ministry of the church of Luke's day. See further Bonnie Bowman Thurston, *The Widows: A Women's Ministry in the Early Church* (Minneapolis: Fortress, 1989).

PASSING THROUGH

The episode ends with allusions to the final destiny of the prophet. The one who would extend divine favor to outsiders is himself about to be cast outside. They lead him to the brow of the hill, but it is on another hill to which he will be led outside the holy city that he is destined to die. This time he passes through their midst unscathed. In Jerusalem, at Passover, Jesus will celebrate with his disciples the passing through the sea under God's protection. There he will go to his death aware that his passing through death is the new liberating act of God for all peoples.[11]

PREACHING POSSIBILITIES

The parable is one that can give courage to those who exercise prophetic ministries today. It shows how illusory is the expectation that preaching or living the gospel will result in adulation. Quite the opposite. A truer measure of success in gospel living is whether one encounters opposition and even deadly hostility. A gospel that does not disturb anyone is not the gospel Jesus preached. A prophet does not seek death, but is realistically prepared that this may be the price for proclaiming good news to those most downtrodden.

The readings, however, do not sound a note of gloom, but rather depict the faithfulness of God, who fortifies the prophet for his or her difficult ministry. On the Fourth Sunday of Ordinary Time both Jesus and Jeremiah derive confident assurance in knowing that God has appointed them to this task. In the first reading (Jer 1:4-5, 17-19) Jeremiah is promised that God will fortify and deliver him and not let him be crushed. The psalmist sings of God's salvation as rock of refuge, stronghold, and safety (Psalm 71). And Paul's hymn to love (1 Cor 12:31–13:13) underscores the cardinal virtue that impels any prophet. On Monday of the Twenty-second Week of Year I Paul

---

[11] Only in the Lukan scene of the transfiguration (9:28-36) do we have the content of the conversation between Moses, Elijah, and Jesus. They speak about his *exodos* that is about to occur in Jerusalem (9:31). *Exodos* has two connotations: death (2 Pet 1:15) and the liberation of the Hebrew slaves from Egypt.

assures the Thessalonians of the hope of new life for all who have fallen asleep in death (1 Thess 4:13-18). In Year II Paul's letter to the Corinthians asserts that there is no power in human wisdom, but only in the wisdom of the cross and the power of the Spirit (1 Cor 2:1-5). This same Spirit vivifies prophets today and impels them to preach the gospel.

In the examples of Elijah, Elisha, and Jesus, who extend God's gracious favor to outsiders, contemporary Christians can find an invitation to identify with those who are outsiders or marginalized and to direct their ministries to them. To any who advocate that one must put one's own house in order first, before turning toward others, the proverbial sayings and the prophetic examples contradict such.

CHAPTER SEVEN

Blind Guides
(Luke 6:39-45)

Eighth Sunday of Ordinary Time

Friday of the Twenty-third Week of Ordinary Time
(Luke 6:39-42)

Jesus told his disciples a parable,
³⁹ "Can a blind person guide a blind person?
Will not both fall into a pit?
⁴⁰ No disciple is superior to the teacher;
but when fully trained,
every disciple will be like his teacher.
⁴¹ Why do you notice the splinter in your brother's eye,
but do not perceive the wooden beam in your own?
⁴² How can you say to your brother,
'Brother, let me remove that splinter in your eye,'
when you do not even notice the wooden beam in your own eye?
You hypocrite! Remove the wooden beam from your eye first;
then you will see clearly
to remove the splinter in your brother's eye.[1]

⁴³ "A good tree does not bear rotten fruit,
nor does a rotten tree bear good fruit.
⁴⁴ For every tree is known by its own fruit.
For people do not pick figs from thornbushes,

---

[1] The *NRSV* translates vv. 41-42 more inclusively: "Why do you see the speck in your neighbor's eye, but do not notice the log in your own eye? Or how can you say to your neighbor, 'Friend, let me take out the speck in your eye,' when you yourself do not see the log in your own eye? You hypocrite, first take the log out of your own eye, and then you will see clearly to take the speck out of your neighbor's eye."

nor do they gather grapes from brambles.
[45] *A good person out of the store of goodness in his heart produces good,*
but an evil person out of a store of evil produces evil;
for from the fullness of the heart the mouth speaks."

LUKAN LITERARY CONTEXT

This series of loosely connected proverbial sayings is found in the middle of Luke's Sermon on the Plain (6:20-49).[2] They come from the Q and L sources and are directed to those who are already Jesus' disciples. The first section (vv. 39-42) highlights proper behavior for Christians in the efforts at guiding, teaching, and correcting one another. The second part concentrates on the visibility of good deeds.

Luke introduces these sayings with the phrase, "then he told them a parable." It is followed by a whole series of parabolic sayings using a variety of images and metaphors. The use of the singular "parable" is easily explained as part of a standard Lukan introduction. "He told them a parable" is found thirteen times in Luke[3] even when it is followed by several parables, as in Luke 15:3.

LITERARY STRUCTURE

Scholars are not agreed on how to divide the Sermon on the Plain. Two different schemas below are illustrative. In the five-part division of Joseph Fitzmyer,[4] today's gospel comprises sections three and four:

1) 6:20-26 Exordium (four beatitudes and four woes)
2) 6:27-36 Love even your enemies.
3) 6:37-42 Judge not one another.
4) 6:43-45 The role of good deeds.
5) 6:46-49 The need to act on these words (with a parable)

---

[2] Luke's Sermon on the Plain corresponds to Matthew's Sermon on the Mount (5:1–7:27). While much of the same material appears in both, each redacts it to his own theological purposes. Matthew's sermon is longer and is directed to both the crowds and Jesus' disciples.

[3] Luke 5:36; 6:39; 8:4; 12:16; 13:6; 14:7; 15:3; 18:1, 9; 19:11; 20:9, 19; 21:29.

[4] Joseph A. Fitzmyer, *The Gospel According to Luke* (AB28; Garden City, N.Y.: Doubleday, 1981) 629.

In the four-part structure of Sharon Ringe[5] the sayings in today's gospel bridge portions of sections three and four:

1) 6:20-26 Blessings and Woes
2) 6:27-35 Relationships with Enemies and Benefactors
3) 6:36-42 Mercy and Judgment
4) 6:43-49 Personal Integrity

The differing structures reflect the variety of ways in which scholars see the thematic clustering of these sayings. Originally disparate, they now form a kind of program for correct Christian living.

There are various motives supplied for why disciples should act in the manner advised. In 6:36 the reason for acting mercifully is that this is how God acts; so, too, Christians are to imitate God's boundless compassion. In 6:37-38 the rules of reciprocity are invoked.[6] One who does not judge or condemn another will not be judged or condemned. Those who forgive and who give gifts will receive the same in kind. The motivation for following the advice offered in the proverbial sayings in 6:39-45, however, seems to rest on simple wisdom that comes from common sense. Almost all the sayings are known to have parallels in other Greek and Jewish literature.

BLIND GUIDES

The first saying has many well-known variations in ancient literature. Sextus Empiricus, a second-century C.E. skeptic, says that an amateur cannot teach an amateur any more than the blind can lead the blind (*Against the Professors* 1.31).[7] Horace, the first-century B.C.E. poet and satirist, writes to Scaeva, a patron: "I have still much to learn, but listen to me anyway, even if I appear to be a blind man giving directions" (*Epistles* 1.17.4). Both

---

[5] Sharon H. Ringe, *Luke* (Westminster Bible Companion; Louisville: Westminster/John Knox, 1995) 91.

[6] On social exchange relations based on reciprocity see Bruce J. Malina and Richard L. Rohrbaugh, *Social Science Commentary on the Synoptic Gospels* (Minneapolis: Fortress, 1992) 325.

[7] This and the following examples come from Frederick W. Danker, *Jesus and the New Age: A Commentary on St. Luke's Gospel* (rev. ed.; Philadelphia: Fortress, 1988) 153–55.

examples speak of blind guides in reference to teaching, the same juxtaposition that Luke makes in 6:39-40. Both Matthew (15:14) and the *Gospel of Thomas* (§34) frame the parable as a conditional statement: "If a blind person leads a blind person, both will fall into a pit." "If a blind person leads a blind person, the two of them fall into a pit."

When seen in the whole context of the Third Gospel, this saying serves to advance an important Lukan theme.[8] Sight is a frequent metaphor in Luke for spiritual understanding that undergirds authentic discipleship. The shepherds, after seeing the newborn Jesus, glorify God for all they had heard and seen (2:20). Simeon rejoices that his eyes have seen the salvation that has been prepared in the sight of all the peoples (2:31). Jesus declares that recovery of sight to the blind is part of his mission (4:18; 7:21), exemplified in 18:35-43. Those who witness the healing of a man who was paralyzed glorify God for the incredible things they had seen (5:26). The Samaritan "saw" that he was healed and returned to Jesus, glorifying God (17:15-16).[9] The centurion who sees Jesus' death glorifies God and declares Jesus upright (23:47). And to convey the post-resurrection understanding of the disciples en route to Emmaus, Luke says "their eyes were opened" (24:31).

The warning about blind guides is akin to two other sayings in Luke. In 8:10 Jesus uses the words of the prophet Isaiah to warn his disciples about looking but not seeing, and hearing but not understanding. He later declares his disciples' eyes blessed for what they see, in contrast to many prophets and kings who desired to see what they see, but did not (10:23-24). The importance of seeing aright is the last note sounded in Luke's two volumes, as he concludes Acts with a return one last time to Isaiah's denunciation of the blindness of those who refuse to convert (Acts 28:26-27; cf. Isa 6:9-10).

---

[8] See Alan Culpepper, "Seeing the Kingdom of God: The Metaphor of Sight in the Gospel of Luke," *CurTM* 21 (1994) 434–43; John J. Pilch, "Blindness," in *The Cultural Dictionary of the Bible* (Collegeville: The Liturgical Press, 1999) 73–75.

[9] See Dennis Hamm, "What the Samaritan Leper Sees: The Narrative Christology of Luke 17:11-19," *CBQ* 56 (1994) 273–87.

DISCIPLES AND TEACHERS

Taken in tandem with v. 39, the saying in v. 40 declares that the follower is only as good as the guide. If the teacher is blind, so will be the student. In Luke 22:27 there is a similar saying about disciples being like and not greater than their teacher, but there it takes on a different meaning. The context for that saying is the Last Supper, where Jesus asks his disciples who is greater: the one who sits at table or the one who serves. He affirms the expected reply but then identifies himself with the one who serves. In this context the disciples' greatness is like their teacher's in their willingness to serve the least. In this aspect a disciple of Jesus cannot surpass the teacher. The saying in 6:40 is uttered toward the beginning of the education of the disciples and points forward to 22:27, where the meaning of "fully trained" unfolds more clearly.

HYPOCRITICAL CORRECTION

The next two verses give a vivid illustration of blindness. Exaggeration and humor drive home the point: those who would correct the faults of others do well to attend to their own shortcomings first. Many similar forms of the proverb are known from antiquity. In the fifth century B.C.E. the Greek philosopher Demokritos wrote, "Better it is to correct one's own faults than those of others" (*Frag.* 60). Previously, Thales, a sixth-century B.C.E. Greek philosopher, who was asked what was easy, replied, "Counseling of others." Diogenes Laertius, a Greek Cynic philosopher who lived in the fourth century B.C.E., advised, "Avoid doing what you find blameworthy in others" (1.36). From Menander, the Greek playwright of the fourth century B.C.E. comes, "Before you charge your neighbor with a flaw, ponder well what deep within yourself you saw" (*Frag.* 710). Petronius, a first-century C.E. satirist, observed, "You manage to see the tiny louse on your neighbor but not the large tick on yourself" (*Satyricon,* 57).[10] The formulation of Matthew 7:3-5 is very similar to that of Luke, as is the form of the saying found in the *Gospel of Thomas* §26 and in the Oxyrhynchus papyri (1:1-4).[11]

[10] Danker, *New Age,* 153–54.
[11] See above, p. 74, n. 8, on the Oxyrhynchus papyri.

The point of the saying is different from that of 6:37, which admonishes disciples to stop judging. Here it is not the act of giving reproof that is proscribed, but the lack of self-criticism by one who would be too ready to correct the faults of others. Such a one is accused of being a hypocrite. In Greek *hypocritēs* denotes, literally, "one who answers," and came to be applied to orators and stage actors. It is from the use of the term for those who donned a false persona on stage in the theater that it came to mean "pretender" in a pejorative sense. It has a consistently negative connotation in the Gospels.[12] In two other instances Luke uses the term to criticize those who know how to interpret signs in the earth and the sky but not the present time (12:56), and to denounce the leader of the synagogue who objects to Jesus' healing on the sabbath a woman who was bent for eighteen years (13:15).

There is speculation that Jesus' use of the term "hypocrite" reflects his familiarity with the theater, from having been raised near the Hellenistic city Sepphoris, a few miles from Nazareth.[13] However, the date of the theater building that has been excavated in Sepphoris is still debated. Some date it to the reign of Herod Antipas, others to the second century. Another possibility is that *hypocritēs* was a term used by the early Greek-speaking Christians of their Jewish opponents, which in time was attributed to Jesus himself.[14] It is notable that Jesus is not criticizing stage actors *per se*, and is himself portrayed as an orator delivering a soliloquy on center stage in this Sermon on the Plain.

GOOD FRUIT

The imagery shifts once again as the next three verses exhort Christians to be like good trees that bear good fruit. The counterparts in Matthew 7:16-20 and 12:34 are similar, as is the saying in *Gospel of Thomas* §45. Fruit is a frequently used meta-

---

[12] The other fourteen instances in the Gospels are: Matthew 6:2, 5, 16; 7:5; 15:7; 22:18; 23:13, 15, 23, 25, 27, 29; 24:51; Mark 7:6.

[13] Richard A. Batey, "Jesus and the Theatre," *NTS* 30 (1984) 564–65; Augustine Stock, "Jesus, Hypocrites, and Herodians, *BTB* 16 (1986) 3–7.

[14] Fitzmyer, *Luke*, 643.

phor in the Bible for deeds.[15] In the Lukan trio of sayings in 6:43-45, the first and third repeat the same message: a good tree produces good fruit (v. 43) as a good person produces good (deeds) (v. 45). The middle verse (v. 44) shifts the focus from what is produced to how the fruit reveals the nature of the producer itself. It is not only the good fruit that is important, but that the tree is known for what it is from its fruit.

The final verse introduces another concept: the centrality of the heart as the place from which all else flows. In the thinking of biblical times the heart is the center of a person's life. It is the seat of the desires, emotions, thoughts, and plans, from which come a person's deeds.[16] It is the place where one meets God, and the locus for conversion.[17] In Luke 6:45 it is imaged as a storehouse of either good or evil. In similar fashion Luke has previously spoken of how Mary treasured all that was revealed to her by God in her heart (2:19, 51). A saying similar to 6:45 appears in 8:15. There Jesus speaks of those who, like rich soil, embrace the word with a good heart and then bear fruit. There are also similarities to the saying in Luke 16:15, where Jesus confronts the Pharisees with the way they justify themselves in the sight of others, while God knows their true hearts. In the context of 6:39-40 the sayings in 6:43-45 can be heard as an admonition that good teaching can only come from good teachers. The emphasis on speaking in v. 45 is balanced by a stress on doing in the subsequent parable in 6:46-49.[18]

PREACHING POSSIBILITIES

Vivid images in the gospel alert disciples to the dangers of ignoring our areas of blindness—those aspects that are yet unredeemed and in need of God's illumination. Worse still is when one who is unaware of their own need for redemption tries to

---

[15] See Hosea 10:13; Isaiah 3:10; Jeremiah 17:10; 21:14.

[16] See Luke 1:51, 66; 2:35; 3:15; 5:22; 9:47; 12:34, 45; 21:14, 34; 24:38.

[17] See Luke 1:17; 8:12; 10:27; 24:25, 32. See Thomas P. McCreesh, "Heart," in *The Collegeville Pastoral Dictionary of Biblical Theology*, ed. Carroll Stuhlmueller (Collegeville: The Liturgical Press, 1996) 422–24.

[18] See below, chap. 22, where this parable is the gospel for Saturday of the Twenty-third Week of Ordinary Time.

lead or correct others. Mutual correction is an important aspect of Christian living, but can only be done by those who know that they, too, are on the same journey as those whose faults they see. Only those who know their own need for conversion are in a position to offer guidance to another. An example of such is the apostle Paul, who, in the letter to Timothy coupled with this gospel on the Twenty-third Friday of Ordinary Time in Year I, is represented as one who has been enabled by God's mercy to turn from a former life of arrogance and persecution to one in which grace is now visible in overflowing measure (1 Tim 1:1-2, 12-14). Preachers might encourage their congregations to consider keeping watch for one day over how many times they find themselves thinking critically or speaking disapprovingly of others. A one-day moratorium on criticizing others could be an opportunity to look inward to the need for one's own conversion in those same areas. Disciples might be invited to examine what it is that fills their hearts that is evident from what they say (v. 45). In what way is the heart in need of transformation so that it is goodness that proceeds from the mouth instead of invidious censure? On the Eighth Sunday of Ordinary Time the first reading from Sirach (27:4-7) also points in this direction: what reveals a person's true character is the way they speak.

The gospel also offers an opportunity to reflect on the need for ongoing education in the teachings of Jesus and of the Church, not only for teachers and official "guides," but for all who follow Jesus' way. One is never "fully trained" (v. 40), but continues to grow in likeness to the Teacher both in intellectual training and in fruitful deeds. A good tree must be fertilized and cultivated in order to continue to bear good fruit.

The object of such study is not only the sayings and deeds of Jesus, but the Teacher himself. A disciple of Jesus who knows only the content of the Gospels without knowing the Teacher himself would be a blind guide. Nor is the objective for a disciple the good deeds themselves. While the "fruit" is important, it is even more essential that the tree be known for what it is (v. 44). The good deeds of a disciple should lead those who enjoy these "fruits" to the source itself. Just as the true nature of the tree is known by its fruit, so the deeds of a disciple reveal the presence of Christ.

The saying in v. 40 can be taken as an admonition to humility on the part of the disciple, recognizing that s/he emulates the Teacher without ever surpassing him. But perhaps more salient is the allusion forward to 22:27 where the likeness of the disciple to the Teacher is visible in the selfless service to the death for those who are lowliest. This same message undergirds the section of Paul's letter to the Corinthians (1 Cor 9:16-19, 22-27) that is coupled with Luke 6 on the Twenty-third Friday of Ordinary Time of Year II. Paul speaks of having made himself a slave to all so as to win over as many as possible.

CHAPTER EIGHT

Seeing Differently
(Luke 7:36–8:3)[1]

Eleventh Sunday of Ordinary Time

Thursday of the Twenty-fourth Week of Ordinary Time
(Luke 7:36-50)

[36] *A Pharisee invited Jesus to dine with him,*
   and he entered the Pharisee's house and reclined at table.
[37] *Now there was a sinful woman in the city*
   who learned that he was at table in the house of the Pharisee.
   Bringing an alabaster flask of ointment,
      [38] *she stood behind him at his feet weeping*
   and began to bathe his feet with her tears.
   Then she wiped them with her hair, kissed them,
   and anointed them with the ointment.
[39] *When the Pharisee who had invited him saw this he said to himself,*
   "If this man were a prophet,
   he would know who and what sort of woman this is
   who is touching him,
   that she is a sinner."
[40] *Jesus said to him in reply,*
   "Simon, I have something to say to you."
   "Tell me, teacher," he said.
[41] *"Two people were in debt to a certain creditor;*
   one owed five hundred days' wages and the other owed fifty.
[42] *Since they were unable to repay the debt, he forgave it for both.*
   Which of them will love him more?"
[43] *Simon said in reply,*

---

[1] See Barbara E. Reid, *Choosing the Better Part? Women in the Gospel of Luke* (Collegeville: The Liturgical Press, 1996) 107–34, where these two episodes are treated in greater detail.

"The one, I suppose, whose larger debt was forgiven."
He said to him, "You have judged rightly."
⁴⁴ *Then he turned to the woman and said to Simon,*
    "Do you see this woman?
    When I entered your house, you did not give me water for my feet,
        but she has bathed them with her tears
        and wiped them with her hair.
⁴⁵ *You did not give me a kiss,*
        but she has not ceased kissing my feet since the time I entered.
⁴⁶ *You did not anoint my head with oil,*
        but she anointed my feet with ointment.
⁴⁷ *So I tell you, her many sins have been forgiven*
        because she has shown great love.
    But the one to whom little is forgiven, loves little."
⁴⁸ *He said to her, "Your sins are forgiven."*
⁴⁹ *The others at table said to themselves,*
    "Who is this who even forgives sins?"
⁵⁰ *But he said to the woman,*
    "Your faith has saved you; go in peace."

¹ *Afterward he journeyed from one town and village to another,*
    preaching and proclaiming the good news of the kingdom of God.
    Accompanying him were the Twelve
        ² *and some women who had been cured of evil spirits and infirmities,*
        Mary, called Magdalene, from whom seven demons had gone out,
        ³ *Joanna, the wife of Herod's steward Chuza,*
        Susanna, and many others who provided for them out of their resources.

LUKAN LITERARY CONTEXT

These two vignettes of ministering women are set in the middle of the Galilean ministry. The first brings to a climax three episodes in Luke 7 in which the question of seeing and believing is central. Also key is the identity of Jesus as a prophet. The whole story of Simon's exchange with Jesus in 7:36-50 is parabolic, not only vv. 41-43, where Jesus poses a parable to Simon. Although the Lectionary links this story with that of Mary Magdalene and the other Galilean women, in the gospel there is a clear change of scene at the beginning of chapter 8. The unnamed woman in Luke 7:36-50 is not to be identified with Mary Magdalene. Nor is this the same story as that of the woman who anoints Jesus for burial (Mark 14:3-9; Matt 26:6-13;

John 12:1-8). In the Western church, traditions about Mary of Bethany, Mary Magdalene, the woman who anointed Jesus for burial, the woman who ministered to Jesus in the home of Simon, and the woman caught in adultery (John 8:1-11) have been interwoven and confused. These Marys and unnamed women have, for the most part, maintained their own identities in the traditions of the Greek church.

TRADITION HISTORY

The story of the nameless woman in Luke 7:36-50 is often confused with that of the woman who anointed Jesus for burial. There are strong parallels between Mark 14:3-9 and Luke 7:36-50. In both the woman is unnamed; she enters the house of Simon; Jesus is reclining at table; the woman carries an alabaster flask of ointment with which she anoints Jesus; observers react negatively, whereas Jesus affirms her action. Luke's account shares other details with the Johannine version: the woman's ministrations are to Jesus' feet, which she also wipes with her hair.

There are also important differences between the Lukan story and the other three. In Luke the setting is Galilee rather than Bethany. In Mark (14:3) and Matthew (26:6) the host is Simon the leper, while in Luke Simon is a Pharisee. In John (12:2) the supper is served by Martha, in the home she shares with Mary and Lazarus. In John (12:3) it is Mary who anoints Jesus, whereas in the Synoptic stories the woman is unnamed. In Matthew, Mark, and John, the anointing occurs shortly before Jesus' passion and is a prophetic action related to his burial; in Luke it happens during the Galilean ministry and the focus is on repentance, forgiveness, and love. In Luke the objection comes from Simon; in John (12:4-6) it is Judas who objects; in Matthew (26:8) "the disciples;" and in Mark (14:4) "some." In Luke Simon's objection centers on the woman's sinful past; in the other three versions the indignity revolves around the extravagance of the anointing when the ointment could have been sold for money to use for the poor.

The best explanation for these similarities and differences is that there are two strands of tradition: one tells of a woman who enters a dinner gathering in Galilee, at which Jesus is a guest. She experiences forgiveness from Jesus and weeps over his feet and dries them with her hair. The other strand relates that a woman at a dinner in Bethany anoints Jesus' head with costly perfume shortly before his passion. Whether the two strands of tradition represent two separate incidents in the life of Jesus or only one that has been variously preserved is impossible to determine. Because the two had many points of similarity, they became intertwined, and details from one passed over to the other in the oral retelling.[2] Each evangelist has further shaped the episode to his own theological purposes. It is important that the preacher focus on the Lukan version and not confuse details from other similar accounts with this one.

DIVIDED RESPONSES

As it stands in Luke's Gospel, the story in 7:36-50 is a moving illustration of the desired response to Jesus' preaching. It comes on the heels of the episode in which the disciples of John the Baptist inquire of Jesus, "Are you the one who is to come, or should we look for another?" (7:20). Jesus replies by reminding them of what they have seen and heard: "The blind regain their sight, the lame walk, lepers are cleansed, the deaf hear, the dead are raised, the poor have the good news proclaimed to them" (7:22). He concludes, "And blessed is the one who takes no offense at me" (7:23). The issue is how one evaluates what one sees and hears concerning Jesus: does it draw you to faith in him? or do you take offense?[3]

The divided response is further illustrated in 7:24-35. There Jesus quizzes the crowds about what they went out to the desert to see (vv. 24, 26) when they followed John. The issue of seeing a prophet is raised in v. 26, preparing for Simon's objection in v. 39, regarding Jesus' identification as a prophet. Verses 29-30 highlight the positive response of "all the people . . . including tax collectors" to John and to the righteousness of God, in contrast

---

[2] See A. Legault, "An Application of the Form-Critique Method to the Anointings in Galilee (Lk. 7.36-50) and Bethany (Mt. 26.6-13; Mk. 4.3-9; John 12.1-8)," *CBQ* 16 (1954) 131–45.

[3] On Seeing and Believing in Luke, see below, chap. 23, p. 271.

to "the Pharisees and scholars of the law, who were not baptized by him" and who "rejected the plan of God for themselves."[4]

A parable in vv. 31-32 continues to contrast actual responses to those desired. Verse 32, "We sang a dirge, but you did not weep" leads into the story in 7:36-50, where the woman who exemplifies the desired response stands behind Jesus, "at his feet weeping" (v. 38). Following the parable, vv. 33-34 return to the issue of seeing. For those determined not to "see" in a way that leads to faith, they will see what they want: in John, who "came neither eating food nor drinking wine," they will see a man "possessed by a demon" (v. 33); in Jesus who "came eating and drinking" they see "a glutton and a drunkard, a friend of tax collectors and sinners" (v. 34).[5]

The central point of the story in Luke 7:36-50 concerns the interaction between Jesus and Simon.[6] The whole story hinges on Jesus' question to Simon in v. 44, "Do you see this woman?" This challenge of Jesus to Simon arises from Simon's misperception of the woman in v. 39. Two perceptions are intimately related: what Simon sees in the woman and her interaction with Jesus determines how Simon sees Jesus. Simon is clear about what he sees: she is a sinner and Jesus is not a prophet. The question that the story poses is: can Simon see differently? Can he see what Jesus sees: a forgiven woman who shows great love (v. 47)? If he can see her this way, then he may perceive Jesus aright: not only as prophet, but also as the agent of God's forgiving love.

GREAT FORGIVENESS LEADS TO LAVISH LOVE

As most often in Luke's Gospel, Jesus' way of getting people to see God's realm as he does, is through parables. And

---

[4] See J. T. Carroll, "Luke's Portrayal of the Pharisees," *CBQ* 50 (1988) 604–21, for further detail on how Luke uses Jesus' encounters with the Pharisees to demonstrate competing understandings of the realm of God.

[5] See also David A. Neale, *None But the Sinners: Religious Categories in the Gospel of Luke* (JSNTSup 58; Sheffield: JSOT, 1991) 135–47, for connections between Luke 7:28-35 and 7:36-50.

[6] Contrary to the assertion by Evelyn Thibeaux, "'Known to Be a Sinner': The Narrative Rhetoric of Luke 7:36-50," *BTB* 23/4 (1993) 151–60, esp. 152, that the main plot is the interaction between Jesus and the woman.

so, Jesus replies to Simon's perception of the woman as a sinner
by telling a parable. What Simon "sees" (vv. 39, 44) frames the
parable of the two debtors in 7:41-43. The parable in vv. 41-43 is
not an allegory that corresponds point by point with the narrative of 7:36-40, 44-50. Nothing is said in the story about Simon
being a sinner or that he is in need of forgiveness. The parable
is not meant to contrast Simon's puny love after being forgiven
little with the woman's lavish love after being forgiven much.
Rather, the parable has a single point: that one who has been
forgiven much loves greatly the one who remitted the debt.

CONTRASTING ACTIONS

Jesus contrasts the behavior of Simon with that of the
woman (vv. 44-46) to show Simon that his actions reveal his
shortsightedness. Simon provided none of the amenities of hospitality, which would express his respect for Jesus and his concern for his guest's comfort.[7] Simon gave no water for Jesus to
wash his feet to refresh himself after walking dry, dusty roads.[8]
He did not greet Jesus with a kiss,[9] nor did he anoint Jesus'
head with oil.[10] The woman, by contrast, went to extravagant

---

[7] G. Bouwman ("La pécheresse hospitalière (Lc. vii, 36-50)," *ETL* 45 [1969]
172–79) asserts that the insertion of elements from John 12:1-11 and the parable
in vv. 41-44 shift the accent of the story: her gestures of contrition have become
expressions of hospitality. He postulates that this episode reflects a tension in
the early Church over women of questionable pasts who offered hospitality to
apostles. However, J. Delobel ("Encore la pécheresse. Quelques réflexions critiques," *ETL* 45 [1969] 180–83) rightly points out that the woman's actions in
7:38 are not about hospitality; it is when they are contrasted with Simon's omis-
sions (vv. 44-46) that that nuance emerges. Furthermore, Jesus is not the guest
of the woman; rather, of Simon. If this theme were a concern to Luke it is odd
that it does not emerge in Acts, where numerous episodes mention hospitality
toward apostles.

[8] In Genesis 18:4; 19:2; 24:32; 43:24 this is part of the hospitality extended to
guests.

[9] It was customary to greet or bid farewell to relatives and friends (of the
same sex or opposite) with a kiss (e.g., Gen 27:26; 29:11,13; 31:28; 1 Sam 20:41;
Luke 15:20). Christians habitually greeted one another with a kiss (Rom 16:16;
1 Cor 16:20; 1 Thess 5:26). It would be expected that Simon would greet Jesus
with a kiss on the cheek. A kiss on the hand would signal even greater respect.

[10] The custom of providing dinner guests with a cone of oil that would drip
down on their heads during the course of the meal is seen in Egyptian repre-

lengths: she bathed his feet with her tears and wiped them with her hair, kissed his feet ceaselessly,[11] and anointed them with ointment.[12]

AN OPEN INVITATION

Jesus points out these actions to Simon so that he can make the same conclusion Jesus has. When presented with the matter in parable form, Simon easily judges rightly (v. 43). In v. 44 the question moves to the real woman that faces Simon. If Simon still does not see the link between the parable and the woman after Jesus recites what he sees (vv. 44-46), he proceeds to interpret it: "So I tell you, her many sins have been forgiven[13]; hence, she has shown great love" (v. 47).[14] The choice lies before Simon: can he let go of seeing her as a sinner and see, rather, her great love? If so, then this will also enable him to perceive Jesus

---

sentations of banquet scenes (ANEP, 209). This would cool and refresh the guests. For the custom among Jews, see H. Strack and P. Billerbeck, *Kommentar zum Neuen Testament* (6 vols.; Munich: Beck, 1922–61) 1.427, 428. Psalm 23:5 and Ecclesiastes 9:7-8 associate anointing of the head with banqueting. Not only was the ointment on the head refreshing, but its fragrance would fill the room (John 12:3), masking other less pleasant odors. In Matthew 6:17 Jesus instructs his disciples to anoint their head and wash their face when fasting.

[11] Kissing the feet was a sign of deep reverence, often extended to leading rabbis (Xen. *Cyr.* vvii.5.32; *Polyb.* xv.1.7; Aristoph. *Vesp.* 608).

[12] Legault, "Anointings," 131–45, asserts that anointing feet is an unheard of action and that this detail is best explained as having crossed into the story from the tradition about the anointing of Jesus' head. However, J. Coakley ("The Anointing at Bethany and the Priority of John," *JBL* 107 [1988] 247) offers eight literary references to anointing of feet.

[13] The perfect passive verb *apheóntai*, "have been forgiven," in vv. 47, 48, connotes a past action whose effects endure into the present. This, coupled with the verb *ēn*, "was," in v. 37, which is in the imperfect tense, connoting "used to be," indicates that she had been forgiven her sins before coming to the home of Simon.

[14] The Greek phrase, *hoti ēgapēsen poly,* is ambiguous. It can be rendered either "because she has shown great love" or "hence she has shown great love." That the latter is the correct meaning is clear from the conclusion in v. 47c, "But the one to whom little is forgiven, loves little," and the parable in vv. 41-43. Both make the point that the love follows the forgiveness. The end of v. 47, "But the one to whom little is forgiven, loves little," does not refer to Simon; it simply provides a contrast to highlight the woman's great love.

correctly: that he is the prophet. Simon's fate rests on whether he can be persuaded to see as Jesus does. In the end, we don't know if he does. As with all good parables, the story is open-ended. It invites the reader to take up the challenge presented to Simon, and to be converted to Jesus' way of seeing.[15]

MINISTERING GALILEAN WOMEN

Linked with the story of the woman who ministers to Jesus in the home of Simon is the notice of the ministry of Mary Magdalene, Joanna, Susanna, and the other Galilean women. Although all four Gospels speak of Mary Magdalene as one of the women who watched Jesus' crucifixion, saw where he was buried, and returned to the tomb on the first day of the week,[16] only Luke introduces her in the context of the Galilean mission. Unlike the Twelve (Luke 6:12-16; 9:1-6), there is no narrative of the women's call to become disciples nor of their being sent on mission. There is no record of how they first came to know Jesus. All that is preserved is that some of them have been healed of evil spirits and infirmities, presumably by Jesus, which leads them to support his mission.

FORMER PROSTITUTES?

The popular notion that Mary Magdalene was a prostitute has no basis whatsoever in the New Testament. In fact, there is no indication that she was a sinner of any kind. The idea that Mary Magdalene was a prostitute probably stems from confus-

---

[15] It is surprising how many commentators and translators reinforce Simon's initial perception of the woman, and never move beyond that. The episode has no title in the Greek text, but modern translators have entitled it: "The Pardon of a Sinful Woman" *(NAB)*; "The Woman Who Was a Sinner" *(NJB, NRSV)*; "A Sinful Woman Forgiven" *(HarperCollins Study Bible)*. *La Nueva Biblia Latinoamericana* confuses matters entirely by making her "La mujer pecadora de Magdala," "The sinful woman from Magdala"! *The Christian Community Bible* is noncommittal: "Jesus, the Woman and the Pharisee." None points the reader to the way Jesus perceives her by entitling it: "A Woman Who Shows Great Love" (v. 47).

[16] Matthew 27:56, 61; 28:1-10; Mark 15:40, 47; 16:1-9; Luke 24:1-12; John 19:25; 20:1-18.

ing her with the woman in 7:36-50,[17] who has commonly been thought to have been a prostitute. However, nothing in the text says that the forgiven woman in 7:36-50 was a prostitute either. While 7:37 says the woman had been a sinner and v. 47 asserts her sins had been many, we are never told the nature of her sins. Verse 37 hints that the whole city knows her as a sinner, but this woman need only have been ill or disabled or have frequent contact with Gentiles to be considered a sinner by Jews in the city. Perhaps she was a midwife or a dyer who Jews would consider sinful from her association with the unclean.

Some commentators believe that the mere presence of this woman at a banquet is a sign that she is a prostitute. In the Roman period, however, respectable women were beginning to attend banquets with men. Moreover, the woman in 7:36-50 does none of the things that banquet courtesans were known to do: engage in witty conversation or discussion with the banqueters, drink with them, recline beside them, dance, act, play the flute or harp, or in any way entertain.[18] Nor is she named by any of the known terms for such women: *pornē,* "prostitute," or "whore," *koinē,* "common," i.e., "shared by all," *gynē pagkoine,* "public woman," *pilasōtos,* "wanton" or *hetaira,* "companion to men," the term for the highest class prostitutes.

Some scholars point to her loosened hair as a sign that she is a "loose woman." The Talmud (*t. Sota* 5.9; *y. Git.* 9.50d) says that a married woman was not to let down her hair in the presence of other men, but a mishnaic text (*m. Ketub.* 2.1) seems to assume that an unmarried woman did not bind up her hair until her marriage. The woman in 7:36-50 might then be unmarried

---

[17] See Esther DeBoer, *Mary Magdalene: Beyond the Myth,* trans. John Bowden (Harrisburg, Penn.: Trinity Press International, 1997); Ingrid Maisch, *Mary Magdalene: The Image of a Woman through the Centuries,* trans. Linda Maloney (Collegeville: The Liturgical Press, 1998); Carla Ricci, *Mary Magdalene and Many Others,* trans. Paul Burns (Minneapolis: Fortress, 1994); Jane Schaberg, "How Mary Magdalene Became a Whore," *BibRev* 8 (1992) 30–37, 51–52; "Thinking Back Through the Magdalene," *Continuum* 2 (1991) 71–90.

[18] See descriptions of banquet courtesans in K. E. Corley, *Private Women, Public Meals: Social Conflict in the Synoptic Tradition* (Peabody, Mass.: Hendrickson, 1993) 38–48; see also Sarah Pomeroy, *Goddesses, Whores, Wives, and Slaves: Women in Classical Antiquity* (New York: Dorset, 1975) 88–92.

and acting decently in a neighbor's house.[19] Her loose hair, rather than a sign of her wantonness,[20] evokes an image of love and loveliness as in the Song of Songs. There the bridegroom-to-be extols the charms of his beloved, among which is her beautiful hair that is "like a flock of goats, streaming down the mountains of Gilead" (4:1; 6:5). Like the bridegroom Jesus sees the woman before him as lovely and loving and attempts to get his host to perceive the same.

For some scholars the expensive alabaster flask of costly perfume is a sign that the woman was a prostitute. They mistakenly believe that this was the only source of wealth for women in antiquity. A woman could inherit money and property from her father if she had no brothers (Num 27:8). And women worked in many kinds of trades. Acts 16:14, for example, tells of Lydia of Thyatira, who was a dealer in purple goods, luxury items. Acts 18:3 speaks of Prisca working together with her husband Aquila at tentmaking. There is evidence of Greco-Roman women employed as weavers, midwives, doctors, hairdressers, wet nurses, masseuses, attendants, and musicians.[21] All we can conclude about the woman in 7:36-50 is that she had access to an expensive flask of perfumed ointment. We know nothing further of how she obtained it.

FORGIVENESS AND HEALING

The story of the unnamed woman in 7:36-50 says that she was a sinner who had been forgiven, but it never specifies what were her sins. There is no clear signal that she was a prostitute.[22]

[19] Coakley, "Anointing," 250.

[20] The idea that a prostitute would have loose hair is mistaken. In fact, had the woman been a prostitute she would have had carefully groomed and elaborately styled hair.

[21] Jane Gardner, *Women in Roman Law and Society* (Bloomington & Indianapolis: Indiana University, 1986) 233–55.

[22] Luise Schottroff (*Let the Oppressed Go Free* [Gender and the Biblical Tradition; trans. Annemarie S. Kidder; Louisville: Westminster/John Knox, 1991] 138–57) offers a different solution. She asserts that the woman is a whore but is not repentant. Because of economic necessity she remains a prostitute, but has experienced and has given love. She believes the story is not about prostitution that can be overcome by Christian repentance. Rather, the issue is mercy and respect toward prostitutes exhibited by Jesus contrasted with prejudice against

The nature of the woman's sins is not the focus of the story and the preacher would do well not to speculate uselessly on them.[23] As for Mary Magdalene there is no evidence whatsoever that she was a prostitute or even a sinner of any sort.[24] What the text does say is that some of the women had been cured of evil spirits and infirmities and that seven demons had gone out of Mary. Seven is a symbolic number for fullness, or completeness. The ancients, not having the benefit of modern medical knowledge, attributed many illnesses to demon possession. What Luke states, then, is that Mary Magdalene had been very seriously ill, and that she had been healed. Luke, in underscoring the gravity of Mary's illness, is more intent on highlighting the greatness of Jesus' power of healing than he is on telling us something about Mary. Rather than speculate on how ill she had been, the preacher would do better to focus on how completely she experienced the liberating, healing power of God. The encounter with Jesus of both the forgiven woman and the healed women lead to their ministerial actions.

FINANCIAL RESOURCES FOR MINISTRY

A common element in the two stories is that these women all had access to financial resources that they used for ministering to Jesus. The woman at the home of Simon directs her ministrations to Jesus alone. The women journeying with Jesus

---

them shown by Simon. Schottroff states that it is the moralizing tendency of Christians that prevents us from accepting such an interpretation.

[23] One has to wonder at the sexism in such speculation when this same gospel presents Peter as a "sinful man" (5:7) in the story of his call, but commentators never muse on the nature of his sins.

[24] It is not clear that any of Jesus' followers were prostitutes. The notion is based on one lone saying in Matthew 21:31-32 which is a warning to religious leaders, who think themselves upright. It contrasts their negative response to Jesus with that of those least expected to be upright: tax collectors and prostitutes. It is a warning to the leaders, set forth in polemical terms, not a historical attestation on the makeup of Jesus' itinerant band of followers. It is also important to note that this Matthean saying is parallel to Luke 7:29-30. If the mention of prostitutes was present in the original Q form of the saying, it is curious that Luke should drop it from his version of the saying. The mention of the positive response of prostitutes to John would have served Luke's interest if, indeed, he had wanted the woman in 7:36-50 to be understood as a prostitute.

through Galilee provided for[25] Jesus and the Twelve[26] out of their resources. That the resources of Mary Magdalene, Joanna, Susanna, and the other Galilean women were monetary is clear from 8:3. The word *hyparchontōn*, "resources," always means possessions, property, money, or goods in Luke and Acts,[27] not time, talent, or domestic service. This kind of support would be crucial since it seems that Jesus did not work for money once he began his ministry of proclaiming the gospel. And those disciples who left behind their occupations to follow Jesus (e.g., Peter, James, and John in 5:11) would need monetary aid. In addition, having rejected him in Nazareth (Luke 4:16-30), it is unlikely that Jesus' family and neighbors would have provided for his support.

The note that Joanna was the wife of Chuza, Herod's steward in 8:3 indicates the source of her wealth, status, and influence. Magdala, Mary's hometown, was a prosperous village noted for its dried and smoked fish, but the gospel gives no explicit information about the source of Mary's money. About Susanna, who is mentioned only here in the Gospels, we have no further information. Whatever the source of their wealth, Luke portrays them as well-to-do patrons who finance Jesus' mission.[28]

Some scholars propose that Mary, Joanna, Susanna, and the other women were not using their own money, but were ad-

[25] The verb *diakonein*, "provide for," literally means "to serve as a go-between." See John N. Collins, *Diakonia: Re-Interpreting the Ancient Sources* (New York: Oxford University Press, 1990). For its various uses and nuances in Luke and Acts see Reid, *Choosing the Better Part?*, 98–101.

[26] There is a textual variant in v. 3 that reads *autō*, "him," attested in ℵ, A, L, Tertullian, Cyprian, etc., instead of *autois*, "them," found in B D K Δ θ etc. However, the greater likelihood is that the singular is a later Christocentric correction in line with Mark 15:41 and Matthew 27:55 (B. Metzger, *A Textual Commentary on the Greek New Testament* [3rd ed.; New York: United Bible Societies, 1971] 144). See R. Karris, "Women and Discipleship in Luke," *CBQ* 41 (1979) 1–20, who accepts the variant as original.

[27] Luke 11:21; 12:15, 33, 44; 14:33; 16:1; 19:8; Acts 4:32.

[28] The relationship of discipleship and use of possessions is an important Lukan theme. While some leave everything to follow Jesus (5:1-11, 27-28) others are well-to-do: Levi (Luke 5:27-32); Zacchaeus (Luke 19:1-10); Barnabas (Acts 4:36-37); an Ethiopian eunuch (Acts 8:27); Mary (Acts 12:12); Lydia (Acts 16:14); prominent women in Thessalonica (Acts 17:4); influential Greek men and women in Beroea (Acts 17:12); Prisca and Aquila (Acts 18:1-11, 18-28).

ministering the common fund (Acts 2:44-45; 4:32–5:11). But the possessive pronoun "their," *autais*, in Luke 8:3 is feminine plural and can only mean that the resources belonged to the women. While the patriarchal system ensured that women would be economically dependent on men, there were some women who had money and control of it.[29] It is possible that the Galilean women were single or widowed and would, therefore, enjoy greater personal and economic independence and would be freer to join Jesus' itinerant movement.[30]

What these women did from day to day or how they interacted with the male disciples is difficult to say, based on the little Luke says in 8:1-3. That women traveling with an itinerant preacher was an unprecedented practice, we cannot say with certainty. Women did travel for feasts, as Luke says Mary did with her family each year for Passover (2:41). Women also traveled to visit family, as Mary did when hearing of Elizabeth's pregnancy (1:39-45). Business women, like Lydia (Acts 16:14) also traveled. But to say that it was unheard of for women to accompany a traveling preacher presumes that we know much more about the practices of religious leaders of Jesus' time than we do. All that can be said with certainty is that this is the only recorded instance of this phenomenon in that time and place.[31] In light of the smallness of the geographic area, the women may have only gone out on day trips, and returned to their own homes each evening. As to the supposed scandal involved, if the practice were so shameful, it is curious that there is no mention or explicit defense of it in the traditions.[32]

---

[29] Inscriptions from Jewish women donors to synagogues show that at least some women had money and the power to donate it. See Bernadette Brooten, *Women Leaders in the Ancient Synagogue: Inscriptional Evidence and Background Issues*, Brown Judaic Studies 36 (Chico, Calif.: Scholars Press, 1982) 143–44.

[30] Although 8:3 mentions Joanna's husband, some speculate that she has left him because she is named again in 24:10 without reference to Chuza. Unlike most women in the Bible, Mary is identified in relation to a city, not a husband.

[31] D. C. Sim, "The Women Followers of Jesus: The Implications of Luke 8:13," *HeyJ* 30 (1989) 61, n. 3.

[32] Schaberg, "Luke," 287. Bruce J. Malina and Richard L. Rohrbaugh (*Social Science Commentary on the Synoptic Gospels* [Minneapolis: Fortress, 1992]) see the scandal averted if these are widows who now serve the surrogate family of Jesus' disciples in place of their biological family.

PREACHING POSSIBILITIES

These texts are rich in possibilities for preaching. Both can provide an opportunity for the preacher to explore how pre-conceived notions can blind one to the presence of God and the response Christ desires. In the story of Simon, his inability to perceive the woman correctly, as one forgiven who loves greatly, blinds him to the true identity of Jesus, as prophet and the Coming One. With the story about Mary Magdalene, false impressions about her having been a prostitute can keep us from seeing the emphasis in the text on her ministry to Jesus. The preacher can explore ways in which sexism, racism, classism, etc. can blind us to seeing Christ present in our midst today. The homilist can, by dislodging false perceptions about these women in the gospel stories, invite the congregation to identify their prejudices and be converted to a different vision. The preacher can show how these women who pour out themselves in ministry are the very image of him who pours out his blood on behalf of those he loves. They are the very embodiment of Jesus, who has come not to be served, but to serve (22:27).[33] Like the prophet Nathan with king David in the first reading (2 Sam 12:7-10, 13), a prophetic preacher skilled in the use of parable can effect dramatic conversion.

Another aspect that emerges in both gospel stories as well as the psalm response (Psalm 32) is the new life and joy that results from forgiveness and healing. The woman at the dinner party poured herself out in lavish demonstrations of love toward Jesus. Mary Magdalene and her companions spent themselves and their monetary resources in service of the mission with Jesus and his companions. Just so, preachers today can invite their congregations to extravagant measures of love and ministry that flow from the exuberance of having experienced healing and forgiveness from Christ. It is important to emphasize that these women did not earn their forgiveness or healing. Rather, their loving ministerial actions flow from the experience of having been forgiven. Although these parts of their stories are not narrated, the forgiveness and healing came first. The second reading, from

---

[33] The same verb, *diakonein,* is used for "serve" in 22:27 as "provide for" in 8:3.

Galatians 2:16, 19-21 sounds a similar note, where Paul insists that one is set in right relation with God not through works of the law but through faith in Christ. The preacher might invite members of the congregation to touch into their own experiences of healing and forgiveness and examine whether their gratitude has taken concrete form in ministerial service.

These two stories of ministering women also offer the opportunity for the preacher to address the topic of ministry as a constituent part of the baptismal call of all disciples. Of equal importance to the apostolic service of the male disciples in the gospel is that of Jesus' female followers. While the Gospel of Luke, written in a patriarchal milieu, portrays the women's roles in ministry as silent, behind-the-scenes support for the male ministers,[34] new questions about ministerial roles must be addressed today in communities of Christians striving for gender equality. As women today continue to minister not only with their financial resources, but with their theological education and their aptitude and willingness to serve in all the ministerial roles, it is important to address the unsettling question of whether a story like that of the Galilean women encourages women to support a system that can exploit them even as they themselves enable it to keep doing so. By providing resources for the mission are women being co-opted into perpetuating a structure in which they can never have access to some of the ministries and to the decision-making power?

The preacher might also explore the relationship of the use of possessions and discipleship. In Luke there is not a two-tiered system in which those who leave everything behind are the "real" disciples. Some do this for the sake of the mission. Others, while not giving everything away, place their possessions at the service of Jesus and the community of believers. In a well-to-do congregation, the preacher might speak of how these resources are given to be poured out in service.

[34] See Reid, *Choosing the Better Part?*; Jane Schaberg, "Luke," *The Women's Bible Commentary*, ed. Carol A. Newsom and Sharon H. Ringe (rev. ed.; Louisville: Westminster/John Knox, 1998) 363–80. Mary Rose D'Angelo, "Women in Luke-Acts: A Redactional View," *JBL* 109/3 (1990) 441–61; Elisabeth Schüssler Fiorenza, in *In Memory of Her: A Feminist Theological Reconstruction of Christian Origins* (New York: Crossroad, 1983) 50.

CHAPTER NINE

Surprising Samaritan
(Luke 10:25-37)

Fifteenth Sunday of Ordinary Time

Monday of the Twenty-seventh Week of Ordinary Time

²⁵ *There was a scholar of the law who stood up to test Jesus*
and said,
"Teacher, what must I do to inherit eternal life?"
²⁶ *Jesus said to him, "What is written in the law?*
How do you read it?"
²⁷ *He said in reply,*
"You shall love the Lord, your God,
with all your heart,
with all your being,
with all your strength,
and with all your mind,
and your neighbor as yourself."
²⁸ *He replied to him, "You have answered correctly;*
do this and you will live."

²⁹ *But because he wished to justify himself, he said to Jesus,*
"And who is my neighbor?"
³⁰ *Jesus replied,*
"A man fell victim to robbers
as he went down from Jerusalem to Jericho.
They stripped and beat him and went off leaving him half-dead.
³¹ *A priest happened to be going down that road,*
but when he saw him, he passed by on the opposite side.
³² *Likewise a Levite came to the place,*
and when he saw him, he passed by on the opposite side.
³³ *But a Samaritan traveler who came upon him*
was moved with compassion at the sight.

^{34} *He approached the victim,*
　　poured oil and wine over his wounds and bandaged them.
　　Then he lifted him up on his own animal,
　　took him to an inn and cared for him.
^{35} *The next day he took out two silver coins*
　　and gave them to the innkeeper with the instruction,
　　'Take care of him.
　　If you spend more than what I have given you,
　　I shall repay you on my way back.'
^{36} *Which of these three, in your opinion,*
　　was neighbor to the robbers' victim?"
^{37} *He answered, "The one who treated him with mercy."*
　　Jesus said to him, "Go and do likewise."

LUKAN LITERARY CONTEXT

This well-known dialogue between Jesus and a scholar of the Law is situated toward the beginning of the travel narrative. Jesus has set his face to Jerusalem (9:51) and has commissioned a further seventy(-two)[1] disciples to precede him to the towns he intended to visit (10:1-12). These have returned (10:17-20) and Jesus utters a word of praise to God (10:21-22). He then addresses the disciples and proclaims their eyes blessed for seeing what they see (v. 23). He remarks that many prophets and kings longed to see and hear what the disciples do but did not see or hear it (v. 24). Here Luke once again emphasizes seeing and hearing as the basis of belief in Jesus, which then results in doing the will of God.[2]

[1] The Greek manuscripts are almost evenly divided on whether the number is seventy or seventy-two. Most likely it is meant to be a round number symbolizing completeness. Luke may be alluding to Exodus 24:1; Numbers 11:16, 24, where Moses chooses seventy elders to assist him.

[2] On Seeing and Believing in Luke, see below, chap. 23. There are a number of scholars (e.g., John R. Donahue, *The Gospel in Parable* [Philadelphia: Fortress, 1988] 134–39; I. Howard Marshall, *Commentary on Luke* [NIGTC; Grand Rapids: Eerdmans, 1978] 450–51) who interpret the parable of the Samaritan in tandem with the story of Mary and Martha, with the former illustrating the doing of Christian service and the latter exemplifying the hearing of the word on which service is based. There is, however, nothing in the text that warrants such a link, and it is problematic for the interpretation of Mary and Martha in 10:38-42. See further Barbara E. Reid, *Choosing the Better Part? Women in the Gospel of Luke* (Collegeville: The Liturgical Press, 1996) 147–48.

The new episode with the scholar of the Law illustrates concretely the obedient doing that leads to life (vv. 25, 28). The parable gives a vivid enactment of three characters who see the same thing (vv. 31, 32, 33), but only one does what is required. The final verse underlines the necessity of seeing in such a way that leads to doing mercy.

WHAT TO DO

There are two parts to the gospel selection for this Sunday. The dialogue between the scholar of the Law and Jesus (vv. 25-28) sets the stage for the parable (vv. 29-37). The question "What must I do?" (v. 25) echoes that of the multitudes (3:10), the tax collectors (3:11), and the soldiers (3:14) who came to John to be baptized. It is the same question that the rich ruler poses to Jesus in 18:18. In each of those instances, however, the question is that of a sincere seeker, whereas here there is hostility.[3]

Jesus responds to the question with a question, an honorable response in the game of challenge and riposte.[4] The scholar's answer[5] combines two commandments: love of God (Deut 6:4-9) and love of neighbor (Lev 19:18). The first, the *Shema^c*, was recited twice daily by faithful Jews (*m. Ber.* 1:1-4). It enjoined love of God with one's whole heart, soul, and strength. The heart *(kardia)* is considered the seat of all emotions; soul *(psychē)* is the vitality and consciousness; strength *(ischys)* is power or might. The gospel tradition adds a fourth element: *dianoia*, "mind," the intelligence.[6] Together, these terms represent the whole of the human person.

The second command is from the Holiness Code in Leviticus 19 where Israel is enjoined to be holy because God is holy

[3] Brad H. Young (*The Parables: Jewish Tradition and Christian Interpretation* [Peabody, Mass.: Hendrickson, 1998] 103) sees no hostility in the exchange, but only the normal mode of inquiry in Jewish learning. This is difficult to maintain, though, in light of the use of *ekpeirazein*, "to test," in v. 25.

[4] On the dynamics of honor and shame in challenge and riposte see B. Malina and R. Rohrbaugh, *Social Science Commentary on the Synoptic Gospels* (Minneapolis: Fortress, 1992) 306–07.

[5] In Mark 12:29-31 // Matthew 22:37-40 it is Jesus who gives the pronouncement about the greatest commandment.

[6] So also Mark 12:30. Matthew 22:37 has *dianoia* in place of *ischys*.

(Lev 19:2). One of the ways in which holiness is made visible is in one's treatment of others. Love of neighbor is a manifestation of love of God. Putting the two commands together says, in effect, that when the whole self is oriented toward love of God, and self-understanding is grounded in the covenant relationship with God, then love of neighbor as oneself (Lev 19:18) is all of a piece of harmonious right relation with God. In biblical worlds a person did not define his or herself in individualistic terms, but rather as one enmeshed in a particular family, clan, or religious group. For peoples operating from a stance of dyadic personality, that is, dependent on others for their sense of self-identity, love of self and of the other is inextricably enmeshed.[7]

Jesus approves this weaving together of the two commandments as the correct answer. When asked what to do, he affirms, "do this" (v. 28). There is more, however, that underlies the exchange. It is significant that it is a scholar of the Law who poses the question to Jesus. A scholar of the Law *(nomikos)* was an expert in Mosaic Law, most probably a Pharisee.[8] Scholars of the Law appear five other times in the Third Gospel, each time along with Pharisees. In 7:30 they are among those not baptized by John who reject the plan of God for themselves. In 11:45, 46, 52 they are denounced by Jesus for imposing burdens on people, for consenting to the killing of the prophets, and for taking away the key of knowledge. In 14:3, with a man suffering from dropsy in front of them, Jesus asks if it is lawful to cure on the sabbath, to which they do not reply.

Here in 10:25-37 the overall negative portrayal of the scholars of the Law is reinforced, as this one approaches Jesus with the purpose of testing him. The same verb, *ekpeirazein*, "to test" is used in reference to the temptations put to Jesus by the devil in 4:12. It is not entirely clear from the text what, exactly, is the

---

[7] See Bruce J. Malina, *The New Testament World: Insights from Cultural Anthropology* (rev. ed.; Louisville: Westminster/John Knox, 1993) chap. 3.

[8] The parallel verses in Mark 12:28-31 make the questioner a scribe *(grammateus),* which is probably a synonym for *nomikos.* In Matthew 22:34-40 the questioner is *nomikos.* Both Mark and Matthew place the incident in a different context and the question is different: which is the first (Mark 12:28) or the greatest (Matt 22:36) commandment? The parable in Luke 10:29-37 is unique to Luke.

point of testing. Sharon Ringe[9] suggests that the scholar of the Law, being a Pharisee who believes in resurrection, may be questioning Jesus to see if he also holds such a belief.[10] However, the answer in vv. 27-28 and the conclusion to the parable in v. 37 stress what must be done, not whether one believes in eternal life.

COMPETING INTERPRETERS

A more likely possibility is that the testing involves divergent understandings of the Law and what must be done to fulfill it. Coupled with this is an underlying question about who is competent to answer such questions authoritatively. Jesus' initial reply to the scholar of the Law queries how he reads what is written in the Law (v. 26). The point at issue is not whether either one of them knows the Law. All Jewish males would have been instructed in the Law and how to keep it. But not all had formal schooling in the Law. Few knew how to read and write or how to debate the fine points of scriptural interpretation. A scholar of the Law has formal education for such. But what about Jesus?

While it would be unusual for a small-town boy from Lower Galilee to obtain formal education in the Law, it is possible that Jesus was literate, having received at least a rudimentary education in Torah in the local synagogue at Nazareth.[11] There is no evidence that he pursued higher studies with a rabbi, as Luke says Paul did with Gamaliel in Jerusalem (Acts 22:3). Certainly all the Gospels portray Jesus as one skilled in interpretation of the Scriptures. Early in the gospel narrative Jesus' teaching provokes astonishment because of its authoritative power (4:32). In the Gospel of Luke people who address Jesus as "Teacher" include the whole spectrum of Jews: Pharisees (7:40; 19:39), scribes (20:21, 39), chief priests (20:21), Sadducees (20:28), scholars of the Law (10:25; 11:45), someone from

---

[9] Sharon Ringe, *Luke* (Westminster Bible Companion; Louisville: Westminster/John Knox, 1995) 156.

[10] See Acts 23:8 where Sadducees and Pharisees are engaged in a fierce row over the issue.

[11] See further John P. Meier, *A Marginal Jew: Rethinking the Historical Jesus* (ABRL; vol. 1; New York: Doubleday, 1991) 268–78.

a synagogue official's house (8:49), a rich ruler (18:18), anonymous persons in a crowd (9:38; 12:13), and Jesus' disciples (21:7). Once Jesus uses it as a self-designation (22:11). Jesus is portrayed as teaching in synagogues (4:15-30, 31; 6:6; 13:10), from a boat (5:3), as he journeys to Jerusalem (13:22), and in the Temple area (19:47; 20:1; 21:37).

In several other episodes that have similarities to 10:25-37 Jesus is pitted against other authoritative teachers of the Law and bests them. In 6:1-5, for example, Pharisees confront Jesus about his disciples plucking and eating heads of grain on the sabbath. As in 10:25-37 the question centers on what is the right thing to do. In this instance it concerns doing what is not lawful on the sabbath. Like in 10:26, Jesus responds with a question about how one reads the Scriptures: "Have you not read what David did when he and those who were with him were hungry?"(6:3). The implication is that Jesus is able to read the Scriptures and interpret them authoritatively. The next episode in Luke 6:6-11 portrays Jesus teaching in a synagogue on the sabbath. He heals a man with a withered hand and then quizzes the antagonistic scribes and Pharisees on whether the command to do good or to keep the sabbath takes precedence. In another episode, in 20:21, agents of the scribes and chief priests set out to trap Jesus but end by being amazed at his answer (20:26). Luke 10:25-37 is one of many episodes in Luke in which Jesus is portrayed as giving an authoritative interpretation of the Law when there are competing readings.[12]

WHO IS NEIGHBOR?

While 10:28 seems to leave Jesus and the scholar of the Law in agreement, this accord does not last as the latter poses another question to Jesus, "And who is my neighbor?" (v. 29). It is not an innocent query, but from a stance of wanting to "justify himself."[13] The verb *dikaiō*, "to justify," means to set in right re-

---

[12] Richard Bauckham, "The Scrupulous Priest and the Good Samaritan: Jesus' Parabolic Interpretation of the Law of Moses," *NTS* 44 (1998) 475–89.

[13] There is a similarity to Luke 16:15, where Jesus excoriates the Pharisees who justify themselves before people, while God knows their real love is for money.

lation. The Law quoted in v. 27 describes right relation with God, self, and neighbor. While both Jesus and the scholar of the Law agree on this definition (v. 28), it is Jesus in Luke and Acts who emerges clearly as the one who does it and who is, therefore, justified. At Jesus' crucifixion, the centurion who sees Jesus die declares him *dikaios,* "just," or "innocent."[14] In Acts of the Apostles *ho dikaios,* "the Just One" becomes a title of Jesus in three key speeches (Acts 3:14; 7:52; 22:14).[15] Part of the twist of the ensuing parable is that it is a Samaritan who demonstrates correct interpretation of the Law and is found justified by his doing of the Law, not the scholar of the Law who is seeking to justify himself and who should know how to interpret the Law.

The commandment about love of neighbor in Leviticus 19 is not difficult to interpret. In v. 18 "neighbor" stands parallel to "any of your own people" *(NRSV).* In Leviticus 19:34 the commandment is expanded to include the *gēr,* the sojourner in the land. A similar commandment is found in the Qumran scrolls, where that community was bound to love all the "children of light" and hate all the "children of darkness" (1QS 1:9-10), that is, the love that was commanded for members of the community was not to be extended to outsiders. The parable that Jesus tells addresses the question, but from a different angle than that posed by the scholar.

THE ROAD TO JERICHO

The scenario of a man falling victim to robbers on the road to Jericho is realistic. According to Josephus (*J.W.* 2:228–30) banditry was widespread in Palestine before the reign of Herod the Great and again in the middle of the first century, prior to the revolt against Rome. The exploitation of the peasants and landless laborers by the ruling elite gave rise to social banditry in which the elite became the targets of brigands.[16] The road from Jerusalem to Jericho would prove a particularly fruitful hideout for bandits, since many of Jerusalem's elite would travel it en

[14] Compare Mark 15:39 where the centurion declares Jesus as Son of God.

[15] See below, chap. 23, for further comments on the use of the term "justify" and its derivatives in Luke.

[16] Malina and Rohrbaugh, *Social Science Commentary,* 403–04.

route to their winter residences in Jericho. Only twenty-three miles from Jerusalem, which has an elevation of 2700 feet, Jericho has a far warmer climate at 770 feet below sea level, the lowest city on earth. Herod the Great had a winter palace there, as did the Hasmoneans.[17]

While most priests and Levites were not among the wealthy aristocracy, many of them resided in Jericho and traversed this road. Traders and merchants also used the road. That the Samaritan is a tradesman with a certain number of resources is indicated by the fact that he journeys (v. 33), has an animal to bear his wares (v. 34), has oil and wine (v. 34), knows the nearby inn (v. 34), and plans a return trip (v. 35).[18]

THEY PASSED HIM BY

As the story progresses, first a priest, then a Levite see the injured man and pass by on the opposite side of the road. They, like the scholar of the Law, held a privileged status among Palestinian Jews because of their roles in the cultic worship in the Temple.[19] Priests were in charge of the sacrificial ritual and served in the Jerusalem Temple twice a year for a week at a time. Presumably the priest in the parable is on his way home after having completed his service. Levites had charge of minor services, such as singing and doorkeeping.

These religious leaders pass by the injured man without attending to him. Rather than presume them callously indifferent, perhaps it is the case that they are weighing conflicting commandments while deciding on their course of action.[20] Which is to be followed in this situation? The commandment to love thy neighbor (Lev 19:18)? Or the command for priests to avoid con-

---

[17] For further description of Jericho see Marianne Race and Laurie Brink, *In This Place: Reflections on the Land of the Gospels for the Liturgical Cycles* (Collegeville: The Liturgical Press, 1998) 143–46.

[18] Douglas E. Oakman, "Was Jesus a Peasant? Implications for Reading the Samaritan Story (Luke 10:30-35)," *BTB* 22 (1992) 117-25.

[19] See Johann Maier, "Self-Definition, Prestige, and Status of Priests Towards the End of the Second Temple Period," *BTB* 23 (1993) 139-51.

[20] So R. Bauckham, "Scrupulous," 475–89; J. Duncan M. Derrett, "Law in the New Testament: Fresh Light on the Parable of the Good Samaritan," *NTS* 10 (1964-65) 22–37.

tracting ritual impurity by contact with a dead body (Lev 21:1-3)? The decision would be compounded by whether the priest thought the victim to be dead or still alive. If already dead then he would be exempt from the obligation to provide him burial since priests were only permitted contact with corpses of close family members (Lev 21:1-3). If still alive, then the command to love the neighbor would apply. But then there was the possibility of him dying while being cared for, which would result in the incurrence of forbidden ritual impurity. That such a debate may well have been a real one in Jesus' day is possible in light of the later debates recorded in the Mishna and Talmud (*b. Meg.* 3b; *m. Nazir* 7.1; *b. Nazir* 48b) in which the obligation to bury an abandoned corpse takes precedent over the obligation to avoid defilement if a priest comes upon such an unfortunate body.

We do not know whether Levites in this period were bound by the same purity laws as priests. A Levite, being of a lower status than a priest, presumably would follow the priest's lead. For narrative effect, it is necessary that there be the usual three characters for the build-up to the punch line. It is also necessary that they both be religious figures who would be looked upon as those who know how to interpret the Law.

A SAMARITAN TRAVELER

Onto the scene comes a layman, one who would be far less skilled in interpretation of the Law. As a Samaritan he knows and observes the same Law of Moses as do Jews. However, the differences between the two, rather than their similarities, were uppermost in the minds of most Jews and Samaritans.[21] The roots of their mutual hatred lie in the eighth century B.C.E., when the Assyrians conquered the Northern Kingdom and deported many of its inhabitants, particularly those of the upper class, and imported non-Jews, who took possession of Samaria, and intermarried with its people (2 Kgs 17:24). Although Samaritans and Jews continued to worship the same God and observed the same Law of Moses, Jews of Judea regarded

---

[21] Sirach 50:25-26 speaks of the loathing that such "degenerate folk" evoke in Jews.

Samaritans as only half Jewish. After the Babylonian exile when Samaritans offered to help rebuild the Temple in Jerusalem, the Jews refused their offer. This was followed by retaliatory efforts of Samaritans to halt the construction (Ezra 4:2-24; Neh 2:19; 4:2-9). Eventually the Samaritans built their own temple on Mount Gerizim in Hellenistic times (see the dialog in John 4:20-24 about the proper place to worship). They also developed their own liturgy and their own form of Scripture, redacted in Hasmonean times, which contained only the Pentateuch.

Around 128 B.C.E. John Hyrcanus destroyed the Samaritan Temple and attempted to impose the Jerusalem version of Judaism on the Samaritans. The latter were freed from the political control of the south by the Romans when they took direct control in 63 B.C.E. But the antagonism between the two was still very tangible in the time of Jesus. Josephus recounts one episode that occurred sometime between 6–9 C.E. when at midnight, during Passover, some Samaritans strewed the bones of a dead person in the Temple, thus defiling it for the feast (*Ant.* 18.30). If this incident was still fresh in the minds of Jesus' audience, then there is a particular irony to the parable that involves the decision of a Samaritan to risk defilement to aid a Jew in need.

Samaria is the area between Judea and Galilee, the territory through which one would pass if going on a direct route between the two. But the tensions between Jews and Samaritans were such that Galileans traveling to Jerusalem would cross to the eastern side of the Jordan River (the Transjordan) and then cross again and approach the holy city by way of the road past Jericho.[22] Despite their common heritage, Jews regarded Samaritans as "foreigners," as is evident from the term *allogenēs* used of the Samaritan leper in Luke 17:18, who returns to thank Jesus for his healing.

Unique to the Gospel of Luke is Jesus' sending of messengers to Samaria (9:51-55) to make ready for his coming there. The Samaritans refused to receive him because "his face was set toward Jerusalem" *(NRSV)*. Luke recounts later in Acts that the mission to Samaria is accomplished by Philip (Acts 8:1-26) and that the Church flourished there (Acts 9:31; 15:3).

[22] Mark 10:1; Matthew 19:1.

Against this background of hostility, the parable of Jesus casts the Samaritan as the hero. While the Jewish religious leaders choose the command to avoid defilement as having precedence over the command to love their neighbor, the Samaritan traveler chooses the opposite. Luke underscores that all three saw the same sight. The difference is that the Samaritan was "moved with compassion" *(esplanchnisthē)* at what he saw. This is the same verb used in Luke 7:13 of Jesus' reaction to the sight of the widow whose only son had died, and in Luke 15:20 of the father's response when he catches sight of his lost younger son returning home. All three stories show how the sight of another who is in deadly circumstances must evoke action that leads to life.

The Samaritan, perhaps a merchant of oil and wine, employs his wares for the healing of the victim. Olive oil, an important product in Palestine both then and now, in addition to its uses in cooking and for lamp fuel, had a curative property as a softener of wounds.[23] Wine, also a prime product in Palestine, is spoken of abundantly in the Bible as a blessing (Gen 27:28; Deut 7:13) that "gladdens the heart" (Ps 104:15). In medicinal use it served as an antiseptic. That the two were used together for medicinal purposes is known from the third century B.C.E. Greek philosopher and naturalist Theophrastus (*Hist. Plant.* 9.11,1) and from later rabbinic tradition in the Mishna (*m. Shabb.* 19.2).

After anointing and bandaging the injured man, the Samaritan takes him to an inn. At this detail, the original hearers of Jesus' parable may have recoiled at this situation, thinking, "out of the fire, into the frying pan." Inns of that time were notoriously dreadful places. One reference from the mid-first century C.E. in Palestine, advises that if one stopped the night at a wayside inn, that one had best make out a will.[24] The Mishnah cautions, "Cattle may not be left in the inns of the Gentiles since they are suspected of bestiality; nor may a woman remain alone with them since they are suspected of lewdness; nor may a man

[23] See Isaiah 1:6; Mark 6:13; James 5:14. Fitzmyer, *Luke,* 888.
[24] From Ramsay MacMullen, *Roman Social Relations 50 B.C. to A.D. 284* (New Haven: Yale University Press, 1974) 4. See Oakman, "Was Jesus a Peasant?" 122, for this and other references.

remain alone with them since they are suspected of shedding blood" (*m. Abodah Zarah* 2.1). For the Samaritan to leave the injured man at an inn was a dangerous prospect, indeed.

The Samaritan, after giving the innkeeper two days' wages for the injured man's care, in essence entrusts him with a blank check for whatever other expenses are incurred. The wounded man is not only in danger for his life from the lowlife lodgers at the inn, but could now be held hostage by the innkeeper for whatever amount he might demand. The concluding verses of the parable (vv. 36-37), however, presume a happy outcome for the endangered victim, adding to the ironic twist of the story.

THE QUESTION INVERTED

As usual, Jesus concludes the story not with a pronouncement on what is the correct interpretation, but he pointedly asks the scholar of the Law to draw his own conclusions. The latter had begun the exchange with the questions, What must I do *(ti poiēsas)*? (v. 25) and Who is my neighbor? (v. 29). Jesus points him toward the answer by inverting the second question, Who became *(gegonetai)* neighbor toward the victim? (v. 36). The answer is clear: the one who did *(ho poiēsas)* mercy. The term mercy *(eleos* in Greek; *ḥesed* in Hebrew) is the word that most completely sums up the whole of who God is. The covenant with Israel is God's manifestation of mercy *(ḥesed)* and faithfulness *(ʾemeth)*. By doing mercy, God's people most faithfully keep the covenantal Law. Not the experts in the Scriptures, but the lay Samaritan, a despised tradesman, exemplifies godliness and faithful enactment of the commandments. To inherit eternal life one must take action to preserve the life of the neighbor who appears on the verge of entering into that eternal life. The question is not answered by defining the limits of who is to be regarded as neighbor. Rather, the boundaries delimiting neighbors are shattered when one can accept mercy from another who acts as neighbor. What one must do and how to do it is modeled by Jesus, who in telling this story is offering his own journey in miniature. [25] As he makes his own way in the reverse

[25] Barbara Green, *Like a Tree Planted* (Collegeville: The Liturgical Press, 1997) 139.

direction, through Jericho, and up to Jerusalem, Jesus does an extraordinary saving act, passing through death itself to bring stranger and friend alike into eternal life.

PREACHING POSSIBILITIES

"Good Samaritan" is a phrase that has become ubiquitous for any person who performs a kind act toward another, particularly a stranger. Stories of heroic acts of mercy by which a person even endangers his or her own life to come to the aid of another continue to hold fascination. Why would anyone do such a thing? The gospel parable gives the answer: because this is how God acts. And so one who wants to keep God's Law does the same.

People often puzzle over what motivates a person to act as the Samaritan did. An important clue as to how such an action is possible emerges when we take into account how the first hearers of Jesus' story would have responded to it. Usually when Christians retell the parable we hear the story as one that advises us to act as the Samaritan did. The point appears to be: do good to your neighbor, even if the one in need is a hated enemy. But the original audience for Jesus' story would have been Jews, presumably Galilean peasants. And in the narrative the one to whom the story is directed is a Jewish scholar of the Law. No Jew who enters into this story would have identified with the hated Samaritan. The character with whom a lay audience would have identified would be the man victimized by the robbers and left for dead. It is from this "view from the ditch,"[26] that the parable invites one to see a hated enemy as the merciful face of God. The parable advances that for some it is only possible to accept this message after having reached the depths of need, having been stripped of all of one's own resources. Accepting godly mercy from one once regarded as a hated enemy

---

[26] Robert Funk, "The Good Samaritan as Metaphor," *Semeia* 2 (1974) 74–81; J. Ian H. McDonald, "Alien Grace," in *Jesus and His Parables*, ed. V. George Shillington (Edinburgh: T. & T. Clark, 1997) 35–51. Douglas Oakman ("Was Jesus a Peasant?" 122–23) speculates that peasants might have initially cheered for the Robin Hood-type bandits. Priests and Levites hearing the story would think those characters the admirable ones.

opens the wellsprings of compassion so that one may come to regard every person as neighbor and in turn be a doer of mercy across boundaries.

It is clear from the rest of the gospel that God acts like the Samaritan, who traverses dangerous territory with unguents and healing means at hand. Like the Samaritan, God takes risky and foolish actions, such as sending Jesus to save life. Eternal life will be able to be inherited only because of the perilous actions Jesus takes on behalf of all who are neighbor. To inherit this life one must "go and do likewise" (v. 37).

Viewing this parable as a story that illustrates a one-time event dulls its edge. It is a true parable in the sense that it has a shocking twist to it that holds out a challenge to the hearer. In the allegorical explanations of this parable that were common among the early Church Fathers[27] the parable becomes an explanation of the faith of the Church, a confirmation of the *status quo,* rather than a provocative invitation to conversion.[28]

On the Fifteenth Sunday of Ordinary Time, when this parable is read in tandem with Deuteronomy 30:10-14, the emphasis on doing God's command is all the more accentuated. In the first reading Moses advises that there is nothing mysterious about the commandment—it only needs to be carried out. The hymn from Colossians emphasizes the universal scope of Christ's reconciling act accomplished through the blood of the cross. When the parable is coupled with the beginning of the book of Jonah on Monday of the Twenty-seventh Week of Ordinary Time in Year I, God's mercy extended to and through foreigners is underscored. However, to try to make a connection between the gospel and the first reading from Galatians 1:6-12 in Year II would be forced.

---

[27] See above, pp. 16–17, for the allegorical interpretation of this parable by Irenaeus.

[28] McDonald, "Alien Grace," 48.

CHAPTER TEN

A Friend in Need
(Luke 11:1-13)

Seventeenth Sunday of Ordinary Time

Thursday of the Twenty-seventh Week of Ordinary Time

¹ *Jesus was praying in a certain place, and when he had finished,*
one of his disciples said to him,
"Lord, teach us to pray just as John taught his disciples."
² *He said to them, "When you pray, say:*
Father, hallowed be your name,
your kingdom come.
³ Give us each day our daily bread
⁴ and forgive us our sins
for we ourselves forgive everyone in debt to us,
and do not subject us to the final test."

⁵ *And he said to them, "Suppose one of you has a friend*
to whom he goes at midnight and says,
'Friend, lend me three loaves of bread,
⁶ for a friend of mine has arrived at my house from a journey
and I have nothing to offer him,'
⁷ and he says in reply from within,
'Do not bother me; the door has already been locked
and my children and I are already in bed.
I cannot get up to give you anything.'
⁸ *I tell you,*
if he does not get up to give him the loaves
because of their friendship,
he will get up to give him whatever he needs
because of his persistence.

⁹ *"And I tell you, ask and you will receive;*
seek and you will find;

> *knock and the door will be opened to you.*
> [10] *For everyone who asks, receives;*
>   *and the one who seeks, finds;*
>   *and to the one who knocks, the door will be opened.*
> [11] *What father among you would hand his son a snake*
>   *when he asks for a fish?*
> [12] *Or hand him a scorpion when he asks for an egg?*
> [13] *If you then, who are wicked,*
>   *know how to give good gifts to your children,*
>   *how much more will the Father in heaven*
>   *give the Holy Spirit to those who ask him?"*

LUKAN LITERARY CONTEXT

There are three segments to this passage, which is set in the context of the journey to Jerusalem. It begins with Jesus at prayer, one of Luke's prominent themes.[1] From the very beginning the gospel is pervaded with an aura of prayer. The first episode of Luke's Gospel is situated in the Temple, where Zechariah is burning incense while the whole assembly of the people is praying outside (1:9-10). The prophet Anna appears in 2:37, never leaving the Temple, worshiping night and day with fasting and prayer. Luke shows Jesus at prayer as a regular occurrence (5:16) and at critical turning points: at his baptism (3:21), before his choice of the Twelve (6:12), before Peter's confession of him as the Messiah (9:18), at the transfiguration (9:28-29), before his arrest on the Mount of Olives (22:39-46), and on the cross (23:46). Jesus assures Peter that he has prayed for him that his faith may not fail (22:32).

The parable in 11:5-8, is framed by teachings on prayer (11:1-4, 9-13)[2] and follows shortly after a spontaneous prayer of

---

[1] Luke inserts references to prayer in his redaction of Markan material in 3:21; 5:16, 33. Eight of the instances in which prayer is mentioned in Luke occur in material peculiar to him: 1:10, 13; 2:37; 18:1, 10, 11; 21:36; 22:32. There are four instances in which the Lukan version of Q material contain a reference to prayer: 6:28; 10:2; 11:1, 2. The Matthean parallels to Luke 10:2 and 11:2 have the references to prayer as well. Five times Luke's mention of prayer comes from the Markan source: 9:18; 20:47; 22:40, 41, 46.

[2] Others incidents in which Jesus instructs the disciples on prayer are: Luke 6:28; 10:2; 18:1-14; 20:45-47; 21:36; 22:40, 46. In Acts the disciples are portrayed

Jesus giving thanks (10:21-23). While the theme of prayer pervades Luke's two volumes, the parable in 11:5-8 may not have been uttered originally as a metaphor for prayer. The surrounding verses now dispose the reader to see it that way, but the link between the parable and the sayings on prayer has been created by Luke. Luke has woven together sayings from the Q source and a parable from L.[3] We will consider the parable first.

A FRIEND IN NEED (vv. 5-8)

The parable opens with a question that Luke employs frequently to initiate parables: *tis ex hymōn*, "which one of you . . . ?"[4] It is a rhetorical question that asks the hearer to imagine an unthinkable situation to which the expected response is an emphatic: "Impossible!"

The story places us in the midst of village life where the unexpected arrival of a guest late at night causes a temporary crisis. Hospitality is of supreme value in the Middle East, both in antiquity as now. A guest must be offered food upon arrival, and the guest must eat, whether hungry or not. Sharing of food is a sign of sharing of life that cannot be overlooked in any exchange between friends. The rules of hospitality demand that a host must supply their best and must provide more than a guest can eat. The scenario in the parable presumes that the host has either an insufficient amount of bread to offer or that the bread at hand was not freshly baked. In such a situation one turns to a neighboring friend in the village.[5]

---

as constantly at prayer: 1:14, 24; 2:42; 3:1; 4:31; 6:4, 6; 7:59; 8:15, 22, 24; 9:11, 40; 10:2, 4, 9, 30, 31; 11:5; 12:5, 12; 13:3; 14:23; 16:13, 16, 25; 20:36; 21:5; 22:17; 26:29; 27:29; 28:8.

[3] The Our Father (Luke 11:1-4) has its parallel in Matthew 6:9-13, as part of the Sermon on the Mount. There is also a version of the Our Father in the *Didache* 8:2, which is longer than the gospel version, and is likely dependent on Matthew. The Matthean version of the sayings found in Luke 11:9-13 is not attached to the Our Father, though they are still part of the Sermon on the Mount in Matthew 7:7-11. The sayings in Luke 11:9-10 also have parallels in *Gos.Thom.* §2, 92, 94.

[4] So also Luke 12:25; 14:5, 28; 15:4; 17:7.

[5] Kenneth E. Bailey (*Poet and Peasant and Through Peasant Eyes* [combined ed.; Grand Rapids: Eerdmans, 1976] 1.122) advances that women in Palestinian

VILLAGE HONOR

What is presumed in the parable is that the honor of the whole village, not just that of the host, is tied up in the treatment of the guest. When the host calls out his need to his friend at midnight, the likelihood is that other surrounding families are also roused. With the honor of all at stake, any who can aid will arise to do so. By the standards of Middle Eastern hospitality no one would think of telling the needy host not to bother them because they are sleeping. The parable expects the reaction that such a situation is unimaginable. In fact, it is an honor, not an annoyance, to be asked to contribute to the reception of a guest. A favorable response by other villagers to the petitioner increases the honor for all.[6]

SHAMELESSNESS

The parable concludes with the observation that if the friend will not give the other the needed loaves out of friendship, which, presumably he would, then he will get up and give him whatever he needs because of his shamelessness *(anaideia autou)*. Here is the most difficult phrase to interpret. Two problems are involved: what is the meaning of *anaideia*? And to whom does *autou* (his) refer?

The literal meaning of *anaideia* is "shamelessness." The word appears only here in the New Testament, but is found fifteen times in the LXX.[7] In every instance the word has a negative sense of "impudence," "insolence," "fierceness," or "indignance." The same is true of other references in classical Greek and early Christian literature.[8] Translators and interpreters of

villages baked bread weekly, not daily, and that they cooperated in the use of a community oven on a rotating schedule. In such a case, everyone would know who had fresh bread.

[6] William R. Herzog II, *Parables as Subversive Speech* (Louisville: Westminster/John Knox, 1994) 201.

[7] Sirach 23:6; 25:22; Deuteronomy 28:50; 1 Kings 2:29; Proverbs 7:13; 21:29; 25:13; Ecclesiastes 8:1; 11; 40:30; Isaiah 56:11; Jeremiah 8:5; Baruch 4:15; Daniel 2:15; 8:23.

[8] See Bailey, *Poet and Peasant*, 125–28; Alan Johnson, "Assurance for Man: The Fallacy of Translating *anaideia* by 'Persistence' in Luke 11:5-8," *JEvThSoc* 22 (1979) 123–31.

Luke 11:8 found this negative connotation problematic, as is evident from Latin translations from the fifth century onward that began to use *importunitatem* rather than *improbitatem* to translate *anaideia*. In light of vv. 9-13, which were taken as advising persistence in seeking and knocking, *anaideia* began to be understood as "persistence," a meaning that it never had elsewhere.

Modern interpreters have recovered the original meaning, "shamelessness." But problems still remain: is this a negative or a positive quality? And to which character does the shamelessness refer—the sleeper or the friend in need? One solution is that shamelessness has a positive sense, that is, avoidance of shame, which is a good thing. The friend aroused from sleep supplies bread for the friend in need out of a sense of honor, thus avoiding shame.[9] Other scholars take shamelessness as a negative quality of the petitioner. It refers to his impudence in begging from his friend and at such a late hour of the night.[10]

While these problems remain unresolved on a lexical level, there is a satisfactory solution to the interpretation of this parable. Attention to the cultural and economic situation of peasants in first-century Palestine moves us closer to understanding the point behind the gospel story. Life was very precarious for rural peasants in Jesus' day—subsistence was the predominant mode of existence.[11] Factors such as drought, famine, floods,

---

[9] So Bailey, *Poet and Peasant*, 133; Bernard Brandon Scott, *Hear Then the Parable* (Minneapolis: Fortress, 1989) 89–90; B. Malina and R. Rohrbaugh, *Social Science Commentary* (Minneapolis: Fortress, 1992) 351; Joachim Jeremias, *The Parables of Jesus* (rev. ed.; New York: Scribners, 1963) 158. The most extensive analysis of the word *anaideia* has been done by Bailey, *Poet and Peasant*, 119–33, but problems with his conclusions still remain. See the critique by Herzog, *Subversive Speech*, 203.

[10] E.g., Joseph A. Fitzmyer, *The Gospel According to Luke* (AB28A; Garden City, N.Y.: Doubleday, 1981) 912; Sharon Ringe, *Luke* (Westminster Bible Companion; Louisville: Westminster/John Knox, 1995) 166; John R. Donahue, *The Gospel in Parable* (Philadelphia: Fortress, 1988) 186.

[11] See Douglas Oakman, *Jesus and the Economic Questions of his Day* (SBEC 8; Lewiston/Queenston: Edwin Mellen, 1986); Herzog, *Subversive Speech*, 204–07; Scott, *Hear Then*, 85–86; James C. Scott, *The Moral Economy of the Peasant* (New Haven: Yale University Press, 1976); Shimon Appelbaum, "Economic Life in Palestine," *The Jewish People in the First Century*, ed. S. Safrai and M. Stern (Compendia rerum Iudaicarum ad Novum Testamentum; Assen: Van Gorcum, 1974–76) 2:631–700.

pestilence, overgrazing, the birth of another child, which resulted in another mouth to feed, could tip the balance and put a small farmer over the edge into debt. Taxation was exorbitant, with Herod, the procurators, and the landlords all taking their cut. In such a system, village solidarity is essential to survival.

RECIPROCAL RELATIONS

One of the mechanisms by which this solidarity was manifest was in reciprocal exchanges. Family members and inhabitants of the same village would lend to one another with the understanding that when the shoe was on the other foot, one could expect the same in return. So when the friend comes begging at midnight, the one roused from sleep will surely accede to the request, since he may need to ask the same kind of help on another day. Village solidarity grounded on reciprocity became even more crucial in Jesus' day as elites were becoming more predatory on peasants and forcing more and more small farmers into tenancy. Worse yet was the situation of one who lost his land to a creditor and was forced into being a day laborer. Each of these steps down the economic ladder was one more step toward loss of status, destitution, and death.

One would turn first to kin to stave off such a dire fate. But if they are not able to provide help, a friend becomes indispensable. A friend would willingly help keep the predators at bay for a time, unless there were no friends or neighbors who were any better off. In such a case, a desperate peasant might seek out a patron and enter into a patron-client relation. This kind of contractual arrangement was, however, very unstable for the peasant, who was in a dependent position, being used by a powerful person who might decide at any time he had no more need for his services.

FRIENDSHIP

Against this backdrop the three-fold emphasis on "friend" (vv. 5-6) and friendship (v. 8) in the parable takes on further significance. In such a strained economic situation, extravagant hospitality is both the best means for survival of villagers and at the same time the most threatened of cultural values. Precisely when the economic need increases, so does the urge to hoard for oneself, to try to insure some measure of security. Moreover, pursuing "friendship" with a powerful patron could prove to be suicidal and could dissolve the bonds between real friends.

The word "friend" in the parable would also have a particular resonance with members of the Jesus movement, where new networks of friends and fictive kin were constructed, with members who were willing to lay down their lives for one another out of friendship on the model of their leader who called them friends and not slaves (John 15:12-17). The gift of hospitality was also a critical component in the spread of the mission, as itinerant preachers depended on the generosity of hosts.

GODLY HOSPITALITY

The parable, then, does not simply state what is obvious in this culture: that one who is asked to supply for the needs of a guest will most certainly do so.[12] Nor is it a reassurance that God hears petitionary prayer and grants requests.[13] Such readings simply reiterate expected mores and have no parabolic twist. Rather, the parable in 11:5-8 is one that affirms extravagant hospitality in precarious economic circumstances where such profligate care of another may seem to foolishly jeopardize one's own security.[14]

Such a model is set by notable figures from the Hebrew Scriptures and by Jesus. Abraham is remembered as hosting heavenly guests (Genesis 18) and is called "friend of God" (2 Chron 20:7; Isa 41:8; Jas 2:23). Moses, through whom manna was provided to the Israelites in the desert (Exod 16:12-36), spoke to God face to face, as one speaks to a friend (Exod 3:11). Woman Wisdom, who is an icon of hospitality, inviting all to her banquet (Prov 9:1-6), passes into holy souls from age to age, producing "friends of God and prophets" (Wis 7:27).[15] In like fashion, Jesus

[12] Herzog, *Subversive Speech,* 209.

[13] This point is made by many other biblical texts, e.g., Psalm 34:18; Sirach 35:13-18; Matthew 6:8; Luke 18:7.

[14] Herzog, *Subversive Speech,* 209–14.

[15] See Elizabeth Johnson, *Friends of God and Prophets* (New York: Continuum, 1998) whose rich study of the communion of saints revolves around this phrase from Wisdom.

offers hospitality toward those most in need, and becomes friends with tax collectors and sinners (Luke 7:34). It is this kind of godly hospitality that the parable in Luke 11:5-8 upholds.

It is in receiving the needy itinerant disciple, or the friend of another in need that the followers of Jesus emulate the incomparable generosity of God, who so foolishly offers everything, even God's own son. In the offer of such hospitality, whether out of godly friendship, or from avoidance of shame, believers use their resources to care for the most vulnerable, thus saving the life of the whole community. To those who used their possessions for their own enhancement, giving banquets to make friends for themselves who could feed their own acquisitive greed, the parable presents an alternate vision. The meals of disciples who receive graciously the sojourner as friend resemble far more closely the messianic banquet than do the great banquets of the elites.[16]

PROVIDENT FATHER (vv. 1-4)

While the central metaphor in vv. 5-8 for relationship in God's realm is friendship with God and one another, the surrounding verses, 1-4 and 9-13 draw on the image of God as father. In vv. 1-4 Jesus teaches his disciples to pray first for the hallowing of God's name. There is an echo of Ezekiel 36:22-28, where the prophet announces that the holiness of God's name will be proven when all the Israelites are gathered from among the foreign nations and brought back to their own land. This scattering of Israel has caused God's name to be profaned among the nations. That God's name is hallowed means that God is recognized and acclaimed as holy and powerful. For Christians, hallowing God's name is centered on recognizing the holiness of God manifest in Jesus and continuing to make that holiness visible in their lives as disciples.

In the prayer that Jesus teaches his disciples in vv. 2-4 Jesus is not revealing a unique divine name by which to call God. Like all ways of addressing God, "Father" is a metaphor that can help us speak of and to God, but does not capture the real-

---

[16] Herzog, *Subversive Speech*, 214.

ity of who God is.[17] In fact, when Moses wanted to know God's name, the divine reply was an enigmatic, "I am who am" (Exod 3:14). While the Gospels do present Jesus several times as speaking of and to God as his father,[18] this is not the only way he speaks of God, nor is it unique to him. There are examples in the Hebrew Scriptures, Qumran texts, Philo, Josephus, and rabbinic literature where God is addressed as father.[19]

It is notable that where "father" appears as a title for God in the ancient Jewish and Christian literature, it is always in a context of a petitioner seeking refuge from affliction or looking for assurance of forgiveness. It is God's *power* as "father" that is invoked, not intimacy and tenderness.[20] In the context of Roman imperial rule, where the emperor claimed the title of *pater patriae* and ruled the empire as the head of a patriarchal family, the application of "father" to God by Jews and Christians presented a challenge to imperial authority: God, not the emperor, is the supreme power. For Christians today, invoking God exclusively as "father" does not have this kind of subversive effect. It does not challenge a patriarchal world view, but rather absolutizes it, transferring male dominance from earth to heaven.

Other images of God, including female images, are found in Jesus' parables of the woman mixing bread dough (Luke 13:20-21) and the woman searching for the lost coin (Luke 15:8-10).[21] Moreover, it is Jesus himself who is the supreme revelation of God, not the metaphor "father." The Gospels portray Jesus as acting with power and authority such as a "father" God would have, but Jesus also speaks of himself in "motherly" terms. When he laments over Jerusalem, he likens himself to a

[17] See Sallie McFague, *Models of God* (Philadelphia: Fortress, 1987); Gail Ramshaw, *God Beyond Gender* (Minneapolis: Fortress, 1995).

[18] Mark 14:36; Matthew 11:25; Luke 23:34; John 17:1.

[19] Sirach 23:1, 4; Wisdom 2:16-20; 14:3; 3 Maccabees 6:3-4, 7-8; Tobit 13:4; 4Q372 1.16; 4Q460; fragment 2 of the *Apocalypse of Ezekiel*; Jos. *Ant.* 2.6.8 #152; Philo, *Op. mund.* 10, 21, 72–75; *m. Yoma* 8:9; *b. Ta'an.* 25b. See further Mary Rose D'Angelo, "*ABBA* and 'Father': Imperial Theology and the Jesus Traditions," *JBL* 111/4 (1992) 611–30.

[20] See James Barr "'*Abba* Isn't Daddy," *JTS* n.s. 39 (1988) 28–47 and "'*Abba* and the Familiarity of Jesus' Speech," *Theology* 91 (1988) 173–79.

[21] See below, chaps. 15 and 25.

mother hen trying to gather her unruly brood under her wings (Luke 13:34; similarly Matt 23:37). This saying equates Jesus' role with that of God, who is likened to a mother eagle in Deuteronomy 32:11-12 and Psalm 91:4. Perhaps the most striking portrait of Jesus in female imagery is found in the Gospel of John, where there are strong parallels between Jesus and Lady Wisdom.[22]

GOD'S RULE

The second petition in the prayer is for the eschatological fulfillment of God's rule, which has already been inaugurated in a new way with the coming of Jesus (Luke 4:43). The term *basileia*, "kingdom," is usually accompanied by the qualifier *tou theou*, "of God" and is often the explicit subject of parables.[23] It is difficult to find an adequate phrase in English to convey the meaning of *basileia tou theou*. Translating it as "kingdom of God" is problematic, first, because it conveys the notion of a locale with fixed boundaries. It has long been recognized that God's *basileia* signifies divine "kingly rule" or "reign," not "kingdom" in a territorial sense.[24] A further difficulty is that it presents an image of God as king, reinforcing a male, monarchical model of God's rule. For communities of believers whose experience of governance is democratic, and who have become conscious of the limitations and dangers of having solely male images of God, "kingdom" is an inadequate term.

Finally, in a first-century Palestinian context the term *basileia* would first call to mind the Roman imperial system of

---

[22] See Raymond Brown, *The Gospel According to John I–XII* (AB29; Garden City, N.Y.: Doubleday, 1966) cxxii–cxxv; Elizabeth Johnson, "Jesus the Wisdom of God: A Biblical Basis for Non-Androcentric Christology," *ETL* 61 (1985) 261–94; Martin Scott, *Sophia and the Johannine Jesus* (JSNTSup 71; Sheffield: JSOT, 1992).

[23] The phrase *basileia tou theou*, "kingdom of God," appears in Luke 4:43; 6:20; 7:28; 8:1, 10; 9:2, 11, 27, 60, 62; 10:9, 11; 11:20; 13:18, 20, 28, 29; 14:15; 16:16; 17:20 [2x], 21; 18:16, 17, 24, 25, 29; 19:11; 21:31; 22:16, 18; 23:51. In 12:31, 32 "his kingdom" refers to the Father's; in 22:29, 30; 23:42 the kingdom is Jesus'. In six instances *basileia tou theou* is associated with a parable: Luke 8:10; 13:18, 20; 14:15; 19:11; 21:31.

[24] G. Dalman, *Die Worte Jesu* (2nd ed.; Darmstadt: Wissenschaftliche Buchgesellschaft, 1965) 283–365.

domination and exploitation. Jesus' annunciation of the *basileia* of God offered an alternative vision to that of the empire of Rome. The *basileia* that Jesus announced was one in which there was no more victimization or domination. This *basileia* was already present incipiently in Jesus' healing and liberative practices, the inclusive table sharing of his followers, and their domination-free relationships. The political threat that such a subversive *basileia* vision presented to the Roman imperial system is clear from the crucifixion of Jesus.[25]

Efforts at alternate translations of *basileia* with these problems in mind include: "kin-dom," "rule," "reign," "realm," "empire," "domain," and "commonweal." These, too, have their difficulties. While no English phrase adequately captures all that *basileia tou theou* signifies, it is important that whatever translation one adopts, it convey the sense of God's saving power over all creation, already inaugurated in a new way with the incarnation and ministry of Jesus, and continued in the faithful ministry of the believing community, but not yet fully manifest. It is authoritative power and empowerment by God-with-us.

DAILY BREAD, FORGIVENESS, TESTING

The second half of the prayer turns from praise of God and anticipation of full establishment of God's reign, to three petitions for human needs. The first is for daily sustenance. This may be understood on two levels of meaning: bread needed for physical subsistence and bread shared at the eucharistic table.[26] The second request is for forgiveness, both as a gift received from God and as manifest in one's relations with others. The prayer concludes with a view toward the eschatological future, pleading that believers not be subjected to the final testing, which might lead them to apostasize. This kind of temptation was already being experienced by members of the

---

[25] Elisabeth Schüssler Fiorenza, *Jesus: Miriam's Child, Sophia's Prophet* (New York: Continuum, 1994) 92–93.

[26] See Fitzmyer, *Luke*, 899–906, for a discussion on the difficulties in understanding *epiousios*.

community who faced accusations from both religious and civil authorities.[27]

Each of these three petitions is cast in the first person plural, making them a communal prayer. When linked with 11:5-8, the parable shows that it is in the practice of extravagant hospitality toward one another that God's answer to this prayer is manifest. Friends provide one another with needed bread, not keeping track of debts owed, but reciprocating freely. They supply aid to one another in time of crisis and so keep their members from facing trials leading to economic devastation. This is a foretaste of the preservation of the community from the final testing.

ASK AND RECEIVE (vv. 9-13)

Appended to the parable is a series of wisdom sayings that are linked with catchwords. In the parable the focus is on the one who receives the request. In vv. 9-10 the sayings switch to the perspective of the petitioner, reassuring that asking, seeking, and knocking result in receiving, finding, and opening. Verse 11 changes to the perspective of the one supplying the request and returns to the image of father. Like the parable, the sayings in vv. 11-12 present totally unthinkable situations. No parent would hand their child a snake in place of a fish or a scorpion instead of an egg.[28] As with the parable, the hearer is meant to respond, "Impossible!"

The concluding verse uses the mode of argumentation that moves from the lesser to the greater: if this is the case with a human father, then how much more will God give good things to those who ask. Luke specifies the "good gift" that the Father will give as the holy Spirit. These concluding verses say nothing about persistence in asking. Nor do they say anything about

---

[27] Luke 12:11-12; 21:12-19; Acts 4:1-22; 5:17-41; 7:54-60; 8:1; 12:1-5; 9:23-35; 13:45-47; 14:1-7, 19-20; 16:40; 17:5-16; 18:12-16; 19:23-40; 20:3; 21:11, 27-36; 22:1–26:32; 28:11-31.

[28] A similarity is implied between the two. Fitzmyer (*Luke,* 915) advances that the first image is of water snakes caught in the Sea of Galilee that feed on small fish and are used as bait. The second envisions a scorpion with its claws and tail rolled up, resembling an egg.

every request being granted. Rather, they simply state that any-one who asks for the gift of the Spirit will, indeed, receive it.[29]

PREACHING POSSIBILITIES

This gospel passage is very rich and offers a number of dif-ferent possibilities to the preacher. It is too much to try to speak adequately about both the parable and the kind of prayer mod-eled in the Our Father. If one chooses to focus on the parable, it is advisable to consider preaching about the theme of extrava-gant hospitality rather than persistence in prayer. The parable was probably not about prayer in its original telling; it is Luke who gives it that cast with the surrounding literary context. Nor is it about persistence. As we have seen, "persistence" is not an accurate translation of *anaideia*. In the parable the friend does not keep calling out to the one asleep—the need is articulated only once, with the presumption that it will be met. Finally, in-terpreting the parable as one about persistence in prayer pre-sents us with a theological difficulty, if the one being petitioned is thought to be God. It would seem to advocate badgering God until one gets one's wish. But texts such as Psalm 138, the re-sponsorial Psalm for the Seventeenth Sunday of Ordinary Time, as well as Psalm 34:18, Sirach 35:13-18, Matthew 6:8, and Luke 18:7, insist that God already knows our needs and is eager to care for them.[30] The first reading (Gen 18:20-32) portrays Abra-ham as pleading repeatedly with God, but there it is on behalf of the people of Sodom and Gomorrah, not for his own needs.

The homilist might instead develop the preaching around the "shamelessness" of contemporary efforts to extend extrava-gant hospitality that builds up community, rather than patterns of greedy acquisition. Collaboration and cooperation presumed in the parable confront a culture where individualism and com-petition thrive. Such a stance reflects godliness in the models of Abraham, Moses, Jesus, and all the countless men and women who have incarnated the Spirit of Wisdom to become friends of God.

[29] The one time when such a request is denied is in Acts 8:18-19, where Simon the magician asks to buy the power of the Spirit.

[30] See below, chap. 19, where a similar difficulty arises with Luke 18:1-8.

The preacher might also take the opportunity to develop the metaphor of God as friend, offered in the parable.[31] In a church that has relied predominantly on the image of God as father, the parable helps expand our capacity for encountering God both in the friend who supplies essential aid and in the needy neighbor.

[31] See McFague, *Models of God*, chap. 6, on God as friend. See also Josephine Massyngbaerde Ford, *Redeemer, Friend, and Mother: Salvation in Antiquity and in the Gospel of John* (Minneapolis: Fortress, 1997) esp. chap. 5, on friendship in the Greco-Roman and Jewish world in relation to the Johannine portrait of Jesus.

CHAPTER ELEVEN

A Rich Fool
(Luke 12:13-21)

Eighteenth Sunday of Ordinary Time

Monday of the Twenty-ninth Week of Ordinary Time

¹³ *Someone in the crowd said to Jesus,*
"Teacher, tell my brother to share the inheritance with me."
¹⁴ *He replied to him,*
"Friend, who appointed me as your judge and arbitrator?"
¹⁵ *Then he said to the crowd,*
"Take care to guard against all greed,
for though one may be rich,
one's life does not consist of possessions."
¹⁶ *Then he told them a parable.*
"There was a rich man whose land produced a bountiful harvest.
¹⁷ *He asked himself, 'What shall I do,*
for I do not have space to store my harvest?'
¹⁸ *And he said, 'This is what I shall do:*
I shall tear down my barns and build larger ones.
There I shall store all my grain and other goods
¹⁹ and I shall say to myself, "Now as for you,
you have so many good things stored up for many years,
rest, eat, drink, be merry!"'

²⁰ *But God said to him,*
'You fool, this night your life will be demanded of you;
and the things you have prepared, to whom will they belong?'
²¹ *Thus will it be for all who store up treasure for themselves*
but are not rich in what matters to God."

LUKAN LITERARY CONTEXT

This parable is couched in sayings that Jesus addresses to his disciples in the hearing of a great crowd. It is set in the midst of the journey to Jerusalem. Jesus has just warned his disciples about the hypocrisy of the Pharisees (12:1) and has encouraged them not to fear anything, even persecution. He assures them of how valuable they are in God's sight—so much so that every hair is counted (12:7). God's vigilant care for them exceeds that of the sparrows, none of whom escapes God's notice (12:6-7). Even if they are dragged before the authorities, the holy Spirit will protect them, giving them the words they need for their defense (12:11-12). Following the parable are further assurances to the disciples not to worry about their life or about anything they need to sustain it. Jesus reiterates how provident is God and how valuable each one is in the eyes of God. Since God supplies every need, the only treasure one should seek to amass is heavenly (12:22-34).

These instructions to the disciples are interrupted by an individual in the crowd who asks Jesus to settle an inheritance dispute (vv. 13-14), to which is appended a saying that cautions against greed (v. 15), which then leads into the parable (vv. 16-21). All of these are unique to Luke, whereas the sayings surrounding 12:13-21 have parallels in Matthew and Mark.[1] Luke's literary construction sets in relief the forces of fear that undergird the vice of greed.

This parable also serves to advance a prominent theme in the Third Gospel. More than any other evangelist, Luke highlights the question of how possessions relate to discipleship. He offers several models of how one's response to Jesus is reflected in the use of material possessions. Some, such as Simon and his

---

[1] The warning against the Pharisees is found in all three: Luke 12:1 // Mark 8:14-15 // Matthew 16:5-6; the assurances in Luke 12:2-9 have a parallel in Matthew 10:26-33; the saying about blasphemy against the holy Spirit is found in all three: Luke 12:10 // Mark 3:28-30 // Matthew 12:31-32; the assurance of the Spirit's help in Luke 12:11-12 has parallels in Mark 13:11 and Matthew 10:19-20; the affirmations about God's providence in Luke 12:22-32 have their counterpart in Matthew 6:25-34. The sayings in Luke 12:13-14 have a parallel in *Gos.Thom.* §72. A variation of the parable (vv. 16-21) is found in *Gos.Thom.* §63.

partners James and John (5:11) and Levi the tax collector (5:28), leave everything behind when called by Jesus. Others, like Mary Magdalene and the other Galilean women (8:3), place their resources at the service of the community or, like Mary of Jerusalem, host the Christian community in their homes (Acts 12:12). Like Barnabas, some sell their property and add it to the communal pool of resources, from which all take according to their need (Acts 2:44-45; 4:32-37). Still others, like Zacchaeus, retain a portion of their wealth, but give the other half as alms (19:1-10). Prominent in Luke are admonitions about the dangers of accumulating riches (6:20; 16:13, 19-23; 18:25).[2] The parable in 12:13-21 gives a vivid illustration of this.

INHERITANCE (vv. 13-14)

The scene is set by a man in a crowd who asks Jesus to arbitrate in a dispute with his brother over their inheritance. The details of their quarrel are not given. That regulations exist both in civil and in religious law for division of property at the death of a father attests to the universality of squabbles within families over such. In Deuteronomy 21:15-17 is the regulation that a double portion of the property goes to the firstborn son. Numbers 27:1-11 legislates that if a man dies without having sons, then his daughters inherit his property (see also Job 42:15). If he has no daughter, then it goes to his brothers; if he has no brothers, then to his father's brothers. If his father has no brothers, then it goes to the nearest relative in his clan. There is a further stipulation in Numbers 36:7-9 that daughters who inherit property are to marry within their own tribe so that the property does not pass into the control of another tribe.

Stories such as the one in Luke 15:11-32 illustrate well the bitterness that was incurred in the division of inheritance among siblings.[3] In contrast, Psalm 133:1 extols how very good it is when brothers and sisters live together in unity,[4] that is, when they remain together on the ancestral property, working

---

[2] See above, pp. 41–42, on Rich and Poor.

[3] See above, chap. 5, on Luke 15:11-32.

[4] Kenneth E. Bailey, *Through Peasant Eyes: More Lucan Parables, Their Culture and Style* (Grand Rapids: Eerdmans, 1980) 59.

the land in a harmonious arrangement. The scenario in today's gospel evokes one more akin to Luke 15:11.

There are also biblical texts that use the term "inheritance" to speak about the relationship between God and the people. Deuteronomy 9:26 speaks of Israel as "the heritage which your majesty has ransomed and brought out of Egypt with your strong hand" (similarly, Ps 28:9). Texts in the New Testament speak of the promised new life of Christians through Christ's resurrection, that is "an inheritance that is imperishable, undefiled, and unfading, kept in heaven" for them (1 Pet 1:4; similarly Acts 20:32; Eph 1:14, 18; Col 3:24; Heb 9:15). Ephesians 5:5 warns that "no immoral or impure or greedy person, that is, an idolater, has any inheritance in the kingdom of Christ and of God." The parable in today's gospel implies a relationship between one's attitude toward material inheritance in this world and heavenly inheritance in the next.

Jesus' response to the person in the crowd[5] dissociates him from making a judgment. The subsequent parable, like many of the parables, asks the person to judge for himself the right course of action. It invites the person to examine whether the dispute is being fueled by his greed, and underscores the dire consequences of storing up treasures for oneself. The word *meristēs*, translated as "arbitrator" in v. 14, literally means "divider." Jesus, whose mission is about reconciling, demurs from the role of divider.[6]

GREED (v. 15)

Sayings that advise against greed *(pleonexia)* abound in the Bible as well as in other ancient literature. Job decries that putting one's trust in gold or rejoicing in great wealth is a crime for condemnation—of which he is innocent (Job 31:24-28). The author of Ecclesiastes finds that in trying to amass silver and gold for himself "all was vanity and a chase after wind, with nothing gained under the sun" (2:11). Plutarch says that *pleonexia* never rests from acquiring more *(to pleon)*.[7] Diodorus

---

[5] The *NAB* and *NSRV* translate *anthrōpos*, inclusively. It is an anonymous person, not a friend *(philos)* of Jesus.

[6] Bailey, *Through Peasant Eyes*, 61.

[7] Plutarch, *On Love of Wealth* 1 (Mor. 523 E).

Siculus calls it "the metropolis of all evil deeds."[8] In Pauline letters greed is featured in vice lists and in hortatory passages.[9] Colossians 3:5 goes so far as to equate greed with idolatry. Greed was seen as particularly vicious in the culture of Jesus' day in light of their perception of limited good. This notion asserts that there is only a limited amount of any good thing, both tangible and intangible. Anything that one acquires is someone else's loss. Contrary to capitalistic notions that all can increase in wealth, in first-century Palestine the operating assumption is that everything is finite and cannot be expanded. If someone's share gets larger, someone else's decreases. Desiring more for oneself was the most insidious of vices, and was utterly destructive of village solidarity.

DIALOGUING ALONE (vv. 16-19)

The parable opens with a rich man whose land produced abundantly. This introduction provides no judgment yet on the morality of this character. Riches in themselves are neutral; it is what is done with them that reveals the heart's true allegiances. In some biblical stories, riches are looked upon as a sign of God's blessing. Abraham, for example, was considered highly favored by God because he had great flocks and herds, a large family, and a great number of servants (Gen 13:2; 26:13-14). In other biblical accounts riches are an insurmountable obstacle to right relation with God.[10]

The soliloquy of the rich man in vv. 17-18 reveals his greed and his isolation.[11] That the man talks only with himself is startling in view of the concept of dyadic personality out of which

---

[8] See BAGD, πλεονεξία, 667, for this and many other references.

[9] Romans 1:29; 2 Corinthians 9:5; Ephesians 4:19; 5:3. See also 2 Peter 2:3, 14.

[10] See Leslie J. Hoppe, *Being Poor* (GNS 20; Wilmington: Glazier, 1987) for analysis of the variety of biblical affirmations about riches and poverty in each section of the Bible.

[11] John R. Donahue, *The Gospel in Parable* (Philadelphia: Fortress, 1988) 177; Bailey, *Through Peasant Eyes*, 66. See Phillip Sellew, "Interior Monologue as a Narrative Device in the Parables of Luke," *JBL* 111 (1992) 239–53, who shows the use of interior monologue in Greek literature to paint vivid and poignant portraits of characters, especially in tragedies and epic poetry. In Lukan parables

Palestinians of the first century operated.[12] One's self-identity is imbedded in that of one's family, clan, village, occupation, and religious group. A modern day Western notion of individuality would be quite foreign to the people of Jesus' world. Moreover, every important decision was made in community, in endless dialogue with others. Every angle is examined, every possibility weighed, every scenario painted, before arriving at a conclusion. The discussion itself is part of the object of the exchange, as it solidifies comradery.

In such a world, the isolation of the rich man in the parable is alarming. A man of means would presumably have a family, slaves, tenants, and an extensive network of patrons and clients.[13] He asks *himself,* "What shall *I* do . . . *I* do not have space . . . *I* shall do . . . *I* shall tear down . . . *I* shall store . . . *I* shall say to *myself* . . ." The focus of his reflection is "*my* harvest . . . *my* barns . . . *my* grain . . . *myself.*" And his solution is shocking: he will tear down his barns and build larger warehouses, where he will stockpile his grain and other goods for many years, presumably waiting until he can charge the most exorbitant prices. The rich man's plan is told in words that echo the call of Jeremiah, whose tearing down and building up (Jer 1:10) consisted of prophetic words and deeds by which he would accomplish God's purposes.[14] The rich man, by contrast, has no thought of God or other people, planning to take his ease and indulge himself in food, drink, and merriment.[15]

---

this device is used with the prodigal son (15:18-19), the steward who is called to account (16:3-4), and the unjust judge (18:4-5) when the character is at a point of crisis or decision. None of the characters who talk to themselves are commendable.

[12] See Bruce J. Malina and Jerome H. Neyrey, "First-Century Personality: Dyadic, Not Individual," in *The Social World of Luke-Acts: Models for Interpretation,* ed. J. H. Neyrey (Peabody, Mass.: Hendrickson, 1991) 67–96.

[13] Mary Ann Beavis, "The Foolish Landowner (Luke 12:16b-20)," in *Jesus and His Parables,* ed. V. George Shillington (Edinburgh: T. & T. Clark, 1997) 63.

[14] Bailey, *Through Peasant Eyes,* 65.

[15] Variations on this stock phrase that capture the ideals of carefree living are found in Isaiah 22:13; Qoheleth 8:15; Sirach 11:19-20; Tobit 7:10; *1 Enoch* 97:8-9; 1 Corinthians 15:32; Euripedes, *Alcest.* 788–89; Menander, *Frag.,* 301; *Gilgamesh* X.iii.

LIFE ON THE LINE (vv. 20-21)

This plan is abruptly aborted when God interrupts. This is a shocking moment in the story—no other parable has a direct appearance by God.[16] Perhaps it is to make all the more dramatic an allusion to Psalm 41:1, where fools say in their hearts, "There is no God." The rich man has been behaving with no thought of God or neighbor. "You fool!" comes the verdict, along with the announcement that this very night his life[17] will be demanded. The critical question that hangs unanswered is: "all the things you have prepared, to whom will they belong?" (v. 20). The rich man's preparations stand in sorry contrast to John the Baptist's efforts to prepare "a people for the Lord" (1:17), and the way of the Lord (1:76; 3:4). What God prepares is salvation (2:31) while the rich man prepares things for himself.[18]

The question "to whom will they belong?" (v. 20) redounds on the person in the crowd who asks Jesus to decide this for him. In biblical mentality, the obvious answer to any question about ownership, particularly if it involves the land, is that it belongs to God. Psalm 24:1, for example, says, "The earth is the Lord's and all it holds, the world and those who live there." Foolishly thinking "there is no God," the rich man is confronted by God, who not only owns the land and produce he is trying to hoard, but also the very life of the man. All of it belongs to God and is merely on loan.[19] The end result of stockpiling is that the rich man has no benefit from his goods and his heirs are left haggling over it at his death. The parable has come full circle.

---

[16] Donahue, *Gospel in Parable*, 178.

[17] The word *psychē*, "soul," in the Greek text should not be understood as the spiritual self, i.e., soul in contrast to the body. Like the Hebrew word *nefesh*, it connotes the whole person as a living being. "It expresses the vitality, consciousness, intelligence, and volition of a human being" (Fitzmyer, *NJBC*, §82:104).

[18] The verb *hetoimazō*, "to prepare," is used in each of these instances, as well as in Luke 9:52, where Jesus' disciples try unsuccessfully to prepare a Samaritan village to receive Jesus.

[19] Donahue, *Gospel in Parable*, 178. Wisdom 15:8 warns against the misspent toil of one who fashions gods out of his own produce, when shortly "the life that was lent him is demanded *(apaitētheis)* back." Other references to life as a loan are found in Cicero, *De Rep.* 1, 3, 4 and Epictetus 4, 1, 172.

The final verse asserts that such a confrontation awaits those who foolishly lay up treasure for themselves, while not being rich toward God. The verses that follow the parable, recommending reliance on God and almsgiving (12:22-34), elaborate on what it means to be rich toward God. Having begun with a question about reparting an earthly inheritance, the parable shifts to the realm of heavenly inheritance. With this parable Luke is providing another part of the answer to the question posed to Jesus by the scholar of the Law, "What must I do to inherit eternal life?"(10:25).[20]

PEASANT PERSPECTIVE

Thus far we have been working to understand the parable as directed to a rich man. But if Jesus' original audience were poor peasants, what might it say to them? They are undoubtedly the ones who work this rich man's land, while he lives in his luxury as an absentee landlord. It is their sweat that produces the abundant harvest. The harder they work, the richer he gets. Unless they are tenant farmers that have a contract to share a percentage of the profit,[21] they will get none of the extra benefits of the abundant harvest. Even more bitter is a scenario in which the land they are working was formerly their own, but has been lost through debt to the rich man. Such a situation adds another ironic twist to the question, "to whom does this belong?" The fury and resentment of hungry peasants clinging to the edge of life for bare subsistence is palpable in the face of their landlord hoarding unused produce.

From this angle, v. 20 takes on a new significance. The verb *apaitousin*, translated in the *NAB* as "will be demanded" is actually a present tense verb in the third person plural, literally, "they demand" or "they will demand." In other words, the peasants, who have reached the breaking point, come at night

[20] See above, chap. 9, on Luke 10:25-37.
[21] This was a risky arrangement, since crop failure due to pestilence or drought was always a possibility. It was safer to agree to a fixed amount. See Douglas Oakman, *Jesus and the Economic Questions of his Day* (Lewiston, N.Y.: Mellen, 1986).

and demand the life of the rich man.[22] The verb *apaiteō* is often used in Hellenistic literature as in Luke 6:30 for demanding back of a loan or stolen property.[23] The question of ownership is put in high relief as the parable ends. What rightfully belongs to the peasants will probably never reach them even if they kill the rich man.[24] The sons of the rich man will inherit his property and the peasants will be even worse off than before. From this perspective the parable warns about the futility of violent attempts to wrest back ownership. While unmasking the injustice, the parable shows that killing the rich man will not result in justice for the peasants. Nor is the taking of his life a just act when all life belongs to God. The parable offers some comfort to poor peasants who are rich in what matters to God that the balance will be rectified at the end time. At the same time, the parable spurs reflection on what nonviolent measures can be taken to confront injustices toward the poor.

PREACHING POSSIBILITIES

The direction of the preaching from this parable depends in large measure on the socioeconomic position of the congregation. If the community is a well-to-do one, the preacher would do well to highlight the dangers of greed, consumerism, and unbridled consumption. Both the gospel and the first reading from Ecclesiastes 1:2; 2:21-23 on the Eighteenth Sunday of Ordinary Time show the weariness of soul and ultimate death that comes not only from vain hoarding of personal possessions, but also from stockpiling of weapons and the exhaustion

---

[22] Beavis, "Foolish Landowner," 65. See Douglas Oakman, "The Countryside in Luke-Acts," in *The Social World of Luke-Acts*, ed. J. H. Neyrey (Peabody, Mass.: Hendrickson, 1991) 168–69, and Richard A. Horsley and J. S. Hanson, *Bandits, Prophets and Messiahs at the Time of Jesus* (San Francisco: Harper & Row, 1985) on peasant uprisings.

[23] Theophr., *Char.* 10, 2; Phalaris, *Ep.* 83, 1; 2; Dit., *Syll.*³ 955, 18; BGU 183, 8; Sirach 20:15; Philo, *De Jos.* 227. See BAGD, ἀπαιτέω, 80, for these and other references.

[24] A similar theme appears in the parable of the wicked tenants in Mark 12:7 // Matthew 21:38 // Luke 20:14, where the subject is also *klēronomia*, "inheritance."

of resources to supply worthless defenses against fear.[25] The verses that precede and follow the parable in Luke underscore that it is fear and anxiety that fuel greedy acquisition. Questions with which those who are economically secure must wrestle are: How much is enough? In what or in whom is my security? What is truly necessary for life? What does one do with excess? To whom does all this belong?

For those wealthy communities that have a strong commitment to social justice and who are actively engaged in endeavors that aim at achieving equitable distribution, the parable provides an opportunity to encourage and further develop these existing efforts. On Monday of the Twenty-ninth Week of Ordinary Time in Year I, when this parable is coupled with Romans 4:20-25, Abraham serves as an example of a rich man whose possessions are not an obstacle to faith, and who is exemplary in his trust in God.

For affluent congregations that need to become more aware and more active in the work of justice, the parable presents an invitation to hear and respond to the seriousness of the current inequities of our world and so move toward a change of heart and deed. It is a challenging task for a preacher to announce God's desire for justice in a way that does not simply lay a guilt trip on the congregation, but results instead in conversion.[26] It is also a challenge for the preacher to be concrete about what becoming "rich in what matters to God" looks like in a contemporary situation, without giving pat answers that cut off potential deeper responses. The parable does not say what the rich man did when he was confronted in the night. Does he actually die? Does he repent and begin to store up heavenly treasure? The open ending is to be completed by the hearer.

If the congregation is a poor one, the parable may be preached from the peasant perspective. It can offer comfort to those who are becoming rich in what matters to God. At the same time, the parable should not be used to reinforce passive

[25] See Barbara Green, *Like a Tree Planted* (Collegeville: The Liturgical Press, 1997) 122–33, whose vivid weaving of the parable of the storehouse with Psalm 39 offers a powerful critique of contemporary patterns of stockpiling.

[26] See Walter Burghardt, *Preaching the Just Word* (New Haven: Yale University Press, 1996).

acceptance of the sinful inequities of this world, by promising heavenly reward. Every effort should be taken to unmask vicious greed and to engage in efforts toward bringing about economic justice. There is an implicit warning in the parable that violence and killing are futile means for achieving just ends.

The parable in Luke, coupled with the second reading from Colossians 3:1-5, 9-11 on the Eighteenth Sunday of Ordinary Time, makes visible the dire consequences of greed. It is destructive of community as it brings conflict between brothers and sisters over ownership. It makes an idol out of possessions, so that one who stockpiles has no thought of the One to whom all things truly belong. It feeds a delusion that power and salvation rest in one's own accomplishments. The reading from Ephesians 2:1-10, paired with this gospel on Monday of the Twenty-ninth Week of Ordinary Time in Year II proclaims it is owing to God's favor that salvation is ours through faith. None of it is our own doing, but is God's gift. The Psalm response that day likewise acclaims that it is God who made us and it is God to whom we belong (Ps 100:2-5).

It is when one rests securely in the arms of the Provider that one is then able to embrace each person as brother and sister, equal heirs to the same promise. Competition and hoarding dissolve as cooperation and equal distribution become realities. Entering into such a stance in this world inaugurates its full expression in the life beyond. The reading from Colossians assures Christians that the power to do this is already given them through the risen Christ. Believers have already died with Christ and are formed anew in the image of the Creator. Christ has dissolved all divisions between peoples—boundaries of ethnicity, religion, and status—so that Christ is everything in all.

CHAPTER TWELVE

Watchful Servants
(Luke 12:32-48)

Nineteenth Sunday of Ordinary Time

Tuesday of the Twenty-ninth Week of Ordinary Time
(Luke 12:35-38)

Wednesday of the Twenty-ninth Week of Ordinary Time
(Luke 12:39-48)

Jesus said to his disciples:
   32 "Do not be afraid any longer, little flock,
   for your Father is pleased to give you the kingdom.
33 Sell your belongings and give alms.
   Provide money bags for yourselves that do not wear out,
   an inexhaustible treasure in heaven
   that no thief can reach nor moth destroy.
34 For where your treasure is, there also will your heart be.

35 "Gird your loins and light your lamps
   36 and be like servants who await their master's return from a wedding,
   ready to open immediately when he comes and knocks.
37 Blessed are those servants
   whom the master finds vigilant on his arrival.
   Amen, I say to you, he will gird himself,
   have them recline at table, and proceed to wait on them.
38 And should he come in the second or third watch
   and find them prepared in this way,
   blessed are those servants.
39 Be sure of this:
   if the master of the house had known the hour
   when the thief was coming,

he would not have let his house be broken into.
[40] *You also must be prepared, for at an hour you do not expect,*
    the Son of Man will come."
[41] *Then Peter said,*
    "Lord, is this parable meant for us or for everyone?"
[42] *And the Lord replied,*
    "Who, then, is the faithful and prudent steward
    whom the master will put in charge of his servants
    to distribute the food allowance at the proper time?
[43] *Blessed is that servant whom his master on arrival finds doing so.*
[44] *Truly, I say to you, the master will put the servant*
    in charge of all his property.
[45] *But if that servant says to himself,*
    'My master is delayed in coming,'
    and begins to beat the menservants and the maidservants,
    to eat and drink and get drunk,
    [46] *then that servant's master will come*
    on an unexpected day and at an unknown hour
    and will punish him severely
    and assign him a place with the unfaithful.

[47] *That servant who knew his master's will*
    but did not make preparations
    nor act in accord with his will
    shall be beaten severely;
    [48] *and the servant who was ignorant of his master's will*
    but acted in a way deserving of a severe beating
    shall be beaten only lightly.
    Much will be required of the person entrusted with much,
    and still more will be demanded of the person entrusted with more."

LUKAN LITERARY CONTEXT

These sayings and parables are part of the instructions Jesus gives his disciples during the journey to Jerusalem. There are five sections to this gospel passage. The first segment, vv. 32-34, completes a theme developed since the beginning of chapter 12. Jesus encourages his disciples not to fear anything and assures them of their value in God's sight and of the assistance of the Spirit in defending themselves should they be brought before the authorities (12:1-12). He then warns them against greed with a parable about a rich fool who stores his possessions, oblivious to God and others (12:13-21).[1] Following the parable are further sayings about God's providence and care (12:22-31). The sayings in 12:32-34 complete this lengthy section on counsel against greed and assurance of God's providence.[2]

The focus shifts in v. 35 as the following four sets of sayings and parables are stitched together by catchwords that revolve around the theme of watchfulness, preparedness, and fidelity. These are loosely joined and the emphasis is slightly different in each. Verses 35-38 are sayings peculiar to Luke and center on watchful servants of an absent master. In vv. 39-40 attention shifts to a watchful master. These sayings have a counterpart in Matthew 24:43-44, where they are part of the eschatological discourse.[3] The transitional verses, 41-42a are composed by Luke to link with vv. 43-46, further sayings from Q, found also in Matthew 24:45-51. The scenario returns to that of a faithful manager in the employ of an absent master. The final section, vv. 47-48, is uniquely Lukan and provides further comment on the previous segment. The final lines are a proverb that may have first circulated independently.[4]

A PARABLE MEANT FOR US? (v. 41)

It is not clear from the context to which parabolic sayings Peter refers when he asks Jesus in v. 41 whether the parable is meant for them or for everyone. It may refer back to the parable of the rich fool in 12:16-21 as well as the intervening sayings. In Luke 12:1 Jesus had been addressing his disciples in the hearing of a large crowd. He is interrupted by a person in the crowd who asks him to arbitrate a dispute over his inheritance (12:13). Jesus responds with a question dissociating himself from the role of judge and divider. He then addresses to "them," presumably the disciples, a saying against greed (12:15), and then

---

[1] See above, chap. 11, on Luke 12:13-21.

[2] A variation of vv. 33b-34 is found in Matthew 6:19-21 as part of the Sermon on the Mount. There is also a version in *Gos.Thom.* §76, where the sayings are linked with the parable of the pearl of great price.

[3] Another form of them is found in Mark 13:35-36 and *Gos.Thom.* §21.

[4] Joseph A. Fitzmyer, *The Gospel According to Luke* (AB28A; Garden City, N.Y.: Doubleday, 1985) 981–93.

directs the parable to "them" (12:16-21). The subsequent sayings are explicitly directed to the disciples (12:22). Peter's question is not answered directly. Jesus replies with another parable. The answer to Peter's question is implied in vv. 47-48: the parable is meant for any who hear, but the one who knows and understands "the master's will" is held to a higher standard of accountability for carrying it out.

Peter is subsequently cast as one who has taken the parable to heart. In Luke 18:18-30 is an episode in which Jesus encounters a rich ruler who becomes sad at the invitation to sell his belongings, give them to the poor, and follow him. Jesus then remarks on how hard it is for a rich person to enter the realm of God (18:24-25). A query is posed by "those who heard" (v. 26): "Then who can be saved?" Jesus affirms, "What is impossible for human beings is possible for God" (v. 27). There is a similar dichotomy in 18:26-27 as in 12:41, between the disciples and others who hear. It is Peter again who is the spokesperson remarking, "We have given up our possessions and followed you" (18:28). In the concluding verses of that episode Jesus assures them of a manifold reward both now and in the age to come. In one more episode, in Acts 5:1-11, Peter confronts Ananias and Sapphira in their deception of the community over their property. He is cast as the leader of the community that has taken Jesus' instructions about greed to heart and who are sharing all their resources together.

The question in 12:41 serves to sharpen the attention of the hearer who may be inclined to dismiss the difficult sayings about avoiding greed, storing treasure in heaven, and being watchful and prepared. They are not meant for only a few, but for any who hear. Those who understand are expected to enact them. Blessing and God's kingdom are promised to those who do (12:32, 37, 38, 43), while punishment and a place with the unfaithful await those who do not (12:46-48).

INEXHAUSTIBLE TREASURE (vv. 32-34)

These verses provide a foil for the story of the rich fool in 12:16-21. They spell out the meaning of the admonition to become "rich in what matters to God"(v. 21) that concludes the parable. Instead of being possessed by fear that results in consuming greed, disciples are to sell their possessions and acquire inexhaustible treasure in heaven. In the parable of the rich man his foolishness was portrayed in terms of not having time to enjoy all that he had stockpiled before his life was demanded. The sayings in vv. 32-34 highlight another aspect of the senselessness of hoarding earthly goods: they wear out and they require vigilance against thieves and other destructive forces. When the heart is set on corruptible things, it is consumed with constant need to guard them, provide for their upkeep, storage, and replacement, leaving no room for compassion and justice. Selling off belongings that hold a grip on the heart opens one to receive all from God as gift, a stance from which one may give just as freely.[5]

Luke gives concrete examples of characters who give alms. Zacchaeus, the chief tax collector, gives half his belongings to the poor (Luke 19:8). Tabitha was "completely occupied with good deeds and almsgiving" (Acts 9:36). Cornelius "used to give alms generously to the Jewish people and pray to God constantly" (Acts 10:2). Paul coordinated a major collection throughout the Gentile churches of alms for the needy community in Jerusalem (Acts 24:17). In one instance in Acts 3:3, a man who was crippled begs alms from Peter and John. But having neither silver nor gold to give, Peter instead gives him a gift of healing.

VIGILANCE (vv. 35-38)

From sayings that censure vigilance over corruptible treasure that consumes the heart, the focus shifts to the need for vigilance for an absent master. The admonition to gird the loins means to tie up one's ankle-length robe so as to be ready for action. It recalls the stance of the Israelites at the first Passover, ready to depart from Egypt (Exod 12:11, 22-23). It is also an expression for readiness for service.[6] Similarly, keeping lamps lit

---

[5] See Fitzmyer, *Luke*, 983, for parallels in secular Greek literature for the proverb in v. 34.

[6] See 1 Kings 18:46; 2 Kings 4:29; 9:1; Job 38:3; 40:7; Luke 17:8; Ephesians 6:14; 1 Peter 1:13.

connotes watchfulness.[7] While the master is away, the servant stands ready to open immediately and to serve him.

There is a startling twist in v. 37b. It is a totally absurd scenario that a master would have his vigilant servants recline at table and then wait on them![8] The metaphor is understandable only in light of Luke 22:27, where at the Last Supper Jesus asks, "who is greater: the one seated at table or the one who serves? Is it not the one seated at table? I am among you as the one who serves."

Verse 38 rounds out this saying, asserting that whenever the master comes, whether at midnight or just before dawn, the servants should be prepared. Twice (vv. 37, 38) these vigilant servants are pronounced blessed. In the Sermon on the Plain (Luke 6:20-26), Jesus declared blessed those who are poor, hungry, weeping, and insulted because of commitment to him. And while en route to Jerusalem Jesus pronounces blessed those who hear the word of God and do it (11:28). To these beatitudes Jesus adds vigilant preparedness.

PREPAREDNESS (vv. 39-40)

The word "prepared" (vv. 38, 40) provides the link for the next saying. From watchful servants, the metaphor now turns to a watchful master. Just as a householder would be especially prepared if he knew the time of a break-in, so must disciples be prepared for the coming of the Son of Humanity. The theme of the unexpected burglar is prevalent in New Testament texts that deal with the parousia, e.g., 1 Thessalonians 5:2-4; 2 Peter 3:10; Revelation 3:3; 16:15. The issue of knowing the timing of God's restorative intervention arises again in Acts 1:6, where the disciples pose the question to Jesus just before his ascension. There he answers them that it is not for them to know the times and seasons that God has set. Like Luke 12:39-40, it asserts that they need to stay always vigilant.

---

[7] So also Luke 8:16; 11:33; Exodus 27:20; Leviticus 24:2; Matthew 25:1.

[8] The absurdity of such is affirmed in the parable in Luke 17:7-10. See below, chap. 18.

SON OF HUMANITY

This expression is an enigmatic one, found in the Gospels only on the lips of Jesus. It occurs in contexts where Jesus speaks of his earthly ministry, his passion, and his future coming and role as judge at the end time.[9] The origin of the phrase *huios tou anthrōpou* ("son of man") is disputed. Some scholars hold that it was an expression used in pre-Christian Jewish apocalyptic writings that was taken over by Christians to refer to Jesus. It is found in Daniel 7:14 and in *The Similitudes of Enoch (1 Enoch 37–71)* to denote an end-time agent of salvation and judgment.

Other scholars argue that *The Similitudes of Enoch,* which do not appear in early versions of *Enoch,* are not pre-Christian, and therefore its use of *huios tou anthrōpou* does not antedate Christian use of the term for Jesus. For them Daniel 7:14 is the only pre-Christian example, and there the expression denotes Israel as a corporate identity. For these scholars, the examples in Daniel and *Enoch* shed no light on the meaning of the expression as used of Jesus.

The meaning of the phrase *huios tou anthrōpou* is likewise debated. It may be understood to reflect a Semitic expression, *ben ʾādām* in Hebrew, or *bar ʾĕnāsh* in Aramaic (literally "son of man"), a phrase that individualizes a noun for humanity in general by prefacing it with "son of," thus designating a single member of the human species. An example of this is found in Psalm 8:5, "What are humans that you are mindful of them, mere mortals[10] that you care for them?" Jesus may have used this phrase as a way of speaking of himself simply as a human being. It could be translated, "a certain person," or "someone" or when used as a self-designation, simply "I."

---

[9] In reference to his earthly ministry see Luke 5:24; 6:5, 22; 7:34; 9:58; 11:30; 12:10; 19:10; in regard to his passion see 9:22, 44; 18:31; 22:22, 48; 24:7; in reference to his future coming see 9:26; 12:8; 17:22, 24, 26, 30; 18:8; 21:27, 36; 22:69. See further, Reginald H. Fuller, "Son of Man," in *Harper's Bible Commentary,* ed. Paul J. Achtemeier (San Francisco: Harper & Row, 1985) 981; Joseph A. Fitzmyer, "The New Testament Title 'Son of Man' Philologically Considered," in *A Wandering Aramean: Collected Aramaic Essays* (Missoula, Mont.: Scholars Press, 1979) 143–60.

[10] The Hebrew *ben ʾādām* and the Greek *huios anthrōpou* in the LXX are singular, i.e., "son of man."

Some scholars who hold that there was a pre-Christian concept of an apocalyptic "son of man," believe that Jesus used the phrase of a coming figure other than himself. In Mark 8:38 and Luke 12:8 Jesus appears to be talking about the "son of man" as someone other than himself who would vindicate his present ministry. In this view, it was Jesus' followers who attributed to him the title from a post-resurrection stance of faith.

Other scholars hold that Jesus did not use the term of himself at all and that all the references to him as *huios tou anthrōpou* arise from the post-Easter insight of his followers. This theory posits that they first applied it to Jesus in an apocalyptic sense, in sayings about his future coming and his role as judge and savior. From this developed the application of the expression to Jesus' earthly ministry and to his passion.

Whatever the provenance and original meaning of the expression, it is clearly used as a christological title in the Gospels. A further difficulty is posed when translating this term into English. There is no felicitous translation that allows for the ambiguity in meaning in the original phrase, nor one that satisfactorily avoids using exclusively male terminology. Some use "Son of Humanity" or "the Human One," but in any case there is not a satisfactory way to capture what it would have originally conveyed.

FAITHFUL STEWARD (vv. 42-46)

One more shift occurs as the image in vv. 42-46 moves to the steward put in charge of other servants in the absence of the master. Whereas the emphasis in vv. 35-40 is on watchfulness for the coming of the master, here the vigilance is over the day-to-day tasks that must be fulfilled in the in-between time. Highlighted is the steward's role of overseeing the feeding of the other servants. A manager whom the master finds exercising this commission faithfully is pronounced blessed, and is given even more responsibility.

But there is another possible scenario. The servant may see the delay as an opportunity to exploit his situation, taking advantage of his temporary power. He may begin to use his authority abusively, and to indulge himself in excessive food and drink. There is an ironic twist as he who had been entrusted with the distribution of food to his underlings instead gorges himself on the provisions. It is another version of the fool who stores up goods for himself. But such a situation will not last long. At the unexpected moment the master will arrive.

The consequences are dire for betraying the master's confidence and misusing his authority. What is translated in the *NAB* as "punish severely, *"dichotomēsei,* literally means "to cut in two." It refers to the dismemberment of a condemned person.[11] In the context of the parable, it is an ironically fitting punishment for the double life that the steward is leading. Furthermore, his place is assigned with the unfaithful. The word for place, *meros,* can mean a portion of property, as in Luke 15:12 and Acts 5:2. It can also carry connotations of a "share" in eternal inheritance, as in John 13:8, where Jesus tells Peter he will have no "part" in him if Jesus does not wash him. The wordplay that frames the parable (*pistos,* "faithful," in v. 42 and *apistos,* "unfaithful," in v. 46) highlights the need for faithfulness in discharging responsibilities while watching attentively for the master's return.

MUCH ENTRUSTED, MUCH REQUIRED (vv. 47-48)

The final verses are linked to the other sayings by the catchwords "servant" (*doulos,* vv. 36, 37, 38, 42, 43, 45, 46, 47, 48) and "prepare" (*hetoimazō,* vv. 38, 40, 47). The topic shifts one more time as the sayings center on the servant who does not do the master's will. What is to be done? Any servant who does not do the master's will is punished, but the severity depends on the level of knowledge the servant has of the master's will. There is an echo of Numbers 15:22-31, where atonement sacrifices are required even for inadvertent transgressions because of the sanctity of the Law. The consequences for one who sins defiantly are far more severe. One who deliberately breaks God's command is cut off from among the people for having despised the word of God (Num 15:30-31).

The proverb that concludes this section points to the increased responsibility of those in positions of leadership. They

[11] BAGD, διχοτομέω, 200.

are entrusted with the tasks of knowing the master's will and acting on it themselves, as well as guiding others to do so.

URGENCY

After a section which offers comfort and security to the disciples, vv. 35-46 inject a new sense of urgency. From exhortations to trust God for all needs, these parabolic sayings press for watchfulness, vigilance, preparedness, faithful stewardship, knowing the master's will and acting on it. There is a resonance with exhortations in the Hebrew Scriptures to be watchful for the eschatological day of Yahweh.[12] Jesus' words about vigilance can be seen in line with those of the prophets who urged Israel to be alert for the coming day of God's judgment. In Jesus' preaching, it is the coming of God's reign that becomes the object of expectation (11:2). By the time the gospel is written, the expected coming is understood to be Christ's parousia and *huios tou anthrōpou* is clearly understood to refer to him as God's eschatological agent of salvation and judgment (v. 40).[13]

PREACHING POSSIBILITIES

At the center of these parabolic sayings stands Peter's query whether these are meant only for some or for all. In various ways the sayings elaborate the need for any who hear the word to take heed and to act on it. There are no higher or lower degrees of discipleship. The radical invitation to sell possessions and give alms is not meant only for some disciples. Nor is it only to a select few that the exhortations to vigilance, preparedness, and faithful enacting of responsibilities apply. These are addressed to all. What does vary is the level of accountability, dependent on the degree of understanding.

The preacher should not shirk from preaching what may be heard as a hard message. The freedom and joy that result from embracing the gospel comes with the price of having to relinquish anything else that clutches at the heart: possessions,

---

[12] E.g., Isaiah 13:6; Ezekiel 30:3; Joel 1:15; 2:1; Amos 5:18; Obadiah 15; Zephaniah 1:14-18.

[13] Fitzmyer, *Luke*, 986–87.

temptation to abuse power, reliance on a false sense that there will be time later to set things aright. For most Christians two millennia of waiting for the parousia have dulled the sense of urgency in watching for it. There is, however, a growing consciousness of the acute need for redistribution of goods globally and for just stewardship. The preacher might stress as the object of vigilance not a vague notion of Christ's return, but his very palpable presence in the needy of our globe, and the urgency for those who have been entrusted with much to respond in justice. The proper time for justice and for right distribution is not only in some future eschatological time when "the master" suddenly arrives, but is the work already being done by the faithful stewards when the critical moment comes (vv. 42-43).

One difficulty with the images presented both in this gospel passage and in the reading from Romans paired with it on Wednesday of the Twenty-ninth Week of Ordinary Time in Year I is that they rely on a world of masters and servants, slaves and overseers familiar to Jesus' original audience, but quite alien to many Christian communities today. A particular challenge for the preacher will be to find a way in which to make the gospel message understandable in a contemporary context without relying on imagery and language of masters and slaves. While neither Jesus nor any of the writers of the New Testament challenged the institution of slavery, accepting it, rather, as the prevailing social structure of their day, for modern Christians it is abhorrent. Nonetheless, metaphors that cast God and Jesus as "master" and disciples as "servants" or "slaves" still abound. There is a particular danger that the use of such language reinforces systems of oppression in our day, giving them theological legitimation. Holding up the ideal of faithful servanthood to people who are caught in the underside of systems of domination only serves to justify human bondage as the will of God. It keeps dominated peoples from recognizing the injustice of their situation and mobilizing to confront it.[14]

---

[14] See Elisabeth Schüssler Fiorenza, "'Waiting at Table': A Critical Feminist Theological Reflection on Diakonia," *Concilium 198. Diakonia: Church for the Others,* ed. N. Breinacher and N. Mette (Edinburgh: T. & T. Clark, 1988) 84–94.

CHAPTER THIRTEEN

Places at Table
(Luke 14:1, 7-14)

Twenty-second Sunday of Ordinary Time

Saturday of the Thirtieth Week of Ordinary Time
(Luke 14:1, 7-11)

¹ On a sabbath Jesus went to dine
at the home of one of the leading Pharisees,
and the people there were observing him carefully.

⁷ He told a parable to those who had been invited,
noticing how they were choosing the places of honor at the table.
⁸ "When you are invited by someone to a wedding banquet,
do not recline at table in the place of honor.
A more distinguished guest than you may have been invited by him,
⁹ and the host who invited both of you
may approach you and say,
'Give your place to this man,'
and then you would proceed with embarrassment
to take the lowest place.
¹⁰ Rather, when you are invited,
go and take the lowest place
so that when the host comes to you he may say,
'My friend, move up to a higher position.'
Then you will enjoy the esteem of your companions at the table.
¹¹ For everyone who exalts himself will be humbled,
but the one who humbles himself will be exalted."
¹² Then he said to the host who invited him,
"When you hold a lunch or a dinner,
do not invite your friends or your brothers
or your relatives or your wealthy neighbors,
in case they may invite you back and you have repayment.

13 Rather, when you hold a banquet,
 invite the poor, the crippled, the lame, the blind;
  14 blessed indeed will you be because of their inability
 to repay you.
For you will be repaid at the resurrection of the righteous."

LUKAN LITERARY CONTEXT

The narrative setting for this banquet is the great journey to Jerusalem. The parabolic sayings in today's gospel are unique to Luke[1] and comprise the second and third parts of four that constitute chapter fourteen. The first part (14:1-6) relates the healing of a man who suffered from dropsy. The Pharisees are watching Jesus, who challenges them about the lawfulness of healing on the sabbath. It parallels the story of Jesus' healing on another sabbath of a woman bent double for eighteen years (13:10-17). In part two (vv. 7-14) the focus shifts to a discussion about places at table. Jesus first addresses the invitees about their choice of seats (vv. 7-10). He then directs his attention in part three to the host, advising him about which guests to invite (vv. 12-14). In the fourth part (vv. 15-24) is another parable,[2] that of the great feast, giving a vivid illustration of what it is like to dine in God's realm.

The parable in 14:7-14 comes as part of the dinner conversation, as Luke 14 takes on the contours of a Hellenistic symposium.[3] To Christian ears banquet settings have eucharistic

---

[1] It is likely that v. 11, which has a close counterpart in Luke 18:14 and Matthew 23:12, comes from Q and has been attached to L material (Fitzmyer, *Luke*, 1044).

[2] See below, chap. 27, on Luke 14:15-24.

[3] In Hellenistic literature from the time of Xenophon to Plato, philosophical discussions were commonly set in the context of a symposium. See Plato, *Symposium*, and the six books of *Table Talk* by Plutarch (*Mor.* 612C–748D). In Jewish literature an example is found in the *Letter of Aristeas*, only here it is Jewish teachers discussing Torah. The Lukan version of the Last Supper (22:14-38) also has elements of a Greco-Roman symposium. Luke, more than any other evangelist, uses meals as a setting for Jesus' teaching. In addition to 14:1-24 see 5:29-39; 7:36-50; 11:37-52; 22:14-28; 24:20-49. See Sharon Ringe, *Jesus, Liberation, and the Biblical Jubilee* (OBT 19; Philadelphia: Fortress, 1985) 54–60, and John Navone, *Themes of St. Luke* (Rome: Gregorian University Press, 1970) 11–37, on the banquet theme in Luke.

overtones and point forward to the eschatological banquet.[4]
This banquet is set in the home of a leading Pharisee, and like
other episodes where Jesus dines with Pharisees, the meal provides a setting for dialogue that brings out conflicts between
Jesus and his hosts and offers them an opportunity to embrace
his vision of the realm of God.[5] Jesus, received here by the
Pharisees as a journeying guest, is offering them a place at his
table in the eternal banquet at which he is host.[6]

WATCHFUL PHARISEES (v. 1)

The story opens with the host and the other Pharisees (and
scholars of the Law, v. 3) watching Jesus closely. The verb
paratēreō, "watch closely," often has a hostile connotation, i.e.,
"to lie in wait for" someone,[7] as in Luke 6:7, where the scribes
and the Pharisees, in a scene very similar to 14:1-6, watch Jesus
closely to see if he would cure a man with a withered hand on
a sabbath. Likewise in Luke 20:20 the scribes and chief priests
observe Jesus closely to try to trap him in his speech in order to
hand him over to the authorities.

In the Gospel of Luke the Pharisees are always a foil to
Jesus. Their understanding of the reign of God is set in contrast
to that of Jesus. Their increasing hostility to Jesus in the narrative
is meant to provoke the opposite response in Luke's readers.
They first appear in Luke 5:17–6:11, where their conflicts with
Jesus center on forgiveness of sins (5:17-26), eating and drinking
with tax collectors and sinners (5:27-32), fasting (5:33-38), plucking grain on the sabbath (6:1-5), and healing on the sabbath
(6:6-11). Jesus dines with Pharisees (7:36-50; 11:37-54; 14:1-24),
but the table discussion is always conflictual. The Pharisees'
warning to Jesus about Herod in 13:31-33 does not cast them in
a positive light, but further illustrates their misapprehension of

---

[4] John R. Donahue, *The Gospel in Parable* (Philadelphia: Fortress, 1988) 140.

[5] Similarly Luke 7:36-50 where Jesus' reception of sinners is the point of
conflict when a woman who had been forgiven expresses lavish love to Jesus at
the home of Simon the Pharisee (see above, chap. 8); and Luke 11:37-52, where
Jesus confronts his Pharisee host about their practices of exterior cleansing
while neglecting justice and love of God.

[6] David P. Moessner, *Lord of the Banquet* (Minneapolis: Fortress, 1989) 158.

[7] BAGD, παρατηρέω, 622.

Jesus' mission. The opposition between Jesus and the Pharisees escalates as Jesus approaches Jerusalem.[8] Curiously, the Pharisees are absent from Luke's passion narrative. In Acts, Pharisees no longer appear as antagonists to the Christian message. Gamaliel persuades the Sanhedrin to let Christianity run its course (5:34-42). Some Pharisees had become believers (15:5), and Paul, himself a Pharisee, is implicitly defended by the Pharisees (23:1-10). In Acts the Pharisees serve to confirm Christianity as a legitimate expression of Jewish faith.[9]

It is important to keep in mind that Luke's literary portrayal of the Pharisees does not entirely match the historical reality. The Pharisees were one group among the many diverse sects of Jews at the time of Jesus. Pharisaism was a lay movement noted for its oral and accurate interpretations of the Jewish Law. Pharisees were less accommodating toward Hellenization than Sadducees, but were not separatists like the Essenes.[10] Disputes over theological interpretations and religious practices would have been common among all the various Jewish sects. The Pharisees were not the prevailing religious force in Jesus' day;[11] this became so only after the destruction of the Jerusalem Temple in 70 C.E. It is this situation that the gospel reflects.

From a hostile introduction in 14:1, and the brewing conflict over a sabbath healing (vv. 2-6), the ensuing parable seems to take on a more irenic tone. What might at first look like common-sense wisdom sayings, akin to Proverbs 25:6-7[12] however, become serious warnings in this literary context.

---

[8] Luke 11:37-54; 12:1; 14:1-24; 15:1-32; 16:14-31; 17:20-21; 18:9-14; 19:37-40. See Moessner, *Lord of the Banquet*, 197–207.

[9] See John T. Carroll, "Luke's Portrayal of the Pharisees," *CBQ* 50 (1988) 604–21.

[10] See Jacob Neusner, *Judaism in the Beginning of Christianity* (Philadelphia: Fortress, 1984) 45–61.

[11] According to Josephus (*Ant.* 17.42) there were six thousand Pharisees in Palestine in Jesus' day. This would make them only about one percent of the Jewish population.

[12] Proverbs 25:6-7 advises, "Claim no honor in the king's presence, nor occupy the place of great men; For it is better that you be told, 'Come up closer!' than that you be humbled before the prince." Similarly, Sirach 3:17-20; *Aboth de R. Nathan* 25.

TAKING PLACES OF HONOR (vv. 7-10)

The assignment of places at table was a critical statement of social status and meals were important occasions used to cement social relations.[13] Normally only people of like status ate together. The Lukan setting implies that the Pharisee, by inviting Jesus to dinner, recognizes him as a social equal. Eating together indicates the sharing of common ideas and values as well.

For special occasions such as a wedding banquet (v. 8), guests and host reclined[14] on couches or mats on their left sides, using their right hands to reach the table in the center. The guest of highest rank would be seated at the central couch, with the next most honored guests at their left, and the host and his family to the right. Choosing a place of honor that is intended for another results in humiliating shame, and banishment to the lowest place. A far better strategy for gaining honor is to take the lowest place and then be invited by the host to take a higher one.

A number of Roman sources describe meals at which guests of differing social rank are seated in separate rooms and served different food and wine according to their social position.[15] Pliny the Younger critiques these discriminatory practices:[16]

> I happened to be dining with a man, though no particular friend of his, whose elegant economy, as he called it, seemed to me a sort of stingy extravagance. The best dishes were set in front of himself and a select few, and cheap scraps of food before the rest of the company. He had even put the wine into tiny little flasks, divided into three categories, not with the idea of giving his guests the opportunity of choosing, but to make it impossible for them to refuse what they were given. One lot was intended for himself and for us, another for his lesser friends (all his friends are graded), and the third for his and our freedmen. (*Letters*, 2:6)

[13] See B. Malina and R. Rohrbaugh, *Social Science Commentary on the Synoptic Gospels* (Minneapolis: Fortress, 1992) 365–68.

[14] So also Luke 7:36; 12:37; 13:29; 24:30.

[15] E.g., Martial, *Epigrams*, 1.20; 3.60; Juvenal, *Satires* 5; Pliny, *Letters* 2.6. See Malina and Rohrbaugh, *Social Science Commentary*, 136, 368.

[16] The following examples are quoted in Jerome Murphy-O'Connor, *St. Paul's Corinth: Texts and Archaeology* (rev. ed.; GNS 6; Collegeville: The Liturgical Press, 1985) 167–68.

Likewise, the Roman satirist Martial writes:

> Since I am asked to dinner, no longer, as before a purchased guest, why is not the same dinner served to me as to you? You take oysters fattened in the Lucrine lake, I suck a mussel through a hole in the shell. You get mushrooms, I take hog funguses. You tackle turbot, but I brill. Golden with fat, a turtledove gorges you with its bloated rump, but there is set before me a magpie that has died in its cage. Why do I dine without you, Ponticus, though I dine with you? The dole has gone: let us have the benefit of that; let us eat the same fare. (*Epigrams*, 3:60)

In Paul's first letter to the Corinthians (11:17-34) there is a similar critique of inequitable dining practices when the Christian community gathers. Paul gives us a glimpse into a situation in which the richer members of the community are enjoying a supper far different from that of the poorer ones. The former are most likely reclining in the triclinium (dining room), while the latter are crowded in the atrium. The rich begin early and eat the best food, while the poor arrive after the day's work and have only sparse fare. Paul is outraged that they make mockery of the Lord's Supper with such practices and advises them to eat their supper at home before coming together for the eucharistic ritual if they cannot share the meal equitably. This vignette from Corinth gives us insight into the struggles that undoubtedly faced the early Christian communities as peoples of differing social rank became believers.[17] With Jews and Gentiles, slave and free, women and men, high ranking and low, all coming together, they would have been faced with difficult problems to resolve about appropriate places at table.

REVERSAL (v. 11)

The saying in v. 11 is a free-floating proverb that is also found in Luke 18:14 and has echoes throughout the Third Gospel. The theme of the lowly being exalted by God and vice versa is first sounded in the Magnificat (1:46-55), and devel-

---

[17] See ibid., 161–78; Gerd Theissen, *The Social Setting of Pauline Christianity* (Philadelphia: Fortress, 1982) 145–74.

oped further with the beatitudes (6:20-26) and other sayings about the greatest in the realm of God (9:46-48; 10:15). The climax comes at the Last Supper, where Jesus speaks of himself as one who has come to serve, not to be served (22:24-30).[18] Within the Lukan narrative, Jesus' remarks about seating at table are not simply words of folk wisdom, but point toward his own practice of seeking out the most marginalized as table companions (Luke 5:29-37; 15:1; 19:7) to indicate who it is that God welcomes. A sensible strategy in terms of the honor-shame exchanges at banquets becomes a subversive image in terms of God's realm.

GUEST LISTS (vv. 12-14)

In the next verses Jesus turns his attention to the host and his guest list. The underlying presumption is that one invites to a meal only those to whom one is indebted or those who can benefit the host in the future.[19] The rules of reciprocity were simple: for anyone of like rank who is not a family member, any invitation or offer of good is expected to be repaid in equal measure. With family members open sharing is based on generosity or need. Repayment can be postponed, or even forgotten.[20]

The guest list Jesus proposes is unthinkable for those concerned about their social status. People who were poor, crippled, lame, and blind, while objects of charity (Deut 14:28-29; 26:11-13) would not be considered as dinner guests. In Leviticus 21:17-21 these are precisely the ones who are thought impure and thus excluded from the priesthood. The Qumran community also excluded them from participation in the eschatological holy war (1QM 7:4) and in the end-time banquet (1QSa 2:5-6). In the gospel, however, it is precisely these kinds of people to whom Jesus directs his mission, as he announced in Luke 4:18, and as he reminds the disciples of John the Baptist in 7:22.

The problem is not only that such persons are unable to reciprocate or to advance the social position of the host, but

---

[18] Eugene LaVerdiere, *Dining in the Kingdom of God* (Chicago: Liturgy Training Publications, 1994) 103.

[19] Charles Talbert, *Reading Luke* (New York: Crossroad, 1988) 197.

[20] Malina and Rohrbaugh, *Social Science Commentary*, 325.

those of high rank who associate with such risk losing their social standing, should they be seen eating with persons of lower rank. For the Christian community the inclusive table companionship that Jesus advocates would have been an exceedingly difficult thing to practice for Christians of higher status. Association with people of lower status could easily result in elites being cut off from their social networks. This, in turn, could have deleterious economic ramifications for the whole community, if the richer members who are acting as patrons to the community lose their connections with other elites. The difficulties posed by inclusive table practices involved more than personal honor.

The sayings conclude with Jesus pronouncing blessed those who are not repaid in the present for their hospitality. Their reward will come at the end time. There are echoes of Luke 13:29, where Jesus tells of people coming from east and west, north and south, to sit together at table in the reign of God. A similar theme of reversal is sounded there as well, as some who are last will be first, and some who are first will be last (13:30).

PREACHING POSSIBILITIES

While the image of jockeying for position at a banquet may not resonate with the experience of contemporary Christians, there are all manner of other examples a preacher can call on to illustrate ways of seeking self-promotion and personal enhancement in contemporary culture. Both the gospel and the reading from Sirach on the Twenty-second Sunday of the Year advocate humility. A preacher can invite believers to reflect on how that virtue is manifest in the life of a disciple, even the small every-day exchanges. What opportunities are there to take a back seat or forego a place at the head of a line? What ways are open to us to seek to serve the needs of others before our own? How do we teach our children to live in this way, when all the advertising that confronts them speaks otherwise?

One danger the preacher will want to be careful to avoid is to reinforce attitudes of false humility and servitude in those who are already on the lowest rungs of society. The example of humility offered by Jesus is directed to those who have status, power, and authority to relinquish. To arrive at a community of equal disciples, strategies of empowerment are needed for those at the bottom of domination systems, while relinquishment of power is incumbent on those at the top.[21]

The second half of the gospel offers an invitation to reflect on the question of who is missing both in our social gatherings and in our eucharistic communities. Who would not feel welcome? Who is left out? How can the congregation take the next step toward greater openness to peoples of diverse socioeconomic strata, ethnic or racial groups, sexual orientation, and the like? What concrete steps would need to be taken to invite those who should be welcome at the table? The blessedness of inclusive table companionship is experienced not only here, but in the fullness of God's realm.

[21] Elisabeth Schüssler Fiorenza, "'Waiting at Table': A Critical Feminist Theological Reflection on Diakonia," *Concilium 198. Diakonia: Church for the Others,* ed. N. Breinacher and N. Mette (Edinburgh: T. & T. Clark, 1988) 84–94.

CHAPTER FOURTEEN

Calculating the Cost
(Luke 14:25-33)

Twenty-third Sunday of Ordinary Time

Wednesday of the Thirty-first Week of Ordinary Time

Great crowds were traveling with Jesus,
   ²⁵ and he turned and addressed them,
      ²⁶ "If anyone comes to me without hating his father and mother,
   wife and children, brothers and sisters,
   and even his own life,
   he cannot be my disciple.
²⁷ Whoever does not carry his own cross and come after me
   cannot be my disciple.
²⁸ Which of you wishing to construct a tower
   does not first sit down and calculate the cost
   to see if there is enough for its completion?
²⁹ Otherwise, after laying the foundation
   and finding himself unable to finish the work
   the onlookers should laugh at him ³⁰ and say,
   'This one began to build but did not have
      the resources to finish.'
³¹ Or what king marching into battle
   would not first sit down
   and decide whether with ten thousand troops
   he can successfully oppose another king
   advancing upon him with twenty thousand troops?
³² But if not, while he is still far away,
   he will send a delegation to ask for peace terms.
³³ In the same way,
   every one of you who does not renounce all his possessions
   cannot be my disciple."

LUKAN LITERARY CONTEXT

The previous verses in Luke 14 comprise the parables about places at table (14:7-14), followed by that of the great banquet (14:15-24).[1] The change of scene between those parables and the sayings on discipleship in vv. 25-33 is abrupt. Jesus is now continuing on the journey to Jerusalem and great crowds are accompanying him. There is a certain parallelism between the obstacles to discipleship Jesus addresses in the parable of the banquet and those he speaks of here to the crowds. The invitation to the banquet was refused by a man who had just purchased a field (14:18), another who had just bought a yoke of oxen (14:19), and a third who had just been married (14:20). These give concrete illustrations of the sayings in today's gospel about the inability to renounce possessions (v. 33) and to relativize all other relationships (v. 26) that impede discipleship. In addition to these two themes that are carried over from the previous parable, there is a reprise of the saying about carrying one's cross (also in Luke 9:23), which is amplified by two short parables, unique to Luke, about being able to complete what one begins.[2]

HATING ONE'S FAMILY (v. 26)

The saying about hating one's family members is jolting at first hearing, both to contemporary ears as well as to Jesus' first audience. In his culture, which operated with the concept of dyadic personality,[3] one would understand his or herself only in relation to the family, clan, village, and religious group to which they belonged. Individual identity was not part of their

---

[1] See above, chap. 13, on Luke 14:7-14; see below, chap. 27, on Luke 14:15-24.

[2] The transitional verse (v. 25) and the concluding verse (v. 33) are composed by Luke. Verses 26-27 derive from Q and have a parallel in Matthew 10:37-38, where the two sayings are part of the missionary discourse addressed to the Twelve. *Gos.Thom.* §55 also has a version of the two sayings together. There is also a form of the first saying in *Gos.Thom.* §101 and at Luke 18:29, which is likely a redaction of Mark 10:29. The parables in vv. 28-32 are unique to Luke.

[3] See Bruce J. Malina and Jerome H. Neyrey, "First-Century Personality: Dyadic, Not Individual," in *The Social World of Luke-Acts: Models for Interpretation,* ed. J. H. Neyrey (Peabody, Mass.: Hendrickson, 1991) 67–96.

consciousness. The extended family was the source of one's honor and status in the community and provided the primary economic, religious, educational, and social network. So it would be unimaginable to think of oneself cut off from family. To break ties with family was tantamount to losing life itself.

This saying in v. 26 must be read in tandem with Luke 8:21, where Jesus' family wants to see him and he replies that his mother and siblings are those who hear the word of God and act on it. Similarly, in 11:27-28, when a woman in the crowd exclaims, "Blessed is the womb that carried you and the breasts at which you nursed," Jesus' response is, "Rather, blessed are those who hear the word of God and observe it." These sayings affirm that it is not blood ties that bind a person to Jesus, but rather obedient response to the word he proclaims. Luke, unlike Mark (3:31-34), leaves open the possibility that Jesus' blood kin can also become disciples. Indeed, in his first two chapters Luke portrays Jesus' mother as one who hears God's word and responds with obedience (1:26-38, 46-56; 2:19, 51). And in Acts Jesus' mother and siblings are present along with the Twelve and all the disciples who are in the upper room awaiting the Spirit given at Pentecost (Acts 1:14).

Read with these previous sayings, v. 26 does not advocate solitary individualism, but rather that a disciple become imbedded in a new family of followers of Jesus. This "surrogate family" of disciples transcends normal categories of birth, class, race, gender, education, and economic and political status. For those born into disadvantaged social positions, an invitation into a fictive family group with those in positions of power would be good news, indeed. But the summons becomes a very difficult one for anyone who is well-connected. For elites it is a very costly decision to give up their social networks and associate with the mixed group of disciples.[4]

The saying in v. 26 insists that a disciple be wholly attached to Jesus and his mission, so that everything else is secondary. Although whole households may become believers together,[5]

[4] B. Malina and R. Rohrbaugh, *Social Science Commentary on the Synoptic Gospels* (Minneapolis: Fortress, 1992) 335–36.

[5] Examples of such are profiled in Acts: Cornelius and his household at Joppa (10:2, 44-49; 11:14), Lydia and her household (16:15), Paul's jailer and his

becoming a disciple of Jesus can also result in divisions between family members, where "a father will be divided against his son and a son against his father, a mother against her daughter and a daughter against her mother, a mother-in-law against her daughter-in-law and a daughter-in-law against her mother-in-law" (Luke 12:53). Jesus is not advising his disciples to seek such division nor to feel hatred for their family members. To "hate" *(misein)* family in v. 26 connotes preferring them less to the family of disciples. It is as Matthew 10:37 renders it, "whoever loves father or mother more than me." This reflects the meaning of the Hebrew verb *śānē,* "to hate," which is, "to leave aside." In Genesis 29:31, for example, Leah is "unloved" (literally, "hated," *śěnû'â*) in comparison to Rachel. In Deuteronomy 21:15 love and hate are the terms used to express preference between two wives, "If a man with two wives loves one and dislikes (literally, "hates," *śěnû'â*) the other." What is expressed in 14:26 is the necessity for a disciple to place first allegiance with the family of disciples over that of their biological family.

A disciple who does not love his or her own family members and who does not recognize God's love revealed in those closest at hand will not very well be able to share that divine love with outsiders. Many disciples are called to remain with their families and to proclaim God's love in that familiar context. Such a story is found in Luke 8:26-39, where a man healed of many demons wants to accompany Jesus on his mission. Instead, Jesus directs him, "Return home and declare how much God has done for you" (8:39). Some disciples are called to leave behind their own world to become missionaries to peoples of other lands (Luke 9:1-6; 10:1-12). Luke 14:26 advises all disciples, whatever their mode of spreading the gospel, that attachment to Jesus will sometimes take one away from beloved family members. But Jesus also assured his disciples, "There is no one who has given up house or wife or brothers or sisters or parents or children for the sake of the kingdom of God who will not receive back an overabundant return in this present age and eternal life in the age to come" (Luke 18:29-30).

_____

household at Philippi (16:31-34), and Crispus and his household in Corinth (18:8).

In both sayings in Luke 14:26 and 18:29, Luke cast the audience as male disciples who leave wives behind. The Matthean parallel to Luke 14:26 advises against loving father or mother, son or daughter more than Jesus (Matt 10:37). The Markan parallel to Luke 18:29 lists houses, brothers, sisters, mother, father, children, and lands (Mark 10:29) as what one might leave behind for the sake of the gospel. While Luke clearly depicts women as disciples (e.g., Mary Magdalene, Joanna, Susanna, and the Galilean women in Luke 8:1-3; 23:44-56; 24:1-12; Tabitha, whom he specifically calls *mathētria*, "disciple," in Acts 9:36; Lydia in Acts 16; Prisca in Acts 18), he shows his androcentric bias in these sayings on discipleship.[6] There are many traditions in the early Church of women disciples who did leave behind their husbands or refused to marry so as to go out and preach the gospel.[7]

CARRYING ONE'S CROSS (v. 27)

The saying in v. 26 about willingness to break ties with family concludes on the sober note that discipleship can demand one's very life. That martyrdom was a real possibility for Jesus' disciples is attested in Acts 7:54-60, where Stephen becomes the first of Jesus' followers to be put to death. He is followed by James (Acts 12:2) and a host of other men and women throughout the Christian centuries.

The next verse (v. 27) must be read in light of the final phrase of v. 26. The exhortation to carry one's own cross is not a reference to bearing with the ordinary trials and tribulations of daily life. That is the lot of any human being. Jesus' admonition refers specifically to the persecution one experiences for being his follower. To "follow" or to "come after" Jesus is part of his

---

[6] See further Barbara Reid, *Choosing the Better Part? Women in the Gospel of Luke* (Collegeville: The Liturgical Press, 1996); Jane Schaberg, "Luke," *The Women's Bible Commentary*, ed. Carol Newsom and Sharon Ringe (rev. ed.; Louisville: Westminster/John Knox, 1998) 363–80.

[7] See Sheila E. McGinn, "The Acts of Thecla," in *Searching the Scriptures*, ed. Elisabeth Schüssler Fiorenza (vol. 2; New York: Crossroad, 1994) 800–28; Virginia Burrus, *Chastity as Autonomy: Women in the Stories of the Apocryphal Acts* (Lewiston, N.Y.: Edwin Mellen, 1987); Bonnie Bowman Thurston, *The Widows: A Women's Ministry in the Early Church* (Minneapolis: Fortress, 1989).

initial invitation to the fishermen in 5:11, to Levi in 5:27, and to a rich official in 18:18-23. At the outset of the journey to Jerusalem there are three potential disciples, two who offer to follow, and one whom Jesus invites to do so. It is unclear whether they actually do or whether their concerns about a place to lay their heads and about family ties are insurmountable (9:57-62). The invitation to follow Jesus means following him all the way to crucifixion, as do the women "who had followed him from Galilee" (23:49). Some may be asked not only to witness and testify to Jesus' crucifixion, but to undergo the same fate themselves, that is, to carry his or her own cross.[8]

While one's physical life may not be demanded in martyrdom, the cost of discipleship for any follower is life itself. To belong to the family of Jesus means that every aspect of life is taken up into this new existence. Relationships, possessions, occupation, time—everything in one's life is directed toward Christ and the community of believers. If the demand seems impossible, v. 27 assures disciples that Jesus goes before them, leading the way through death to new life.

TOWER BUILDER (vv. 28-30) AND WARRING KING (vv. 31-32)

The two parables at the center of the difficult sayings on discipleship, unlike many of the parables that have an unexpected twist, are straightforward bits of common sense wisdom. Both make the same point: anyone who begins an enterprise will first weigh the cost to complete it before starting. Both examples come from a world of power and privilege. The first envisions a landowner who would build a watchtower to guard his house and land, as the vineyard owner in Mark 12:1. Or perhaps the parable calls to mind the palace Herod built in Jerusalem with its three towers named for his friend Hippicus, his brother Phasael, and his wife Mariamne. The parable emphasizes not only the imprudence of beginning

---

[8] On crucifixion in the Greco-Roman world see Martin Hengel, *Crucifixion* (Philadelphia: Fortress, 1977). See further Josephine Massyngbaerde Ford, *Redeemer, Friend and Mother: Salvation in Antiquity and in the Gospel of John* (Minneapolis: Fortress, 1997) 50–72, who explores crucifixion of women as well as of men and its significance.

something that the builder cannot complete, but also the shame incurred when onlookers laugh at his incomplete project. It would be a foolish waste to put valuable resources into a partial tower; only a finished turret serves the purpose. The second image is of a king at war who needs to strategize whether his troops are sufficient to successfully engage his opponent. If his resources are only half what he needs he would obviously not go forward to battle. He would send a delegation to ask for conditions of peace. The same phrase, *ta pros eirēnē*, is used here as in Luke 19:42, where Jesus weeps over the city Jerusalem because it does not know the "things that make for peace" *(NRSV)*. As Luke makes clear, it is Jesus who brings peace, through his ministry of healing, forgiveness, and reconciling—a peace that is of a different nature than that of the emperor's *pax romana.*[9]

The parables, by using images of powerful people with expendable resources at their disposal, sharpen the focus of the previous sayings on discipleship to direct them to those potential disciples who are well-to-do and powerful. For elites the cost of discipleship is higher in terms of loss of honor, status, prestige, privilege, and social networks. This must be considered before anyone begins the journey with Jesus. Moreover, for any who are attracted to follow Jesus, the parables affirm that entering into the community of believers is not something that can be done casually or occasionally. It is not a social club that people can attend when it suits them. It will cost everything—a price that must be considered before embarking on the way of Jesus.

RENOUNCING POSSESSIONS (v. 33)

A familiar Lukan theme sounds one more time in this concluding saying, and reinforces the sense that these sayings are directed primarily to the richer disciples. In the Third Gospel the theme that possessions can pose an obstacle to discipleship is a constantly recurring one. Other sayings about possessions are found in Luke 12:15, where Jesus warns, "Take care to guard

---

[9] Luke 1:79; 2:14, 29; 7:50; 8:48; 10:5, 6; 12:51; 19:38, 42; 24:36.

against all greed, for though one may be rich, one's life does not consist of possessions." In 12:33 he counsels, "Sell your belongings and give alms." The first fishermen called to be disciples leave everything behind to follow Jesus (5:11) as does Levi (5:28). The rich ruler, however, seems unable to do so (18:23). Zaccheus is exemplary for giving half his belongings to the poor (19:8). The Galilean women use their financial resources to support the mission of Jesus (8:3). In Acts 2:43-47 and 4:32-37 the community of believers sell their possessions and goods and distribute them to all, as any have need. Letting go of possessions has as its aim both to free the heart from being centered on them (12:34) and to ensure that there are none in need while others are sated (Acts 4:34).

PREACHING POSSIBILITIES

The parables of the tower builder and the warring king are simple enough, but the sayings on discipleship that surround them are some of the most radical in the gospel. They are not difficult to understand, but are immensely demanding to practice. The preacher will want to be wary of compromising the gospel message by spiritualizing it or interpreting the hard sayings in a metaphorical way. The gospel says that to be a disciple of Jesus, one must be willing to let go of what one values most: familial relationships, possessions, and even one's own life. Jesus names three of the strongest attachments that would be difficult for anyone to leave aside when called into the community of believers and to participate in the mission of Jesus. The cost is particularly high for any who have riches, power, privilege, and status.

To a congregation that is well-to-do, a preacher may speak words that invite them to reflect on what has been the cost of their identification with the Christian community. Have their works of seeking justice and giving alms cost them property or reputation or possibilities for advancement? What role do their possessions play in their lives as disciples? Are they obstacles to deeper discipleship or are they put to use as ministerial resources? Has the congregation made efforts to include those most disadvantaged so that their family of disciples reflects the diversity of persons with whom Jesus associated? Where the answers to such questions are affirmative, the preacher can offer a word of encouragement to continue such efforts. Alternatively, a word of challenge to consider the further cost of completing the endeavor on which they have embarked may be in order.

Concrete examples of how these counsels are acted upon are found in the Pauline letters that are paired with this gospel in the Lectionary. On the Twenty-third Sunday in Ordinary Time the second reading from Philemon (9-10, 12-17) offers the example of Paul, who is suffering imprisonment for the sake of the gospel. Moreover, he speaks to Philemon about receiving the slave Onesimus as a brother in the Lord—a specific illustration of how the new family of God crosses lines of status and power, making all members brothers and sisters in Christ, children of the same God. On Wednesday of the Thirty-first Week of Ordinary Time in Year II, Paul's letter to the Philippians (2:12-18) speaks of how he is "poured out as a libation upon the sacrificial service of your faith," another way of articulating "carrying his own cross."

In a congregation where the members are economically disadvantaged or where they are victimized by systems of domination, there is a danger of using the sayings about renunciation of possessions and about carrying one's cross to reinforce passive acceptance of injustice. While it is important for Christians to find meaning and comfort by identifying their present suffering with that of Jesus, when injustice is the source of suffering, the preacher is compelled to offer a word of challenge to such. In this case the second parable might offer an image of how the community who is in a disadvantaged position, with fewer resources, might strategize how to confront the one who has double the resources and negotiate for "what makes for peace," that is, for just distribution so that all may live peaceably as brothers and sisters in the family of God.

CHAPTER FIFTEEN

Joyful Finding
(Luke 15:1-32)

Twenty-fourth Sunday of Ordinary Time (Luke 15:1-32)

Feast of the Sacred Heart (Luke 15:3-7)

Thursday, Week 31 of Ordinary Time (Luke 15:1-10)

¹ *Tax collectors and sinners were all drawing near to listen to Jesus,*
² *but the Pharisees and scribes began to complain, saying,*
    "This man welcomes sinners and eats with them."
³ *So to them he addressed this parable.*
⁴ *"What man among you having a hundred sheep and losing one of them*
    would not leave the ninety-nine in the desert
    and go after the lost one until he finds it?
⁵ *And when he does find it,*
    he sets it on his shoulders with great joy
    ⁶ *and, upon his arrival home,*
    he calls together his friends and neighbors and says to them,
    'Rejoice with me because I have found my lost sheep.'
⁷ *I tell you, in just the same way*
    there will be more joy in heaven over one sinner who repents
    than over ninety-nine righteous people
    who have no need of repentance.

⁸ *"Or what woman having ten coins and losing one*
    would not light a lamp and sweep the house,
    searching carefully until she finds it?
⁹ *And when she does find it,*
    she calls together her friends and neighbors
    and says to them,
    'Rejoice with me because I have found the coin that I lost.'

[10] *In just the same way, I tell you,*
   there will be rejoicing among the angels of God
   over one sinner who repents."

[11] *Then he said,*
   "A man had two sons, [12] *and the younger son said to his father,*
   'Father, give me the share of your estate that should come to me.'
   So the father divided the property between them.
[13] *After a few days, the younger son collected all his belongings*
   and set off to a distant country
   where he squandered his inheritance on a life of dissipation.
[14] *When he had freely spent everything,*
   a severe famine struck that country,
   and he found himself in dire need.
[15] *So he hired himself out to one of the local citizens*
   who sent him to his farm to tend the swine.
[16] *And he longed to eat his fill of the pods on which the swine fed,*
   but nobody gave him any.
[17] *Coming to his senses he thought,*
   'How many of my father's hired workers
   have more than enough food to eat,
   but here am I, dying from hunger.
[18] *I shall get up and go to my father and I shall say to him,*
   "Father, I have sinned against heaven and against you.
[19] *I no longer deserve to be called your son;*
   treat me as you would treat one of your hired workers."'
[20] *So he got up and went back to his father.*
   While he was still a long way off,
   his father caught sight of him,
   and was filled with compassion.
   He ran to his son, embraced him and kissed him.
[21] *His son said to him,*
   'Father, I have sinned against heaven and against you;
   I no longer deserve to be called your son.'
[22] *But his father ordered his servants,*
   'Quickly bring the finest robe and put it on him;
   put a ring on his finger and sandals on his feet.
[23] *Take the fattened calf and slaughter it.*
   Then let us celebrate with a feast,
      [24] *because this son of mine was dead, and has come to life again;*
   he was lost, and has been found.'
   Then the celebration began.
[25] *Now the older son had been out in the field*

and, on his way back, as he neared the house,
he heard the sound of music and dancing.
[26] *He called one of the servants and asked what this might mean.*
[27] *The servant said to him,*
'Your brother has returned
and your father has slaughtered the fattened calf
because he has him back safe and sound.'
[28] *He became angry,*
and when he refused to enter the house,
his father came out and pleaded with him.
[29] *He said to his father in reply,*
'Look, all these years I served you
and not once did I disobey your orders;
yet you never gave me even a young goat to feast on with my friends.
[30] *But when your son returns*
who swallowed up your property with prostitutes,
for him you slaughter the fattened calf.'
[31] *He said to him,*
'My son, you are here with me always;
everything I have is yours.
[32] *But now we must celebrate and rejoice,*
because your brother was dead and has come to life again;
he was lost and has been found.'"

A BELOVED STORY

The frequency with which the lost and found parables from Luke 15 appear in the Lectionary attests to their perennial attraction. All three parables convey a similar message but with different images. This chapter will focus on the first two parables in the trilogy. See above, chapter five, for comments on the parable of the father and his two lost sons (vv. 11-32).

LUKAN LITERARY CONTEXT

The narrative setting for these parables continues to be the great journey to Jerusalem. In the previous chapter Jesus had been dining at the home of one of the leading Pharisees (14:1). There Jesus told pointed parables about places at table (14:7-14) and about unconventional guest lists (14:15-24).[1] Jesus not only

---

[1] See above, chap. 13, on Luke 14:7-14 and below, chap. 26, on Luke 14:15-24.

speaks about eating with people who are poor and marginalized, but he is also portrayed as doing so. The complaint of the Pharisees that Jesus eats with tax collectors and sinners (15:1) has previously been voiced in 5:30, where Jesus attends a banquet given by Levi, the tax collector. Similarly, in 7:34 Jesus confronts those who have labeled him a friend of tax collectors and sinners.[2] In another episode Jesus receives a forgiven sinner at a dinner given by Simon, a Pharisee (7:36-50),[3] and is likewise criticized. It is to those religious leaders who complain about his inclusive table practices that Jesus addresses the parables about the lost and found.[4] As usual, it is the Pharisees who provide a foil to Jesus.[5]

PURITY AND FOOD

It is commonly thought that Jesus' table practice of eating with tax collectors and sinners was part of his mission to free the common people from the oppressive Pharisaic purity regulations, especially those involving meals. However, the Jewish purity laws did not for the most part affect table companionship. Purity rules deal with system and order, defining boundaries and anomalies. The intent is that Israel, by maintaining its boundaries, reflects the holiness of God by its social wholeness and completeness. The purity regulations found in the books of Leviticus and Numbers are the concrete ways in which Israel strives to be holy as God is holy (Lev 11:44). Ritual impurity is incurred in any number of ways: e.g., from emissions of bodily fluids, touching a corpse, or eating unclean foods. When a person becomes ritually impure the process for cleansing usually involves a time lapse, ritual washing, and for some types of uncleanness, sacrificial offering.[6] It is important to remember that

---

[2] See below, chap. 23, on Luke 7:31-35.

[3] See above, chap. 8, on Luke 7:36–8:3.

[4] The parables of the lost coin and the lost sons (15:8-32) are unique to Luke. The parable of the lost sheep comes from Q and has a parallel in Matthew 18:12-14 as well as in *Gos.Thom.* §107. In Matthew the parable is directed to Jesus' disciples, not to Pharisees and scribes. It is part of the ecclesiastical discourse.

[5] See above, pp. 159–60, on Luke's literary portrayal of the Pharisees.

[6] See "Clean and Unclean: Understanding Rules of Purity" in Bruce J. Malina, *The New Testament World: Insights from Cultural Anthropology* (rev. ed.;

most Jews of Jesus' day were ritually impure most of the time. The only time that it was essential to be ritually pure was when entering the Temple. It is for this reason that regulations for priestly purity were more stringent.

As for table practices, notions of purity regulated both the food eaten and the persons with whom one eats. With regard to the food, there were three ways in which it would be classified as clean or unclean: (1) certain foods were automatically declared unclean (Lev 11:1-47; Deut 14:3-21); (2) preparation of the food needed to be done in a certain way; (3) tithes needed to be paid on them.[7] There were certain Jews, *haberim*, who voluntarily took on themselves stricter ritual observance and more rigid tithes on food (e.g., as the Pharisee depicted in Luke 18:12). This resulted in their shunning table companionship with those outside their group. Their concern was not about the morality of such persons, but the avoidance of eating untithed food. The *haberim* represented a very small percentage of the Jewish population. Though some Pharisees belonged to this group, it is doubtful that they should be entirely identified with them. Once again, the Pharisees in Luke 15:1 are a caricature for those whose vision of the reign of God is opposed to that of Jesus.

EATING WITH SINNERS

The charge that Jesus received sinners and ate with them had to do, then, with his attitude toward sinners, not with his failure to avoid association at table with people who did not observe strict purity regulations about food. At meals, likes eat with likes; meals are means of celebrating group cohesion. Jesus' eating with sinners signifies that God extends an invitation to them for forgiveness and for membership in the covenanted people.

Those who are considered "sinners" include those who commit an individual wrong act; those who live without regard

---

Louisville: Westminster/John Knox, 1993) 149–83.

[7] Jerome H. Neyrey, "Ceremonies in Luke-Acts: The Case of Meals and Table Fellowship," in *The Social World of Luke-Acts*, ed. Jerome H. Neyrey (Peabody, Mass.: Hendrickson, 1991) 365.

for the will of God and consequently sin routinely;[8] and those caught in a power opposed to God, such as sickness or demon possession.[9] In Judaism sin could be inadvertent "missing the mark," offenses for which ritual sacrifices are able to atone. There is also willful rebellion against God's covenant. In this case repentance and conversion of heart are necessary. The debate in John 9:24-34 over whether or not Jesus was a sinner rests on the notion that flagrant disregard for the Law makes one a sinner. The same story also reflects the notion that sickness or disability is a punishment for sin. Jesus' response to his disciples' question about who sinned—the man born blind or his parents—clearly ruptures the connection between sin and suffering (John 9:2-3). Certain professions were considered sinful because they opened the way by which their practitioners could transgress the law with ease.[10]

Tax collectors as a whole were considered sinful because they were notoriously greedy and corrupt. There is a distinction between tax collectors and toll collectors. Direct taxes, such as the land tax and the poll tax were under the direct supervision of Herod Antipas in Galilee and the Roman prefects and procurators in Judea. Collectors of these taxes were bureaucrats who were accountable to the government. The *telōnai* of the gospels, however, were toll collectors in charge of indirect taxes, such as tolls, imposts, customs, and tariffs. These positions were leased out by contract and the amount to be collected had to be paid in advance. The toll collector had to then secure that amount and make some profit for his own survival. Because the system was open to extortion and greed, the Talmud most often groups toll collectors with robbers.[11] The reason for hatred of toll collectors

---

[8] This would include Gentiles, who, since they did not know the Law, could not possibly keep it, and therefore lived continually without regard for the Law.

[9] E. P. Sanders, "Sin, Sinners," *ABD* 6, 40–47; K. Rengstorf, *"hamartōlos,"* *TDNT* 1 (1964) 325–28.

[10] Joachim Jeremias, *Jerusalem in the Time of Jesus* (Philadelphia: Fortress, 1969) 303–12.

[11] See John R. Donahue, "Tax Collectors and Sinners: An Attempt at Identification," *CBQ* 33 (1971) 39–61; William R. Herzog II, *The Parables as Subversive Speech* (Louisville: Westminster/John Knox, 1994) 187–89. See below, chap. 20, on the Pharisee and the toll collector in Luke 18:9-18.

is more for their thievery than the fact that they are quislings of Rome or that their work makes them ritually impure.

Luke, however, portrays toll collectors in a very positive light. They are among those who come to be baptized by John (Luke 3:12; 7:29). That Luke knows their reputation for extortion is evident in John's directive, "Stop collecting more than what is prescribed" (3:13). Levi, the toll collector, leaves everything, follows Jesus, and hosts a great banquet for him (5:27-32). Zacchaeus, a chief toll collector, asserts that he does not defraud anyone and gives half his belongings to the poor (19:8). In one of Jesus' parables a toll collector is exemplary in his prayer (18:9-14).[12] Luke shows Jesus' practice of eating with toll collectors and sinners as a successful part of his missionary strategy.

What offended other Jews was that Jesus evidently offers forgiveness to sinners and admission into his community without making the normal demand of restitution and commitment to the law.[13] Jesus' offer of forgiveness was not novel: in Judaism one could always turn to God, repent, and be saved. Nor was Jesus' offense that he offered forgiveness to sinners before they performed acts of restoration and amended their way of life rather than vice versa. If Jesus were bringing people to repentance and to a life conformable to the Law, this theological distinction would not be such an offense as to evoke mortal hostility from other Jews. The novelty and offense of Jesus' message was his affirmation that sinners who heeded him would be included in the reign of God even though they did not repent by making restitution, sacrifice, and turning to obedience to the Law. Jesus' companionship with such people was a sign that God would save them, and implied, moreover, a claim to know whom God would include. Concrete examples of this are found in the stories of Levi (5:27-32) and Zacchaeus (19:1-10). Neither one is asked to relinquish his sinful profession. To the Pharisees and scribes who complained about Jesus' eating with Levi and a large crowd of tax collectors Jesus replies, "I have not come to call the righteous to repentance but

[12] See below, chap. 20, on Luke 18:9-14.
[13] E. P. Sanders, *Jesus and Judaism* (Philadelphia: Fortress, 1985) 174–211. See also David A. Neale, *None But the Sinners: Religious Categories in the Gospel of Luke* (JSNTSup 58; Sheffield: JSOT, 1991).

sinners" (5:32). Likewise, to Zacchaeus he says, "Today salvation has come to this house because this man too is a descendant of Abraham" (19:9). He then elaborates that he has come "to seek and to save what was lost" (19:10). The parables in Luke 15 offer one more illustration of such.

SEEKING A LOST SHEEP (vv. 4-7)

The first parable takes us into the world of shepherds and sheep. But it is not a gentle, bucolic story. The opening line would have been jarring to Pharisees and scribes. By asking, "What man among you . . . ?" Jesus invites the Pharisees and scribes to imagine themselves as the shepherd who loses the sheep. Although "shepherd" was a familiar metaphor for God (Psalm 23), and for religious leaders (Ezekiel 34), real shepherds were disdained. They were thought to be dishonest and thieving, leading their herds onto other people's land and pilfering the produce of the herd.[14] It is a shock for respected religious leaders to be asked to think of themselves as lowly shepherds.

The story begins with a shepherd who loses one sheep out of the hundred that are in his[15] care. Most probably a herd that size belongs to several members of his clan.[16] Or, if they all belong to one person, the owner is rich enough to hire the shepherd to do the dirty work of herding. In either case, the shepherd is answerable to others if any sheep is lost. The parable is framed in such a way that the expected answer to the question, "Wouldn't you leave the others and go after the lost one?" is an emphatic, "of course!" The point of the story is not about putting ninety-nine others in danger for the sake of retrieving one. A flock that size would ordinarily have more than one shepherd,[17] and the audience imagines the others will care for the ninety-nine. What the story presumes is that a sheep is

---

[14] Jeremias, *Jerusalem in the Time of Jesus,* 303–05, 310, cites examples from the Mishnah that list herdsmen among the despised trades.

[15] It is also common for girls and women to engage in shepherding. However, the masculine verb endings in vv. 4-6 imply that the shepherd is male.

[16] Kenneth E. Bailey, *Poet and Peasant: A Literary-Cultural Approach to the Parables in Luke* (Grand Rapids: Eerdmans, 1976) 148.

[17] Ibid., 149.

so valuable that it would be unthinkable not to go in search of a lost one.

The parable also makes it clear that it is the shepherd who expends great effort to retrieve the lost sheep. Traversing the craggy hillsides of Palestine in search of the lost sheep is no easy task, particularly if it has taken refuge in a cave, where it might not be plainly visible. And though the sheep may hear the shepherd call out to it, if it has become frightened it will not be able to get up and go to the shepherd. All it may do is bleat until the shepherd finds it. When the shepherd does find the lost sheep, he then hoists it up and sets it on his shoulders, hauling it all the way back home. It is no small thing to lug a seventy-pound sheep over rocky, hilly terrain—and he does it with great joy!

DOUBLE JOY

Finding the lost sheep is only half the joy. Upon arrival home the shepherd calls together all his friends and neighbors to rejoice with him. Both the losing and the finding are a communal affair. The sheep likely belongs to them all; its loss would be loss to all; its gain is profit for all. The joy in finding is replicated in the joyful community celebration of restoration of the lost. The parable ends by comparing the joy of this community to that of the great joy in heaven over one sinner who repents.

REPENTANCE

There is a disjunction, however, between the contours of the parable and the notion of repentance. The verb *metanoeō*, "to repent," (v. 7) means, literally, to turn, to change one's mind.[18] In

---

[18] BAGD, μετανοέω, 511–12. This word is a particular favorite of Luke and is often inserted by him into his source. He alters Mark's conclusion of the call of Levi, so that Jesus declares as his mission, "I have not come to call the righteous to repentance but sinners" (Luke 5:32). The Matthean parallel of Luke 15:7 (Matt 18:14) has no mention of repentance. Warnings about repentance appear in other passages unique to Luke: 13:3, 5; 16:30. In Luke 17:3-4, unlike the corresponding sayings in Matthew 18:15, 21-22, repentance is a condition for forgiveness of one's brother or sister. Finally, the concluding instruction of the Lukan Jesus to his disciples as he is about to ascend, is to proclaim "repentance and forgiveness

the story, however, the lost one does not do the turning or initiate the change. It is the shepherd who does all the work of finding, lifting, and carrying home the lost one. The parable is presenting an image of how God, like a shepherd, pays the great cost to bring back the lost. Repentance, then, takes on a new definition. It begins with God offering to the sinner the free gift of forgiveness and restoration to the community. For the sinner it means being able to accept this kind of God, to enter into the joy of being found, and to then live from that grace.[19]

SEEKING A LOST COIN (vv. 8-10)[20]

The second parable has the same structure and tells the very same story as that of the shepherd and the sheep.[21] In both stories the main character loses, searches, and finds the lost object, and then celebrates with friends and neighbors. Both conclude with a comparison to the heavenly joy over a repentant sinner.

---

of sins" (Luke 24:47). Repentance is a particular theme of the Third Evangelist, which he inserts into the tradition wherever forgiveness appears.

[19] Kenneth E. Bailey, *Finding the Lost: Cultural Keys to Luke 15* (Concordia Scholarship Today; St. Louis: Concordia, 1992); *Poet and Peasant*, 144–56; "Psalm 23 and Luke 15: A Vision Expanded," *IBS* 12 (1990) 54–71.

[20] See also, Barbara E. Reid, *Choosing the Better Part? Women in the Gospel of Luke* (Collegeville: The Liturgical Press, 1996) 179–89.

[21] Susan Durber ("The Female Reader of the Parables of the Lost," *JSNT* 45 [1992] 59–78) sees subtle but significant differences from the parable of the lost sheep. The shepherd's rejoicing is compared with "greater joy in heaven" (v. 7) while the woman's with "joy among the angels of God" (v. 10). For her this circumlocution signals that the woman is less easily compared with God. The address in v. 4 is, "If one of you . . . " whereas in v. 8 it is, "if a woman . . . ." She sees the reader invited to take the position of the shepherd, but not that of the woman. The woman is just a woman, someone different from the reader. On this point, Kenneth Bailey (*Finding the Lost: Cultural Keys to Luke 15* [Concordia Scholarship Today; St. Louis: Concordia, 1992] 93–94) also recognizes the difference between the addressees in vv. 4 and 8, but remarks that in a patriarchal Middle Eastern culture a speaker cannot compare a male audience to a woman without giving offense. But is that any more offensive than comparing religious leaders to shepherds? Durber concludes that women discover that they must either read as men or admit that they are excluded. Her cautions are well taken. However, I propose that there is a third option: recognizing the male perspective of the text, women can read against its intent, and unleash its liberating potential for inclusivity.

Despite these obvious similarities, it is startling that some commentators depict the woman searching for the lost coin as miserly[22] or her action as trivial, important only to her women friends.[23] Rather, it portrays a poor woman[24] who goes to great lengths to find one drachma, one day's wage, because it is extremely valuable. For people living at subsistence level, one drachma means the difference between eating for a day or going hungry. Women in the first-century Mediterranean world exercised control over the private sphere of the home and derived support from female networks. The woman in the parable has charge of the household finances. Her power and status derive from maintaining orderly household management.[25]

Another interpretation that has become popular is that the lost coin was part of a set of decorative coins on a bridal headdress or a necklace. This approach makes the coin valuable because it is part of the woman's dowry, or because the whole necklace loses its value if it is missing one coin. This imaginative interpretation, however, comes from practices of modern nomadic Bedouin women, not Jewish women of the first century. Of the myriad coins that have been unearthed in excavations, none has yielded evidence that they were used in this decorative way in antiquity. Moreover, this line of interpretation assumes that there must be a special motive for the woman's search. The point of the story is that the woman has lost a valuable coin and she expends every effort to find it, just as the shepherd who loses the prized sheep, and the father whose precious sons are lost.

Like the shepherd in the previous parable, the woman goes to great lengths to seek[26] the lost. Since houses in first-century Palestine were dark, with small, high windows, she has to use precious oil to light a lamp for her search. Floors of houses were

---

[22] Joseph A. Fitzmyer, *The Gospel According to Luke* (AB28A; Garden City, N.Y.: Doubleday, 1981) 1080.

[23] The nouns *philas*, "friends," and *geitonas*, "neighbors" in v. 9 are feminine.

[24] Susan Praeder, *The Word in Women's Worlds: Four Parables* (Zacchaeus Studies, New Testament; Wilmington: Glazier, 1988) 42.

[25] Carol Scherstsen LaHurd, "Rediscovering the Lost Women in Luke 15," *BTB* 24 (1994) 66–76.

[26] In v. 8 the verb *zēteō*, "seek," is the same used in 19:10, were Jesus tells Zacchaeus he has come to seek the lost in order to save them.

usually of packed dirt. Some were paved with stones, between which were cracks where a coin could easily lodge. She expends much energy in sweeping the house and searching carefully in the cracks and corners. Like the shepherd in vv. 3-7 and the father in vv. 11-32, she extends herself greatly to find the lost and restore it. Her celebration with friends and neighbors similarly replicates the joy of heaven over a sinner who repents.

GODLY SHEPHERD AND HOUSEHOLDER

These two parables present images of God that both serve to justify Jesus' inclusive table practices and pose a challenge to religious leaders. Like God who shepherds the flock with great care (Psalm 23), so should religious leaders go out in search of the lost. And like Woman Wisdom who seeks out the simple ones among all humans (Prov 1:20-23; 8:1-5) and invites all to her banquet (Prov 9:1-11), Jesus, by eating with toll collectors and sinners, reaches out to the lost in the same way, to bring them to restored life. Implied is a critique of Pharisees and scribes for not acting thus, akin to that of the prophet Ezekiel (34:1-16), who had harsh words for Israel's "shepherds" who cared only for their own comfort and not the good of the people. Furthermore, in order to be good shepherds of God's flock, they needed first to be able to accept the kind of costly love God offers them. But thinking themselves righteous (*dikaiois*, v. 7),[27] they do not see themselves as needing what God has to offer them through Jesus.[28]

PREACHING POSSIBILITIES

All three parables in Luke 15 follow the same contours and invite a similar response. Any one of the three provides rich fare. The preacher might do best to develop only one of them as the central image. Since the first and third tend to be the more

[27] In Luke 16:15 Jesus charges the Pharisees with justifying themselves before people while God knows their hearts. In Luke 18:14 the toll collector rather than the Pharisee returns home from the temple justified.

[28] In Matthew the parable (18:12-14) is directed to Jesus' disciples to instruct them on the kind of leaders they must be.

frequently used, and because of the great need for retrieval of female images of God, the homilist might consider using the images of the second parable as the focus. It is still difficult for many contemporary Christians to embrace a female image of God, even though there are ample instances in the Scriptures. In Deuteronomy 32:18 and Isaiah 42:14 God is portrayed as a mother giving birth. Isaiah speaks of God's tenderness as that of a mother consoling her child (Isa 49:15; 66:13). Isaiah 66:9 and Psalm 22:10-11 portray God as a midwife, drawing Israel forth from the womb. The Psalmist talks of God's care for humans like that of a mother eagle for her brood (Ps 91:4). Jesus uses this same image in Luke 13:34 to express his care for Jerusalem. He also tells a parable about a woman mixing dough (Luke 13:20-21) to speak of God's activity in the realm of God.[29] By entering into the figurative world of the parable of the woman searching for the lost coin, the preacher can invite both female and male believers to expand their repertoire of God images and more fully apprehend the divine mystery. The woman seeking the lost coin is a metaphor that is equally apt for speaking of God as is "shepherd" or "father."

These parables are both comforting and challenging. For those who feel lost, the parables offer immense relief at being found by God who is willing to expend so much effort to bring back any who are lost. From the perspective of the one who is in trouble, all that is necessary as a first step—which is often the hardest—is to be willing to accept such gratuitous love and let oneself be embraced by God's great tender arms. It lifts a huge burden when it is not up to the sinner to put things right or to find one's own way back. For those in need of healing and forgiveness, the preacher can help move the congregation into letting go of trying to earn reconciliation and to abandon themselves into God's searching mercy. On the Twenty-fourth Sunday of Ordinary Time the second reading from 1 Timothy

[29] See further Sallie McFague, *Models of God: Theology for an Ecological, Nuclear Age* (Philadelphia: Fortress, 1987); Elizabeth Johnson, *She Who Is: The Mystery of God in Feminist Theological Discourse* (New York: Crossroad, 1992); Rosemary Radford Ruether, *Sexism and God-Talk* (Boston: Beacon, 1983); Gail Ramshaw, *God Beyond Gender* (Minneapolis: Fortress, 1995); Sandra Schneiders, *Women and the Word* (New York: Paulist, 1986).

(1:12-17) also speaks eloquently of God's immense grace and mercy toward one who was a sinner. And while the first reading from Exodus (32:7-11, 13-14) at first portrays God as wrathful and wanting to inflict punishment on Israel for its sin, Moses invokes God's unchanging gracious promises, which causes God to relent in mercy. On Thursday of the Thirty-first Week of Ordinary Time in Year II when the first reading is from Philippians 3:3-8a, Paul is portrayed as a perfect example of a leader in the Church who was blameless in righteousness based on the Law, but for whom all that became nothing when he accepted the free gift of righteousness from God through faith in Christ. He is the perfect counterpart to the Pharisees in the gospel, as he forsakes his Pharisaic observance for discipleship with Christ.

For those who are leaders, or for a congregation that is complacent about their own situation, the preacher might emphasize the need to actively search out those who are missing from the community, for whatever reason, and become catalysts in their restoration to the community. The fact that some are lost is not only tragic for the individual, but for the whole community that remains incomplete without them. Just as the joy in the parable is shared by all the friends and neighbors, so the restoration of any who have been alienated is a cause of communal celebration. On the Feast of the Sacred Heart, Luke 15:3-7 is paired with Ezekiel 34:11-16, which reinforces the image of God as shepherd who cares well for the sheep and seeks out the lost, in contrast to Israel's leaders who tend to their own interests while the people languish. On Thursday of the Thirty-first Week of Ordinary Time in Year I when these first two parables are linked with Romans 14:7-12, the emphasis is on the accountability of how one responds to the graciousness of God.

By the time Luke was writing, it is probable that he was not so concerned with what constituted Jesus' offensive table practice in the eyes of other Jews of his day. Rather, Luke has in mind the tensions of his own day surrounding table companionship. As a Gentile Christian, writing for communities that were a mix of Gentile and Jewish Christians, with Gentiles increasingly becoming the majority, his concern was to help settle struggles between the two components. In his second volume, in Acts 15, he recounts some of the difficulties in the early Church over dietary regulations and how they came to be resolved. In Luke's communities the parables that vindicated Jesus' practice of eating with sinners would have been understood as justification for Jewish Christians eating with Gentile Christians who did not adopt the dietary practices of Judaism. While this issue is long settled for contemporary Christians, there are yet many other sources of division that become evident when we gather at the eucharistic table. The parables in Luke 15 provide opportunity for the preacher to address those and to help move the hearers to greater inclusivity.

CHAPTER SIXTEEN

Rewriting the Script
(Luke 16:1-13)

Twenty-fifth Sunday of Ordinary Time

Friday of the Thirty-first Week of Ordinary Time
(Luke 16:1-8)

[Jesus said to his disciples,]
¹"A rich man had a steward
who was reported to him for squandering his property.
² He summoned him and said,
*   'What is this I hear about you?*
* Prepare a full account of your stewardship,*
*   because you can no longer be my steward.'*
³ The steward said to himself, 'What shall I do,
*   now that my master is taking the position of steward away from me?*
* I am not strong enough to dig and I am ashamed to beg.*
⁴ I know what I shall do so that,
*   when I am removed from the stewardship,*
*   they may welcome me into their homes.'*
⁵ He called in his master's debtors one by one.
* To the first he said,*
*   'How much do you owe my master?'*
⁶ He replied, 'One hundred measures of olive oil.'
* He said to him, 'Here is your promissory note.*
* Sit down and quickly write one for fifty.'*
⁷ Then to another he said, 'And you, how much do you owe?'
* He replied, 'One hundred kors of wheat.'*
* The steward said to him, 'Here is your promissory note; write one for eighty.'*
⁸ And the master commended that dishonest steward for acting prudently.
* "For the children of this world*

> *are more prudent in dealing with their own generation*
> *than are the children of light.*
> [9] *I tell you, make friends for yourselves with dishonest wealth,*
>   *so that when it fails, you will be welcomed into eternal dwellings.*
> [10] *The person who is trustworthy in very small matters*
>   *is also trustworthy in great ones;*
>   *and the person who is dishonest in very small matters*
>   *is also dishonest in great ones.*
> [11] *If, therefore, you are not trustworthy with dishonest wealth,*
>   *who will trust you with true wealth?*
> [12] *If you are not trustworthy with what belongs to another,*
>   *who will give you what is yours?*
> [13] *No servant can serve two masters.*
>   *He will either hate one and love the other,*
>   *or be devoted to one and despise the other.*
>   *You cannot serve both God and mammon."*

ENDLESS INTERPRETIVE DIFFICULTIES

Almost every commentary or article on this parable begins by listing the difficulties in trying to interpret it. Each offers a slightly different solution. None resolves all the problems entirely. The questions about the parable include: How can a dishonest steward be praised by his master? Who is the master *(ho kyrios)* in v. 8? Is he Jesus? Or the rich man (v. 1) whom the steward calls "my master" *(ho kyrios mou)* in vv. 3 and 5? Is this about lost honor or lost income? What is the economic system presumed in the story? Does it concern usury? Or the steward's commission? What does *diaskorpizein* ("squandering") signify? Is the charge true or false? Who are the debtors? Is the master a sympathetic character or a villain? Is the steward someone to be emulated or is he a picaresque character designed to give us a chuckle in a comic story? Where does the original parable end?

EARLY HOMILY NOTES (vv. 8b-13)

The only thing about which there is substantial agreement among scholars is that the sayings at the conclusion of the parable are loosely linked to it and function like notes for four different homilies by the parable's first interpreters.[1] Most scholars regard v. 8a as the ending of the parable.[2] The subsequent verses are sayings attached by catchwords that provide four different variations on the theme of the right use of money. None really captures the import of the parable proper. Verse 8b is linked with v. 8a by the word *phronimōteroi/phronimōs*, "more prudent"/"prudently." It makes a dualistic contrast between "children of the light" and "children of this world," much like the phrases found in Qumran literature contrasting "children of light" and "children of darkness," dividing those inside the community from those outside.[3] The effect of this saying is to encourage Christians to be more shrewd than nonbelievers[4] in worldly dealings. But this kind of dualistic contrast does not fit the structure nor the story told in vv. 1-8a.

In v. 9 the catchword "dishonest" *(adikias)* is the link, as the same word is used to describe the steward in v. 8. Verse 9 is generally interpreted as an exhortation to use money shrewdly to one's own advantage to ensure a lasting place in the end. The reference to eternal dwellings brings in an eschatological flavor. But is the summons to accountability in the parable a reference to the apocalyptic crisis?[5] A further difficulty is how to

---

[1] C. H. Dodd, *The Parables of the Kingdom* (London: Collins, 1961) 26.

[2] A few dissent: e.g., Joachim Jeremias, *The Parables of Jesus* (rev. ed.; New York: Scribners, 1963) 45–47; John Dominic Crossan, *In Parables* (New York: Harper & Row, 1973) 109. These resolve the difficulty of Jesus seeming to approve dishonesty by interpreting v. 8a as the narrator's voice, not that of Jesus: *kyrios* in v. 8a refers to Jesus, not the rich man in the parable. However, when Luke changes speakers he usually gives a clearer signal, as in 12:35-37; 18:6-7; 19:12-28, as Bernard Brandon Scott has observed (*Hear Then the Parable* [Minneapolis: Fortress, 1989] 257–58). Moreover, there seems to be no conclusion to the parable if the ending is v. 7.

[3] See especially the Scroll of the War Rule concerning the war which the "sons of light" (i.e., the Qumran community) were to fight at the end of time against the "sons of darkness," i.e., the wicked as represented by all the heathen nations. The phrase "all the children of the world" is also found in the Damascus Document from Qumran (CD 20:34) to designate outsiders.

[4] In Luke *genea*, "generation" is usually pejorative: 7:31; 9:41; 11:29-32, 50-51; 17:25.

[5] John Kloppenborg, "The Dishonoured Master (Luke 16,1-8a)," *Bib* 70 (1989) 478–79, points out that nothing in the parable evokes an apocalyptic situation. The crisis is not precipitated by a returning master and does not need to be so allegorized in order to make it intelligible. The phrase *apodidonai ton logon,*

understand the meaning of "dishonest" *(adikias)* wealth. Is it wealth gained unjustly? In that case we face the difficulty of explaining how such an admonition could be consonant with Jesus' preaching in the rest of the gospel. More likely is that it means money that could lead to dishonesty. This latter theme is very much at home in Luke and points toward the evangelist's composition of the saying.

The next verses, 10-12, go in yet another direction with the catchword phrase, "dishonest wealth" (vv. 9, 11). In vv. 10-12 "dishonest," *adikios/adikǭ* (vv. 10, 11) is placed in antithetical parallelism with "faithful," *pistos* (vv. 10 [2x]) and *pistoi* (vv. 11, 12), and there is a wordplay with the verb "entrust," *pisteusei* (v. 11). New contrasts are introduced: small matters vs. great matters (v. 10); dishonest wealth vs. true wealth (v. 11); what belongs to another vs. what is your own (v. 12). The first is a simple proverb, but it does not really correspond to what happens in the parable. The second and third pick up on the movement toward eternal realities introduced in v. 9, making "true wealth" and "what is yours" references to imperishable treasure, akin to 12:33. This saying does not recognize, however, that the master praises the steward in v. 8a.[6]

Finally, the catchwords "master," and "mammon" link the final verse (v. 13) to the previous ones. Verse 13 constructs yet another contrast between serving God and serving mammon. The parable did not treat such a dilemma. This saying, from Q,[7] is consonant with Luke's concern about being rich toward God (12:21).[8] Luke consistently warns about becoming enslaved to money and he provides counter examples of wealthy believers who instead use their possessions to serve God, e.g., Levi, who gives a banquet for Jesus (5:29); the woman who uses her expensive ointment to anoint Jesus (7:36-50); the Galilean women who minister out of their monetary resources (8:3); Zacchaeus,

---

"give an account" (v. 2) is found in Matthew 12:36 and 1 Peter 4:5, but there the context clearly points to its eschatological meaning. See similar expressions in an apocalyptic context in Matthew 25:19 and Romans 14:12.

[6] As noted by Kloppenborg, "The Dishonoured Master," 475.

[7] This verse has a parallel in Matthew 6:24, where it is part of the Sermon on the Mount.

[8] See above, chap. 11.

who gives half his possessions to the poor (19:8); Barnabas, who donates to the community the proceeds from the sale of his property (Acts 4:36-37); and Mary, who makes her home available to the community in Jerusalem (Acts 12:12).

While all these appended sayings in vv. 8b-13 have verbal links with the parable, none of them elucidates the meaning of vv. 1-8a. All of them domesticate the parable, dulling its startling twist by reducing it to proverbial platitudes. The parable proper concludes in an unexpected manner in v. 8a and it still remains to try to ascertain what message it conveys.

PRUDENCE, NOT DISHONESTY

One way to resolve the difficulty of Jesus or the evangelist seeming to approve dishonesty in v. 8a is to see the master's praise not as an affirmation of his wrongdoing, but as approval of prudence in knowing what steps to take in a crisis.[9] But this line of interpretation fractures the narrative logic and creates a further difficulty by having Jesus affirm that a good end justifies unrighteous means. Moreover, if the steward's dishonesty is known, on what grounds would he be hoping that others would welcome him into their homes (v. 4)? If these others are thought to be potential employers, why would they hire someone known to mismanage his master's property? If they are fellow underlings, why would they jeopardize their own position vis-à-vis the rich man on whom they would be economically dependent?[10]

Another tack is to interpret the steward's actions as a prudent move, in which he was not guilty of any wrongdoing by reducing the amounts of the debts. The steward, who had been guilty of usury, prohibited by the Law,[11] when found out by his master, rectifies his wrongdoing by erasing the illegal interest, thus coming into conformity with the Law and bringing praise to the master.[12] Another variation is that the amount reduced by

[9] E.g., Alfred Plummer, *The Gospel According to S. Luke* (5th ed.; ICC; Edinburgh: T. & T. Clark, 1981) 380; Jeremias, *Parables,* 182; Dodd, *Parables of the Kingdom,* 17.

[10] John R. Donahue, *The Gospel in Parable* (Philadelphia: Fortress, 1988) 164.

[11] Deuteronomy 15:7-8; 23:20-21; Exodus 22:24; Leviticus 25:36-37.

[12] J.D.M. Derrett, "The Parable of the Unjust Steward," *NTS* 7 (1960-61) 198–219.

the servant is the interest he would take on the loans. Thus, he is not hurting his employer by reducing the debts, but is simply foregoing his own commission.[13] The parable, from this angle, shows that sometimes the "children of this world" act according to God's Law, even if they are brought to it out of an interest in self-preservation. Their prudence sets an example for Christians on the right use of possessions in view of the crisis of the kingdom preaching of Jesus.

Unresolved questions remain with this interpretation. It is not specified in the parable that the master and his steward are Jews. If the master is one of the "children of this world" (v. 8b) who is not an observer of Jewish Law, why would he not expect the usurious practices[14] and be anticipating the profit they would bring him? Would not a rich man be happy to have an industrious steward keep making more money for him? And how would the steward then get away with keeping the commission? Furthermore, how can we reconcile Jesus' approval of the steward's efforts to save himself when elsewhere he has advised that those who wish only to save their life will lose it (9:24; 14:26)?[15] Does this interpretation of the parable as an illustration of prudent behavior or an exhortation to ethical use of wealth capture the impact of the twist in v. 8a? Why the need for haste in v. 6?

A COMIC ROGUE

A different approach is to read the parable in light of comic stories of picaresque slaves common in ancient literature, who are able to survive by their wits in difficult situations. In Aesop's fables, for example, the typical pattern is that the slave gets into trouble with his master, takes clever action to remedy the situation to his own advantage, and in the end gets the bet-

---

[13] Joseph A. Fitzmyer, *The Gospel According to Luke* (AB28A; Garden City, N.Y.: Doubleday, 1981) 1098.

[14] Ibid., 1097–98. Fitzmyer details the widespread practice of agents, such as the estate manager in this parable, to add a commission or an interest to the principal in promissory notes or bonds on loans made from a master's property. These notes mentioned only the amount owed, i.e., the principal plus the interest.

[15] Kloppenborg, "The Dishonoured Master," 478.

ter of his master. Such stories provide a "moral holiday" in which everyday relations are temporarily overturned.[16]

From this angle, the accusation against the slave[17] is a false one[18] and the steward is wrongfully dismissed. Such a situation would evoke great sympathy on the part of the hearers who know that turning him out into the world without home, friends, or employment is tantamount to a death sentence.[19] In the face of such a dire situation the steward avenges himself by doing exactly what he was accused of: mishandling the master's affairs to the benefit of the debtors. The story presumes that the debtors have not yet heard of the steward's dismissal (thus the need for haste, in v. 6) and think that he still acts with the authority of the master. By rewriting the scripts the steward gains public praise for the master, thus outsmarting him and winning his approval. The master can hardly revoke the rewritten notes since he would then lose the public honor that is coming to him as a great benefactor.[20] This interpretation further presumes that the master's approval indicates the steward's reinstatement in his position.

---

[16] Mary Ann Beavis, "Ancient Slavery as an Interpretive Context for the New Testament Servant Parables with Special Reference to the Unjust Steward (Luke 16:1-8)," *JBL* 111 (1992) 37–54.

[17] B. Malina and R. Rohrbaugh (*Social Science Commentary on the Synoptic Gospels* [Minneapolis: Fortress, 1992] 373) note that the estate managers employed by rich landowners were often slaves born in the household and that they had the authority to rent property, make loans, and to liquidate debts in the name of the master.

[18] Fitzmyer, *Luke*, 1099, notes that the verb *diaballō* (v. 1) often connotes "to bring charges with hostile intent," either falsely (e.g., 4 Macc 4:1; OxyP 900:13; Jos., *Ant.* 7.11, 3 §267) or correctly (LXX of Dan 3:8; 2 Macc 3:11). While he opts for the latter meaning in Luke 16:1, Beavis chooses the former.

[19] Beavis suggests that the verb *skaptein* ("dig") in v. 3 indicates he was in danger of being imprisoned and sent off to hard labor in the quarries, an even worse fate. Fitzmyer, *Luke*, 1100, understands v. 3 as a true recognition by the slave who has been doing a white-collar job, that he does not have the physical strength for hard, physical labor.

[20] Variations of this interpretation are given by Beavis, "Ancient Slavery," 37–54; Dan O. Via, *The Parables: Their Literary and Existential Dimension* (Philadelphia: Fortress, 1967) 155–62; Scott, *Hear Then*, 255-66; Malina and Rohrbaugh, *Social Science Commentary*, 373–75; Kenneth E. Bailey, *Poet and Peasant and Through Peasant Eyes* (combined ed.; Grand Rapids: Eerdmans, 1976) 86–110.

A question that remains with this line of interpretation is how a type of story that functions simply to entertain in Greco-Roman literature is meant to be understood within a gospel context. Scott advances that by presenting a counterworld to the hearer's normal world of power in the hands of rich patrons and injustice toward the vulnerable, the parable forces the hearer to reconsider stereotypes. They must ask whether masters are cruel or not. Are victims right in retaliating? Scott sees the parable as breaking the bond between power and justice and showing, instead, that the kingdom is for the vulnerable, "for masters and stewards who do not get even."[21] But this explanation falters because the parable portrays a steward who *does* get even! Bailey finds the meaning in the master's generosity in not immediately throwing the steward into prison. For him the master reveals the generosity of God on which Christians should stake everything.[22] But does this interpretation place too much stress on a minor detail of the story?[23] Is the master really such a good character?

LUKAN LITERARY CONTEXT

Another approach is to rely on the literary context of Luke for the interpretive clues. William Loader, who also sees the parable as a rogue tale, understands it as a means to defend Jesus' own behavior to those who would see him as a rogue, a would-be servant of God who took it upon himself to offer forgiveness of sin without proper authorization.[24] When taken together with the parables on finding the lost that immediately precede it in Luke 15, this parable continues Jesus' self-defense of his offer of forgiveness of sins outside the prescribed means of the Law.[25]

---

[21] Scott, *Hear Then*, 266.

[22] Bailey, *Poet and Peasant*, 86–118.

[23] William Loader, "Jesus and the Rogue in Luke 16,1-8A: The Parable of the Unjust Steward," *RB* 96 (1989) 525.

[24] Ibid., 518–32. A similar tack is taken by L. John Topel, "On the Injustice of the Unjust Steward: Luke 16:1-13," *CBQ* 37 (1975) 216–27.

[25] Loader, "Jesus and the Rogue," 532. See above, pp. 181–84, on Jesus' attitude toward sinners, and E. P. Sanders, *Jesus and Judaism* (2nd ed.; Philadelphia: Fortress, 1985) 174–77.

The twist in v. 8a is that God, like the master, does, indeed, approve the actions of Jesus as he releases sinners from their debts. In a similar vein, John R. Donahue outlines the parallels between Luke 15:11-32 and 16:1-8: both parables are introduced with Luke's typical formula *anthrōpos tis,* "a certain person" (15:11; 16:1); in both the central character determines the narrative flow and speaks the final verse (the father in 15:11, 32; the master in 16:1, 8); in both the character who provides the dramatic interest squanders *(dieskorpisen)* the property (15:13; 16:3) and then confronts life-threatening alternatives (15:15-17; 16:3) which begin to be resolved in a soliloquy that reveals his self-centeredness (15:17-19; 16:3-4); in both the hope for a changed fortune is couched in the form of acceptance into a "house"; in both there is heightened tension through use of literary devices: the journey home of the son and the negotiations of the steward; in both cases the plan is not realized but transcended by the surprising acceptance by the character introduced in the first verse; both parables are open-ended—we do not know if the older brother went in to the feast or if the steward was restored to his position.[26] As in Luke 15:11-32, where it is the father who is the focus of attention and the one who conveys God's costly love, so in 16:1-8 the focus is on the "foolish master" who does not operate according to the normal expectations of one in power. It reveals God not as one who exacts punishment, but who "gives time and cancels debts in the midst of human machinations."[27] Whereas the parables in Luke 15 are directed toward the Pharisees to counter their rigidity, this parable is for disciples (16:1) to assure them of God's graciousness and to encourage similar behavior in Christian leaders.[28]

REWRITING SOCIAL SCRIPTS

Another approach to this parable is to see it as a rewriting of accepted social scripts. John Kloppenborg[29] sees the honor of

[26] Donahue, *Gospel in Parable,* 167–68.
[27] Ibid., 168.
[28] Note the use of "steward" for Christian disciples and ministers in Luke 12:41-48; 1 Corinthians 4:1-2; Titus 1:7; 1 Peter 4:10.
[29] Kloppenborg, "The Dishonoured Master," 474–95.

the master as the focal point of the parable. The steward's scattering of the master's property has been reported to him by others (v. 2) and what is at stake is the master's honor. It is clear not only to him, but to others that he has someone in charge of his household who is not under control, which shames him publicly. It does not matter whether the charges are true or false—his public face is already affected. It is not so much the squandering of the money, as it is the affront to the master's honor, that causes the steward's immediate dismissal. The steward then does the only thing he can to ensure a welcome elsewhere: he gathers clients with the rewriting of the promissory notes and expects from them a favorable reception as their patron. At the end of the story the audience expects only one thing: the master must retrieve his honor, undoubtedly at the expense of the steward. But here is the twist: the master shifts attention from his own dishonor and honors the very one who was its cause! For Kloppenborg, the master's "laughing" at his own dishonor serves to shatter the honor-shame codes of Jesus' cultural world. "It celebrates the master's 'conversion' from the myopia of his society's system of ascribed honour" and invites the listener to doubt the absoluteness of this pivotal value.[30]

A problem with this interpretation is that the steward's actions of rewriting the notes of the debtors would not make him a patron. The debtors only respond to the rewriting if they perceive the steward as an authorized representative of the master. It is the master who remains the patron. A more serious difficulty is that the motivation for such a supposed shattering of the cultural values is not given in the story. Why would a master behave in such a way? What does this reveal about the realm of God? Also, to speak of Jesus telling a parable bent on shattering the codes of honor and shame of his day comes dangerously close to sounding like Christian anti-Judaism.

William R. Herzog II also sees the parable as one that rewrites the social scripts of elites and debtors that gives a glimpse of another world order.[31] While for him the parable is

---

[30] Kloppenborg, "The Dishonoured Master," 493.
[31] William R. Herzog II, *The Parables as Subversive Speech* (Louisville: Westminster/John Knox, 1994) 233–58.

not necessarily one about the reign of God (i.e., none of the characters stands for God or Jesus), it depicts how the weapons of the weak may produce a temporary victory for debtors in a world in which they usually come out losers.[32] Herzog outlines the expected social scripts with which the parable begins: "masters distrust stewards; peasants hate stewards; stewards cheat both tenants and masters."[33] The world of the parable is one in which elites exploit and prey on those beneath them. There is endless war between landowners and peasants, merchants and stewards, all trying to keep what they have and all bargaining to get a little more. The steward is just doing his job and the charges brought against him refer to an alleged inefficient use of the master's property to make more profits, which would be grounds for dismissal. The master has no concern about the steward's profits from the interest rates hidden in the contracts, so long as the steward keeps the master's yield high.

The crisis in the parable is an episode of back stabbing, to which the steward must respond by developing a new strategy. Because of the amount of the debts and the apparent literacy of the debtors, Herzog sees them as merchants, not tenant farmers, with whom the steward negotiated for the monetization and transport of the wheat and oil from the estate. The *grammata*, "documents," then, were IOUs ("promissory notes," vv. 6, 7), not tenant leases. The rumors against the steward could be initiated either by the merchants who think they are not receiving the volume of goods anticipated because the steward is taking too large a cut, or by the villagers who think they are left with too little after everyone above them gets their share. It may also be that the steward's "squandering" (*diaskorpizein*, v. 1) is conspicuous consumption that is inappropriate to his social status, whereby the steward dishonors his master by trying to compete with him. The accusatory rumors against the steward are typical tactics of villagers or merchants aimed at undermining the steward and strengthening their own bargaining position.

---

[32] Paul Trudinger, "Exposing the Depth of Oppression (Luke 16:1b-8a)," in *Jesus and His Parables*, ed. V. George Shillington (Edinburgh: T. & T. Clark, 1997) 121–37, takes a similar tack to Herzog, but sees the parable's function as told by Jesus in anger to expose the depth of oppression inflicted on the poor.

[33] Herzog, *Subversive*, 257.

The steward's action proves his worth to his master. While the owner may experience a temporary loss in the hidden interest erased from the debts, he will recoup it in other ways, since the steward has now bound the debtors even more deeply to the patron who has shown them beneficence. The steward has exposed his anonymous enemies and has ensured his position with his master for a while longer by showing his resourcefulness in assuring long-term gains while taking a short-term loss. The story ends with a reversal of the usual scripts. "At the close of the parable, peasants are praising the master, the master commends the steward, and the steward has relieved the burden on the peasants and kept his job."[34] The result of all the twisted machinations and scheming is a temporary forgiveness for debtors, from which comes rejoicing.

PREACHING POSSIBILITIES

None of the interpretations sketched above resolves completely all the interpretive difficulties with this parable, which makes this an even more challenging parable for the preacher. The appended sayings in vv. 8b-13 do not entirely capture the force of the parable and the preacher would probably do better to wrestle with the meaning of vv. 1-8a.

One of the challenges that faces the preacher is to make meaning of a story that presumes an economic setting and social scripts far removed from that of most contemporary congregations. In his or her interpretation the preacher will need to be wary of presuming modern Western values from capitalistic systems. S/he will most likely need to elucidate the presumed world of the parable for the congregation, but at the same time will want to avoid making the homily into a Bible study lesson. Moreover, the homily is not the place to outline debates about the interpretive difficulties. The preacher needs to choose one line of interpretation and follow it through.

If the preacher decides to emphasize the virtue of prudence s/he will want to do so in a way that does not convey the message that good ends justify unrighteous means. If the preacher

---

[34] Ibid., 257.

decides on a variation of the rogue interpretation it will be important to find the thread where the good news of the gospel emerges. Humor can be very effective in preaching, but there is the danger that the comic story is heard only as entertainment. This parable may show that Jesus has a sense of humor, but as embedded in the gospel, the story conveys more than that.

For a congregation engaged in serious hard work for social justice, the comic reversals in the parable and the rewriting of social scripts can give a respite of joy and a hope for a more just future. On the Twenty-fifth Sunday of Ordinary Time, the parable is read in tandem with Amos 8:4-7, where the prophet rails against those who daily trample on the needy and chomp at the bit for the end of the sabbath so they can resume their unjust scheming. The preacher can pick up on the intersection of the moral holiday in the parable and the notion in Amos of sabbath as rest from injustice and speak about a renewed observance of sabbath as a foretaste of a differently ordered world of God's making.[35] Another direction is to speak from the parable about the complexity of systems, whether moral or economic or ecological, and how God does not intervene to "fix things" when they go awry.[36] The resourcefulness of the steward toward his survival in an ambiguous situation can be a paradigm for Christian actions toward survival of the planet and of the most vulnerable in society in a world in crisis.

For people who struggle with rigidity in accounting for sins, or who try to earn forgiveness, the preacher might take the tack of interpreting the parable as vindication for Jesus' profligate release from debt for sinners—a missionary tactic of which God approves! For those who imagine God or Jesus at work only in the transcendent, the parable might provide a vehicle for conveying the ways in which God is revealed in the midst of human machinations in an imperfect world.

In the very act of interpreting, the preacher is rewriting the script once again, whether emphasizing the rewriting of social

---

[35] See the April–June 1998 issue of *Living Pulpit* devoted to the topic of sabbath.

[36] See Barbara Green, "The Ecosystem: Psalm 7 and Luke 16:1-9," in *Like a Tree Planted* (Collegeville: The Liturgical Press, 1997) 89–107.

scripts, the rewriting of debts so as to bring forgiveness, or rewriting the parable's message, as in the early appended sayings of vv. 8b-13. The important thing is for the preacher to be clear about where the good news is in the script being written and read now.

CHAPTER SEVENTEEN

Beggar at the Gate
(Luke 16:19-31)

Twenty-sixth Sunday of Ordinary Time

Thursday of the Second Week of Lent

Jesus said to the Pharisees:
    [19] *"There was a rich man who dressed in purple garments and fine linen*
      and dined sumptuously each day.
[20] *And lying at his door was a poor man named Lazarus, covered with sores,*
    [21] *who would gladly have eaten his fill of the scraps*
    that fell from the rich man's table.
    Dogs even used to come and lick his sores.
[22] *When the poor man died,*
    he was carried away by angels to the bosom of Abraham.
    The rich man also died and was buried,
    [23] *and from the netherworld, where he was in torment,*
    he raised his eyes and saw Abraham far off
    and Lazarus at his side.
[24] *And he cried out, 'Father Abraham, have pity on me.*
    Send Lazarus to dip the tip of his finger in water and cool my tongue,
    for I am suffering torment in these flames.'
[25] *Abraham replied,*
    'My child, remember that you received
    what was good during your lifetime
    while Lazarus likewise received what was bad;
    but now he is comforted here, whereas you are tormented.
[26] *Moreover, between us and you a great chasm is established*
    to prevent anyone from crossing who might wish to go
    from our side to yours or from your side to ours.'
[27] *He said, 'Then I beg you, father,*
    send him to my father's house, [28] *for I have five brothers,*
    so that he may warn them,

lest they too come to this place of torment.'
²⁹ But Abraham replied, 'They have Moses and the prophets.
  Let them listen to them.'
³⁰ He said, 'Oh no, father Abraham,
  but if someone from the dead goes to them, they will repent.'
³¹ Then Abraham said, 'If they will not listen to Moses and the prophets,
  neither will they be persuaded if someone should rise from the dead.'"

LUKAN LITERARY CONTEXT

Between this lengthy parable and that of the steward who rewrites the promissory notes in 16:1-8 and its appended sayings in vv. 9-13 are several other sayings directed to the Pharisees (16:14-18). While the connection is loose, there is a thread that runs through all the parables and sayings in Luke 15-16: Jesus' defense of those most vulnerable to victimization by the rich and powerful.[1] Luke depicts the Pharisees as "lovers of money" who sneer at Jesus' words (v. 14),[2] setting them up as the audience for the parable in vv. 16-31. In v. 15 their penchant for self-justification and their wrongly centered hearts align them with the rich man in the following parable. The sayings in vv. 16-18 on the enduring value of the Law and the prophets point ahead to Abraham's response in vv. 29 and 31.[3]

This parable also serves to further Luke's recurrent theme of possessions in relationship to discipleship. In the opening stories of Luke's Gospel Mary sings of God's goodness in filling the hungry with good things and sending the rich away empty (1:52-53). Jesus is born in lowly circumstances (2:1-7) and his first visitors are despised shepherds (2:8-20). His parents offer the sacrifice of poor people at his presentation in the Temple (2:24). Jesus announces good news to the poor at the inauguration of his mission (4:17-19) and is portrayed doing so. Jesus pro-

---

[1] See John R. Donahue, *The Gospel in Parable* (Philadelphia: Fortress, 1988) 172–74, for the relationship of vv. 14-18 to the surrounding parables.

[2] Donahue (ibid., 172) notes that historically, Pharisees, unlike Sadducees and many of the scribes, were not from the upper class. Whenever Luke wants an opponent to Jesus the Pharisees take the role.

[3] As Donahue (ibid., 174) points out, the saying on divorce is not as out of place in v. 18 as it may at first seem since in the cultural milieu of the gospel divorce is more an economic issue than a breakup of an interpersonal relationship.

nounces the poor blessed (6:20), and in Luke's version he adds a woe against the rich (6:24-26). Unique to Luke are the parables of the rich fool (12:13-21) and that of the rich man and Lazarus. While possessions is a constant theme in Luke, there is no one prescription for how a disciple is to use them. Some, like the first fishermen and Levi, leave everything to follow Jesus (5:11, 28). Others, like Mary Magdalene, Joanna, Susanna, and the other Galilean women, use their monetary resources to finance Jesus' mission (8:1-3). Zacchaeus, the chief tax collector (19:1-10), is approved for giving half his possessions to the poor. In Acts (2:42-47; 4:32-36) disciples hold everything in common, selling their possessions and dividing them according to need. Other well-to-do disciples use their riches to host the community, as Mary in Acts 12:12 and Lydia in Acts 16:15, 40. What is constant in the message of the Lukan Jesus is that it is not possessions in themselves that are good or evil, but what one does with them. They can either be an obstacle to discipleship, as in the case of the rich ruler (18:18-23), or they can be placed at the service of the mission. It is within this context that we have this parable of the rich man and Lazarus that puts human faces on wealth and poverty and conveys a powerful message.[4]

ORIGIN OF THE STORY

There are a number of stories in antiquity that parallel this one of reversals of fortune in the afterlife. An Egyptian folk tale dated to 47 c.e. tells about a reincarnated Egyptian who takes his father on a tour of the realm of the dead. There he sees a rich man who had died, shrouded in fine linen and given an elaborate

[4] Donahue (ibid., 175) outlines the Lukan texts on rich and poor in relation to 16:19-31. For more detailed studies of the theme see Luke T. Johnson, *The Literary Function of Possessions in Luke-Acts* (SBLDS 39; Missoula: Scholars Press, 1977) where he shows that riches in Luke are both literal and metaphoric. Luke is concerned both about actual poor people as well as poverty as a symbol of vulnerability. See also David P. Seccombe, *Possessions and the Poor in Luke-Acts* (Studien zum Neuen Testament und Seiner Umwelt. Series B. vol. 6; Linz: 1982); W. Stegemann, *The Gospel and the Poor* (Philadelphia: Fortress, 1984); John Gillman, *Possessions and the Life of Faith* (Zacchaeus Studies: New Testament; Collegeville: The Liturgical Press, 1991); Walter Pilgrim, *Good News to the Poor* (Minneapolis: Augsburg, 1981).

burial, as well as a poor man who was brought unmourned on a straw mat to a common necropolis of Memphis. The former was in torment while the latter was seated on a throne, adorned in the rich man's fine linen. The story concludes with the son wishing a similar fate for his father.[5] Another parallel story is found in Greco-Roman literature in Lucian of Samosata's *Gallus and Catalpus,* in which a poor shoemaker, Micyllus, is contrasted with a rich man.[6] There are also similar Jewish legends, one, for example, which transforms the characters into a poor Torah scholar and a rich toll collector (*y. Sanh.* 6.23c and *y. Hag.* 2.77d). That Jesus composed his parable along the lines of known popular folk tales is altogether possible.

What is more debatable is the source of the ending. Jeremias holds that vv. 27-31 were added by Jesus to make the parable into a warning to those who were unaware of the impending judgment.[7] Others believe that v. 31 makes no sense except in a post-resurrection context.[8] William Herzog proposes that it does if it refers to "the return of Lazarus's ghostly apparition, not to the resurrection of Jesus."[9] For him the whole of vv. 16-31 come from Jesus.

HUMAN FACES OF WEALTH AND POVERTY (vv. 19-21)

While the theme of the blessedness of the poor and the warnings of woe to the rich runs throughout the gospel, it is never so vividly portrayed as in the parable of the rich man and Lazarus. While sayings about the dangers of riches may catch the hearer's attention, the graphic details of the parable pull at the heart.

[5] J. A. Fitzmyer, *The Gospel According to Luke* (AB28A; Garden City, N.Y.: Doubleday, 1981) 1126.

[6] See Ronald F. Hock, "Lazarus and Micyllus: The Greco-Roman Backgrounds to Luke 16:29-31," *JBL* 106 (1987) 447–63.

[7] Joachim Jeremias, *The Parables of Jesus* (6th ed.; New York: Scribner's Sons, 1963) 180–87.

[8] E.g., John Dominic Crossan, *In Parables: The Challenge of the Historical Jesus* (New York: Harper & Row, 1973) 66–68, holds that the verses are pre-Lukan but post-resurrectional.

[9] William R. Herzog II, *The Parables as Subversive Speech* (Louisville: Westminster/John Knox, 1994) 126.

The story has three parts.[10] It opens with a sketch of the life situation of two opposite characters (vv. 19-21). First we are introduced to the rich man whose manner of dress and eating habits are typical of royalty or of the very wealthy. Purple is worn by kings (Judg 8:26; Esth 8:15), is used for hangings that adorn their palaces, and is the color of sacred vestments (Sir 45:10) and accouterments for God's sanctuary (Exod 26:1, 31, 36). Fine linen and purple are often paired to describe the very finest attire (Prov 31:22; Jos., *Ant.* 3, 154; Rev 18:12; Esth 1:6). In addition to adorning himself in splendid clothes the rich man feasts on sumptuous fare every day. The verb *euphrainō* (v. 19) is the same one that is used for the celebration at the return of the younger son in 15:23, 29. There the reference is to a special banquet; here the rich man gorges on such every day.[11] He clearly belongs to the urban elite who control the political and economic lives of the city and surrounding countryside.[12]

The description of the poor man could not paint a starker contrast. He is destitute and his purple covering is that of ulcerated skin. He is "thrown down" at the gate[13] of the great mansion of the rich man, hoping for whatever might be thrown down to him to eat. His plight evokes that of the younger son in 15:16 who longed to fill his belly with the pods on which the swine fed, but no one gave him any. There is also an echo of the story of the Canaanite woman who pleads with Jesus for her daughter, "Please, Lord, for even the dogs eat the scraps that fall from the table of their masters" (Matt 15:27).[14] The scraps here may refer not to leftovers, but to pita bread used as a napkin by

[10] Donahue, *Gospel in Parable,* 170. Cf. R. Bultmann, *History of the Synoptic Tradition* (Oxford: Blackwell, 1963) 178, 196, and others consider that it has two basic sections: 1) vv. 19-26 based on a folkloric account of reversals in the afterlife, and 2) vv. 27-31 a polemic against the need for signs to augment the Law and the Prophets.

[11] This is also what the suddenly rich fool in 12:19 does: eat, drink, and be merry *(euphrainou).*

[12] Herzog, *Subversive,* 118.

[13] The Greek verb *ebeblēto* in v. 20 translated as "lying" by the *NAB,* means literally "cast down" or "thrown down." *Pylōn,* translated as "door" in the *NAB,* refers to the large gate at the entrance of a temple, palace, or city (Acts 14:13; Rev 21:25).

[14] Also Mark 7:28. Luke omits this story from his gospel.

the rich on which to wipe their hands. These bread pieces would then be thrown under the table. This detail adds to the picture of conspicuous consumption of the rich man, who can afford to squander what would be sustenance to another.[15]

The poor man has to compete with the hungry street dogs for the garbage thrown out from the rich man's house. The dogs, like the poor man, know the pickings will be good, and while they lurk in wait they lick at Lazarus' sores. How Lazarus came to be in such a wretched condition is not narrated. The first hearers of the parable undoubtedly saw in him a familiar face of one who had fallen into irredeemable debt through vicissitudes such as pestilence, drought, or over-taxation. If he had lost his land to a predator such as the rich man, he might have tried first to enter into a tenancy arrangement. Falling even deeper into debt, he may next have been reduced to the precarious situation of a day laborer. The downward spiral quickened as there was not enough work and he became weaker and weaker through malnourishment. Having succumbed to disease, death was not far off.[16]

BLESSING AND CURSE

As the scene is set in the parable, the sympathy of the hearers would go toward one or the other of the two contrasting characters. At the outset well-to-do Christians in Luke's community might have thought the rich man the hero of the story. Wealth was typically regarded as a sign of God's favor, as in the case of Abraham, who was rich in flocks and herds, and therefore, thought to be blessed by God (Gen 24:35).[17] It is likely that they would have looked with disdain at the poor man in the parable. Perhaps they would have thought him lazy or accursed.[18] Like Jesus' disciples, who react with astonishment at

---

[15] Herzog, *Subversive*, 118.

[16] Ibid., 119.

[17] See also Job 42:10-17; Ecclesiastes 3:10-13; 1 Timothy 4:4-5, for example. See further Leslie J. Hoppe, *Being Poor* (GNS 20; Wilmington: Glazier, 1987).

[18] Herzog, *Subversive*, 119, suggests there may be an echo of 1 Kings 21:19, where Elijah tells Ahab, "In the place where the dogs licked up the blood of Naboth, the dogs shall lick up your blood, too." This fate is also to befall Jezebel (v. 23) and all of Ahab's wicked line (v. 24).

Jesus' remark on how difficult it is for a rich person to enter the reign of God (Luke 18:25), rich hearers will be caught off guard with the ending of this parable.

Those of Jesus' first audience or those in Luke's community who struggled to hold poverty at bay would most likely see their own possible fate in that of Lazarus. They would be all too familiar with the exploitation of the rich and the unjust economic systems that victimized the likes of Lazarus. Like him they have cried out to God, trusting that God would be their refuge (Ps 34:6). Or they may have thought themselves punished by God and may have prayed for forgiveness. It is possible that both rich and poor hearers of the parable were surprised by what came next.

FATHER ABRAHAM (vv. 22-26)

In part two (vv. 22-26) both characters die and the chasm between them in earthly life is continued into the beyond. The rich man has a fitting burial, but there is none such for the poor man. However, angels come and carry him to a place of high esteem, to the bosom *(kolpos)* of Abraham.[19] As in John 13:23, where the beloved disciple reclines on the bosom *(kolpos)* of Jesus at the Last Supper, and in John 1:18, where the only Son is said to be at the Father's side *(kolpos)*, Lazarus enjoys a place of intimacy and honor with father Abraham in the afterlife. The scene evokes the way in which Jacob, Aaron, and Moses, each "was gathered to his fathers" upon his death (Gen 49:33; Num 27:13; Deut 32:50).[20]

The rich man, by contrast, is in torment in Hades. Luke uses the Greek term, Hades,[21] for the netherworld, as also in 10:15 and Acts 2:27. It is roughly equivalent to the Hebrew

---

[19] This is not a common motif in Jewish literature before the mid-second century, though see Shepherd of Hermas, *Vis.* 2.2, 7; *Sim.* 927.3; *T.Asher* 6:4-6.

[20] This expression most likely comes from the custom of gathering the bones of family members together in the same ossuary after the flesh has decayed.

[21] The Greek word *hadēs* derives from the name of the Greek god who was god of the netherworld, the place of the dead (Homer, *Il.* 15.188). In time the name was applied to the place where the dead dwell. See Fitzmyer, *Luke*, 855; Daniel Harrington, "Sheol," *CPDBT*, 904–05.

word Sheol. The latter, however, is not a place of punishment, but a place of shadowy existence (Isa 14:9) beneath the earth (Job 26:5-6). It is a place of darkness, where praise of God is no longer possible (Ps 6:6). It has separate locales for the righteous and for the wicked (*1 Enoch* 22:3-13). Several texts associate fire with the fate of sinners in the netherworld (Sir 21:9-10; Isa 66:24). Whereas on earth the rich man enjoyed flashy clothes, his raiment is now burning flames. The tongue that had savored sumptuous food daily now longs for a drop of water to quench his savage thirst. In anguish, the rich man raises his eyes and sees Abraham far off and Lazarus at his bosom. The one whom he seemed not to see at his gate daily suddenly comes clearly into his vision—still not as brother, but as one who could serve his needs.

Curiously, only the poor man's name is given in the parable, and v. 24 indicates that the rich man knows it. The name Lazarus is a shortened Greek form of the Hebrew or Aramaic name *ʾElʿāzār*, which means "God has helped." The truth of his name is borne out in the afterlife. The rich man whose name would have been widely known during his lifetime fades into anonymity in the afterlife.[22]

The rich man calls out, "Father Abraham, have pity on me *(eleēson me),*" the same words used by the ten lepers (17:13) and by the man who was blind (18:39). He claims kinship with Abraham as the basis for a hearing. But John the Baptist had warned in 3:8, "Produce good fruits as evidence of your repentance; and do not begin to say to yourselves, 'We have Abraham as our father,' for I tell you, God can raise up children to Abraham from these stones."[23] In Luke, it is the marginalized who are shown to be true children of Abraham, such as the woman who was healed of her bent condition after eighteen years (13:16), and Zacchaeus the tax collector (19:9). The one who did not give alms *(eleēmosynē)* to the beggar at his gate cannot expect that his cry for mercy *(eleēson)* will be sufficient to get him through the narrow gate (13:24). The parable enacts the reversal

---

[22] The man's name is popularly said to be Dives, which comes from a misunderstanding of the Latin Vulgate, "Homo quidam erat dives." See H. J. Cadbury, "A Proper Name for Dives," *JBL* 81 (1962) 300–402.

[23] There is a similar theme in the Fourth Gospel (John 8:31-59).

spoken of in 13:30, of some who were first being last, and some who ate and drank in Jesus' company now wailing and grinding their teeth, seeing others reclining at table with Abraham and all the prophets (13:26-29).

Abraham still recognizes the rich man as "my child" (v. 25), but like the father in the parable of the lost sons, who addresses his son the same way (15:31), he cannot force him to choose the good. In the latter story, the son still has time to turn to the father. In the case of the rich man, death has fixed the chasm that the rich man established in his lifetime. Now it cannot be crossed (v. 26).[24]

BROTHERS (vv. 27-31)

In the last section (vv. 27-31) the yawning gap between the rich man and Lazarus is sealed by the wealthy man's perduring inability to perceive Lazarus as his brother. Even when he sees Lazarus resting in the bosom of their mutual father, he does not yet see him as his sibling.[25] Instead, he turns his attention to his five rich brothers who he wants to spare from torment. He wants Lazarus to serve him as his messenger and warn (*diamartyromai*) them. There is great irony in the word Luke uses in v. 27. Throughout Acts *diamartyromai* is used for "bearing witness" to the risen Jesus.[26] The desired response is to repent (*metanoein*, v. 30)[27] and believe (*peithō*, v. 31).[28]

The final verses underscore that the rich man is irrevocably blind to the poor man, his brother. Moses and the prophets repeatedly admonish care for the poor.[29] And Lazarus sits at

[24] Matthew sounds a similar theme with the closed door to the foolish virgins in 25:1-13 and the separation of the sheep and the goats in 25:31-46.

[25] Herzog, *Subversive*, 123.

[26] Acts 2:42; 8:25; 10:42; 18:5; 20:21, 23, 24; 23:11; 28:23.

[27] On repenting and converting in Luke and Acts see Barbara E. Reid, *Choosing the Better Part? Women in the Gospel of Luke* (Collegeville: The Liturgical Press, 1996) 27.

[28] While the more frequent term for "believe" is *pisteuein*, in Acts 13:43; 14:19; 17:4; 18:4 the term *peithō*, "to convince," is used of those who come to faith. See Reid, *Choosing the Better Part?*, 25–27, for references in Luke and Acts on the theme of believing.

[29] E.g., Exodus 22:21-22; Leviticus 19:9-10; Deuteronomy 10:17-19; Amos 2:6-8; Hosea 12:7-9; Jeremiah 5:25-29, and numerous other places.

every gate. If one will not heed the Torah and put it into practice when given repeated opportunities, not even an apparition
from the dead Lazarus will melt the hardened heart.[30] Right to
the end of the parable the rich man continues to bargain with
Abraham and to claim a privileged position. What is necessary
is for him to relinquish his status and power and privilege so as
to claim Lazarus as his brother. What is already clear in the Law
and the prophets is spoken and enacted repeatedly by Jesus in
the new age.[31] Now it is Jesus' word that must be heard and
obeyed (9:35; 16:16).[32]

This final dialogue in vv. 27-31 makes the parable not simply
one of reversal of fortune of the rich and poor, but sharpens the
focus on the necessity of perceiving God's word and responding
to it. The invitation is through Jesus and all his brothers and sisters visible in the concrete faces of poor people. Not to respond
is a matter of life and death both here and in the beyond.

PREACHING POSSIBILITIES

As with the original telling of the parable, responses to it
in a contemporary congregation will vary, depending on their
socioeconomic position. For those who are made poor the parable obviously offers hope. It gives assurance of their blessedness, portraying poverty not as a curse for wrongdoing, but as
a result of greed and of inequitable systems of distribution. It
portrays a picture of ultimate bliss for those who endure destitution and degradation in this life. On the other hand, the parable challenges the notion that abundance of possessions is a
sign of God's blessing. Neither having nor lacking possessions
is blessed. It is how one uses possessions that determines
blessedness or woe. Pitfalls a preacher will want to avoid are

---

[30] Herzog, *Subversive*, 126, takes the reference in v. 31 to Lazarus' ghostly
apparition, not to the resurrection of Jesus. In later Christian retelling, it would
naturally be taken as a reference to the latter. Other examples of messengers
from the dead are found in 1 Samuel 28:7-20; Plato, *Resp.* 10.614D; Lucian, *De-
monax* 43; Cicero, *Republic*, 6:9-26; Philostratus, *Life of Apollonius of Tyana*, 8:31.

[31] See Peter's speech in Acts 3:11-26.

[32] On hearing and obeying the word see Luke 5:1, 15; 6:17, 27, 47-49; 7:29;
8:8-15, 18, 21; 9:35; 10:16; 11:28; 14:35; 19:48; 21:38; Acts 2:22, 37; 3:22-23; 4:4; 7:2;
15:7; 18:8.

both the romanticizing of poverty or the canonizing of poor people and vilifying riches or wealthy people. The dualistic contrast in the parable is for narrative effect. Neither is good or bad in itself. And real life is always somewhere in between. The ideal is not to make oneself destitute for the sake of poverty. The ideal Luke presents is all having what they need when possessions are shared (Acts 2:44-45; 4:34). This entails relinquishment on the part of those who have property, power, privilege, status, and empowerment by those who are lacking. It is significant that Abraham figures prominently in this parable. He is a rich man who remains rich, but who is remembered as blessed for his generous hospitality (Gen 18:1-15).[33]

For a well-to-do congregation, the preacher would do well not to spiritualize the message of the parable. That material wealth can pose a great danger to discipleship is clear from this and numerous other episodes in Luke's Gospel. The first reading from Amos 6:1a, 4-7 reinforces the same. The gospel parable shows how riches can blind a person not only to the needs of those at their gate, but to the fact that all people are brothers and sisters of the same parent God and of the same ancestors in the faith. The rich man in the parable never sees Lazarus as his brother, even when he can see him resting in Abraham's bosom.

A preacher might take the direction of the vividness of this parable to put names and real faces on the abstract noun "poverty." The general sayings in the gospel about rich and poor do not stir the heart and stay in the memory nearly as powerfully as the graphic descriptions of the two characters in this parable. Likewise, the homilist would do well not to speak of "the poor" in the abstract, but to relate the message using names and real stories, much like news reporters put human faces on their facts when going for a human interest angle. The preacher might also counter the exclusively male world presented in the parable by highlighting how in today's world it is women and children who are the majority of poor people.

Another pitfall the preacher should avoid is to reinforce passive acceptance of unjust structures that keep some people destitute while others have an overabundance of wealth. To

[33] Herzog, *Subversive*, 130.

emphasize the promise of heavenly reward and to ignore the need to work for justice now is not to take seriously Jesus' announcement that the reign of God is already in our midst (Luke 4:18-21). The preacher can help channel the responses of the congregation toward social justice ministries that aim at undoing systemic causes of poverty, not only charitable outreach. The preacher will want to move hearts to respond with action, not to instill fruitless guilt. On Thursday of the Second Week of Lent, when the parable is paired with Jeremiah 17:5-10, what stands out is how deeds are what reveal the true heart of a person. One whose heart rests in God need not fear the fate of the rich man who begs for a drop of water to cool his tongue. Such a one, says the prophet, fears not the heat, because they are like a tree planted beside the waters whose roots stretch to the stream.

CHAPTER EIGHTEEN

What Is Expected
(Luke 17:5-10)

Twenty-seventh Sunday of Ordinary Time

Tuesday of the Thirty-second Week of Ordinary Time
(Luke 17:7-10)

[5] *The apostles said to the Lord, "Increase our faith."*
[6] *The Lord replied,*
"If you have faith the size of a mustard seed,
you would say to this mulberry tree,
'Be uprooted and planted in the sea,' and it would obey you.
[7] *"Who among you would say to your servant*
who has just come in from plowing or tending sheep in the field,
'Come here immediately and take your place at table'?
[8] *Would he not rather say to him,*
'Prepare something for me to eat.
Put on your apron and wait on me while I eat and drink.
You may eat and drink when I am finished'?
[9] *Is he grateful to that servant because he did what was commanded?*
[10] *So should it be with you.*
When you have done all you have been commanded,
say, 'We are unprofitable servants;
we have done what we were obliged to do.'"

LUKAN LITERARY CONTEXT

As the travel narrative begins to draw to a close we find in chapter seventeen a collection of isolated sayings. They are unrelated to one another except that each addresses an aspect of discipleship. The sayings that precede today's gospel selection treat of stumbling blocks or scandals (17:1-3a), reproof of a fellow

Christian, and unlimited forgiveness (17:3b-4).[1] These continue to flesh out what it is that disciples are called to do. The verses that follow address the question of how they are able to do it.[2]

The saying in vv. 5-6 about little faith being able to do great things has parallels in Matthew 17:20; 21:21 and Mark 11:22-23. The context and the wording in these parallels are slightly different from Luke's. In Mark 11:22-23 Peter remarks about the fig tree that has withered after Jesus cursed it, and Jesus tells his disciples, "Truly I tell you, if you say to this mountain, 'Be taken up and thrown into the sea,' and if you do not doubt in your heart, but believe that what you say will come to pass, it will be done for you." The following verse relates the saying to disciples believing that they receive whatever they ask for in prayer. Matthew 21:21 is found in the same context and has similar wording. It focuses more explicitly on the question of how this happened. The import of the saying both in Mark and in Matthew is to explain how Jesus was able to do this powerful deed, and to assure the same ability to faith-filled disciples.[3] Luke omits this episode about the withered fig tree.

Matthew has another rendition of the saying in 17:20, where it is part of Jesus' response to the disciples' inability to cast out a demon just after the Transfiguration. All three Synoptic Gospels have this episode, and in all three Jesus addresses his followers as a "faithless generation" (Mark 9:19; Matt 17:17; Luke 9:41) but only Matthew elaborates on the disciples' "little faith" (17:20)[4] with the saying about faith as a grain of mustard (17:21). Luke's version of this saying (17:6) is in a different context and changes the image from a mountain that moves "from here to there" to a sycamine tree that is uprooted and planted in the sea.[5]

---

[1] Parallel sayings for Luke 17:1-2 are found in Matthew 18:6-7 and for Luke 17:3-4 in Matthew 18:15, 21-22.

[2] Charles H. Talbert, *Reading Luke: A Literary and Theological Commentary on the Third Gospel* (New York: Crossroad, 1988) 160.

[3] Ibid., 161.

[4] The theme of "little faith" *(oligopistia)* is a favorite of Matthew: 6:30; 8:26; 14:31; 16:8; 17:20.

[5] R. K. Bultmann *(The History of the Synoptic Tradition.* Trans. J. Marsh [rev. ed.; New York: Harper and Row, 1968] 75) thinks that the Matthean form of the

POWERFUL FAITH (vv. 5-6)

The saying in v. 6 is introduced by a request from the apostles to the Lord to increase their faith. The audience for the sayings in vv. 1-4 is the disciples; in v. 5 it is apostles. Luke tends to equate the apostles with the Twelve,[6] although in Acts 14:4, 14 he names Paul and Barnabas as apostles.[7] The designation of Jesus as "Lord" is a post-resurrection title retrojected into the narrative of his earthly ministry.[8]

The request of the apostles is, literally, "add faith to us." This can be understood in two ways: "add more faith to what we already have" or "add faith to the other gifts that we have received."[9] The former makes more sense since it would be presumed that apostles, those sent to proclaim good news, already have faith. While the request seems to be for a greater quantity of faith, Jesus' reply and the literary context focus on the nature of faith.

The image in v. 6 is a strange one. A sycamine tree (*sycaminos*, translated in *NAB* as "mulberry")[10] is one that is very large and has an extensive root system. The hyperbole is meant to underscore the seeming impossibility of the project. A similar image is used by the first-century Roman satirist Petronius, who has one of his characters speak of moving bushes from Mount Ida to the sea (*Satyricon*, 134).[11]

Q saying is more original. Joseph A. Fitzmyer (*The Gospel According to Luke* [AB28A; Garden City, N.Y.: Doubleday, 1981] 1142) argues that the Lukan form with the sycamine tree preserves the original form and Matthew has assimilated the saying in 17:20 to the form of the saying derived in 21:21 from Mark.

[6] Luke 6:13; 9:10, 22:14 (the parallel in Mark 14:17 has the twelve); 24:9-10; Acts 1:26. See further Fitzmyer, *Luke*, 254–55.

[7] In Pauline letters the designation "apostle," that is, "one sent," is given to Paul (Gal 1:1, Rom 1:1; 1 Cor 1:1; 9:1; 2 Cor 1:1; Eph 1:1; Col 1:1; 1 Tim 1:1; 2:7; 2 Tim 1:1; Titus 1:1), Andronicus and Junia (Rom 16:7), Apollos (1 Cor 4:6, 9), Barnabas (1 Cor 9:5-6); Epaphroditus (Phil 2:25), Silvanus and Timothy (1 Thess 1:1 with 2:7).

[8] See Fitzmyer, *Luke,* 202–03.

[9] Ibid., 1143.

[10] In the LXX *sykaminos* is found in 1 Kings 10:27; 1 Chronicles 27:28; 2 Chronicles 1:15; 9:27 as the Greek translation of the Hebrew *šiqmāh*, "sycamore tree." Luke uses *sykomorea* for sycamore in 19:4.

[11] F. W. Danker, *Jesus and the New Age: A Commentary on St. Luke's Gospel* (rev. ed.; Philadelphia: Fortress, 1988) 288.

Verse 6 is usually understood to say that the apostles do not have faith; but if they had even a little bit, they would be able to do impressive things.[12] But in the Greek text the conditional clause begins with a present tense verb in the protasis, *ei echete,* "If you have," which expresses a real condition, rather than a contrary-to-fact condition. The second part, the apodosis, is unreal, which is called for by the subject matter. In other words, the apostles *do* have faith the size of a mustard seed, and therefore *are* able to do wondrous things, but they would not use this faith to transplant trees into the sea.[13]

What this saying conveys, as well as its variations in Matthew and Mark, is that faith in Jesus becomes manifest in visibly awesome ways. Faith is not magic, but is the response of a person to the gracious invitation of God. It is not manifest in flashy, impressive displays of power such as uprooting trees and transplanting them into the sea. In fact, to revel in such pointless, grandiose gestures of power is precisely one of the temptations that Satan poses to Jesus in Luke 4:9-12. He wants Jesus to prove he is the son of God by throwing himself down from the parapet of the temple and letting God's angels rescue him. Instead Jesus' power is manifest in the work of healing, preaching, exorcising, and forgiving. In like manner, the saying in 17:6 assures disciples that with the faith they have, however little, they share in Jesus' power for good. What seems impossible to do is entirely within their ability as given by Christ. Coming on the heels of 17:3-4, an example of the phenomenal power that Jesus' disciples have is that they can forgive a seemingly impossible number of times, knowing that they are continually being forgiven. The point, then, is that those who have faith and who are continually seeking to live more deeply from that faith are given the ability to do this.[14]

---

[12] E.g., Fitzmyer, *Luke,* 1142.

[13] Maximillian Zerwick, *Biblical Greek* (Scripta Pontificii Instituti Biblici 114; Rome: Biblical Institute, 1963) §310; Talbert, *Reading Luke,* 161; Sharon Ringe, *Luke* (Westminster Bible Companion; Louisville: Westminster/John Knox, 1995) 219.

[14] Talbert, *Reading Luke,* 162–63.

WHAT IS REQUIRED (vv. 7-10)

The second cluster of sayings in today's gospel can be considered a parable in the form of a simile. It begins like several other parables, "Who among you . . . ?"[15] The last verse makes it a similitude, "so should it be with you."[16] Verses 7-9 invite the hearer to take the stance of the master who has a servant who has responsibilities both in the field and in the kitchen.[17] The questions in vv. 7-9 are phrased so as to elicit the expected responses. In a world of masters and slaves, patrons and clients, would a slave come in from work in the field and expect to sit down immediately to be fed? Of course not! Would the slaves not first serve the master and only later have their own meal? Of course! Is there any special favor owed to one who just does what is expected? Of course not! The final verse shifts to the perspective of the slaves, advising that this is how it is with disciples who do all that is expected.

There are two words that need to be further explored in vv. 9 and 10. In v. 9 the expression *"echei charin,"* translated "is he grateful?" literally means "does he have favor?" Forms of the word *charis,* "favor," occur a number of times in the Gospel of Luke. Mary is favored by God (1:28, 30) and the favor of God is upon Jesus (2:40, 52). He speaks favorable words *(logois tēs charitos)* which astonish the crowd at his first proclamation of his mission (4:22). There are a number of times in Luke and Acts where *charis* has the sense of "reward" or "merit." In the Sermon on the Plain Jesus asks his followers if they love those who love them, do good only to those who do good to them, or lend only to those from whom they expect repayment, what credit *(charis)* is that to them? (6:32, 33, 34). In Acts 7:10 Stephen describes Joseph as having gained favor or merit *(charis)* with Pharaoh so as to be put over his household. It is likely that the

---

[15] So also Luke 11:5, 11; 12:25; 14:28; 15:4, 8.

[16] "Just so," *houtōs,* is used in the parables of the rich fool (12:21); the finding of the lost sheep (15:7) and the lost coin (15:10), and the parable of the fig tree (21:31).

[17] The master need not be thought of as a rich person, since even relatively poor families had slaves. This master apparently has only one slave, who works both outside and inside the house (B. Malina and R. Rohrbaugh, *Social Science Commentary on the Synoptic Gospels* [Minneapolis: Fortress, 1992] 378).

sense of *echei charin* in 17:9 also has the sense of gaining merit or credit, rather than gratefulness.[18] The sense of v. 9, then, is: Does a master give any extra credit to a slave because he did what was commanded? Or is the master indebted to the slave or does he owe him anything for doing what is expected? The anticipated answer is, Of course not.[19]

The concluding verse affirms the same: just so disciples earn no extra merit when they do what they are expected to do. There is another difficulty in v. 10. Translating the phrase *douloi achreiai* as "unprofitable servants," as does the *NAB* is problematic. The adjective *achreios* can have the connotation, "useless" or "worthless," as it does in Matthew 25:30. It is a term often used of slaves.[20] But a slave is not "worthless"; to the contrary, a slave is valuable to a master because of the service he or she performs. There are instances where *achreios* has the connotation, "miserable" or "unworthy," as in 2 Samuel 6:22 (LXX).[21] But a better understanding of the term in Luke 17:10 comes from recognizing it as the adjective *chreios*, "needy," or "obligated," with an alpha privative suffix that negates the meaning.[22] The sense of v. 10, then, is "We are servants and we have no need," that is, we are not owed anything.[23]

Together the saying in vv. 5-6 and the similitude in vv. 7-10 say that with faith disciples are able to perform visibly power-

---

[18] Kenneth E. Bailey, *Through Peasant Eyes: More Lucan Parables, Their Culture and Style* (Grand Rapids: Eerdmans, 1980) 121–22; Malina and Rohrbaugh, *Social Science Commentary*, 378; Luke T. Johnson, *The Gospel of Luke*. Sacra Pagina 3 (Collegeville: The Liturgical Press, 1991) 259. There are other instances where the expression *echein charis* does mean "to be grateful": 1 Timothy 11:12; 2 Timothy 1:3; Romans 7:25; 2 Corinthians 9:15.

[19] Questions introduced with the particle *mē* expect a negative response. See *BDF* §427.2.

[20] Fitzmyer, *Luke*, 1147, notes these instances: Ps.-Plato, *Alcib* 1.17 122B; Achilles Tatius, *Erot.* 5.17, 8. The *NRSV* translates *achreios* as "worthless"; *NJB* as "useless" in Luke 17:10.

[21] BAGD, 128.

[22] Similarly, in English, "amoral" is the opposite of "moral."

[23] John J. Kilgallen ("What Kind of Servants are We? [Luke 17,10]," *Bib* 63 [1982] 549–51) argues for this interpretation on grounds of both etymology and literary structure. It is also supported by the seventh-century Harclean Syriac version, the expression which is translated *la ḥoshḥo*, "without need," or "owed nothing." See also Bailey, *Through Peasant Eyes*, 124; Malina and Rohrbaugh, *So-*

ful deeds, but not because of any merit they have accumulated. Demonstrable deeds are what are expected of the disciple. Faith and the ability to act from it are a gift from God. Faith is not merited, nor does it increase by one's working harder for it.[24]

PREACHING POSSIBILITIES

One of the difficulties this parable poses is that it presumes a world of masters and slaves, which is a metaphor that ought not be used in a contemporary context. While neither Jesus nor any of the writers of the New Testament challenge the institution of slavery,[25] but rather accept it as the prevailing social structure of their day, for modern Christians it is abhorrent. Nonetheless, metaphors that cast God and Jesus as "master" and disciples as "servants" or "slaves" still abound. The use of such language reinforces systems of oppression and victimization, giving them theological legitimation. Holding up the ideal of faithful servanthood to people who are caught in the underside of systems of domination only serves to justify human bondage as the will of God. It keeps dominated peoples from recognizing the injustice of their situation and mobilizing to confront it. Language and imagery of "service" is liberating only when those who have power, status, and privilege relinquish it in the service of their disadvantaged brothers and sisters.

The parable does not say that it is unnecessary to thank people for the work they do. Gratitude is a fundamental Christian virtue, and the expression of thanks is one of its manifestations, as the story that follows this parable well demonstrates. In Luke 17:11-17 Jesus recognizes the exemplary thanksgiving

---

cial Science Commentary, 378; Ringe, *Luke,* 219. The *REB* rightly translates, "We are servants and deserve no credit."

[24] A similar saying is attributed to Rabbi Johanan ben Zakkai, "Even though you have been faithful in carrying out the Law, claim no special merit, for to that end you were created" (SB 2:235). And in *Pirke Aboth* 1:3 is the admonition: "Be not like servants who serve the master for condition of receiving a gift, but be like servants who serve the master not on condition of receiving a gift. And let the fear of heaven be upon you."

[25] Luke makes frequent use of master-slave stories and sayings: 12:35-40, 42-48; 13:25-27; 14:16-24; 16:1-13.

of the one leper who returned to express his gratitude. Rather, the point of the parable in vv. 7-10 is that when disciples are doing what they are called to do they do not gain any extra credit; they are being what they are meant to be and doing what they have been empowered by their faith to do. This happens neither because of any merit on the part of the believer, nor is the Christian owed anything for doing what their faith emboldens them to do. All is grace. The preacher will want to stress this gratuitous aspect of the saying and the parable. Living out one's faith is not about living from a sense of obligation. Rather, having received all as gift, a believer is invited continually to move deeper and deeper into the being of the Giver, becoming what they are intended to be and doing what they are intended to do, making the power of that gift visible in their work and being. There is no need to cry out for more faith (17:5) or for God to intervene, as in the first reading from Habakkuk (1:2-3; 2:2-4) on the Twenty-seventh Sunday of Ordinary Time. Faith to move insurmountable obstacles has already been given. And from the faith that has been given a believer grows in right relation with God, i.e., as a "just one" (Hab 2:4) and lives.

One of the other emphases the preacher might make is that the astonishing power of Jesus is manifest not in spectacular displays of supernatural prodigies, but in every act of forgiveness, healing, reconciliation, justice, and peacemaking—this is far more impressive than transplanting trees into the sea! Moreover, the faith on which such abilities rest is not faith that I can do wonders, but faith that God can do what seems to be impossible. When the faith of the littlest in the realm of God is unleashed it has the potential to transform the world. This gospel gives hope to those who feel it is impossible to confront seemingly insurmountable obstacles posed by systems of injustice. People of faith who "stir into flame" the gifts God has given (as the second reading, on the Twenty-seventh Sunday of Ordinary Time from 2 Tim 1:6-8, 13-14 advises), working together to eradicate those tangled roots of injustice, are doing exactly what they are commanded to do; no more, no less. It is by grace and by faith that such efforts can succeed.

CHAPTER NINETEEN

Persistently Pursuing Justice
(Luke 18:1-8)

Twenty-ninth Sunday of Ordinary Time
Saturday of the Thirty-second Week of Ordinary Time

¹ Jesus told his disciples a parable
 about the necessity for them to pray always without becoming weary.
He said, ² "There was a judge in a certain town
 who neither feared God nor respected any human being.
³ And a widow in that town used to come to him and say,
 'Render a just decision for me against my adversary.'
⁴ For a long time the judge was unwilling, but eventually he thought,
 'While it is true that I neither fear God nor respect any human being,
 ⁵ because this widow keeps bothering me
 I shall deliver a just decision for her
 lest she finally come and strike me."'
⁶ The Lord said, "Pay attention to what the dishonest judge says.
⁷ Will not God then secure the rights of his chosen ones
 who call out to him day and night?
Will he be slow to answer them?
⁸ I tell you, he will see to it that justice is done for them speedily.
 But when the Son of Man comes, will he find faith on earth?"

UNJUST JUDGE OR PERSISTENT WIDOW?

This parable, situated in the eschatological section of Luke 17:11–19:44, is unique to the Third Gospel. Like many parables, it paints a vivid picture of two opposing characters, one of which is exemplary and who invites the hearers into a new understanding of the realm of God. But which character does

227

that in this parable? A sampling of titles shows that there is no consensus among commentators and translators on which character is the focus of the story. For many it is "The Parable of the Unjust Judge."[1] For others the focus is "the Persistent Widow."[2] Some give it a title that keeps both characters in view, labeling it "The Parable of the Widow and the Judge."[3]

Nor is there a consensus about what message the parable conveys. Is it about how "You Can't Keep a Good Woman Down"?[4] Or is it about "Persistence in Prayer"?[5] Is it a comic parable meant to make us laugh at the ludicrous picture of a powerful judge cowering before a helpless old widow? Or is it a deadly serious portrait of one small victory for justice in the face of shameless systems of rampant injustice? What were the hearers of this parable supposed to hear? What in this story is a disciple of Jesus supposed to emulate?

LAYERS OF INTERPRETATION

Some of these questions can be resolved by recognizing Luke's hand in the earliest layers of interpretation of the parable. Although we have no other version by which to trace Luke's redactional changes, it is clear that v. 1 and vv. 6-8 are secondary additions that reflect early Christian attempts to understand the story. Most scholars agree that the original parable of Jesus is found in vv. 2-5.

There are tell-tale signs of Luke's hand in v. 1. Luke alone among the evangelists consistently introduces parables with an expression that uses the verb *legein:* "he told *(elegen)* them a par-

---

[1] Joachim Jeremias, *The Parables of Jesus* (New York: Scribner's, 1972) 248. Similarly, Joseph A. Fitzmyer (*The Gospel According to Luke* [AB28A; Garden City, N.Y.: Doubleday, 1981] 1175), who names him the "Dishonest Judge"; and Alfred Plummer (*The Gospel According to S. Luke* [ICC; Edinburgh: T. & T. Clark, 1981] 411), who has "the Unrighteous Judge."

[2] As titled in the *NAB.*

[3] Sharon Ringe, *Luke* (Westminster Bible Companion; Louisville: Westminster/John Knox, 1995) 223.

[4] Bernard Brandon Scott, *Hear Then the Parable: A Commentary on the Parables of Jesus* (Minneapolis: Fortress, 1988) 175.

[5] F. W. Danker, *Jesus and the New Age: A Commentary on St. Luke's Gospel* (rev. ed.; Philadelphia: Fortress, 1988) 294.

able."⁶ Also, Luke introduces one of his favorite themes: prayer. Luke, more than any other evangelist, shows Jesus at prayer as a regular practice (5:16) and at critical turning points: at his baptism (3:21), before his choice of the Twelve (6:12), before Peter's declaration of Jesus as the Messiah (9:18), at the Transfiguration (9:28-29), before his arrest on the Mount of Olives (22:39-46), and on the cross (23:46). There is a spontaneous prayer of Jesus giving thanks in 10:21-23, followed by his teaching the disciples to pray (11:1-13). The Lukan Jesus prays for Peter that his faith may not fail (22:32).⁷ The theme of prayer continues to be prominent in Acts, where mention of the disciples praying is made some thirty-two times.⁸ It is apparent that the evangelist has composed v. 1 to further a favorite theme. It also seems to have been fashioned with v. 8b in view.⁹

The concluding verses, 6-8, add various other applications and secondary interpretations of the parable. The absolute use of *ho kyrios* ("the Lord") in v. 6 is out of step with the narrative flow and is a sign of later interpretation. Calling Jesus "Lord" is a post-resurrection insight that has been retrojected into the time of Jesus' ministry. Verse 7 wrestles with the disturbing portrait presented in the parable while at the same time relates the story to the situation of the Lukan community.

---

⁶ In Luke 18:1 as well as 5:36; 13:6; 14:7 the verb is in the imperfect *(elegen de parabolēn autois)*. In Luke 6:39; 8:10; 12:16; 15:3; 18:9; 19:11; 20:19; 21:29 the verb is in the aorist *(eipen)*, in 20:9 it is in the infinitive *(legein)*. In only one instance each do Matthew (22:1) and Mark (3:23) use the verb *legein* with the plural *parabolais* ("parables"). Instead, Matthew and Mark use the verbs *lalein* ("to speak, express oneself") in Matthew 13:3, 10, 13, 33, 34; Mark 4:33, 34; 12:1; *paratithēmi* ("put before," i.e., in teaching) in Matthew 3:24, 31; and *didaskein* ("teach") in Mark 4:2.

⁷ Five times Luke's mention of prayer comes from Mark: 9:1; 20:47; 22:40, 41, 46. Three times Luke inserts references to prayer in his redaction of Markan material: Luke 3:21; 5:16, 33. In four instances prayer appears in Q material (Luke 6:28; 10:2; 11:1, 2). Eight of Luke's references to prayer occur in uniquely Lukan material: 1:10, 13; 2:37; 18:1, 10, 11; 21:36; 22:32.

⁸ Acts 1:14, 24; 2:42; 3:1; 4:31; 6:4, 6; 7:59; 8:15, 22, 24; 9:11, 40; 10:2, 4, 9, 30, 31; 11:5; 12:5, 12; 13:3; 14:23; 16:13, 16, 25; 20:36; 21:5; 22:17; 26:29; 27:29; 28:8.

⁹ Fitzmyer, *Luke*, 1175–78.

DOES GOD HEAR PRAYER?

Two questions surface in these concluding verses: Does God hear the prayers of the chosen ones who call out day and night? (v. 7a). Theologically speaking, a believer can only answer this in the affirmative. Yet common experience is that God often does not seem to answer prayer. So a second question arises: Is the explanation that God's response has been delayed? (v. 7b). Various biblical texts reflect different solutions to these perennial questions. The parable about the friend who comes at midnight (Luke 11:5-13)[10] assures believers that God, indeed, wants to give all good to those who ask, as does Sirach 35:14-19, which asserts that God will listen to the prayer of one who is wronged. God "is not deaf to the wail of the orphan, nor to the widow when she pours out her complaint" (35:14). In Luke 18:7b-8a the answer given is that God's timing is different from that of the seeker. Also in view for the Lukan community is the question of the delay of the second coming.[11] Verse 8a assures the answers to both questions: God will vindicate those who cry out to God, and God will do so speedily. While these are theologically correct notions, they ill fit the dynamic of the parable in 18:2-5, particularly if the judge is seen as the character who is supposed to represent God. The final half of v. 8 takes the applications even further afield by asking if the Son of Humanity[12] will find faith on earth at his coming. It links loosely to the notion of delay in vv. 7b-8a, but is unrelated to the parable proper, which makes no mention of faith. It appears to be a transplant from the discussion of the coming of the Son of Humanity in Luke 17, which immediately precedes the parable.

In sum, vv. 1 and 6-8 are secondary interpretations added by Luke to a puzzling parable told by Jesus. The parable proper, which is most probably closer to that which Jesus told, is found in vv. 2-5, and is not necessarily about praying.

---

[10] See above, chap. 10.
[11] See above, pp. 36–37, on Lukan eschatology.
[12] On the meaning of this phrase see above, pp. 151–52.

BREAKING STEREOTYPES

The two characters are introduced in vv. 2 and 3. Neither fits the expected stereotypes. A judge who neither fears God nor respects human beings is not acting according to the expected script given in 2 Chronicles 19:6-7, where Jehoshaphat is appointing judges. He instructs them to take care what they do, for they are judging, not on behalf of human beings, but on behalf of God, who judges with them. He explicitly admonishes them to let the fear of God be upon them. He reminds them to act carefully because with God there is no injustice, no partiality, and no bribe-taking. While the original hearers of this parable would undoubtedly know well the reality that judges' decisions were bought and were tilted in favor of the most influential supporters, it would be startling to have judges so portrayed in a biblical story.

Moreover, it is alarming to encounter a character who does not act according to the prevailing codes of honor and shame. Twice (vv. 2 and 4) the text underscores that this judge eschews honor, whether in regard to the divine or the human. The original hearers of the parable would likely be uneasy. What can be expected from such a story?

The portrait of the judge only gets more unsettling as the story proceeds. He remains utterly unmoved by the widow's persistent pleas. He is supposed to be representing God (as sketched in 2 Chron 19) but he is acting totally contrary to what Sirach 35:14-19 says of God, who is not deaf to the cry of the widow, and who judges justly and affirms the right without delay. The final incongruity is that a powerful judge is afraid (v. 5) that a seemingly poor, defenseless widow will come and give him a black eye! The verb *hypōpiazein* (v. 5b) is a boxing term that means literally "to strike under the eye."[13] Paul uses the term with this meaning in 1 Corinthians 9:26-27, "I do not fight as if I were shadowboxing. No, I drive [*hypōpiazō*] my body and train it. . . ." The word also has a figurative sense, meaning "to slander," or "to besmirch one's character." Some translations of v. 5 take the metaphorical meaning in a weakened sense and

---

[13] BAGD, 848.

render the verb "annoy greatly" or "wear out" (so the *NRSV* and *NEB*). However, Luke 18:5 is the only known example where *hypōpiazein* is thought to have this nuance, a fact that makes this interpretation suspicious. Furthermore, to propose this connotation dilutes the irony that the literal meaning "blacken the eye" conveys, which is part of the intentional twist of the story.

No less startling is the character of the widow. Biblical references to widows most often cast them as poor and defenseless.[14] They are usually mentioned in the same breath with orphans and aliens, that is, those who are most vulnerable and without resources, a woman in a financially precarious position as well as without social status, at the mercy of her nearest male relative, who was responsible to take on her care. The Hebrew Scriptures are replete with admonitions to make widows objects of special concern. Cursed was anyone who violated the rights of a widow (Deut 27:19; Isa 10:2).

The widow in this parable, however, does not fit this portrait at all. She boldly faces the impervious judge, voicing her demands until she achieves justice on her own behalf. She marches into the arena of adjudication—clearly the domain of men by the mores of her culture. The irony is that her complaint may be against the very man who should have been her provider! As to the nature of her complaint, Jeremias advances, based on a text from the Babylonian Talmud that since the widow brings her case to a single judge and not before a tribunal, it would appear to be a money matter: a debt, a pledge, or a portion of an inheritance, that is being withheld from her.[15]

The parable ends with a soliloquy by the judge which follows a long time of resistance by him. Verses 3 and 4 indicate

---

[14] In the New Testament Luke has the most stories about widows and the most references to them, probably reflecting their growing prominence in ministry in the early Church. In addition to 18:1-8 see 2:37; 4:25-26; 7:11-17; 20:47; 21:1-4; Acts 6:1-6; 9:39, 41. See further Robert Price, *The Widow Traditions in Luke-Acts: A Feminist-Critical Scrutiny* (SBLDS 155; Atlanta: Scholars, 1997); Bonnie Bowman Thurston, *The Widows: A Women's Ministry in the Early Church* (Minneapolis: Fortress, 1989).

[15] Jeremias, *Parables*, 153, cites *b. Sanh.* 4b (Bar.): "An authorized scholar may decide money cases sitting alone."

that the widow kept coming again and again in a relentless pursuit of her claim. This is indicated with the imperfect tense of the verb *ērcheto* ("kept coming" rather than "used to come" as rendered by *NAB*) in v. 3 and followed by "for a long time he resisted, but eventually . . . " (v. 4).

Lest the hearer think the judge has a change of heart, a conversion effected by the widow's dogged efforts, v. 4 repeats: he still has no fear of God nor any respect for human beings. It is because the widow causes him so much trouble (*parechein kopon*, v. 5)[16] that he decides to give her what she wants—he simply wants to be rid of her. The final comment that he is afraid she will blacken his eye almost makes the story ridiculous. Like most of Jesus' parables, it is open-ended, leaving the hearer to puzzle over its meaning. This parable, with its unusual characters and startling ending, jolts the hearer into a new way of seeing. It asks one to leave behind stereotypes and wrestle with unfamiliar notions about what God is like and what justice in the realm of God looks like and how it is achieved. It invites one to emulate such a pursuit of justice in efforts to embody the reign of God here and now while awaiting future fulfillment.

A GODLY WIDOW

Most commentaries on this parable turn instinctually to the character of the judge as the figure who reveals something about God. But all such efforts falter because the judge clearly does not reflect what we believe about God hearing and responding to the cries of the poor. Moreover, the text itself underlines twice that the judge neither fears God nor respects human beings. The signals could not be clearer that the judge is *not* like God. Most commentators settle, however, for an understanding of the parable as a negative example, or one that makes its point by the argument *a minori ad maius* (from the lesser to the greater): if an unjust judge would give in to the

---

[16] The phrase *parechein moi kopon* means, literally, "to present me with work." The translation of the *NJB*, "she keeps pestering me," has an overtone that is sexist, which is only partially reduced in the *NRSV* and the *NAB* that render it "keeps bothering me."

relentless pleas of a widow, how much more will God, who is upright.[17]

There is a far simpler way to understand the parable. It is the widow who is cast in the image of God and who is presented to the disciples as a figure to emulate. This interpretation not only resolves the difficulties just named, but also settles an important theological issue that surfaces when one tries to see the judge as representing God. When the judge is seen as the God figure, the story suggests that if one badgers God persistently enough, one can eventually wear God down and get a positive response. Such a notion is theologically abhorrent and is flatly contradicted by texts such as Luke 11:9-13 and Sirach 35:14-19, which insist that God is eager and willing to give all good things to those who ask, particularly to those who are poorest.

POWER IN SEEMING WEAKNESS

When the widow is seen as the God-like figure, then the message of the parable is that when one doggedly resists injustice, faces it, names it, and denounces it until right is achieved, then one is acting as God does. Moreover, it reveals godly power in seeming weakness. The persistence of one apparently powerless widow achieves the victory for right. There is also in v. 5 a comment on the methods to be used in accomplishing a just end. The ludicrous image of a powerful judge fearing a seemingly helpless widow may be Jesus' wry comment on the futility of resorting to violence in the work for justice. This message achieves its fullest force in the passion, death, and resurrection of Jesus. His seeming helplessness in the face of his executioners is transformed into the very defeat of the powers of sin and death. Followers of Jesus are invited to take up this same stance: to draw on the power of apparent weakness to overcome death-dealing powers.

Finally, it is important to recognize Luke's concern to tame this story of an unconventional woman and cast her in a docile and acceptable role as an example of praying always, much

---

[17] E g., Fitzmyer, *Luke*, 1177.

like Anna, who spent eighty-four years praying in the Temple (Luke 2:36-38). This parable of the widow and the judge is one more example of the mixed message that the third evangelist gives about women in the Christian community.[18] Although Luke preserves the most stories with female characters, for the most part they are given silent, passive roles. Luke's redaction of this parable and the translations and interpretations of subsequent scholars have tamed, and even trivialized, a powerful portrait of a godly widow persistently pursuing justice.

PREACHING POSSIBILITIES

There is a great liberating potential in this parable. With a tradition that has overlooked and downplayed female images of God,[19] his parable gives the preacher a good opportunity to speak about how women and men embody the mission of Jesus when they emulate this widow by persistently pursuing justice. By abandoning futile attempts to make the judge into a God-figure, preachers can unmask sexism and help their congregations take one more step toward greater gender inclusivity. The preacher can help dislodge sexist stereotypes such as that of Jeremias who portrays the judge as a beleaguered man who is "tired of her perpetual nagging and wants to be left in peace."[20] When preached as a widow persistently pursuing justice, the parable can serve to animate women who have been socialized not to put themselves forward, and to wait patiently in hope, and with prayer, to take bold, public steps toward the pursuit of justice.[21]

---

[18] See Barbara E. Reid, "Luke's Mixed Message for Women," *Chicago Studies* 38/3 (1999) 283–97; *Choosing the Better Part? Women in the Gospel of Luke* (Collegeville: The Liturgical Press, 1996); Jane Schaberg, "Luke," in *The Women's Bible Commentary,* ed. Carol A. Newsom and Sharon H. Ringe (rev. ed.; Louisville: Westminster/John Knox, 1998) 363–80; Turid Karlsen Seim, *The Double Message: Patterns of Gender in Luke-Acts* (Nashville: Abingdon, 1994).

[19] See above, pp. 188–89, for female images of God found in the Hebrew Scriptures.

[20] Jeremias, *Parables,* 145.

[21] Ivoni Richter, "El Poder de una Protagonista. La oración de las personas excluidas (Lk 18,1-8)," *Ribla* 25 (1997) 59–68.

In a culture that measures power in terms of acquisition of wealth, this parable underscores the paradoxical power of seeming weakness. It shows that the initiative in seeking justice comes from the one who has been wronged, and her power is in doggedly raising her voice day after day after day. The parable portrays not violence, but persistent naming and confronting injustice as the means to accomplish righteousness. Further, she can encourage those who are intimidated at the enormity of the challenge in dismantling interlocking systems of racism, sexism, militarism, and economic imbalance. A seemingly helpless widow has power far beyond that of a corrupt judge. This image is not so foreign to biblical readers who know of Ruth and Tamar, widows who took bold steps that ensured God's plan for the continuance of Israel.[22]

The preacher can also raise the necessity for persistence in confronting injustice. The image of the widow can encourage Christians who become weary in their repeated efforts toward justice. The parable keeps a disciple realistic, however, about not expecting to transform whole systems of injustice at once. The judge remains as ungodly and as shameless as ever—but the widow achieves at least one small victory for justice. The other two readings on the Twenty-ninth Sunday in Ordinary Time also underscore persistence. While the first reading from Exodus 17:8-13 gives an image of Moses persevering in his intercession on behalf of Israel, with his arms upraised, the second, from 2 Timothy 3:14–4:2 emphasizes persistence in proclaiming the word.

Perhaps the preacher might encourage his or her congregation to complete the parable, not as Luke attempted in vv. 6-8, but more akin to the finale of the parables of the lost and found sheep, coin, and sons. Like the shepherd, the woman, and the father whose joy in finding overflows in partying with their friends and neighbors (15:6, 9, 23-24, 32), a celebration to conclude this and each victory for justice could underscore the good news the parable presents and give strength and freedom of spirit to its hearers for their next confrontation with injustice.

---

[22] Don C. Benjamin, "The Persistent Widow," *TBT* 28 (1990) 212–19.

CHAPTER TWENTY

Acceptable Prayer
(Luke 18:9-14)

Thirtieth Sunday of Ordinary Time

⁹ Jesus addressed this parable
to those who were convinced of their own righteousness
and despised everyone else.
¹⁰ "Two people went up to the temple area to pray;
one was a Pharisee and the other was a tax collector.
¹¹ The Pharisee took up his position and spoke this prayer to himself,
'O God, I thank you that I am not like the rest of humanity—
greedy, dishonest, adulterous—or even like this tax collector.
¹² I fast twice a week, and I pay tithes on my whole income.'
¹³ But the tax collector stood off at a distance
and would not even raise his eyes to heaven
but beat his breast and prayed,
'O God, be merciful to me a sinner.'
¹⁴ I tell you, the latter went home justified, not the former;
for whoever who exalts himself will be humbled,
and the one who humbles himself will be exalted."

LUKAN LITERARY CONTEXT

This parable brings to a close the uniquely Lukan portion of the travel narrative that began in 9:51. The journey to Jerusalem continues to 19:27, but at 18:15 Luke picks up again with the Markan source. The parable of the Pharisee and the toll collector is unique to Luke, and like the preceding parable, it contrasts two characters in a dualistic fashion. The parable proper is found in vv. 10-14a, while the opening and closing verses are from Luke's hand, framing the parable with an interpretive overlay.[1] The saying in v. 14b about those who exalt themselves becoming humbled and vice versa is identical to the saying that concludes the parable of the places at table in 14:11. It is a free-floating proverb that is also found in Matthew 23:12.

The first verse and last verses bring forward the theme of righteousness. This term in English has a pejorative tone to it, as it is often associated with "self-righteousness," a connotation reinforced by this parable. But the word in biblical parlance is one that expresses right relation with God, which is the ultimate goal of the believer. In the First Testament righteousness is expressed in terms of faithfulness to the covenant. In the New Testament Paul formulates it most succinctly: it comes from faith in Christ, which is a gift from God, not by works of the Law (Rom 3:21-26). The issue of righteousness is also explicitly connected to the parables of the children in the marketplace (7:29-35), the good Samaritan (10:29-37); and that of the steward who rewrites his master's accounts (16:1-13).[2] The parable of the Samaritan is directed to a scribe who wants to justify himself (10:29); that of the steward is followed by a saying of Jesus directed at Pharisees who justify themselves in the sight of others (16:14-15). Luke puts a similar slant on the parable in 18:9-14. Jesus addresses the parable to those who believe that they are just (*dikaioi*, v. 9) and ends with a surprising twist affirming the toll collector as justified (*dedikaiōmenos*, v. 14a).[3]

---

[1] R. K. Bultmann, *The History of the Synoptic Tradition.* Trans. J. Marsh (rev. ed.; New York: Harper & Row, 1968) 193; Joseph A. Fitzmyer, *The Gospel According to Luke* (AB28A; Garden City, N.Y.: Doubleday, 1981) 1183; John R. Donahue, *The Gospel in Parable* (Philadelphia: Fortress, 1988) 187.

[2] See chaps. 23, 9, and 16, respectively.

[3] The word in 18:9 is the plural adjective *dikaioi;* in v. 14a it is the perfect passive participle of the verb *dikaioō.* Elsewhere Luke uses the adjective *dikaios* to describe Zechariah and Elizabeth (1:6), Simeon (2:25), Joseph of Arimathea (23:50), and Cornelius (Acts 10:22). It occurs in nine other sayings about the upright: Luke 1:17; 5:32; 12:57; 14:14; 15:7; 18:9; 20:20; Acts 4:19; 24:15. Most notable is that Luke changed the climactic declaration of the centurion at the death of Jesus from "Truly this man was God's Son!" (Mark 15:39) to "Certainly this man was innocent *(dikaios)"* (Luke 23:47). In Acts of the Apostles "the Righteous One" *(ho dikaios)* becomes a title of Jesus in three key speeches (Acts 3:14; 7:52; 22:14). The adverb *dikaiōs,* "just,"occurs in Luke 23:41 where it refers to the two criminals who have been justly condemned. The noun *dikaiosynē,* "justification," occurs in Zechariah's prayer (Luke 1:75) and four times in Acts: 10:35;

THE PHARISEE'S PRAYER

While Luke's introduction in v. 9 does not specify the Pharisee as the one who believes in his own righteousness, his overall treatment of the Pharisees leads the hearer to understand him this way. Throughout the gospel Luke casts the Pharisees as Jesus' opponents,[4] and has already reprimanded them for justifying themselves in the sight of others while such human esteem is an abomination in the sight of God (16:15). Because of Luke's literary portrayal of the Pharisees as a foil to Jesus, we are ready to identify them as condemnably self-righteous. For Jesus' original audience, however, the Pharisee would be the character who would be expected to offer exemplary prayer. As pious lay religious leaders, Pharisees were known for surpassing others in their observances of piety and in their exact interpretation of the law."[5]

Nor would the prayer of this Pharisee necessarily have sounded objectionable to Jesus' first audience. A prayer that thanks God[6] for preserving him from sin and that gives an account of his fidelity is not unlike this prayer from the Talmud:

> I thank thee, O Lord, my god, that thou hast given me my lot with those who sit in the seat of learning, and not those who sit at the street-corners; for I am early to work, and they are early to work; I am early to work on the words of the Torah, and they are early to work on things of no moment. I weary myself and they weary themselves to no profit. I run and they run; I run towards the life of the Age to Come, and they run towards the pit of destruction.[7]

13:10; 17:31; 24:25. The verb *dikaioō* appears in Luke 7:29, 35; 10:29; 16:15 and Acts 13:38-39.

[4] See above, pp. 159–60, on the Pharisees in Luke, and John T. Carroll, "Luke's Portrayal of the Pharisees," *CBQ* 50 (1988) 604–21.

[5] Josephus, *J.W.* 1.5, 2 §110. See Anthony J. Saldarini, *Pharisees, Scribes and Sadducees in Palestinian Society: A Sociological Approach* (Wilmington: Glazier, 1988).

[6] Fitzmyer, *Luke*, 1186, notes that the phrase *eucharistō soi*, addressed to God in the second person singular, occurs on the lips of Jesus in John 11:41 and often in the Qumran Thanksgiving Psalms, e.g., 1QH 2:20, 31; 3:19, 37; 4:5; 7:34, and also in Judith 8:25; 2 Maccabees 1:11.

[7] *b. Ber* 28b. This reference is noted by Donahue, *Gospel in Parable*, 188–89; Joachim Jeremias, *The Parables of Jesus* (New York: Scribner's, 1972) 142; Bernard Brandon Scott, *Hear Then the Parable: A Commentary on the Parables of Jesus* (Minneapolis: Fortress, 1989) 95; and others.

The Talmud does not view this prayer negatively, but as one that appropriately thanks God for the privilege and opportunity to study the Torah. Another similar prayer is found in the Tosephta:

> Rabbi Judah said: One must utter three praises every day: Praised be the Lord that he did not make me a heathen, for all the heathen are as nothing before Him (Isa 40:17); praised be He, that He did not make me a woman, for woman is not under obligation to fulfill the law; praised be He that He did not make me an uneducated man, for the uneducated man is not cautious to avoid sins.[8]

Although these prayers post-date Jesus' time, it is probable that the values they embody were current in the first century as well. In the Psalms are also examples of prayers that extol the prayer's accomplishments:

> My mouth has not transgressed as humans often do.
>> As your lips have instructed me,
>>> I have kept the way of the law.
>> My steps have kept to your paths;
> my feet have not faltered (Ps 17:4-5).

And from the Qumran community we have a psalm that reads:

> "I praise you, O God, for you have not allowed my lot to fall among the worthless community, nor assigned me a part in the circle of the secret ones."[9]

The Pharisee also mentions his exemplary fasting and tithing. The only fasting prescribed in the Torah is for one day of the year: Yom Kippur, the day of Atonement (Lev 16:29; 23:27). There are a few references in the Hebrew Scriptures to fasting on other occasions. In Psalm 35:13 there is mention of fasting accompanying prayer so as to make a prayer of supplication more efficacious. And there is mention of David (2 Sam 12:13-25) and Ahab (1 Kgs 21:27) fasting as an expression of penance. David also fasts as a sign of mourning at the death of

---

[8] *t. Ber.* 7.18; Scott, *Hear Then*, 95; Eta Linnemann, *Jesus of the Parables: Introduction and Exposition* (New York: Harper & Row, 1966) 59.

[9] 1QH 7:34. This example is cited by Donahue, *Gospel in Parable*, 189; Jeremias, *Parables*, 142, n. 55.

Saul (2 Sam 1:12) and at the death of Abner (2 Sam 3:36). In Daniel 10:3 and later apocalyptic literature fasting is practiced to make one open to divine revelation or visions.

Certain Jewish sects contemporary with Jesus were known for their fasting. The Essenes, who were likely the group at Qumran, fasted, as did the Therapeuts in Egypt.[10] As for the practice of fasting twice a week, of which the Pharisee boasts, it is not certain whether this practice can be dated to pre-70 C.E. Pharisaism. Our earliest reference to the Pharisaic practice comes from the *Didache* (8:1), where Christian fast days are set forth as Wednesday and Friday, in contrast to the Jewish fast days of Monday and Thursday.[11] Luke says that Anna "worshiped night and day with fasting and prayer" (2:37) and mentions this as a practice of the early Christians in Acts 13:2-3 and 14:23. And in 5:33-39 he contrasts the frequent fasting of the disciples of John the Baptist and of the Pharisees with the lack of such by Jesus and his followers.[12] The import, then, is that the fasting of the Pharisee in Luke 18:12 would be looked upon as laudatory.

As for tithes, Deuteronomy 14:22-23 prescribed tithes for seed, grain, wine, oil, the firstborn of the herd and flock, to be offered annually at the harvest festival. If one did not live close enough to the Temple to bring the goods, they could be converted to money and that could be offered instead (Deut 14:25-27). Certain groups of Pharisees, the *ḥaberim*, voluntarily took upon themselves stricter ritual observance involving more rigid tithes on food. As a result they shunned table companionship with those outside their group. The *ḥaberim* represented a very small percentage of the Jewish population, and although some Pharisees belonged to this group, it is doubtful that they should be entirely identified with it.[13]

[10] Josephus (*J.W.* 2.8.5) speaks of the Essenes fasting; Philo (*VitaCont.* 34) tells that the Therapeuts fasted.

[11] The final form of the *Didache* dates to the first half of the second century. The Jewish fast days, Monday and Thursday, are attested in *b. Ta'an.* 12a, the final redaction of which dates to approximately 450 C.E. Thursday and Monday are said to be the days on which Moses ascended and descended Mount Sinai. See further John Muddiman, "Fast, Fasting," *ABD*, 2.773–76.

[12] See below, chap. 21, on Luke 5:33-39.

[13] See E. P. Sanders, *Jesus and Judaism* (2nd ed.; Philadelphia: Fortress, 1985) 174–211.

At first blush, the form of prayer of the Pharisee, and the extraordinary practices of fasting and tithing are most exemplary. But there are other details in the description of the Pharisee and his prayer that reveal that his righteousness is not all it seems. One cannot help but notice that although the prayer begins with an address to God, every other pronoun is "I": "I thank you . . . I am not like . . . I fast . . . I pay . . . ." His whole prayer is centered on himself and his accomplishments. While he does begin by acknowledging God as the source of his blessings and achievements, his prayer sounds to contemporary Western ears like one of self-congratulation and self-aggrandizement. He seems to need nothing from God.

A further difficulty with the Pharisee is not only that his relation with God seems out of kilter, but there is a yawning gulf that he has placed between himself and all "the rest of humanity" (v. 11).[14] He labels others as rapacious *(harpages)*,[15] unjust *(adikoi)*, and adulterers *(moichoi)* and keeps apart from the toll collector. In so judging others he has usurped God's prerogative. All that he has received from God has not served to give him a compassionate heart toward others.[16] His stance appears to be one of entitlement rather than gratitude, by which he might recognize all as gift, and to see himself as inextricably bound with all of humanity as brothers and sisters. He is neither in right relation with God nor with other people.

---

[14] Scholars debate whether the phrase *pros heauton,* "to himself," modifies *statheis,* "stood," or *proseucheto,* "prayed." Donahue, *Gospel in Parable,* 188, and Fitzmyer, *Luke,* 1186, fault the Pharisee for praying to or about himself; for Kenneth E. Bailey (*Through Peasant Eyes: More Lucan Parables, Their Culture and Style* [Grand Rapids: Eerdmans, 1980]) the problem is that he "stood by himself." Jeremias, *Parables,* 140, finds him arrogant because he "took up a prominent position." Perhaps it is not important to decide one way or the other. The ambiguity of the referent allows us to see the Pharisee's alienation both from God and from other people.

[15] This term is used in Genesis 49:27 and Matthew 7:15 of ravenous wolves, to which Benjamin and false prophets are compared. Ironically, in Luke 11:39 Jesus accused the Pharisees of washing the outside of the cup, while inside being full of rapaciousness *(harpagēs)* and evil.

[16] Barbara Green, *Like a Tree Planted: An Exploration of Psalms and Parables Through Metaphor* (Collegeville: The Liturgical Press, 1997) 62.

THE TOLL COLLECTOR'S PRAYER

The toll collector, by contrast, stands apart because he knows he is despised by the Pharisee. Law-observant Jews would have considered him greedy, sinful, unclean, dishonest, and a quisling of Rome.[17] He does not lift his eyes to heaven, which bespeaks his compunction.[18] He beats his breast, a sign of sorrow and mourning,[19] a gesture more typical of women than of men in Middle Eastern culture.[20] His prayer is a simple cry for mercy, in the spirit of Psalm 51, "Have mercy on me, God, in your goodness; in your abundant compassion blot out my offense" (v. 3).[21] His plea *hilasthēti* literally means, "make atonement for me." His hope is that the atonement sacrifices offered in the temple may apply to him.[22]

Although he has made no restitution for any offenses—and probably could not find all the people he has cheated even if he wanted to—he returns home justified. He is righteous because he recognizes who he is in relation to God and that any good that comes to him is by God's mercy.

LUKAN PORTRAITS OF PRAYER

Luke adds this portrait to his depiction of many forms of prayer. He has shown Mary (1:46-55), Simeon (2:29-32), Anna (2:38), and Jesus (10:21-22) praying in thanksgiving. Prayers of praise have been offered by Zechariah (1:67-79), the heavenly host (2:13-14), and shepherds (2:20). Jesus has taught his disciples intercessory prayer (11:1-4). Jesus has instructed his followers to pray for their enemies (6:28) and exemplifies it with

---

[17] See above, pp. 182–83, on toll collectors.

[18] Fitzmyer, *Luke*, 1188, notes that in *1 Enoch* 13:5, "they did not raise their eyes to heaven out of shame for the sins for which they had been condemned." Generally one would lift the face (Job 22:21-30; John 6:5; 11:41; 17:1; Luke 12:28; 16:23) or hands (Lam 2:19; Pss 119:48; 134:2) or eyes (Ezek 18:6; Ps 123:1) in prayer.

[19] As the people who had gathered to watch Jesus' crucifixion in Luke 23:48.

[20] Bailey, *Through Peasant Eyes*, 153.

[21] Similar prayers are known from Qumran: 1QS 11:3-5, 10-12; 1QH 11:15-22.

[22] Bailey, *Through Peasant Eyes*, 154. This is different from others who ask for mercy from Jesus, as the lepers in 17:13, who plead, *eleēson me*.

his prayer for forgiveness for those who crucify him (23:34).[23] To this portrait he adds the humble prayer of the toll collector who knows his need for mercy.

By coupling this story with that of the widow and the judge in 18:1-8, Luke provides a fuller picture of righteousness. Right relation is expressed in both prayer for God's mercy and persistent action in the pursuit of justice. Both stories overturn stereotypes and startle the hearer. A widow who is expected to be helpless and acquiescent is a powerful force who successfully moves a corrupt judge toward a just act. A toll collector, despised by others and expected to be likewise despised by God, exemplifies right relation in prayer. In him we see an image of the crucified One, who seemingly cursed by God (Deut 21:23) is actually God's Righteous One (Luke 23:47). It is the despised[24] One who is chosen by God.

TEMPLE TOLL COLLECTOR

The fact that this episode takes place in the Temple is also significant. People could go to the Temple at any time to pray, but two times were reserved for public prayer: the third hour of the day, about 9 A.M. (Acts 2:15) and the ninth hour, 3 P.M. (Acts 3:1).[25] But far more than simply a place to gather to pray, the Temple was the prime redemptive symbol for Jews. It represented the institutionalized aspects of religious observance. It was the Jerusalem Temple that was the power base for the aristocratic Sadducees and the priestly class.[26]

The upkeep of the Temple and the Jerusalem elites was accomplished through an elaborate system of taxes and tithes. There was an annual offering of first fruits of the produce. In addition was the annual first tithe, which provided support to the priests and Levites. A second tithe was used for various

---

[23] Donahue, *Gospel in Parable*, 192.

[24] The verb *exoutheneō* ("despised," v. 9) is used of the action of Herod and his soldiers toward Jesus in Luke 23:11, and in Acts 4:11 it describes the stone rejected contemptuously by the builder, alluding to Jesus.

[25] Fitzmyer, *Luke*, 1186.

[26] The following is from William R. Herzog II, *Parables as Subversive Speech: Jesus as Pedagogue of the Oppressed* (Louisville: Westminster/John Knox, 1994) 173–93.

purposes during the six-year cycle between sabbatical years. Contributing these tithes to the Temple was seen as an important way to acknowledge God's goodness and to ensure continued good crops. But in addition to Temple taxes and tithes there were exorbitant Roman taxes. Romans and the elites among the Jews collaborated to keep peasants in a cycle of indebtedness. Many people in first-century Palestine lived from hand to mouth and would have been unable to meet all the demands. Peasants who did not pay their Temple taxes would be stigmatized as lax in Torah observance and would find themselves branded as threatening the well-being of the land.

In this light, the Pharisee in the parable, who emphasizes the importance of tithes in his prayer, reveals himself as a toll collector of another sort—one who sanctions the importance of the Temple tithes and who despises those who cannot meet the exorbitant demands. The toll collector is a convenient target for his deprecation toward the socially vulnerable. Rather than haughty quislings, toll collectors might better have been described as low-level functionaries who formed a constantly changing and socially unprotected group of men. They were subsistence-level wage earners with no bargaining power and only stooped to such a job in desperation when no other work could be found. Their extortionary practices kept them from the brink of starvation, but made them hated by all.[27]

Seen in this way the Pharisee's attempt to shame and publicly label the toll collector is deflected by the latter's appeal to a higher source: God. In so doing he demystifies the Temple tax system and its claim to mediate redemption. Such an act allows one who is oppressed and dehumanized by the Temple system to name this and unmask its pretensions. Like Jesus' confrontation with the merchants in the Temple (Luke 19:45-48), the parable exposes corruption, inviting renewal so that the Temple can yet be the place of God's saving action, as hoped for by the toll collector.[28]

---

[27] Herzog, *Subversive*, 188; Luise Schottroff and Wolfgang Stegemann, *Jesus and the Hope of the Poor*, trans. M. J. O'Connell (Maryknoll: Orbis, 1986) 8–9.

[28] Michael Farris, "A Tale of Two Taxations (Luke 18:10-14b)," in V. G. Shillington, ed., *Jesus and His Parables: Interpreting the Parables of Jesus Today* (Edinburgh: T. & T. Clark, 1997) 23–33.

PREACHING POSSIBILITIES

Preachers of this parable often pick up the theme of humility before God as the stance for prayer, rather than self-congratulation or self-aggrandizement. People are usually invited by the preacher to emulate the toll collector, who we usually see as a sympathetic and falsely maligned figure. We instinctually despise the Pharisee whom we see despising all other human beings. A new twist might be for the preacher to stop us in our tracks and invite us to see how in the very act of judging the Pharisee we are ourselves exemplifying the judgmentalness we despise in him.[29] A startling aspect of the parable is to invite those who are good church-going people to stand with the Pharisee, an upstanding religious person, one who goes beyond what is required in religious observance, and to be challenged to see how much we may be like him. The preacher may invite reflection on how to move from a stance of entitlement to one of utter dependence on God at all times, with gratitude for all that has been given, and with complete trust for all that is needed. From such a place where all is seen as gift, right relation with God, self, others, and all creation flows. From this position, there is no smugness of superiority toward any other; all are seen as brothers and sisters of the same gracious God.

This stance speaks both to how an individual approaches God in personal prayer and to the manner of expressing our public communal prayer. Moreover, there is no dividing line between prayer and action. The link between prayer and action to confront injustice is inextricably made. In prayer one shares the tender heart of God toward all brothers and sisters, and one becomes sensitized to systems of injustice. This moves a person to act with the passion of God, who desires right relation for all of creation. Coupled with the first reading from Sirach 35:12-14, 16-18, the parable assures that God hears and accomplishes the good for one who prays in such a fashion.

One pitfall the preacher should avoid is emphasizing the humility of the toll collector to people who are already downtrodden. To people who are oppressed, exalting humble ac-

---

[29] Green, *Like a Tree Planted*, 69.

ceptance of their circumstances, or offering it to God in prayer short-circuits the process of prayer that moves into action for justice.[30] Prayer and justice (righteousness) go hand in hand.

[30] F. G. Downing ("The Ambiguity of 'The Pharisee and the Toll-collector' [Luke 18:9-14] in the Greco-Roman World of Late Antiquity," *CBQ* 54 [1992] 80–99) argues that neither the toll collector nor the Pharisee is exemplary. The Pharisee is right in thanking God, but not for his own deeds. The toll collector is likewise blameworthy for keeping a distance from God and for praying with self-deprecating despair, an attitude that is nowhere encouraged in the Scriptures. For Downing both characters are sure God's welcome is restricted and conditional; both are sure God holds public offenders at arm's length; and both are wrong. Jesus repeatedly demonstrates God's unconditional welcome. Both are warnings about false attitudes in prayer. Downing's interpretation does not work for the redaction of the parable as it now stands in Luke. He advances that vv. 9 and 14 (in its entirety) are Lukan additions, which set up the anticipation that one character is approved and the other not.

CHAPTER TWENTY-ONE

Feasting and Fasting
(Luke 5:33-39)

Friday of the Twenty-second Week of Ordinary Time

[33] *[The scribes and the Pharisees said to Jesus]:*
  "The disciples of John fast often and offer prayers,
  and the disciples of the Pharisees do the same;
  but yours eat and drink."
[34] *Jesus answered them,*
  "Can you make the wedding guests fast
  while the bridegroom is with them?
[35] *But the days will come,*
  and when the bridegroom is taken away from them,
  then they will fast in those days."

[36] *And he also told them a parable.*
  "No one tears a piece from a new cloak
    to patch an old one.
  Otherwise, he will tear the new
    and the piece from it will not match the old cloak.
[37] *Likewise, no one pours new wine into old wineskins.*
  Otherwise, the new wine will burst the skins,
  and it will be spilled,
  and the skins will be ruined.
[38] *Rather, new wine must be poured into fresh wineskins.*
[39] *[And] no one who has been drinking old wine desires new,*
  for he says, 'The old is good.'"

LUKAN LITERARY CONTEXT

This exchange takes place within the context of the banquet given by Levi for Jesus (5:29-32). There the Pharisees and scribes complain to Jesus' disciples, asking why they eat and drink with tax collectors and sinners (v. 30). The controversial dialogue continues in vv. 33-35, as the issue of eating and drinking[1] shifts to practices of fasting. Luke frequently employs banquet scenes with dialogue that confronts the hearer with an invitation to conversion.[2]

Luke's episode follows closely that found in Mark 2:18-22, though Luke makes a number of redactional changes.[3] There are three parts to the selection. The first (vv. 33-35) is a controversy dialogue, followed by two similitudes (vv. 36-38), which Luke dubs a parable.[4] The section concludes with a proverb (v. 39) that is unique to Luke. The disparate pieces are held together by the common theme of the old versus the new.

CONTROVERSY OVER FASTING (vv. 33-35)

As the controversy dialogue opens in v. 33 the ones who question Jesus are unnamed. Presumably the challengers are the last ones mentioned in v. 30: "the Pharisees and their scribes," that is, scribes who belonged to the Pharisee party.[5] As throughout the Third Gospel, the Pharisees are cast as a foil to Jesus.[6] Echoes of their challenge here are also found in 7:33-34, where they complain that John the Baptist, who came neither eating nor drinking, was possessed; and that Jesus, who does eat and drink, is "a glutton and a drunkard, a friend of tax collectors and sinners" (7:34). The same complaint surfaces from

---

[1] Luke's addition of the phrase "eat and drink" in v. 33 (cf. Mark 2:18) clearly links vv. 33-35 with vv. 29-32.

[2] Luke 7:36-50; 9:10-17; 11:37-54; 14:1-24; 19:1-10; 22:4-38; 24:29-32.

[3] The incident is also found in Matthew 9:14-17 and there are parallels in *Gos.Thom.* §104 and §47bc. The latter are clearly dependent on the Lukan form of the sayings. See Joseph A. Fitzmyer, *The Gospel According to Luke* (AB28; Garden City, N.Y.: Doubleday, 1981) 594–95, for detailed analysis of Luke's redactional changes.

[4] See above, p. 14, for the various kinds of sayings and stories included under the rubric of *parabolē*, "parable."

[5] This creates narrative tension, however, with "the disciples of the Pharisees" in v. 33b.

[6] See above, pp. 159–60, for how the historical Pharisees in Jesus' day differed from their literary function in the Gospel of Luke.

the Pharisees and scribes in 15:2, and from the generic "they" in 19:7. The point of conflict in those episodes is Jesus' inclusive table practices that signified the acceptance of marginalized people in God's realm. In 5:33-35 the issue is more sharply focused on the failure of Jesus' disciples to fast, in contrast to those of John and those of the Pharisees. While Luke redacts the challenge in v. 33a to involve both fasting and prayer,[7] it is only the former that is the focus of Jesus' response in vv. 34-35.

DISCIPLES OF JOHN AND OF THE PHARISEES

Mention of disciples of John the Baptist is made not only here, but also in Luke 7:18-35, where the imprisoned John sends two of his disciples to ascertain whether Jesus is the one who is to come. And in 11:1, Jesus' disciples ask him to teach them to pray as John taught his disciples. These texts, as well the stepparallelism of the infancy narratives (Luke 1–2), and Acts 19:1-7, may reflect a rivalry in the early Church between disciples of Jesus and those of John.[8] But more to the point of Luke's agenda is that for him John the Baptist is a transitional figure between the old age and the new. John is the hinge figure that bridges the time of the Law and the Prophets and the new inbreaking of the reign of God with the coming of Jesus. (Luke 16:16).[9]

The "disciples of the Pharisees" is a curious phrase and scholars puzzle over its meaning. The best explanation for its origin is that in Luke 11:19 (// Matt 12:27) there is a query by Jesus to the Pharisees, "If I drive out demons by Beezebul, by whom do your own people (*hoi huioi hymōn*, literally, "your sons") drive them out?" Here "your sons" denotes members of a group, that is, those belonging to the Pharisees. It stands in parallelism to *tous huious tou nymphōnos*, "sons of the bridegroom" (translated "wedding guests" in v. 34). It is probable that the phrase "disciples of the Pharisees" was constructed by Mark (Luke's source) for the sake of parallelism with "the

---

[7] Prayer is a favorite theme of Luke (see above, pp. 229, 243–44) and the combination of fasting and prayer occurs also in Luke 2:37; 18:12; Acts 13:2-3; 14:23; 27:9.

[8] So also John 1:6-8, 15, 19-23; 3:25-26; 4:1-2.

[9] See above, pp. 35–36, on Luke's historical framework.

disciples of John" and for contrast with "your [Jesus'] disciples" (Mark 2:18).

NOT NOW BUT THEN

In Luke's narrative Jesus is portrayed as fasting in the desert in preparation for his mission (4:2), but elsewhere he is eating and drinking, as are his disciples. In this they clearly stand out from the disciples of John and of the Pharisees. The Jewish practice of fasting is long-standing. However, the only day on which fasting is required of all is Yom Kippur, the Day of Atonement (Lev 16:29; 23:27). This tradition likely dates to pre-exilic times. Other examples of fasting in the Hebrew Scriptures are individuals who fast so as to make their prayer of supplication more efficacious (Ps 35:13), or do so as an expression of penance (2 Sam 12:13-25; 1 Kgs 21:27) or mourning (2 Sam 1:12; 3:36). In Daniel 10:3 and later apocalyptic literature, fasting is practiced to make one open to divine revelation or visions.

Among Jesus' contemporaries the Essenes were noted for their fasting, as attested by Josephus (*J.W.* 2.8.5), so also the Therapeuts in Egypt, as described by Philo (*VitaCont.* 34). In the story of the Pharisee and the toll collector (Luke 18:9-18) the Pharisee prides himself on his twice-weekly fasting (v. 12). It is not certain whether this practice dates to pre-70 c.e. Pharisaism. Our earliest reference to the Pharisaic practice comes from the *Didache* (8:1),[10] where Christian fast days are set forth as Wednesday and Friday, in contrast to the Jewish fast days of Monday and Thursday.[11] Against such a backdrop, Jesus' nonfasting requires explanation.

THE BRIDEGROOM

Jesus' reply equates his disciples with wedding guests and himself with the bridegroom. This image recalls the many times in the prophetic literature where Yahweh is presented as the groom or the husband of the people of the covenant (e.g., Hos

[10] The final form of the *Didache* dates to the first half of the second century.

[11] John Muddiman, "Fast, Fasting," in *Anchor Bible Dictionary*, ed. David N. Freedman (New York: Doubleday, 1997) 2.773–76.

2:19; Isa 54:3-6; 62:5; Jer 2:2; Ezekiel 16). One implication, then, is that Jesus is on a par with God who is also cast as bridegroom in the Hebrew Scriptures.[12] The use of the image, however, is not the same. In the prophetic texts, Yahweh is portrayed as faithful husband to perfidious Israel. The prophets urge Israel to repentance and return to their God who never breaks covenant trust. In Luke 5:34-35 the bridegroom's presence evokes joy and calls for suspension of all penitence.

There is also a stress on timing—the time of Jesus' earthly ministry is unique. The inbreaking of the reign of God brought by Jesus is like a marriage feast. It demands a temporary stop to all grieving and penitence. There is already a foretaste of Isaiah's prophecy about the messianic age, "On this mountain the LORD of hosts will make for all peoples a feast of rich food, a feast of well-aged wines, of rich food filled with marrow, of well-aged wines strained clear" (Isa 25:6).

THE DAYS WILL COME

In v. 35 there is a somber shift. The expression "the day will come" is often used in the Scriptures to introduce an oracle of woe (e.g., 1 Sam 2:31; Amos 4:2; Jer 38:31; Luke 17:22; 21:6). The reference to the taking away of the bridegroom is the first allusion in the gospel to the death of Jesus. It carries an echo of Isaiah 53:8, where the suffering servant, "oppressed and condemned . . . was taken away." Most scholars doubt whether Jesus himself uttered this saying so early in his ministry. For them this verse reflects the post-crucifixion experience of the early Church. After the death of Jesus it became appropriate for his disciples to fast.[13]

---

[12] Other New Testament texts in which Jesus is presented as bridegroom or alluded to as such include: Matthew 22:1-14; 25:1-13; John 2:9-10; 3:29; 2 Corinthians 11:2; Ephesians 5:22-32; Revelation 18:23; 19:7, 9; 21:2, 9; 22:17.

[13] Other New Testament references to fasting include Matthew 6:16-18 where Jesus gives instructions on appearances when fasting. In Luke 2:27; Acts 13:2-3; 14:23, fasting accompanies prayer. In 2 Corinthians 6:5; 11:27 Paul mentions hunger among the hardships he endures for the sake of the gospel. It is unclear whether he means involuntary hunger or fasting.

INCOMPATIBILITY OF NEW AND OLD (vv. 36-37)

Linked to the controversy dialogue are two parabolic say-ings in vv. 36-37 that bring to a climax the contrast between the new way of Jesus and the way of other religious leaders. Two illustrations involving new cloth and new wine bring home the point of the incompatibility of Jesus' new way with the old. In v. 36 Luke shifts the image somewhat from that presented in Mark. Luke moves the focus from the old garment to the new, as it is from the new garment that a piece is torn for the patch on the old.[14] The consequences are two-fold in Luke and center on the new garment: the new will be torn and the piece from the new will not match the old.[15]

The second simile (v. 37) matches Mark's version (2:22) more closely and envisions destruction of both the new wine and the old wineskins when new is poured into the old. Metaphorically, both images convey the message that Jesus' teaching is not a younger, more contemporary version of older teaching; it is something radically new, demanding a new re-sponse. While Luke retains these sayings from his Markan source,[16] he more often stresses the continuity between Chris-tianity and Judaism. He consistently portrays Jesus and his mis-sion in terms of fulfillment of prophecy from the Scriptures,[17] and the continuity of God's saving action from the days of the covenant into the new age.

The final verse (v. 39) is unique to Luke. At first glance it may seem to contradict the previous sayings. A better explana-tion, however, is that this comment explains the reason why many were slow to accept Jesus' new teaching and follow his new way. In a culture that prizes traditional ways over innova-tions, new ideas and ways of doing things are not readily

---

[14] In Mark 2:21 there is no mention of the source of the piece of unshrunk cloth sewn to the old garment.

[15] In contrast, the consequence in Mark 2:21 is that the new patch tears away from the old garment and a worse tear results.

[16] He drops, however, the Markan exclamation of the amazed crowd in the synagogue who cry out: "What is this? A new teaching with authority!" (Mark 1:27). The Lukan parallel has them simply ask, "What is there about his word?" (4:36).

[17] On this theme see Fitzmyer, *Luke*, 180–81.

adopted. Like the Athenians, who enjoyed nothing more than telling or hearing something new (Acts 17:21), they like to talk about new ideas, but do not adopt them readily, as is evident in Paul making only a few converts there (Acts 17:34). Sirach 9:10 enshrines a similar attitude:

> Discard not an old friend,
> for the new one cannot equal him.
> A new friend is like new wine
> which you drink with pleasure only when it has aged.

PREACHING POSSIBILITIES

The question of the incompatibility of the new with the old is a theme that needs careful handling. A preacher must be wary of any remarks that suggest superiority of Christianity over Judaism or the replacement of the latter by the former. It is critical that Jesus always be understood as an observant Jew whose mission was directed to first-century Palestinian Jews. His first followers were Jews who understood themselves as one of the diverse streams of pre-70 C.E. Judaism, where Pharisees, Sadducees, Essenes, Zealots, and followers of the Way all co-existed within the chosen people. There was no univocal "orthodox" Judaism in Jesus' day; there were many valid expressions of first-century Judaism. The Jesus movement most likely understood itself as a prophetic renewal movement.[18] Its focus on emancipation for those most oppressed and marginalized proved a threat to those Jewish and Roman authorities whose power was derived from systems of domination. Thus did they conspire to do away with Jesus and put an end to its momentum.

A preacher must take care not to foment Christian anti-Judaism by speaking of Christianity as a "reform movement" within Judaism. Judaism was not superseded or replaced by Christianity. Nor should Christianity be thought of as an "outgrowth" of Judaism. Rather, early Judaism and emergent

---

[18] See Elisabeth Schüssler Fiorenza, *Jesus: Miriam's Child, Sophia's Prophet* (New York: Continuum, 1994) 88–92.

Christianity were twin siblings of the same mother.[19] In their inception they were two coexisting streams of the same religion. The Gospels often retroject into the time of Jesus the later conflicts between Jews of the synagogue and those who followed Jesus. It was not until the 80s that these tensions resulted in a split between the two, when Christians were no longer welcome in the synagogue and had to choose one or the other.

It is in this context of increasing struggle for Christian self-understanding that Luke presents the Jesus movement as incompatible with emergent Pharisaic Judaism. A preacher today who chooses to focus on the theme of incompatibility must decide what the contrasting pole will be. With what is present-day Christianity incompatible?

A related question that could be expanded on by the preacher is the issue of Christian self-definition. How are Christians different from others? Do our practices set us visibly apart from others? What are those practices? In a culture where comfort and self-gratification is the norm, is there an invitation in this text to a renewal of the practice of fasting on a regular basis, not only during Lent? In a culture with high consciousness of diet and weight-loss, a preacher needs to articulate the motivations for fasting that are biblically based and different from these. Fasting accompanies prayer, makes one more open to God, and puts one in solidarity with those whose hunger is not voluntary. It can also be a sign of penitence or mourning.

The gospel also gives an example of a process of reinterpretation of tradition in a new context that posed new questions. Verse 35 shows how the early Christians were able to theologize the adoption of a practice that differed from that of Jesus. Part of the question is timing; what was done when the earthly Jesus was alive was different from what was proper after his death. In our changed time and circumstances what traditional practices require reinterpretation?

The final verse also offers food for thought on what our cultural stance is toward what is new and what is old. For the

---

[19] Alan F. Segal, *Rebecca's Children* (Cambridge: Harvard University Press, 1987); Hayim G. Perelmuter, *Siblings: Rabbinic Judaism and Early Christianity at their Beginnings* (New York: Paulist, 1989).

most part American culture values the newest, the latest, the most updated versions of almost every commodity. In this we differ from the traditional culture of Jesus' day and many contemporary cultures, where what is tried and true is best, and where the elderly are held in higher esteem as wisdom figures. Even as Jesus' contemporaries struggled to accept the new manifestation of God in Christ, the preacher might reflect on new ways in which God is acting in our day that call for a change in our attitudes or practices. By so doing we are faithful to tradition as it is embodied in a new way.

CHAPTER TWENTY-TWO

A Firm Foundation
(Luke 6:43-49)

Saturday of the Twenty-third Week of Ordinary Time

[Jesus said to his disciples:]
43 *"A good tree does not bear rotten fruit,*
  nor does a rotten tree bear good fruit.
44 *For every tree is known by its own fruit.*
  For people do not pick figs from thornbushes,
  nor do they gather grapes from brambles.
45 *A good person*
  out of the store of goodness in his heart
produces good,
  but an evil person
  out of a store of evil produces evil;
  for from the fullness of the heart the mouth speaks.
46 *"Why do you call me, 'Lord, Lord,'*
  but not do what I command?
47 *I will show you what someone is like*
  who comes to me, listens to my words, and acts on them.
48 *That one is like a person building a house,*
  who dug deeply and laid the foundation on rock;
  when the flood came,
  the river burst against that house
  but could not shake it because it had been well built.
49 *But the one who listens and does not act*
  is like a person who built a house
  on the ground without a foundation.
  When the river burst against it,
  it collapsed at once and was completely destroyed."

LUKAN LITERARY CONTEXT

These verses form the fourth (vv. 43-45) and fifth (vv. 46-49) sections of the Sermon on the Plain (Luke 6:20-49). The portion that precedes this has the great command on love of enemies (6:27-36), which then moves to admonitions not to judge others and to forgive (6:37-42). The sayings in vv. 43-49 come from Q[1] and conclude the Sermon on the Plain with counsel about putting Jesus' teaching into practice. Luke frames the Sermon with references to all who come to Jesus (6:18, 47). But he stresses that there is more needed than just coming to listen. The efficacy of Jesus' words is attested by the quality of the fruit borne (vv. 43-44) and the enactment of Jesus' words (vv. 45-49) by those who hear them.

A TREE KNOWN BY ITS FRUIT (vv. 43-45)

The metaphor of "fruit" for a person's deeds is a familiar one from the prophets. Hosea rails against Benjamin and Judah, announcing that the injustice they have reaped is the fruit of their lies (Hos 10:13). Isaiah tells the innocent that they shall eat the fruit of their labors (Isa 3:10). Jeremiah says that God gives to all "according to the fruit of their doings" (Jer 17:10, *NRSV*), and will likewise punish all "according to the fruit of their doings" (Jer 21:14, *NRSV*). Luke employs this metaphor in several places. John the Baptist warns that every tree that does not bear fruit will be cut down and thrown into the fire (3:9). In the parable of the sower/seed/soil/harvest[2] and its interpretation (8:4-15), mature fruit is what comes from the good soil, that is, the ones who hear and embrace the word with a good heart (v. 15). The same metaphor is employed in the parable of the fig tree (13:6-9).[3] In the most profound use of the metaphor, Elizabeth proclaims as blessed Jesus, who is the "fruit" of Mary's womb (1:42).

---

[1] Verses 43-44 have parallels in Matthew 7:16-20. The parallel to Luke 6:45 is found not in the Sermon on the Mount, but in Matthew 12:34-35, in reverse order. Luke 6:43-45 also has a parallel in *Gos.Thom.* §45. Luke 6:46-49 has a counterpart in Matthew 7:21, 24-27.

[2] See below, chap. 24.

[3] See above, chap. 4.

The contrast between a good *(kalos)* tree and a rotten *(sapros)* one may refer either to healthy or good-quality trees as compared to bad ones of the same species, or to useful as contrasted to useless trees.[4] An example of the latter may be the *Calotropis procera*, popularly called "Sodom's Apple," a low, unattractive tree that grows near the shore of the Dead Sea and in the lower Jordan Valley. Its fruit looks edible, but the rind is deadly poisonous, the interior of the fruit is filled with seeds covered with tufts of hair, and it crumbles when handled. The sap is very irritating to the skin. Josephus says that this inferior tree is one of the results of the wicked end of Sodom and Gomorrah.[5]

The impossibility of getting good fruit from anything but a good tree is illustrated with a ridiculous image of looking for figs from thornbushes and grapes from brambles. While the saying is meant to emphasize that such is impossible, the illustration does not derive from fig trees resembling thornbushes or grapevines looking like brambles. Rather, vine and fig are often paired in the Bible (e.g., Isa 34:4; Mic 4:4) as are thorns and thistles (Gen 3:18; Hos 10:8; Heb 6:8).[6] The former symbolizes prosperity, the latter are metaphors for snares and difficulties (e.g., Prov 22:15; Luke 8:14).

The agricultural truisms have their equivalent in human terms in v. 45. In biblical parlance the heart is not only the center of emotions, thoughts, and passions, but is also the seat of the will. It is the place of encounter with God and where conversion takes place. A good person produces good out of the "good treasure" *(ek tou agathou thēsarou)* of their heart,[7] and an evil person produces evil. In the last phrase goodness is identified more specifically as what the mouth speaks. The parallel to the previous verses in Matthew 7:16-20 are warnings against false teachers and prophets. Luke's reference to speaking in v. 45 may be meant to allude to the same. The topic of speaking

[4] I. H. Marshall, *The Gospel of Luke: A Commentary on the Greek Text* (NIGTC; Grand Rapids: Eerdmans, 1978) 272. The adjective *sapros* can mean both "unusable" and "decayed," or "rotten" (BAGD, σαπρός, 742).

[5] B. Malina and R. Rohrbaugh, *Social Science Commentary on the Synoptic Gospels* (Minneapolis: Fortress, 1992) 323.

[6] Marshall, *Luke*, 273.

[7] Luke 12:34 also juxtaposes treasure and heart, with a different point, "For where your treasure is there also will your heart be."

leads easily into the next verses that begin with a contrast between saying and doing (v. 46).

ACTING ON THE WORD (vv. 46-49)

Jesus poses a question that contrasts saying "Lord, Lord," with doing the will of God (v. 46). Although this is the only instance where the double address "Lord, Lord" is found in Luke, there are a number of healing stories in which the person who is suffering, or another who intercedes for them, approaches Jesus and addresses him as "Lord": a man with leprosy (5:12); friends of a centurion whose slave is ill (7:6); and a man who is blind (18:41). When Martha wants Jesus to intervene for her she addresses him as "Lord" (10:40), as does Peter when he asks for interpretation of a parable (12:41) and when he professes his willingness to die with Jesus (22:33). Disciples who want to learn to pray (11:1) and apostles who want more faith (17:5) address Jesus this way. In these incidents, the supplicants implore Jesus as "Lord," to use his power to alleviate their suffering or to answer their need. In this context Luke 6:46 warns that one must not only recognize and call upon Jesus' saving power when in need, but must also be actively engaged in doing what he has told them.

Luke's community may also have heard resonances of their liturgical gatherings in the phrase "Lord, Lord." From Paul's letters we know that "Jesus is Lord" was a common liturgical acclamation of early Christians (Rom 10:9; 1 Cor 12:3; Phil 2:11). From this perspective Luke 6:46 asserts that a lasting relationship with Jesus requires much more than simply proclaiming him as "Lord," or regularly participating in communal worship. Doing God's will must accompany such proclamation.

The theme of doing, or acting on the word that is heard, is a prominent one in Luke. Jesus declares that whoever hears the word of God and does it is family to him (8:21). And whoever hears the word and does it is proclaimed blessed (11:28).

ADDRESSING JESUS AS "LORD"

In New Testament texts the term "Lord" is used for both God and Jesus. In the First Testament Exodus 3:14 recounts that

YHWH was the name revealed by God when Moses insisted on knowing the divine name. Out of reverence, pious Jews never pronounce this name. In Hebrew the four-lettered YHWH (meaning roughly, "I AM the One who causes to be") is written without vowel pointing, reinforcing that it is unpronounceable. In oral reading of a text where YHWH is written, a Jew would pronounce "Adonai," meaning "Lord." New Testament texts often refer to God as "Lord."[8] In one of Jesus' prayers he addresses God, "Father, Lord of heaven and earth" (Matt 11:25 and Luke 10:21).

A significant step was taken by early Christians after the resurrection when they applied the same term, "Lord," (*kyrios* in Greek; *mārê* or *māryā* in Aramaic) to Jesus.[9] However, the Greek address, *kyrie*, does not always carry a religious significance. It was a term of respect, proper for speaking to teachers. When people called Jesus *kyrie* during his earthly ministry, it was a polite form of address, such as "Sir," that did not carry connotations of divinity.[10] In a number of instances the evangelists retroject this post-resurrection title into the phase of Jesus' earthly ministry.[11] It is likely that the title was first applied to Jesus in reference to his return at the parousia (as in Matt 24:42). We see this use in the early Christian Aramaic prayer, *māranā* *thā*, "O Lord, come!" preserved in Greek form in 1 Corinthians 16:22.[12]

---

[8] In Matthew's Gospel see 1:20, 22, 24; 2:13, 15, 19; 5:33; 21:9; 22:37; 23:39; 27:10; 28:2.

[9] E.g., in Luke 3:4; 4:12 the evangelist applies to Jesus texts from Isaiah and Deuteronomy where "Lord" originally referred to God.

[10] For this reason the *NRSV* translates *kyrie* as "Sir," not "Lord" when addressed to Jesus in Mark 7:28; John 4:11,15, 19, 49; 5:7; 12:21. In addition to these instances the *NAB* (with revised NT) translates *kyrie* as "Sir" in John 6:34; 8:11; 9:36; 20:15. Pilate is addressed as *kyrie*, "Sir," by the chief priests and Pharisees in Matthew 27:63.

[11] In addition to the many gospel texts in which Jesus is addressed as *kyrie*, there are those in which the earthly Jesus is called "the Lord," e.g., Mark 5:19; 11:3; Luke 1:43; 7:13, 19; 10:1, 41; 11:39; 12:42; 13:15; 17:5, 6; 18:6; 19:8, 31, 34; 22:61; John 6:23; 11:2.

[12] As a Christological title "Lord" was a favorite of the apostle Paul—it occurs some 250 times in the letters attributed to him. On the background of the title see further Joseph A. Fitzmyer, "New Testament *Kyrios* and *Maranatha* and Their Aramaic Background," in *To Advance the Gospel: New Testament Studies* (New York: Crossroad, 1981) 218–35; "The Semitic Background of the New Testament

For contemporary believers "Lord" is still a very popular term of address both for God and for Christ. Yet today there are serious difficulties with this address.[13] In English, the term evokes an image of feudal times replete with lords and ladies and courtly airs. Although there is a certain romantic fascination with royalty, the question must be posed: What are the effects of using this language for God and Christ?

The original Anglo-Saxon word "lord" denoted the male authority figure who was obligated to provide food and protection for his community. In the Middle Ages it acquired its connotation of feudal power. What is problematic about using "Lord" for God or Christ today is that the term is androcentric, archaic, and domination-oriented. Whereas the divine name YHWH or "I AM" has no gender, "Lord" is always male. Moreover, "Lord" derives from an economic system in which a powerful man was looked to as provider for his subservient vassals. More often medieval times found the reverse was true: powerful lords consumed disproportionately the produce of peasants. However, the issue is not whether lords were benevolent or abusive. The problem is that "Lord" reinforces patterns of inequality and domination.

The challenge in the present is to find or create language that is able to express the idea of divine providence, mercy, and power in ways that do not support earthly systems of domination and submission. One proposal, offered by the National Council of Churches, is to use "the SOVEREIGN ONE" to render the Hebrew YHWH and "the Sovereign Jesus Christ" for *kyrios*.[14]

Kyrios-Title," *A Wandering Aramean* (SBLMS 25; Chico, Calif.: Scholars Press, 1979) 115–42.

[13] See further Gail Ramshaw, *God Beyond Gender: Feminist Christian God-Language* (Minneapolis: Fortress, 1995) 47–58.

[14] This proposal was made by the committee of the NCC in their inclusive language revision of the *Revised Standard Version*. See *An Inclusive-Language Lectionary*, ed. the Inclusive-Language Lectionary Committee, Division of Education and Ministry, National Council of the Churches of Christ in the U.S.A. (Atlanta: John Knox, 1984) 10–11. It should be noted, however, that this is not an entirely acceptable solution. Many African American Christians, for example, insist that calling both God and Jesus "Lord" is essential for their piety, and that for them it is liberating to address God, not white masters, as "Lord."

Another proposed title is "the Living One."[15] This phrase has the advantage of encompassing both genders and captures the life-giving and life-sustaining power of "I AM." Further, it speaks of God's power to release all from suffering and death, expressed in and exercised by Christ, who is also well-named, "the Living One."

TWO BUILDERS

The parable of the Two Builders (vv. 47-49) contrasts two characters, but in it the point shifts from "saying and doing" to "hearing and doing." The simile is straightforward. Its meaning is not elusive. Everyone who hears and acts on Jesus' words is likened to a person who builds a house on a rock foundation (v. 48). Such an abode does not collapse when the river[16] floods its banks and endangers the house. But anyone who listens yet does not act on the words of Jesus is like someone who does not know how to build a house. Without a foundation the river sweeps it completely away.

At the outset of the Sermon on the Plain people were coming to Jesus to hear him and be healed (6:18). At the close of the sermon, Jesus emphasizes that they must not only come and listen, but must act on the word they hear (6:49). There is an emphasis on "these words of mine" (v. 47) and the pronoun is in an emphatic position—it is *Jesus'* interpretation of the Law that is to be acted upon. There are echoes of the First Testament where the same two actions—hearing and doing—are required of Israel at the giving of the Law. Their response was, "All that the LORD has said, we will heed and do" (Exod 24:7). The close connection between hearing and doing is again underscored in Moses' final instructions for the reading of the Law. He charges Joshua to read the law aloud in the presence of all Israel "that they may

---

[15] Ramshaw, *God Beyond Gender,* 54–57. She also suggests "the Name" and "I AM" as more moderate proposals (57–58).

[16] Joseph A. Fitzmyer, *The Gospel According to Luke* (AB28; Garden City, N.Y.: Doubleday, 1981) 644, notes that Matthew's rain, wind, and torrents is more probably original and is closer to what would happen in a Palestinian setting. He queries whether Luke's "river" alludes to floods caused the overflow of a river like the Orontes near Antioch in Syria, a possible locale for the Lukan community. In Palestine wadis flood seasonally, and funnel powerful torrents.

hear it and learn it, and so fear the LORD, your God, and carefully observe all the words of this law" (Deut 31:11-12). For
Jesus' followers, it is his words that require the same response.

As is often the case in the New Testament, language used
of God in the First Testament is now applied to Jesus. The
image of rock is used frequently in the Hebrew Scriptures to
speak of God's steadfast faithfulness, strength, and protection
(e.g., Deut 32:4,18, 31; Ps 18:2, 31; 27:5; 28:1; Isa 17:10). In the
Christian Scriptures Luke 6:48 is one of several instances where
the rock is now said to be Jesus.[17]

The image of the flood is polyvalent. For dwellers along
the Nile, who depended on the annual flooding of the river for
raising their crops, flooding is a yearly blessing. Luke uses it
here, however, as a means by which the good fruit are distinguished from the evil. Like the flood in the time of Noah, which
was a sign of God's purifying action in the world, to which
Luke refers in 17:27, so the flood in the parable separates one
who acts on the word from one who does not.

A FAMILIAR CONCERN

The theme of speaking well but not putting the words into
action is a familiar motif that recurs not only in biblical literature,[18] but also in contemporary Hellenistic philosophy.[19] In addition, there are rabbinic parables with the same theme. A
parable attributed to Rabbi Elisha ben Avuyah (c. 110 C.E.) is
very similar to the gospel parable of the two builders:

---

[17] E.g., Paul identifies the "spiritual rock" from which the Israelites drank
during the Exodus as Christ in 1 Corinthians 10:4. The first letter of Peter invites
Christians, "Come to him [Christ], a living stone" (2:4-5). Close to the parable
in Luke 6:47-49 is 1 Corinthians 3:10-11 where Paul says, "like a wise master
builder I laid a foundation, and another is building upon it. But each one must
be careful how he builds upon it, for no one can lay a foundation other than the
one that is there, namely, Jesus Christ." Note that in each of these instances
Jesus himself is the foundation, whereas in Luke 6:47-49 it is Jesus' teaching that
is the foundation.

[18] See especially James 2:14-26.

[19] Seneca, *Moral Epistles* 20:1 and *Sentences of Sextus*, 177, as noted by Luke
T. Johnson, *The Gospel of Luke*. Sacra Pagina 3 (Collegeville: The Liturgical
Press, 1991) 114.

A man who has good deeds to his credit and has also studied much Torah, to what is he like? To one who builds [a structure and lays] stones below [for the foundation] and bricks above, so that however much water may collect at the side it will not wash it away. But the man who has no good deeds to his credit, though he has studied Torah, to what is he like? To one who builds [a structure and lays] bricks first [for the foundation] and then stones above, so that even if only a little water collects it at once undermines it.[20]

This rabbinic story follows the same contours as the gospel parable, but the debate is framed in terms of Torah study plus good deeds. The conclusion is the same in both: action must result from study of Torah for the rabbis; from heeding Jesus' interpretation of Torah for Christians.

PREACHING POSSIBILITIES

There are several possible emphases that emerge from the parable. One is the necessity for coherence between the inner person and the outer deeds of a disciple. One cannot produce good "fruit" if the inner storehouse is rotten. Nor can one cultivate only their inner relationship with God without having it flow into visible deeds of godly action. Both conversion of heart and outward action are constituent of a disciple. The gospel presents both poles: one must not only speak to and about Jesus, but must also enact his teaching (v. 46). Likewise, one cannot simply listen, but must put the word into practice.

In v. 45 the "fruit" is identified specifically as what the mouth speaks from the fullness of the heart. The preacher might take the theme of the speech of a believer as revelatory of their heart. In a culture where even public discourse has degenerated into crude exchanges, a particular identifying mark of Christians could be their manner of speaking that builds up others and invites conversation partners to speak reverently of one another. What kind of "fullness of the heart" do gossip or

---

[20] ʾAbot R. Nat. ver. a, chap. 24, quoted from Brad Young, *Jesus and His Jewish Parables: Jewish Tradition and Christian Interpretation* (Peabody, Mass.: Hendrickson, 1988) 257.

vulgar speech reveal? Or what does silence bespeak when there is injustice that needs to be denounced?

The preacher may take the opportunity to offer other images or language for Jesus and for God than "Lord." It is always a delicate business to try to alter long-used, cherished names of God. It is extremely important for preachers to understand the genesis of our names for God and how language about God and Christ functions in the contemporary context. The preacher plays a critical role in either reinforcing the *status quo* or opening new horizons. Attentive, consistent use of inclusive and liberating names for God and Christ in the liturgy works best when accompanied by respectful and clear adult education. The ideal is a community that can study together and wrestle jointly with misgivings and apprehensions, while clearly journeying toward liberating praxis in worship.

CHAPTER TWENTY-THREE

Wisdom's Children Justified
(Luke 7:31-35)

Wednesday of the Twenty-fourth Week
of Ordinary Time

[Jesus said]
³¹ *"Then to what shall I compare the people of this generation?*
    What are they like?
³² *They are like children who sit in the marketplace*
        and call to one another,
    'We played the flute for you, but you did not dance.
    We sang a dirge, but you did not weep.'
³³ *For John the Baptist came neither eating food nor drinking wine,*
    and you said,
        'He is possessed by a demon.'
³⁴ *The Son of Man came eating and drinking*
    and you said,
        'Look, he is a glutton and a drunkard,
        a friend of tax collectors and sinners.'
³⁵ *But wisdom is vindicated by all her children."*

LUKAN LITERARY CONTEXT

This parable comes as the third in a series of units taken from Q.[1] In the first unit (7:18-23) John the Baptist sends some

---

[1] There are few differences between the versions of Luke and Matthew (11:16-19). Minor variations in wording are not greatly significant until the last verse. There Matthew concludes, "Wisdom is justified by all her deeds," thus portraying Jesus as Wisdom incarnate. For detailed analysis of the differences in the two versions and a reconstruction of the text from Q, see Wendy J. Cotter,

of his disciples to Jesus to ascertain if he is "the one who is to come"[2] or whether they should look for another. Jesus replies by instructing John's disciples to report to him what they have seen and heard: how those who were blind now see, those who had been lame walk, those with leprosy are cleansed, those who were deaf now hear, dead people have been raised, and those made poor have had the good news proclaimed to them (Luke 7:22). For the reader of Luke's Gospel this litany recalls Jesus' initial proclamation of his mission in Luke 4:18 (modeled on Isa 61:1-2) and subsequent episodes in which Jesus has been carrying this out by healing people who were blind (7:21), paralyzed (5:17-26), leprous (5:12-16), and all who were sick with various diseases (4:40). Jesus has also been depicted as raising dead people (7:11-17) and proclaiming good news (4:43).

Jesus' response to John's disciples underscores how their seeing should answer their question about the one for whom they are looking. Against the background of Isaiah 35:5-6,

> Then the eyes of the blind shall be opened,
> and the ears of the deaf unstopped;
> then the lame shall leap like a deer,
> and the tongue of the speechless sing for joy.
> For waters shall break forth in the wilderness,
> and streams in the desert

it should be evident that Jesus is, indeed, the one issuing in the messianic era. Jesus' concluding word, "Blessed is the one who takes no offense at me" (7:23) points ahead to the parable, which contrasts the desired response with the petulant refusal of the children in the marketplace. It furthers the recurring theme of the divided responses to Jesus' deeds.

"The Parable of the Children in the Market-Place, Q(Lk) 7:31-35: An Examination of the Parable's Image and Significance," *NovT* 29/4 (1987) 289–304. For analysis of the tradition history of the parable see Joseph A. Fitzmyer, *The Gospel According to Luke* (AB28; Garden City, N.Y.: Doubleday, 1981) 677–79; John P. Meier, *A Marginal Jew: Rethinking the Historical Jesus* (ABRL; Garden City, N.Y.: Doubleday, 1994) 2.144–54.

[2] This expression does not appear in the Hebrew Scriptures as a messianic title. But see Psalm 118:26; Malachi 3:1; Isaiah 59:20.

SEEING AND BELIEVING

The theme of seeing and believing is particularly pronounced in the Gospel of Luke and is central to each of the four units in Luke 7:18-50. While restoring physical sight is part of Jesus' mission (4:18), seeing is also a metaphor for perceiving the word of God.[3] Seeing Jesus' deeds of power is meant to lead one to glorify God (Luke 5:26; 17:15-16; 18:35-43; 23:47)[4] and to follow Jesus (18:35-43). This theme is already sounded in the infancy narratives and is carried through all the way to the resurrection appearance stories. The shepherds, after seeing the newborn Jesus, "returned, glorifying and praising God for all they had heard and seen" (2:20). Simeon declares, "my eyes have seen your salvation, which you have prepared in the presence of all peoples" (2:30-31). The post-resurrection understanding of the disciples en route to Emmaus is described as "their eyes were opened" (24:31).

Seeing does not, however, always lead to believing. Jesus warns his disciples about the dangers of looking but not seeing, and hearing but not understanding (8:10). He later tells them, "Blessed are the eyes that see what you see! For I tell you that many prophets and kings desired to see what you see, but did not see it, and to hear what you hear, but did not hear it"(Luke 10:23-24). In Luke 7:18-23 the reader is confronted with all the evidence to confirm the identification of Jesus as the one who is to come.

LOOKING FOR A PROPHET (vv. 24-30)

Central to each of these three episodes is the identification of both John and Jesus as prophets. The first episode, with the allusion to Malachi 3:23, which speaks of the return of Elijah before the coming day of the Lord, establishes that Jesus is the Coming One to whom the prophets pointed.[5] The second unit

[3] See Alan Culpepper, "Seeing the Kingdom of God: The Metaphor of Sight in the Gospel of Luke," *CurTM* 21 (1994) 434–43.

[4] See Dennis Hamm, "What the Samaritan Leper Sees: Narrative Christology of Luke 17:11-19," *CBQ* 56 (1994) 273–87.

[5] Very few prophets besides Jesus appear in the Third Gospel. Zechariah prophesies as he speaks his canticle (1:67). Gabriel announces that John the

turns to the identification of John as a prophet "and more than a prophet" (Matt 11:9 // Luke 7:26).

Three times Jesus poses to the crowd the question, "What did you go out to see?" If they have objections to John's unbending asceticism, as opposed to a reed shaken by the wind, or are offended by his rugged dress (Matt 3:4) in contrast to those decked out in gorgeous apparel, Jesus tells the crowds they are looking for the wrong thing in the wrong places. Those seeking a prophet will not only find one, but the very prophet of whom Malachi spoke, the messenger who prepares the way for the coming one. While there is differentiation in their roles,[6] both John and Jesus are presented here as powerful prophets of God. The third unit will underscore that the two prophets suffer the same divided response to their ministry as does every messenger of God.

TRANSITION (vv. 29-30)

Leading into the parable, Luke 7:29 states that "all the people who listened, including the tax collectors, and who were baptized with the baptism of John, acknowledged the justice of God *(edikaiōsan ton theon)*." Balancing this statement is the conclusion of the parable about the children in the marketplace, "Nevertheless, wisdom is vindicated *(edikaiōthō)* by all her children" (7:35). The verb *dikaioō* ("to justify") frames the parable and sharpens its impact. In Luke 7:29-30 the contrast is clearly set forth: there are those who are in right relation with God and those who are not. Those who rightly perceived John the Baptist as God's prophet, and accepted his baptism, are in right re-

---

Baptist "will be called prophet of the Most High" (1:76; see also 3:2; 20:6). Anna is the last prophet (2:36) mentioned before Jesus assumes this role. Luke casts Jesus as the promised "prophet like Moses" of Deuteronomy 18:15 (Luke 9:28-36; Acts 3:22-23; 7:37). He also emulates the prophets Elijah and Elisha in his miracle working (Luke 4:25-27; 7:11-17; 9:8, 10-17, 19, 30-33, 51). A particular Lukan theme is that of Jesus as rejected prophet (Luke 4:24, 39; 13:33; 24:19-20; Acts 7:52). See further Fitzmyer, *Luke*, 213–15; Robert O'Toole, "The Parallels Between Jesus and Moses," *BTB* 20 (1990) 22–29; Raymond E. Brown, "Jesus and Elisha," *Perspective* 12 (1971) 84–104.

[6] The subordination of John to Jesus, while stated in Luke 7:28, is not the main focus here. Both are prophets who have a similar reception and rejection.

lation with God (7:29). The Pharisees and scholars of the law who did not so respond rejected God's purposes (7:30). The parable then further elaborates on the rejection by "this generation" of the offer made by God through John and Jesus (7:31-34). The concluding verse (7:35) affirms that despite this rejection, divine justification prevails.

THE CHILDREN IN THE MARKETPLACE (vv. 31-35)

The parable opens with a simile (vv. 31-32), followed by an explanation (vv. 33-34) and a concluding saying (v. 35). Like many parables, the introductory verses set up a comparison, using the verb *homoioō*, "to liken," and the adjective *homoios* ("like").[7] The Aramaic *lᵉ* underlies these expressions and should be translated "It is the case with . . . as with. . . ."[8] Thus, the comparison is not only between the characters "this generation" and "children," but involves the whole situation described. As will be clear below, there are two groups of children envisioned, one of which is the cipher for "this generation."

"The people of this generation" *(genea)* are compared to children sitting in the marketplace calling to one another. In most instances Luke uses the word *genea*, "generation," in a pejorative sense. Disciples who are unable to cast out a demon are dubbed a "faithless and perverse generation" (9:41). Jesus declares "this generation" that seeks signs an "evil generation" that will be condemned (11:29-32).[9] Likewise, Jesus asserts, "this generation" will be "charged with the blood of all the prophets shed from the foundation of the world" (11:50-51). And he predicts to his disciples that he will suffer and be rejected by "this generation" (17:25).[10] While God offers mercy "from generation

---

[7] So also Mark 4:30; Luke 6:47-49; 12:36; 13:18-21; Matthew 7:24, 26; 11:16; 13:24, 31, 33, 44, 45, 47, 52; 18:23; 20:1; 22:2; 25:1.

[8] Joachim Jeremias, *The Parables of Jesus* (2nd rev. ed.; New York: Scribner's Sons, 1972) 101.

[9] This passage makes a similar juxtaposition as Luke 7:31-35 of a reference to Wisdom and a condemnation of "this generation" for not responding positively to the prophets sent by God.

[10] The pejorative use of *genea* continues in Acts. In his Pentecost speech Peter admonishes, "Save yourselves from this corrupt generation" (2:40). In Acts 8:33; 14:16 *genea* is used of past generations whose purposes were opposite

to generation" (1:50), the predominantly pejorative use of *genea* signals a likely negative response in this parable.

The parable likens "this generation" to a group of children who stubbornly refuse to play with another group. No matter what the one group offers, whether pretending at wedding, or at funeral, the other refuses to participate.[11] The explanation in the next two verses relates this metaphor to the negative reception of the invitations issued by John and Jesus. "This generation" responded to neither John's "dirge" nor to Jesus' "flute."

The children seated in the marketplace introduce an image connected with court proceedings.[12] As the center of public life, the *agora*, "marketplace," was the locale for commercial, social, religious, and civic interchange. One might expect children in the *agora* to be running and chasing after one another in their play, not sitting while voicing their complaint about their unresponsive potential playmates. The verb *kathēmai*, "sit," is frequently associated with judgment, as in Matthew 27:19, for example, where Pilate sits on the *bēma* when Jesus is brought before him.[13] That the *agora* was used for court proceedings is evident from Acts 16:19, where Paul and Silas were dragged into the *agora* to be judged by the magistrates. In addition the verb *prosphōneō* ("to call out to") connotes formal address, such as would take place in a court context (Luke 23:20; Acts 21:40; 22:2).

God's. There is a more positive nuance in two instances: God offers mercy from "generation to generation" (Luke 1:50), and "all generations" recognize Mary's blessedness (Luke 1:48). More neutral uses of *genea* occur in Luke 16:8; 21:32; Acts 13:36; 15:21.

[11] Some see the figure in Luke's account as two groups of children, each wanting to play a different game. One group wants to pretend at wedding, the other at funeral, but they cannot agree. Matthew clearly has one group offering two different games to another unresponsive group. It is likely that Luke also is to be understood this way.

[12] Cotter ("Children," 289–304) equates "the children who call" with "this generation," who falsely sit in judgment on John and Jesus. Because of the association of the verb *prosphōneō* ("to call out to") with Jesus and the application of the parable to John and Jesus in vv. 33-34 I understand Jesus and John to be the ones calling and the agents of judgment.

[13] For other examples of such usage see BAGD, 389 and Cotter, "Children," 299–301.

The image, then, presented in the opening line of the parable introduces a note of judgment. It makes clear that John and Jesus' invitation is not merely a game in which children can participate or not as they will. Rather, it points toward the serious consequences that incur for those who refuse their call. The final verse, using another term from the legal world, *dikaioō*, "to justify," completes the court proceedings with the handing down of the verdict.

CALLING AND BANQUETING

The auditory imagery of voices calling, flutes playing, dirges being sung (v. 32) shifts to a culinary theme (vv. 33-34). Both themes are associated with Wisdom's invitation to life and point forward to the final verse (v. 35). Just as Wisdom sent out servant girls, calling from the highest places in the town (Prov 9:3), so John called out his invitation in the desert (Luke 3:4) and Jesus called out his message for anyone with ears to hear (Luke 8:8). Wisdom's invitation, like that of Yahweh (Isa 25:6; 55:1; Ps 23:5) is cast in terms of eating her bread and drinking her wine (Prov 9:5). In like manner, banqueting with Jesus is associated with response to his invitation to discipleship.[14]

But just as Wisdom is rejected by the foolish (Sir 5:7-8) so John is dismissed as having a demon (as is Jesus in Luke 11:15) and Jesus is accused of being a glutton and a drunkard. This charge alludes to Deuteronomy 21:20, where the phrase refers to a rebellious son. The final verse shows that this perception is false: Luke asserts that Jesus is a true son of Wisdom. The additional slur that he is a friend of toll collectors and sinners surfaces a charge that reappears in the Gospel of Luke. Jesus' table companionship with toll collectors and sinners is part of his missionary strategy to bring all into right relation. This is especially evident in the call of Levi (Luke 5:27-32) and in Luke 15:1-32, where the objection to Jesus' eating with tax collectors and sinners is voiced by his opponents.

[14] This theme is prominent in Luke (5:30, 33; 7:36-50; 10:7; 11:37; 12:19, 22, 29, 45; 13:26; 14:7-24; 15:2; 17:8, 27, 28; 22:7-20, 30; 24:43).

WISDOM'S CHILDREN (v. 35)

The parable advances the theme of justification, or right relation. While Paul and Matthew are more noted for this theme, it also plays an important role in the Third Gospel. In addition to Luke 7:29, 35, the verb *dikaioō*, "to justify," occurs five more times in Luke and Acts. Twice in the gospel it is used in a pejorative way to depict characters who try to justify themselves: the scholar of the Law in 10:29 and the Pharisees in 16:15. In Luke 18:14 the toll collector returns home from the Temple justified. In Acts 13:38-39 Paul speaks of all who were not able to be justified by the Law of Moses who are now justified by belief in Jesus.

The adjective *dikaios*, "righteous," describes Zechariah and Elizabeth (1:6), Simeon (2:25), Joseph of Arimathea (23:50), Cornelius (Acts 10:22), and occurs in nine other sayings about the upright.[15] The adverb *dikaiōs*, "just," occurs once in Luke 23:41 where it refers to the two criminals who have been justly condemned. The noun *dikaiosynē*, "justification," occurs once in the Third Gospel, in Zechariah's prayer to serve God in holiness and righteousness (1:75).[16]

Most notable is that Luke changed the climactic declaration of the centurion at the death of Jesus from "Truly this man was God's Son!" (Mark 15:39) to "Certainly this man was innocent *(dikaios)*" (Luke 23:47). In Acts of the Apostles "the Righteous One" *(ho dikaios)* becomes a title of Jesus in three key speeches (Acts 3:14; 7:52; 22:14).

The parable has both a sorrowful edge to it, yet a note of triumph. While there seems little hope in the gospel that "this generation" will respond positively to the invitation offered by God's prophets, John and Jesus, the invitation continues to be put forth. Right relation with God, personified as Wisdom,[17]

---

[15] Luke 1:17; 5:32; 12:57; 14:14; 15:7; 18:9; 20:20; Acts 4:19; 24:15.

[16] It occurs four other times in Acts: 10:35; 13:10; 17:31; 24:25.

[17] It is in the final verse of the parable that there is the most significant divergence between Matthew and Luke. Most scholars hold that Luke has the more original wording: "Yet Wisdom is justified by all her children." The divine is portrayed as Lady Wisdom, whose justification is made evident by her children, preeminently, John and Jesus. Unlike the Gospel of Matthew, Luke does not identify Jesus with Wisdom. There are only a few explicit associations of

will ultimately prevail, as some will heed her call, and will banquet with her, as her true, upright children. Her child John embraced his mission "to turn the hearts of parents to their children, and the disobedient to the wisdom of the righteous, to make ready a people prepared for the Lord" (Luke 1:17). Her son Jesus went to his death trying to gather Jerusalem's children under his wings, despite their unwillingness (Luke 13:34). To these exemplary children of Wisdom are added all those[18] who have embraced her invitation and who in turn speak it in their day.

PREACHING POSSIBILITIES

One of the functions of this parable in its original context was to confirm that Jesus is the Coming One who ushers in the messianic age. There were likely still circles of followers of John the Baptist in the purview of the Lukan community who thought their leader was the awaited one. This parable may serve to clarify that it is Jesus, not John, who is the Coming One. For contemporary Christians who have already accepted Jesus as the Messiah, the questions leading into the parable may be recast in terms of an invitation to come to deeper belief. The unit to which the parable belongs raises questions such as: What have you seen? What are you looking for? Where are you looking? How will you respond? The preacher might reflect on how predetermined attitudes and expectations can keep some from perceiving correctly the One who is the envoy of Wisdom, or even holy Wisdom herself. Moreover, the parable makes clear that the consequences of blindness or petulance are not neutral: judgment will ensue and these will not be counted among Wisdom's children.

Jesus with Wisdom in the Third Gospel. The infancy narratives assert that the child Jesus was filled with and grew in wisdom (Luke 2:40, 52) and in Luke 21:15 Jesus promises to give his disciples "words and a wisdom" that none of their opponents will be able to withstand or contradict. In Luke 11:49 it is unclear whether the reference to the "Wisdom of God" speaking is to God or to Jesus.

[18] Luke's addition of "all" in v. 35 reflects his tendency to universalize, as also in 4:15, 5:26; 7:16; 9:43; 18:43; 19:37.

In the Lukan community, where a prime tension point was inclusive table companionship, the parable most likely served to further their discussion of this issue by anchoring the community's inclusive practice in that of the just Jesus, Wisdom's child. In a congregation that struggles with inclusivity, the preacher might take the parable in this direction.

When Luke portrays Jesus as another in the long line of Sophia's prophets who announce justice, right order, and well-being for all God's creatures, especially those most marginalized, he gives hope to all those who today continue to proclaim and work for justice. The parable makes clear that the opposition and rejection Jesus and John experienced was the response expected by every prophet. The preacher can use the parable as one of encouragement to Christians who take prophetic stances. They can be assured that resistance or rejection are not signs of their failure, but can be seen as signs of legitimation for those who follow in the footsteps of the rejected Jesus and his predecessor. The divine presence and power to free is experienced in the midst of the struggles against oppression as Sophia accompanies disciples and leads them through the suffering to victory.

Finally, the parable brings to the fore the image of Sophia as the female personification of the Divine.[19] The Wisdom traditions in the books of Job, Proverbs, Sirach, Wisdom of Solomon, and Baruch portray Sophia as the female personification of God's creative and saving action in the world. "She fashions all that exists and pervades it with her pure and people-loving spirit. She is all-knowing, all-powerful, and present everywhere, renewing all things. Active in Creation, she also works in history to save her chosen people, guiding and protecting them through the vicissitudes of liberating struggle. Her powerful words have the mark of divine address, making the huge claim that listening to them will bring salvation while dis-

---

[19] In addition to providing a rich resource for female language for God, Elisabeth Schüssler Fiorenza has shown that the retrieval of Jewish and Christian discourses on Divine Wisdom also provides a framework for developing a feminist ecological theology of creation and a religious ethos that is inclusive of other religious visions. See "The Sisters of Wisdom-Sophia: Justified by All Her Children," in *Sharing Her Word* (Boston: Beacon, 1998) 160–83.

obedience will bring destruction. She sends her servants to proclaim her invitation to communion. By her light, kings govern justly and the unjust meet their punishment. She is involved in relationships of loving, seeking, and finding with human beings. Whoever loves her receives what in other scriptural texts is given by God alone."[20]

All these characteristics and activities ascribed to Sophia in the biblical Wisdom traditions are elsewhere attributed to Yahweh. The preacher would do well to take the opportunity offered in this parable to speak of the Divine in female terms so as to bring forth a fuller understanding of God and of her children, female and male made in the divine image. While no metaphor adequately encompasses the reality of God, to speak of the Divine without female metaphors overlooks whole strands of biblical tradition and results in a greatly impoverished theology. This parable offers a good opportunity to help the congregation stretch their imagination toward a fuller image of God.

---

[20] Elizabeth Johnson, *She Who Is: The Mystery of God in Feminist Theological Discourse* (New York: Crossroad, 1992) 91. See also her article, "Jesus, the Wisdom of God," *ETL* 61 (1985) 261–94.

CHAPTER TWENTY-FOUR

Subversive Seeds
(Luke 8:4-15)

Saturday of the Twenty-fourth Week of Ordinary Time

⁴ *When a large crowd gathered,*
with people from one town after another journeying to him,
he spoke in a parable.
⁵ *"A sower went out to sow his seed.*
And as he sowed, some seed fell on the path
and was trampled,
and the birds of the sky ate it up.
⁶ *Some seed fell on rocky ground,*
and when it grew,
it withered for lack of moisture.
⁷ *Some seed fell among thorns,*
and the thorns grew with it and choked it.
⁸ *And some seed fell on good soil,*
and when it grew,
it produced fruit a hundredfold."
After saying this, he called out,
"Whoever has ears to hear ought to hear."

⁹ *Then his disciples asked him*
what the meaning of this parable might be.
¹⁰ *He answered,*
"Knowledge of the mysteries of the kingdom of God
has been granted to you;
but to the rest, they are made known through parables
so that 'they may look but not see,
and hear but not understand.'
¹¹ *"This is the meaning of the parable.*
The seed is the word of God.
¹² *Those on the path are the ones who have heard,*

> but the devil comes and takes away the word from their hearts
> that they may not believe and be saved.
> [13] Those on rocky ground are the ones who,
> when they hear, receive the word with joy,
> but they have no root;
> they believe only for a time and fall away in time of trial.
> [14] As for the seed that fell among thorns,
> they are the ones who have heard,
> but as they go along,
> they are choked by the anxieties and riches and pleasures of life,
> and they fail to produce mature fruit.
> [15] But as for the seed that fell on rich soil,
> they are the ones who, when they have heard the word,
> embrace it with a generous and good heart,
> and bear fruit through perseverance.

LUKAN LITERARY CONTEXT

This parable begins a new section in the Gospel of Luke, where the third evangelist returns to his Markan source after a section of uniquely Lukan material from 6:20–8:3. The seed parable and its interpretation follow closely the Markan version, with a few variations.[1] Luke has edited the parable and its interpretation, making it more streamlined and coherent than his source.[2] In the verses immediately preceding, Jesus is traveling through cities and villages preaching and bringing good news (8:1). With him are the Twelve, Mary Magdalene, Joanna, Susanna, and many other Galilean women who "provided for them out of their resources" (8:3).[3] Presumably, they are still part

---

[1] This parable has parallels in Mark 4:1-20; Matthew 13:1-23; and *Gos.Thom.* §9. The latter does not have the allegorical explanation (Luke 8:11-15) nor is the concluding exhortation to hear attached to this parable, but has a parallel at *Gos.Thom.* §8 and 24.

[2] Mark's parables discourse has three clear divisions with a shift in audience and scene at Mark 4:10 (// Luke 8:9) and Mark 4:13 (// Luke 8:11). See further Joseph A. Fitzmyer, *The Gospel According to Luke* (AB28; Garden City, N.Y.: Doubleday, 1981) 699–700.

[3] In Luke and Acts the Greek word *hyparchontōn* always refers to money, possessions, property or goods (Luke 11:21; 12:15, 33, 44; 14:33; 16:1; 19:8; Acts 4:32). The verb *diakonein* and the related noun *diakonia* cover a range of ministries: apostolic service (Acts 1:25), financial aid (Luke 8:3; Acts 11:29; 12:25), ministry of the table (Acts 6:2), ministry of the word (Acts 6:4). See further John

of the large crowd that gathers and hears the parable. Following the seed parable is the parable of the lamp (8:16-18) and the episode with Jesus' family (8:19-21). In the latter instance Luke's redaction dilutes Mark's harsh criticism of Jesus' mother and siblings. Mark places this episode immediately before the seed parable and casts Jesus' family as outsiders and the crowd seated around him as the insiders who may become his disciples (Mark 3:31-35). In Luke, Jesus' family are examples of those who may hear and respond to the word; in fact, he has already portrayed Mary as a prime example of one who does so (1:26-38).

The parable advances Luke's theme of hearing the word and acting on it. The admonition to hear in v. 8 recalls the *Shema*ᶜ, the prayer from Deuteronomy 6:4-5, prayed by observant Jews three times daily, "Hear, O Israel! The LORD is our God, the LORD alone! Therefore, you shall love the LORD, your God, with all your heart, and with all your soul, and with all your strength."[4] While this prayer underscores Israel's unique relationship with God, Jesus' parable widens the audience to any who will attend to his words.

But what is the meaning of his words? The parable allows for a variety of interpretations, depending on from which angles one approaches it. Various translators and commentators title the parable differently, showing that it can be understood to have more than one point of emphasis. Depending on which "character" is chosen as the focus, it could be the Parable of the Sower;[5] the Parable of the Seed,[6] the Parable of the Soil; or the Parable of the Harvest.[7]

N. Collins, *DIAKONIA: Re-interpreting the Ancient Sources* (New York: Oxford University Press, 1990); Barbara E. Reid, *Choosing the Better Part? Woman in the Gospel of Luke* (Collegeville: The Liturgical Press, 1996) 96–106, 124–34.

[4] Birger Gerhardsson, "The Parable of the Sower and its Interpretation," *NTS* 14 (1968) 165–93 interprets the whole parable in light of the Deuteronomic referent. For him the seed devoured by birds represents those who do not love God with their whole heart; those on rocky ground are those who do not love God with their souls; those choked by thorns are those who fail to love God with their whole might.

[5] So *NAB, NJB, La Nueva Biblia Latinoamericana, Christian Community Bible*.

[6] So 1970 edition of *NAB*.

[7] The *NRSV* wisely avoids titling the parable, allowing for any of the various interpretations. The *Revised English Bible* simply titles the chapter "Parables." No parable is entitled in the Greek text.

THE PARABLE OF THE SEED

Luke's redaction shifts the focus slightly from Mark's version. Whereas Mark had called attention to the sower in his first lines (Mark 4:3-4), Luke's addition of "his seed" in v. 5 and his omitting of an explanation of the character of the sower and moving right away to talking about the seed in v. 11 (cf. Mark 4:14) makes the seed slightly more prominent than the sower. In v. 11 the seed is equated with the word of God. The parable shows that the seed is reliable—it is able to bring forth a good yield. Though it appears at first that there will be no harvest, the end result confirms the seed's efficacy. The parable assures that God's word does accomplish its purpose, even though much of it falls on deaf ears.

The parable may well be a recasting of Isaiah 55:10-11: "For as from heaven the rain and snow come down, / and do not return there until they have watered the earth, / making it bring forth and sprout, / giving seed to the sower and bread to the eater, so shall my word be that goes forth from my mouth; / it shall not return to me empty, / but shall accomplish that which I propose, / and succeed in the thing for which I sent it" (NRSV).[8]

In the context of Jesus' ministry, the parable encourages his disciples that, despite the lack of an overwhelmingly positive response, Jesus' preaching of God's word does, finally, achieve God's purpose. Christians today can take the same assurance from the parable; despite lack of apparent initial results, their efforts at spreading God's word will eventually bring forth fruit.

THE PARABLE OF THE SOWER

If Jesus' original audience were peasant farmers who saw the sower as their landowner, they might react with disdain toward the sloppy and wasteful manner of sowing.[9] Alterna-

---

[8] C. A. Evans ("A Note on the Function of Isaiah 6:9-10 in Mark 4," *RB* 99 [1981] 234–35) analyzes the Markan version of the parable as a midrash on Isaiah 6:9-13 and 55:10-11. See also J. W. Bowker, "Mystery and Parable: Mark 4:1-20," *JTS* 25 (1974) 300–17, who sees Mark 4:1-20 as a midrash on Isaiah 6:13.

[9] There is some debate whether the custom was to plow after sowing, as this parable envisions. Some ancient texts refer to plowing before sowing: Isaiah

tively, if they saw the sower as a tenant farmer or a day laborer like themselves, their reaction would be sympathetic. They would know all too well the amount of seed and effort expended that never bears fruit because of the difficult conditions.[10]

The sower is usually interpreted as representing God or Jesus, though Luke omits Mark's phrase that identifies the sower as the one who sows the word (Mark 4:14; cf. Luke 8:11). From this perspective the story centers on how God acts. God is like a profligate farmer who indiscriminately sows seed on every type of ground. The story is an illustration of God's all-inclusive love. The point is that God knowingly scatters the seed on all types of soil. God offers the word to all people, regardless of their potential for accepting it. Although not all will accept the word and bring it to fruition, it is offered to all. If the sower is Jesus, the point is the same. Jesus preaches the word to all, offering God's inclusive love indiscriminately to all kinds of people.

In the first-century Palestinian world of Jesus this crossing of boundaries and mixing of peoples would be shocking.[11] If Jesus' peasant audience has regarded the sower with hostility, seeing in him the figure of a wasteful landlord, there is a challenge to them that God can be manifest even in the one they regard as despicable. If they were to exercise God's all-inclusive love, it must extend even to one who exploits them. Such inclusive love does not mean that exploitation goes unchallenged. Rather, it creates an opportunity for an oppressor to repent; it does not simply cut off such a one as unredeemable. Alternatively, if the peasants identify with the sower as one like themselves, the challenge is for them to understand that in their own actions they emulate God whenever their actions of sowing God's word extend beyond their own circles of friends and relations.

28:24-26; Jeremiah 4:3; Ezekiel 36:9; *Gos.Thom.* 20; Pliny, *Nat.Hist.* 18.176. Others speak of plowing after sowing: *Jub.* 11.11; *m. Šabb.* 7.2; *b. Šabb.* 73a-b.

[10] B. Malina and R. Rohrbaugh, *Social Science Commentary on the Synoptic Gospels* (Minneapolis: Fortress, 1992) 202.

[11] Ibid., 192–94; David Rhoads, "Social Criticism: Crossing Boundaries," in *New Approaches in Biblical Studies,* ed. J. C. Anderson and S. D. Moore (Minneapolis: Fortress, 1992) 135–61.

From the narrative perspective of the gospel text, the invitation to the crowds who are not yet followers of Jesus is to receive and respond to the gracious word he preaches. If they are Jews who think they already know and are obedient to God, Jesus invites them to expand their perception of who it is God invites to be among the chosen ones. For people in the crowd who see themselves outside the bounds of Israel, or not addressed by Israel's God, a door is now opened to them.

From the standpoint of Luke's community the parable justifies the inclusion of marginal Jews and Gentile members among the faithful, a favorite Lukan theme. The sower has scattered seed among those formerly not regarded as "good soil." For contemporary Christian communities that struggle with inclusivity, the parable can function the same way.

THE PARABLE OF THE HARVEST

Another point emerges if the focus of the parable is the harvest. The narrative creates a dynamic in which expectations rise with each arena of sowing. From the footpath, hopes of harvest are immediately dashed as what is not trodden underfoot is instantly devoured by the birds. From the rocky ground, hope springs up immediately with the sprouting seed, but, again, is short-lived for lack of moisture. From the thorn patch, hope endures a bit longer, as the seed and the thorns both grow up. But in the end the thorns triumph. Finally, from the good soil comes grain that reaches maturity.

But the story does more than build to an expected climax. It is not simply an assurance of eventual success in the face of repeated failure. The staggering amount of the harvest shatters open the parable, and propels the hearer into an eschatological scenario. The image of harvest is often used to speak of the end time,[12] as is hyperbole.[13] The amounts of the harvest are astro-

---

[12] So also Mark 4:29; Matthew 13:30, 39; 21:34, 41; Luke 20:10; Revelation 14:15.

[13] Irenaeus (*Adv. Haer.* 5.33.3–4) asserts that Papias foretold that in messianic times "a grain of wheat shall bring forth 10,000 ears, and every ear shall have 10,000 grains." The rabbinic tractate *Ketub.* 111b-112a says it will take a ship to carry one grape in the messianic age.

nomical. If a good harvest for a Palestinian farmer yields up to ten-fold, one that produces one-hundred-fold is unimaginable.[14] This explosive scale symbolizes the overflowing of divine fullness, which surpasses all human measure.[15]

Considered from this perspective, whether the context is Jesus' preaching, or Luke's community, or contemporary proclamation of the gospel, the parable leaves the hearer overwhelmed at the inconceivable abundance of God's graciousness manifest in the end times. It evokes awe and praise of God, as the miraculous harvest is clearly the work of God, surpassing anything that is possible from human efforts. A peasant farmer who has labored mightily against adverse conditions hears in this story good news of God's loving providence toward those in need, and assurance of great reward in the end time.[16]

In view of Jesus' proclamation in Luke 4:21 that liberty to oppressed people is already being fulfilled in the mission of the earthly Jesus, some commentators read the abundant harvest as articulating the hopes of oppressed people for a present re-ordering of relationships.[17] It is not just wishful dreaming for the future, but has a subversive function in the present. The bumper crop could shatter the vassal relationship between peasant and landlord. With such a surplus a farmer who formerly struggled just to eat and pay his debts could think formerly outrageous thoughts of even buying the land himself. His oppressive servitude to the landowner could come to an end.

[14] Joachim Jeremias (*The Parables of Jesus* [2nd rev. ed.; New York: Scribner's Sons, 1972] 150, n. 84) asserts that a good harvest yields up to ten-fold; an average one seven and a half.

[15] A similar point is found in Genesis 26:12, "Isaac sowed seed in that land, and in the same year reaped a hundredfold. The Lord blessed him."

[16] John J. Pilch (*The Cultural World of the Gospel: Sunday by Sunday Cycle A* [Collegeville: Liturgical Press] 109) notes that if Jesus' audience heard the parable as telling of a wasteful owner who realized such an enormous profit, it would hardly be good news. We wonder, then, why Jesus would tell such a story that depicts the way things are in an oppressive situation without offering any hopeful alternative.

[17] Ched Myers, *Binding the Strong Man: A Political Reading of Mark's Story of Jesus* (Maryknoll, N.Y.: Orbis, 1988) 177.

THE MEANING OF THE PARABLE (vv. 9-10)

In a transition from the parable proper (vv. 4-8) to its allegorical explanation (vv. 11-15), the disciples[18] question Jesus about the meaning of the parable. Jesus replies that they have been given a gift by God[19] to see and understand what is mysterious about God's realm. Unlike the scholars of the Law who "take away the key of knowledge" (11:52), not entering God's realm and preventing others from doing so as well, Jesus' disciples are given the opportunity to understand the mystery. The fuller gospel narrative with Acts makes clear that complete understanding does not come, however, until after the resurrection (Luke 24:27, 31; Acts 1:3).

While the Markan theme of insiders versus outsiders does not play out in Luke in the way that it does in the Second Gospel, there is a line drawn here between those who understand and those who do not. To the latter the mysteries are made known through parables, but they are unable to understand. Using the words of the prophet Isaiah (6:9) Jesus seems to leave little hope for those who do not perceive or understand (v. 10).

Scholars have wrestled mightily with the meaning of these verses.[20] Are the parables meant to be unintelligible? Does Jesus intend to keep some people on the outside? If so, how can this be reconciled with his universal saving purpose?

One explanation is that Jesus is following an established rabbinical parable pattern in which there are four parts: 1) a question posed by an opponent; 2) a public retort, in veiled language, sufficient to silence the questioner, but not giving a straight answer; 3) a request by the followers for elucidation after the opponent's departure; 4) a private explanation to them

---

[18] At this point in the narrative Mark has a change of scene. Jesus is alone with those who were about him and the twelve (Mark 4:10). In Luke, presumably the disciples ask their question in the hearing of the crowd (Fitzmyer, *Luke,* 706).

[19] The theological passive "it has been given" is a circumlocution that understands God to be the giver.

[20] For a detailed study of the Markan version see Mary Ann Beavis, *Mark's Audience: The Literary and Social Setting of Mark 4.11-12* (JSNTSup 33; Sheffield, JSOT Press, 1989).

in clear language.[21] Several difficulties are left unresolved with this explanation. It is not certain that a form known from rabbinical literature was familiar to the composer of the gospel. Nor is there any evidence of opponents to Jesus in this particular passage. Finally, it still does not resolve the disturbing image of Jesus declaring that some are destined to be on the "outside."

Joachim Jeremias, in studying Mark's version of these verses (Mark 4:10-12), which Luke follows, offers another solution. He proposes that an Aramaic substratum (Jesus' original language) underlies the text of the Greek New Testament and that the Aramaic word *dil^ema* has been misunderstood. Accordingly, the last part of v. 12 should read, *"unless they turn and God will forgive them."*[22] Jeremias bases his reconstruction on parallels between Mark 4:12 and the translation of Isaiah 6:10 in the Aramaic Targum of Isaiah. This is problematic because the extant text of the Targum dates only to the fourth or fifth century C.E.

Other commentators have interpreted these verses as a composition of the early Church, who explained Israel's lack of acceptance of Jesus as having been God's predetermined plan. Similar sayings can be found in Romans 9:16-29; 10:16-21; 11:7-10; John 12:37-41; Acts 28:25-28.[23] This explanation is problematic because in the parable of the wicked tenants (Mark 12:12 // Luke 20:19), Jesus' Jewish opponents understand the parable perfectly well as spoken against them.

The best explanation is that Jesus speaks as a prophet, who experiences the same mixed reception of his message as the prophets of old. Jesus does not speak in parables so that some will not understand; their incomprehension is the result of their choice not to join those who struggle to follow him. The "mysteries" of the reign of God entrusted to those who become disciples are not things that remain incomprehensible, but refers to the paradoxical plan of God, now being revealed in Jesus, that salvation comes through one who is rejected and crucified.[24] To

[21] David Daube, *The New Testament and Rabbinic Judaism* (New York: Arno Press, 1973) 141–43.

[22] Jeremias, *Parables*, 17.

[23] John R. Donahue, *The Gospel in Parable: Metaphor, Narrative, and Theology in the Synoptic Gospels* (Philadelphia: Fortress, 1988) 41.

[24] Ibid., 42–46.

those who choose to remain with Jesus the meaning of the mystery will be gradually unfolded. But those who choose otherwise have deliberately closed their eyes and ears so that they may not understand.

THE PARABLE OF THE SOIL (vv. 11-15)

Most scholars believe that the explanation of the parable in vv. 11-15 is a secondary interpretation by the early Church.[25] With the exception of the weeds in the field (Matt 13:24-30, 36-43), no other gospel parable has an allegorical explanation. It is more likely that Jesus left his stories with open-ended challenges. A linguistic analysis shows this to be the only instance in the Gospels of the absolute use of *ho logos*, "the word," a technical term for "the gospel" that occurs often in the Pauline letters and Acts.[26] Also, the parallel in *Gospel of Thomas* §9 does not have the interpretation, a sign that at one time the parable circulated without it. Moreover, the interpretation misses the eschatological point of the parable; it becomes, instead, an exhortation to self-examination.[27] Nonetheless, these verses offer an important insight into how the early Church preached this parable of Jesus, and they give one direction for how it might yet be preached.

The allegorical explanation in vv. 11-15 clearly focuses on the varying levels of receptivity of the four different types of soil, that is, four types of hearers of the word.[28] The kinds of ob-

---

[25] For arguments for this position see Jeremias, *Parables*, 77–79; Donahue, *Gospel in Parable*, 46–47. Michael P. Knowles ("Abram and the Birds in *Jubilees* 11: A Subtext for the Parable of the Sower?" *NTS* 41 [1995] 145–51) argues on source-critical grounds for an organic link between the parable and its interpretation in light of parallels with a story in *Jubilees* 11. David Flusser (*Die rabbinischen Gleichnisse und der Gleichniserzähler Jesus 1. Teil: Das Wesen der Gleichnisse* [Bern: Peter Lang, 1981] 20, 63, 119–20) also holds that interpretations of parables are not later additions but belong to the original accounts by Jesus.

[26] E.g., 2 Corinthians 11:4; 1 Thessalonians 1:6; 2:13; 2 Thessalonians 1:6; 2 Timothy 1:8; 2:9; Colossians 1:6, 10; Acts 6:7; 12:24; 17:11; 19:20.

[27] Jeremias, *The Parables of Jesus*, 28.

[28] Joel Marcus ("Blanks and Gaps in the Markan Parable of the Sower," *BibInt* 5 [1997] 247–62) points out that the one element that is not explained in the allegorical interpretation is the identity of the sower. Is it God? Christ? the Christian preacher? Marcus proposes that this "gap" in the narrative allows for

stacles that a farmer would face from birds, rocks, trampling, thorns, and lack of moisture are likened to stumbling blocks one faces, once having received the word. Deficient understanding, the work of the evil one, lack of rootedness in oneself, tribulation and persecution on account of the word, worldly concerns, and the lure of riches, all stand in the way of God's word[29] taking deep root and bearing fruit.[30]

From this vantage point the emphasis is on the hearer; each is exhorted to cull out all impediments and become "good soil." The parable not only explains why some hearers of the word "bear fruit" and others do not, but it calls those who hear to cultivate themselves for maximum receptivity and understanding. Luke underscores faith and perseverance with his additions in vv. 12 and 15. He also adds the phrase in v. 15 about embracing the word with a generous and good heart, characteristics found in Hellenistic literature that indicate a noble character.[31] Several other sayings in the gospel refer to the heart: it is the place where goodness or evil is stored (6:45), and lies where one's treasure is (12:34). Disciples in pre-resurrection attempts to understand are "slow of heart" to believe the prophets (24:25).

PREACHING POSSIBILITIES

The task of the preacher is to discern which of the many possible points, the four outlined above, or others still, conveys

---

an identity of the Christian with God and Christ when preaching the word (similar to Mark 13:11).

[29] Some scholars have advanced that the "seed" in Mark 4:15 // Luke 8:11 can represent not only the "word" but also the people who hear the word and who are destined for the eschatological reign of God. They call on Hosea 2:25; Jeremiah 31:27 and 4 Ezra 8:41 for scriptural background for the double duty metaphor of seed as people. See Heil, "Reader Response," 278; L. Ramoroson, "'Parole-semence' ou 'Peuple-semence' dans la parabole du Semeur?," *ScEsp* 40 (1988) 91–101.

[30] There is a similar passage in the Mishnah that speaks of four different kinds of hearers as: those who are slow to hear and swift to lose; those who are slow to hear and slow to lose; those who are swift to hear and slow to lose; and those who are swift to hear and swift to lose (*m.ʾAbot* 5.10-15).

[31] Luke T. Johnson, *The Gospel of Luke*, Sacra Pagina 3 (Collegeville: The Liturgical Press, 1991) 133, notes the same combination in Aristotle, *Nichomachean Ethics* 1, 8, 13.

the message that their congregation needs to hear at this time and place. Does the community struggle with inclusivity? Then the preacher would do well to focus on the sower's profligate and indiscriminate sowing of the word. Is there discouragement over lack of results from efforts toward evangelization and justice? The parable provides a word of encouragement about the assured efficacy of the seed, the word, and the bountiful harvest at the end time. Are there people in the congregation who are caught in impossible webs of oppression? Then the revolutionary image of an out-of-bounds harvest can give hope to an upturning of systems of domination.

Is the assembly growing lax in their efforts to cultivate themselves as receptive "soil" for the word? An exhortation to clear away the "rocks" and "thorns" and all other obstacles would be in order. The parable warns disciples that their initial good reception of the word can falter in the face of deterrents to faith. More is required than an initial decision to follow Jesus.

In Year II the reading paired with this one from 1 Corinthians 15:36-37, 42-49 also uses the image of seed that is sown, but the metaphor is not the same. Paul speaks of the seed as the body that dies and comes to life again as he is trying to explain the manner of body with which the dead will be raised.

CHAPTER TWENTY-FIVE

Mischievous Mustard and Lasting Leaven
(Luke 13:18-21)

Tuesday of the Thirtieth Week of Ordinary Time

¹⁸ *Then [Jesus] said,*
"What is the kingdom of God like?
To what can I compare it?
¹⁹ *It is like a mustard seed*
that a person took and planted in the garden.
When it was fully grown,
it became a large bush
and 'the birds of the sky dwelt in its branches.'"

²⁰ *Again he said,*
"To what shall I compare the kingdom of God?
²¹ *It is like yeast that a woman took*
and mixed (in) with three measures of wheat flour
until the whole batch of dough was leavened."

LUKAN LITERARY CONTEXT

The parable of the mustard seed is found in all three Synoptic Gospels, but the Lukan literary context is unique. Mark (4:3-32) and Matthew (13:31-33) each have a chapter in which a collection of parables is clustered together. Luke retains most of these parables and parabolic sayings, but does not have a structured parables discourse; rather, he interjects the parables into various contexts. Luke, like Matthew, pairs the parable of the mustard seed with that of the leaven. In Mark's Gospel the parable of the mustard seed is paired with the parable of the growing seed (Mark 4:26-34). Mark does not have the parable of the leaven; that tradition comes from Q. It is likely that the parables of the mustard seed and the leaven were already paired in the Q source, but the fact that they have parallels in the *Gospel Thomas* (§20 and 96) that are not joined indicates that at one time they circulated independently.[1]

A notable feature of Luke is his technique of pairing parallel stories, often with one featuring a male protagonist and the other with a female.[2] The two stories make an identical point and serve the same function. Examples include two annunciations, one to Zachariah (1:5-23), one to Mary (1:26-38); two canticles, one of Mary (1:46-56), one of Zachariah (1:67-79); two prophets in the Temple, Simeon (2:25-35) and Anna (2:36-38), etc.[3] Some pairs are found already linked in Luke's source. In a number of instances the story with the male character comes from Mark or Q while the one with the female character is special to Luke. The parables of the mustard seed and the leaven are already paired in Q.[4]

Luke places this pair of parables on the heels of the episode in the synagogue where he cures a woman who had been bent double for eighteen years. As is typical in the gospel, the response to Jesus' sabbath healing is divided: Jesus' adversaries are humiliated while the crowd rejoices at all his glorious deeds (13:17). Luke has intentionally linked the parables to this epi-

---

[1] *Gos.Thom.* §20 reads: "The followers said to Jesus, 'Tell us what heaven's kingdom is like.' He said to them, 'It is like a mustard seed. <It> is the smallest of all seeds, but when it falls on prepared soil, it produces a large plant and becomes a shelter for birds of heaven'" (translation from Marvin Meyer, *The Gospel of Thomas* [HarperSanFrancisco, 1992] 33). This form follows the Markan tradition more closely, but omits making the mature mustard into a shrub (Mark 4:32) or a tree (Luke 13:19).

[2] Constance F. Parvey, "The Theology and Leadership of Women in the New Testament," in *Religion and Sexism,* ed. Rosemary Radford Ruether (New York: Simon & Schuster, 1974) 139-40; Mary Rose D'Angelo, "Women in Luke-Acts: A Redactional View," *JBL* 109 (1990) 443-48.

[3] For a full list see Mary Rose D'Angelo, *Women and Christian Origins,* ed. Ross Shepard Kraemer and Mary Rose D'Angelo (New York: Oxford University Press, 1999) 181-84.

[4] D'Angelo (ibid., 181-84) also delineates another kind of paired stories in Luke and Acts in which two similar stories are told in different contexts to bind the narrative together and to manifest the coherence of God's plan.

sode by constructing the phrase, "he said, therefore *(oun).*"[5] The parables continue to unfold the meaning of the way in which Jesus' mission of liberation is accomplished.

MISCHIEVOUS MUSTARD (vv. 18-19)

For the parable of the mustard seed Luke uses both the Markan source and Q. He relies primarily on the latter, and takes little from Mark's version.[6] One notable difference in Luke's version is that he omits the detail of the smallness of the seed (cf. Mark 4:31 // Matt 13:32). Because of the influence of the other two versions and because of our familiarity with the proverbial smallness of the mustard seed, as is evident in the saying in Luke 17:6 (// Matt 17:20) about having faith its size, it is often thought that the parable in Luke 13:18-19 is meant to be taken as one that contrasts a small beginning to a great outcome. Thus, Jesus is thought to have spoken this parable to his discouraged disciples to reassure them that although his ministry did not seem to amount to much at the outset, there would come a time when he would have a huge, universal following. He would be vindicated in the end, and it would be his critics who would be shown to be in the wrong. This interpretation of the slow, but inevitable growth of the Church as the locus of the reign of God was most popular in the nineteenth century with the rise of evolutionary science.

Another detail that is puzzling in Luke's version is that the mustard seed grows into a tree *(dendron),* in whose branches birds make their nests. It is a botanical impossibility for mustard to become a tree;[7] this may be a simple case of hyperbole so as to make a point. More likely, however, is that the detail of the

[5] The *NAB* translation omits "therefore" which makes the link to the preceding story.

[6] Matthew does the reverse, basing his version mostly on Mark and conflating details from Q (Matt 13:31-32 // Mark 4:30-32). On the Markan version see Barbara E. Reid, *Parables for Preachers: Year B* (Collegeville: The Liturgical Press, 1999) 61–74.

[7] In Mark the seed grows to become the greatest of shrubs *(lachanon)* and the birds make their nests in its shade rather than in its branches (4:32). Matthew conflates the two: the seed grows into the greatest of shrubs *(lachanon)* and becomes a tree *(dendron)!* in whose branches the birds nest (13:32).

sheltering tree is meant to evoke images from the Hebrew Scriptures where a tree with nesting birds symbolizes a powerful nation gathering other peoples under its sway. In Daniel 4:7-9 the strong tree whose top touched the heavens and in whose branches the birds of the air nested represents the power of Nebuchadnezzar, King of Babylon, whose rule extended over the whole earth (Dan 4:19). Similar imagery is found in Ezekiel 17:22-24, where Yahweh plants a cedar shoot atop the mountain heights of Israel.[8] It becomes a majestic tree beneath which birds of every kind shall dwell. This prophecy envisions the end-time gathering in of all the Gentile nations, like nesting birds, under the sheltering embrace of Israel. In light of these passages, commentators have understood Jesus' parable of the mighty mustard with its nesting birds to point toward the end-time when all will be drawn into the bosom of the Christian way.

More recently, scholars have followed the lead of Robert Funk, who proposed that the parable is really a burlesque of Ezekiel's cedar figure with a comic twist.[9] Funk proposes that Jesus' parable is meant to contrast mustard, the common garden weed, with cedar, the most majestic tree, as an image of God's reign. The reign of God does not have to be imported from far-away Lebanon,[10] nor does it come with an impressive power. Rather, it is found in every back yard, erupting out of unpretentious ventures of faith by unimportant people—but which have potentially world-transforming power!

Furthermore, wild mustard, often regarded as a pesky weed, is impossible to eradicate once it has infested a field.[11] So, too, is the tenacious faith of those who seem to be of no account. From this perspective another point emerges: the reign of God, like wild mustard that menaces the cultivated field, is a threat

---

[8] Fortuitously, when the Markan version of the mustard seed parable appears in the Lectionary for the Eleventh Sunday in Ordinary Time, the first reading is from Ezekiel 17:22-24.

[9] Robert Funk, "The Looking Glass Tree is for the Birds," *Int* 27 (1973) 3–9.

[10] See 1 Kings 5:15-25, where Solomon imported cedar wood from Lebanon for the building of the Temple.

[11] D. E. Oakman, *Jesus and the Economic Question of His Day* (Lewiston/Queenston: Edwin Mellen, 1986) 125. See Pliny *NH* 19.171, who distinguishes three kinds of mustard and describes the uncontrollable growth of wild mustard.

to the upper classes who live off the toil of the poor cultivator.[12] Not only is the mustard dangerous, but also the needy birds it attracts, who can also be destructive to the crop. The weed-like reign of God poses a challenge to the arrangements of civilization and those who benefit from them. This interpretation poses a disturbing challenge to the hearer: Where is God's reign to be found? With what kind of power is it established? Who brings it? Who stands to gain by its coming? Whose power is threatened by it?

One objection to this last interpretation for Luke's version is that Luke has made the sowing deliberate and seemingly in a more controlled environment: a man takes the seed and casts *(ebalen)* it into his garden *(kēpos)*. In contrast, Mark uses a passive construction, "when sown" (4:31), and Matthew has the man sow *(speirō)* the seed in his field *(agros)*. While it is not possible to know certainly whether Matthew or Luke preserves the more original form of the wording from Q, Luke probably has redacted it to fit an urban context with houses that have modest vegetable and herb gardens.[13]

LASTING LEAVEN (vv. 20-21)[14]

This is one of three Lukan parables that feature women protagonists,[15] in which the hearers are invited to take the perspective of a female character. The majority of gospel parables and narratives reflect the experience of men and revolve around male characters, so that women disciples have to read as if they were men. Here the reverse is true.

Luke begins this parable with the same rhetorical question as the preceding parable.[16] Both give an image of the reign of

---

[12] Ibid., 127–28.

[13] Joseph A. Fitzmyer, *The Gospel According to Luke* (AB28A; Garden City, N.Y.: Doubleday, 1981) 1017, notes that *m. Kil.* 2:9, 3:2 advises that mustard was not to be grown in a field but in a garden bed.

[14] An earlier version of the following is in Barbara E. Reid, *Choosing the Better Part? Women in the Gospel of Luke* (Collegeville: The Liturgical Press, 1996) 169–78.

[15] For the parable of the woman searching for a lost coin (15:8-10) see above, chap. 15; for the widow and the judge (18:1-8) see chap. 19.

[16] The wording of Matthew's version (13:33) is almost identical to Luke's, with the exception of the introduction, where Matthew begins with a statement

God *(basileia tou theou)*.[17] It is difficult to capture well in English the meaning of the Greek expression *basileia tou theou*. Most frequently it is translated "the kingdom of God." This English phrase conjures up the notion of a place, usually thought of as belonging to another sphere of time and locale (e.g., "up in heaven" and "the next life") in which God dwells and rules as monarch. But such images of God and the divine realm do not entirely cohere with those attached to this symbolic phrase in the synoptic sayings.[18] By translating *basileia tou theou* as "the reign of God" or "the realm of God" one can avoid reinforcing some of the male-centered monarchical imagery that "kingdom of God" evokes and further allow the parables to take our imaginations into the rich meanings attached to the symbol *basileia*.

The most common interpretation of the parable in Luke 13:20-21 focuses on the small amount of yeast that one would mix with flour to produce a loaf of bread. The point is said to be the astonishing growth of something small into something that permeates a large entity. In this interpretation, the leaven is thought to be Jesus' preaching, or the word of God, which grows phenomenally in its efficacy throughout time and history.[19] In the version of the saying found in *Gospel of Thomas* there is such a contrast between the "bit of leaven" used and the "big loaves" it made. However, there is no reference in the Lukan or Matthean versions of the parable to the amounts involved. Knowledge of Paul's proverbial statement, "A little yeast leavens the whole batch of dough" (Gal 5:9; similarly 1

---

rather than a question. Similarly, *Gos.Thom.* §96 reads: "The father's kingdom is like [a] woman. She took a little yeast, [hid] it in dough, and made it into large loaves of bread. Whoever has ears should hear" (translation by Meyer, *The Gospel of Thomas*, 61).

[17] Matthew's version says "the kingdom of heaven" *(basileia tōn ouranōn)* rather than "kingdom of God" *(basileia tou theou)*. Like pious Jews who refrain from using the name of "God," Matthew substitutes "heaven" as a circumlocution. See below, pp. 306–07, on Reign of God.

[18] Sallie McFague *(Models of God: Theology for an Ecological, Nuclear Age* [Philadelphia: Fortress, 1987] especially 63–69) shows the inadequacies of the monarchical metaphor for God.

[19] E.g., Joachim Jeremias, *Rediscovering the Parables* (New York: Charles Scribner's Sons, 1966) 116–17.

Cor 5:6), may also influence one to read a contrast of amounts into the parable.

The Markan parable of the mustard seed does emphasize a contrast between small beginnings and a large outcome (Mark 4:30-32). Matthew's rendition (13:31-32) also has this contrast, but Luke's (13:18-19) omits it. Because the parable of the mustard seed immediately precedes that of the leaven in Matthew and in Luke, the interpretation of the Markan version of the former has influenced that of the latter. However, in the *Gospel of Thomas* the two parables are not connected. Mark's Gospel does not have the parable of the leaven. Thus, at one stage of the tradition, the two stories circulated separately and do not necessarily have the same point. This is especially true for the Lukan versions: neither story has a small-large contrast in the text.

CORRUPTION

Important to the meaning of the parable is the fact that in every other instance in Scripture in which leaven occurs, it represents evil or corruption. In Exodus 12:15-20, 34 the Passover ritual prescribes that unleavened bread be eaten for seven days. This recalls the Israelites' hasty departure from Egypt, with no time to wait for dough to be leavened. Eating unleavened bread becomes a sign of membership in God's holy people. Grain offerings are to be unleavened (Lev 2:11), equating unleavened with sacred. In Mark 8:15 (similarly Matt 16:6, 11, 12) Jesus cautions his disciples, "Watch out, guard against the leaven of the Pharisees and the leaven of Herod." In his version of this saying Luke (12:1) defines the leaven of the Pharisees as "hypocrisy." Twice Paul uses leaven as a symbol for corruption. He admonishes the Corinthians, "Do you not know that a little yeast leavens all the dough? Clear out the old yeast, so that you may become a fresh batch of dough, inasmuch as you are unleavened. For our paschal lamb, Christ, has been sacrificed (1 Cor 5:6-7). To the Galatians he quotes the proverb, "A little yeast leavens the whole batch of dough," warning them not to be misled by those preaching a different message from his own.[20]

[20] In other Greek writers, e.g., Plutarch, *Mor.* 289 E-F and 659 B, leaven also connotes corruption.

For some interpreters such a singular positive use of leaven in Jesus' parable is the unexpected twist in the story. However, if leaven is meant to connote corruption, the startling message is that the reign of God is like a batch of dough that has been permeated by what societal standards would consider a "corruptive yeast." In other words, Jesus' story presents an image of God's realm as one that reverses previous notions of holiness: no longer unleavened, but leavened is the locus of the sacred. It proclaims that God's realm thoroughly incorporates persons who would have been considered corrupt, unclean, or sinners according to prevailing interpretations of the Jewish purity regulations.

To understand the parable this way accords well with Jesus' other teachings and actions, particularly in the Gospel of Luke, in which Jesus continually extends himself to people who are poor, outcast, or marginalized. The challenge of the parable for those who are on the fringes is to begin to see themselves as "leaven," a vital component of the believing community. For those who are privileged, it is a summons to change their attitude toward those they consider "corrupt" and to see them as the very ones who provide the active ingredient for the growth of the community of God's people.[21]

As Luke's predominantly Gentile community retold the story in their day, they may have been thinking of how Gentile Christians, who began as a hidden minority mixed into the batch of predominantly Jewish Christian communities, were now beginning to permeate the whole. To Jewish Christians, this "corrupting" influence would have had a disturbing effect on their prevailing theology and praxis. Having let a few Gentiles mix in, these now were changing the character of the whole community!

---

[21] So e.g., Robert W. Funk, "Beyond Criticism in Quest of Literacy: The Parable of the Leaven," *Int* 25 (1971) 149–70; Susan Praeder, *The Word in Women's Worlds: Four Parables* (Zacchaeus Studies: New Testament; Wilmington: Glazier, 1988) 32; Bernard Brandon Scott, *Hear Then the Parable: A Commentary on the Parables of Jesus* (Minneapolis: Fortress, 1989) 329.

HIDDENNESS

An odd detail in this parable is the hiddenness of the leaven. The parable says that the woman took and hid *([en]ekrypsen)* leaven in three measures of flour. The verb *(en)kryptō* is nowhere else attested in a recipe for "mixing" dough.[22] Some scholars understand the point of the parable to be that the reign of God, like leaven, works silently, imperceptibly within, surely bringing about transformation.[23] This interpretation is not far removed from that of the small-to-large contrast. But there is something more to be explored in this detail.

Forms of the verb *kryptō* ("to hide") occur several other times in Luke. In one instance, Jesus rejoices in the Holy Spirit and says, "I thank you, Father, Lord of heaven and earth, because you have hidden *(apekrypsas)* these things from the wise and the intelligent and have revealed them to infants" (10:21). In another, the twelve do not grasp what Jesus says to them about his coming passion: "what he said was hidden *(kekrymmenon)* from them" (18:34). In another, Jesus laments over Jerusalem, saying, "If you, even you, had only recognized on this day the things that make for peace! But now they are hidden *(ekrybē)* from your eyes" (19:42).

In each of these instances full understanding of some aspect of the mystery of the divine realm is concealed by God (the passive voice of the verb *kryptō* in 18:34 and 19:42 is a theological passive, that is, God is understood to be the subject).[24] These examples provide further clues to the meaning of the parable in Luke 13:20-21. In this instance also, there is something hidden in the reign of God and the one who does the concealing is God.

---

[22] Praeder, *Women's Worlds*, 35. Elizabeth Waller ("The Parable of the Leaven: A Sectarian Teaching and the Inclusion of Women," *USQR* 35 [1979–80] 99–109) proposes that the verb *enkryptō*, "to hide," came into the leaven parable by its similar sound to the noun *enkrypsias*, "cakes," found in Genesis 18:6. Waller asserts that the story in Genesis 18:1-10 stands behind the leaven parable. Both concern a woman who mixes three measures of dough for an epiphany.

[23] E.g., C. H. Dodd, *The Parables of the Kingdom* (rev. ed.; New York: Charles Scribner's Sons, 1961) 155–56; Fitzmyer, *Luke*, 1019.

[24] Similar uses of *kryptō* occur in Matthew: "I will open my mouth to speak in parables; I will proclaim what has been hidden *(kekrymmenō)* from the foundation

Two things are startling in this image: that God is portrayed as a woman, and that she conceals rather than reveals.

The latter point most likely reflects the struggle of the early Christian communities to explain the paradoxes which framed their faith. They declared that a crucified criminal was the Messiah (Acts 2:36), that death was the way to life (Acts 17:3), and that suffering was the path to glory (Luke 24:26). For people who readily attributed all things to God, the incomprehensibility of these seeming contradictions could be explained in terms of God concealing their full meaning until the propitious time of revelation.

A FEMALE IMAGE OF GOD

The parables of the woman mixing dough (13:20-21) and of the woman who searches for a lost coin (15:8-10) are two of the clearest instances in which Jesus invites believers to envision God as a woman.[25] Although God does not have a gender, when we picture a personal God, our human experience of persons being either male or female enters our imagination. All language about God is metaphorical; no image adequately expresses who God is.[26] God is like a woman hiding leaven in bread dough, a woman searching for a lost coin, a shepherd going after a lost sheep, but God *is* not any of these. However, the language and images we use for God are extremely important because they work in two directions: what we say about God reflects what we believe about human beings made in

---

of the world" (13:35); and "The kingdom of heaven is like a treasure buried *(kekrymmenō)* in a field, which a person finds and hides *(ekrypsen)* again, and out of joy goes and sells all that he has and buys that field" (Matt 13:44).

[25] Interestingly, in the version of the parable in the *Gospel of Thomas*, the focus of the story clearly shifts away from the leaven to the woman. Waller ("Leaven," 102–03) believes that Thomas' version of the introduction is earlier than that of Matthew or Luke. Her arguments for such are not convincing. Her desire to make the figure of the woman central to the story can be achieved without resorting to an earlier date for the version of Thomas.

[26] See Elizabeth Johnson, *She Who Is: The Mystery of God in Feminist Theological Discourse* (New York: Crossroad, 1992); Sandra Schneiders, "God Is More Than Two Men and a Bird," *U.S. Catholic* (May 1990) 20–27; *Women and the Word* (New York: Paulist, 1986).

God's image. Genesis 1:27 asserts that male and female are made in God's image. But when we use predominantly male metaphors for God, then being male is equated with being god-like. Consequently, women are not thought to be like God, and are regarded as less holy than men. Jesus' teaching and praxis contradicts such a notion and invites believers to envision God in such a way that women and men are both seen to reflect God's image equally. When the parable of the woman mixing bread dough is paired with that of the man who sowed mustard seed in his garden it shows that women and men both act in the divine image to bring about the realm of God.

EPIPHANY BAKING

One other startling element in the story is the grandiose amount of flour, three measures, or approximately fifty pounds! The woman is preparing bread for a feast fit for a manifestation of God. In fact, the very same amount of flour is used by Sarah when she bakes for Abraham's three heavenly visitors (Gen 18:6). Gideon uses this amount, too, when preparing for an angel of God (Judg 6:19), as does Hannah when making the offering for the presentation of Samuel in the Temple at Shiloh (1 Sam 1:24). In each of these instances, the large-scale baking prepares for an epiphany. So, too, the parable in Luke 13:20-21 portrays the work of a woman as a vehicle for God's revelation.

PREACHING POSSIBILITIES

Both parables in this gospel present a number of preaching possibilities. The preacher would do well to focus on only one main point. One of the tasks of the preacher is to discern which of the many possible points is the one that needs to be preached at this time and place. In another moment and place the choice might be very different.

While the small-to-large contrast is not Luke's emphasis, the hiddenness of the seed sown or the leaven mixed into the dough could be the central image. The preacher might focus on assurance that God is at work, even when the divine action seems imperceptible or unintelligible. In its original setting these parables may have assured followers of Jesus that the word he preached would eventually become impressive in the visible growth of the body of the believers, even if the beginnings seemed very modest.[27] In Year I when this reading is paired with Romans 8:18-25, the theme of hope and trusting in what is not seen comes to the fore.

From the mustard parable the preacher could also choose to focus on the locale of the reign of God and its manner of coming. It is not imported from far off, but comes with every small venture of faith by ordinary believers who act in the power of the crucified and risen Christ. Such ventures pose a challenge to oppressive systems of power just as mustard run wild can overtake cultivated fields. These kinds of efforts also shelter the little ones who, like the birds of the air, depend on God's benefaction for existence (Luke 12:24). This subversive power of radical faith, like mustard gone to seed, is impossible to root out once it has taken hold and is impossible to control within confined plots of land.

The parable of the leaven likewise poses a challenge about crossing boundaries. As Luke's community may have understood the parable to speak to their experience of including "corrupt" Gentiles, for believers today the message may be a challenge to discard attempts at keeping the faith community a flat, "unleavened," mass of homogenous people, and to enthusiastically embrace an image of God's reign that includes persons of diverse races, ethnic origin, class, gender, age, sexual orientation, differing physical and mental abilities, who energize and transform the whole.

The parable of the leaven provides a rare opportunity for the preacher to speak of God in female terms and of the ministry of women as leaven, the critical ingredient for vitality and transformative action in the life of the church and the reign of God. The image of the agitating action of leaven could be a vehicle to articulate how for some women's entry into ministries traditionally reserved for males and the use of female images of God is

---

[27] Herman Hendrickx, *The Parables of Jesus* (rev. ed.; San Francisco: Harper & Row, 1986) 40; Eugene LaVerdiere, "Teaching in Parables," *Emmanuel* 94 (1988) 453.

the ruination of the unleavened bread, the Church. Others will thrill with the fermentation that causes the whole loaf to rise and be transformed into fulfilling fare for the whole community of believers. The preacher might lead the congregation in reflecting how it was that leaven, a good thing, which brings taste and texture to the loaf, came to be used exclusively as a symbol of corruption and evil. Similarly, we may ask how it was that women's leadership in ministry, so vital to the Church's early life, came to be regarded as a corrosive element and increasingly restricted. To have leavened bread is what is normal. It was the crisis situation of having to flee hastily from Egypt, with no time to wait for bread to be leavened (Exod 12:15-20, 34) that gave rise to the Jewish custom of eating unleavened bread in remembrance at Passover. Likewise, the restriction of women from the ministry of presiding at the breaking of the bread might be considered to have arisen from a crisis situation in the first Christian decades, where for the survival of the fledgling communities in a patriarchal and imperial world, these roles were taken over by men. What would be needed to return to a situation of leavened bread, where the mix of women with men in the same ministerial roles is considered "normal"?

In Year II when this gospel is paired with Ephesians 5:21-33, where women are admonished to be submissive to their husbands, it is particularly imperative that the preacher clarify the patriarchal world out of which these household codes arose. The preacher should both show the danger of legitimizing attitudes and structures of domination and at the same time offer an alternate vision of the empowerment of women from the parable of the leaven.

The context of these parables shows that these are not peaceful stories about birds and plants and baking bread. Rather, they pose difficult challenges and invite conversion. The hearer is faced with a choice to side with Jesus' opponents who complain that he does not observe the Law (13:14) or with those who magnify God for his powerful deeds (13:17) and become his followers.

EXCURSUS: THE REIGN OF GOD

The parables of the mustard seed and the leaven are explicitly about the reign of God. The phrase *basileia tou theou*, "kingdom of God," appears thirty-two times in the Gospel of Luke and six times in Acts.[28] It is difficult to find an adequate phrase in English to convey the meaning of *basileia tou theou*. Translating it as "kingdom of God" is problematic, first, because it conveys the notion of a locale with fixed boundaries. It has long been recognized that God's *basileia* signifies divine "kingly rule" or "reign," not "kingdom" in a territorial sense.

A further difficulty with the translation "kingdom of God" is that it presents an image of God as king, reinforcing a male, monarchical model of God's rule. For communities of believers whose experience of governance is democratic, and who have become conscious of the limitations and dangers of having solely male images of God, "kingdom" is an inadequate term.[29]

Finally, in a first-century Palestinian context the term *basileia* would first call to mind the Roman imperial system of domination and exploitation. Jesus' annunciation of the *basileia* of God offered an alternative vision to that of the empire of Rome. The *basileia* that Jesus announced was one in which there was no more victimization or domination. This *basileia* was already present incipiently in Jesus' healing and liberative practices, the inclusive table sharing of his followers, and their domination-free relationships. The political threat that such a subversive *basileia* vision presented to the Roman imperial system is clear from the crucifixion of Jesus.[30]

Recognizing that no phrase adequately captures all that *basileia tou theou* signifies, alternative translations of *basileia* include: "kin-dom," "rule," "reign," "realm," "empire," "domain," and "commonweal." With adequate explanation, some leave it untranslated, as *basileia*. While none of these terms is

---

[28] Luke 1:43; 6:20; 7:28; 8:1, 10; 9:2, 11, 27, 60, 62; 10:9, 11; 11:20; 13:18, 20, 28, 29; 14:15; 16:16; 17:20 [2x], 21; 18:16, 17, 24, 25, 29; 19:11; 21:31; 22:16, 18; 23:51; Acts 1:3; 8:12; 14:22; 19:8; 28:23, 31.

[29] See McFague, *Models of God.*

[30] Elisabeth Schüssler Fiorenza, *Jesus: Miriam's Child, Sophia's Prophet* (New York: Continuum, 1994) 92–93.

perfect, it is helpful for a preacher to experiment with new phrases to jog the hearers into wrestling with the meaning of the phrase.

It is important that whatever translation one adopts, it convey the sense of God's saving power over all creation, already inaugurated in a new way with the incarnation and ministry of Jesus. It is continued in the faithful ministry of the believing community, but not yet fully manifest. It is not a fixed place located in the beyond. Nor is it coterminus with the Church. It is authoritative power and empowerment by God-with-us.

CHAPTER TWENTY-SIX

Godly Guests
(Luke 14:15-24)

Tuesday of the Thirty-first Week of Ordinary Time

^{15} One of his fellow guests on hearing this said to him,
  "Blessed is the one who will dine in the kingdom of God."
^{16} He replied to him,
  "A man gave a great dinner to which he invited many.
^{17} When the time for the dinner came,
  he dispatched his servant to say to those invited,
  'Come, everything is now ready.'
^{18} But one by one, they all began to excuse themselves.
  The first said to him,
  'I have purchased a field and must go to examine it;
  I ask you, consider me excused.'
^{19} And another said,
  'I have purchased five yoke of oxen and am on my way to evaluate them;
  I ask you, consider me excused.'
^{20} And another said,
  'I have just married a woman,
  and therefore I cannot come.'
^{21} The servant went and reported this to his master.
  Then the master of the house in a rage commanded his servant,
  'Go out quickly into the streets and alleys of the town
  and bring in here the poor and the crippled, the blind and the lame.'
^{22} The servant reported,
  'Sir, your orders have been carried out and still there is room.'
^{23} The master then ordered the servant,
  'Go out to the highways and hedgerows
  and make people come in that my home may be filled.

[24] *For, I tell you,*
   none of those men[1] who were invited will taste my dinner.'"

TRADITION HISTORY

The parable in vv. 16-24 has parallels in Matthew 22:2-14, *Gospel of Thomas* §64, and in rabbinic literature.[2] The setting for the Matthean version is entirely different: it is the third of three parables that Jesus tells after having already reached Jerusalem, following the parable of the two sons (Matt 21:28-32) and that of the wicked tenants (Matt 21:33-46). Matthew has highly allegorized the parable, making the host a king and the banquet a wedding feast for his son. Typical of Matthew, he extends the parable to address the ethical demands of discipleship by adding vv. 11-14 about wearing appropriate garments. Matthew's parable takes a deadly turn when the servants delivering the invitation are murdered and the king retaliates with slaughter of the murderers and burning of their city (vv. 6-7).

In the *Gospel of Thomas* the story is simpler, and has four refusals by businessmen and merchants. The form is closer to Luke's while the ending is more similar to Matthew's. For some scholars the Lukan version represents the form of the parable closest to that of Jesus; for others the version of Thomas. Still others attempt a hypothetical reconstruction of a Q parable that underlies the various redactions.[3] It is clear that each version is carefully crafted to advance each evangelist's particular theological themes.

---

[1] The Greek word used here is the genitive plural of *anēr*, which refers specifically to males, in contrast to *anthrōpos*, which refers to human beings. What is envisioned in the parable is the world of first-century urban elite men. While customs were beginning to change in the Roman world of the first century, banquets were, in many circles, still the exclusive domain of males. See Kathleen Corley, *Private Women: Public Meals* (Peabody, Mass.: Hendrickson, 1993).

[2] Joachim Jeremias (*The Parables of Jesus* [New York: Scribner's, 1972] 178–79) cites a rabbinic parable (*j. San.* 6.6) as the source of the gospel tradition. It is a story of a tax collector who invited poor people to dinner so the food would not go to waste. The form and function of this story, however, is much different than the one in the gospel, as shown by Bernard Brandon Scott (*Hear Then the Parable: A Commentary on the Parables of Jesus* [Minneapolis: Fortress, 1989] 171–72).

[3] For more detailed treatment of the tradition history of the parable see Joseph A. Fitzmyer, *The Gospel According to Luke* (AB28; Garden City, N.Y.: 1981) 148–57; Scott, *Hear Then,* 161–68; John Dominic Crossan, *The Dark Interval: Towards a Theology of Story* (Niles, Ill.: Argus Communications, 1975) 108–19.

LUKAN LITERARY CONTEXT

This familiar parable is the fourth and last part of the interchange that is set at a sabbath dinner in the home of a leading Pharisee (14:1). In the first section (vv. 1-6) Jesus heals a man suffering from dropsy and confronts the scholars of the Law and the Pharisees present with a question, to which they do not reply, about the lawfulness of healing on the sabbath. In the second part (vv. 7-11) Jesus addresses guests about their choice of places at table, which is followed by advice to the host about his guest list (vv. 12-14).[4]

This parable is part of the great journey narrative, which is punctuated with banquet scenes at every juncture. In addition to the dinner in 14:1-24 is another in the house of a Pharisee (11:37-54), the one that follows the finding of the lost son (15:23-24), and the banquet at the home of Zacchaeus (19:1-10). The parable of the great dinner is part of the dinner conversation after the meal, cast like a Hellenistic symposium.[5] In the Gospel of Luke the after-dinner conversations always concern issues of discipleship. The topic of conversation at the dinner is further directed to a wider audience in the last half of Luke 14 (vv. 25-33).[6] At v. 25 the scene shifts to a continuation of the journey, with great crowds traveling with Jesus. Not only for the scholars of the Law and the Pharisees with whom Jesus is dining (vv. 1-24), but for any (vv. 25-33) relational attachments (v. 26) and possessions (v. 33) can be obstacles to discipleship.

DINING IN THE KINGDOM[7] (vv. 15, 24)

The opening and closing verses give the parable an interpretive frame that makes the parabolic dinner (vv. 16-23) an image

---

[4] On Luke 7:7-14 see above, chap. 13. Charles H. Talbert (*Reading Luke: A Literary and Theological Commentary on the Third Gospel* [New York: Crossroad, 1988] 196) sees a chiastic pattern in the four parts with sections one and four addressing unconcern about others while giving the appearance of being religious; parts two and three counter self-seeking of guests and hosts.

[5] See above, p. 158, n. 3, for references on Greco-Roman symposia.

[6] Richard Rohrbaugh, "The Pre-Industrial City in Luke-Acts: Urban Social Relations," in *The Social World of Luke-Acts* (Peabody, Mass.: Hendrickson, 1991) 137.

[7] See Eugene LaVerdiere's book by this title (*Dining in the Kingdom of God* [Chicago: Liturgy Training Publications, 1994]) which examines all the banquet

for the reign of God. There are clear links with 14:13-14, where the guest list of poor, crippled, lame, and blind people (v. 13) parallels that of v. 21. And v. 14 points to eschatological fulfillment, as it speaks of repayment at the resurrection of the righteous, as does v. 24, where "my dinner" signals the eschatological feast.[8] The image of a banquet for end-time feasting to celebrate God's ultimate triumph over evil is elaborated by Isaiah:

> On this mountain the LORD of hosts
> will provide for all peoples
> A feast of rich food and choice wines,
> juicy, rich food and pure, choice wines (Isa 25:6).[9]

The topic of reversals at end-time dining has already been raised in Luke 13:28-29, where Jesus proclaimed that people from every direction would recline at table in the reign of God and some who are first will be last.

DOUBLE INVITATIONS

The parable opens with a rich man giving a great banquet, with many people invited. The setting is clearly the world of urban elites, as will become clearer in vv. 21-23. Such a feast need not have any particular occasion, but is a means of solidifying social status and ingratiating the host with those of his class. Perhaps he is reciprocating for other banquets where he has been a guest; perchance he is initiating the event to obligate others to himself. In either case, in Jesus' world, as in the world of Luke, likes eat with likes and social classes are not crossed. Eating together signifies shared values and social position.[10]

As v. 17 indicates, invitations had already been issued previously. The custom of a double invitation is seen in Esther 5:8;

---

episodes in the Third Gospel in relation to the origins of the Eucharist according to Luke.

[8] Willard M. Swartley, "Unexpected Banquet People (Luke 14:16-24)," in *Jesus and His Parables*, ed. V. George Shillington (Edinburgh: T. & T. Clark, 1997) 187.

[9] See also Isaiah 55:1-2; 65:11-13; Deuteronomy 12:4-7; Psalms 22:27; 23:25; *1 Enoch* 62:14; *2 Enoch* 42:5.

[10] B. Malina and R. Rohrbaugh, *Social Science Commentary on the Synoptic Gospels* (Minneapolis: Fortress, 1992) 367.

6:14 and is also known from ancient papyri.[11] It served the purpose of allowing the potential guest to ascertain who else is coming and whether all was being done appropriately in arranging the dinner. It would also give the invitee time to determine if he could afford to reciprocate in like manner.[12] From the perspective of the host, the time lapse allows him to determine the amount of food he will need to prepare.[13]

TRIPLE EXCUSES

As the servant goes out to tell the invited guests that all is ready, they all stand united against the host. The phrase *apo mias* in v. 18, translated "one by one" in the *NAB*, literally means "from one" and most likely captures an underlying Aramaic expression. What it signifies is that either all the invitees will come or none will. None in the tightly knit circles of elites[14] will break ranks. They have decided all together to shun the host. The reason for this is not entirely clear from the excuses they offer.

Some commentators have noted a similarity between the excuses offered by the potential guests and the stipulations in Deuteronomy 20:5-7 for why a man may be excused from military service in the event of a holy war: "Then the officials shall say to the soldiers, 'Is there anyone who has built a new house and not yet had the housewarming? Let him return home, lest he die in battle and another dedicate it. Is there anyone who has

[11] Chan-Hie Kim, "The Papyrus Invitation," *JBL* 94 (1975) 391–402. R. L. Rohrbaugh, "The Pre-Industrial City in Luke-Acts: Urban Social Relations," in *The Social World of Luke-Acts: Models for Interpretation,* ed. J. H. Neyrey [Peabody, Mass.: Hendrickson, 1991] 141, notes also that a later rabbinic commentary on Lamentations also attests to this (*Lam. R.* 4:2).

[12] For the social and geographical arrangements presumed in this parable I rely chiefly on Rohrbaugh, "Pre-Industrial City," 125–49.

[13] Kenneth E. Bailey, *Through Peasant Eyes: More Lucan Parables, Their Culture and Style* (Grand Rapids, Mich.: Eerdmans, 1980) 94, estimates that for 2–4 guests he would kill a chicken or two, for 5–8 a duck, for 10–15 a kid, for 15–35 a sheep, and for 35–75 a calf.

[14] That the first two guests are rich is evident in their ability to purchase land and animals. The first is evidently an absentee landlord who has bought a field outside the city. The second has oxen enough to plow some one hundred acres of land (as estimated by Luise Schottroff and Wolfgang Stegemann, *Jesus and the Hope of the Poor* [Maryknoll: Orbis, 1986] 101).

planted a vineyard and never yet enjoyed its fruits? Let him return home, lest he die in battle and another enjoy its fruits in his
stead. Is there anyone who has betrothed a woman and not yet
taken her as his wife? Let him return home, lest he die in battle
and another take her to wife.'"[15] Similarly, Deuteronomy 24:5
exempts a new groom from military service for one year.

While such excuses may apply to war, there is no relevance
to a banquet invitation. The excuses are patently flimsy. Anyone
who purchases a field looks it over very carefully *before* he completes the transaction. The same is true of anyone buying yoked
oxen. Before agreeing to the purchase, the buyer would be very
careful to test them out beforehand to make sure they are healthy
and well-paired. The bridegroom may have legitimate reason to
refuse if he has accumulated too many social obligations to be
able to repay. But in the context all three excuses are insulting to
the host and show that he is being deliberately shunned.[16] There
is an interesting literary interplay as the host who is left out becomes enraged (v. 21) and invites in social "losers," while in the
next chapter the elder brother becomes infuriated (15:28) at a
banquet given for his lost brother, to which he is invited.

SOCIAL SUICIDE

The reaction of the host turns the whole social configuration on its head. Having been shunned by his rich associates he
breaks ranks with them irrevocably in a socially suicidal move.
He commands his servant to go into the streets *(plateias)* and alleys *(rhymas)* of the town and bring in people who are poor,
crippled, blind, and lame. In contrast to modern cities, where
the poorest live in the inner city and the rich live in outlying
suburbs, the reverse was true in antiquity. The elite, who made
up some five to ten percent of the total population, lived in the
center of the city. It was they who controlled the political, economic, and religious systems. Physically and socially they were
separated from the non-elite who served their needs. These latter often lived clustered in ethnic and occupational groups.

---

[15] E.g., J.D.M. Derrett, *Law in the New Testament* (London: Darton, Longman & Todd, 1970) 126–55.

[16] Bailey, *Through Peasant Eyes*, 95–99.

Walls and gates, often with watchmen, ensured control of traffic and communication between sections.

The servant of the rich man goes into the wider streets *(plateias)* and the narrow alleys *(rhymas)*, along which the poorest live. Rohrbaugh describes, "Most streets were unpaved, narrow, badly crowded and would not have allowed passage of wheeled vehicles. Many would have been choked with refuse and frequented by scavenging dogs, pigs, birds, and other animals. Shallow depressions in the streets allowed some drainage, but also acted as open sewers. Large, open spaces were few in most cities and those that did exist were often at intersections of the few paved thoroughfares. Such open squares often served as gathering places for ceremonies or public announcements."[17]

We might envision the servant calling out the invitation in these intersections, in stark contrast to the private, genteel manner in which the first rich potential guests had been summoned. The kinds of guests now being sought out correspond to the list of those who the Qumran community thought excluded from the messianic banquet. For them no one who was paralyzed, lame, blind, deaf, mute, or who had skin blemishes would find a place at the final in-gathering (1QSa 2:11-22). However, it is precisely these to whom Jesus' mission is directed, as articulated in Luke 4:18, when Jesus makes the words of Isaiah 61:1-2 his own (so also Luke 6:20-22; 7:22; 14:13).

Having made one foray into the world of the marginalized non-elite, the servant reports that there is yet room at the banquet. So the rich master sends him out again, this time to the highways *(hodous)* and hedgerows *(phragmous)*. The way *(hodos)* has the literal connotation of "roadway" but it also is a metaphor in Luke for the journey of Jesus and those who follow him. John the Baptist sets the tone at the beginning of the gospel when he uses the words of Isaiah (40:4) to invite people to prepare the way of the Lord (Luke 3:4). In Acts "the Way" becomes an expression for the followers of Jesus.[18] The term *phragmos* is used for hedges or fences that enclose fields or property. The slave is sent to the area immediately outside the city where outcasts such as tanners, traders, beggars, and prostitutes live. These are people whose

---

[17] Rohrbaugh, "Pre-Industrial City," 135.
[18] Acts 9:2; 18:25, 26; 19:9, 23; 24:14, 22.

services are needed in the city, but who are not permitted to live in it. They are socially vulnerable, having neither the protection of the city walls, nor that of a village network.[19]

The detail that the servant must compel these people to come into the elite man's home is true to life. Rather than eager recipients of a generous handout, the parable portrays them as wary outsiders who are well aware of the social gulf between them and the rich man, and would not easily cross this gulf.[20] There is more at stake in this scene than the Middle Eastern custom of politely declining an unexpected invitation.[21] It is an undoing of the social boundaries, which would be met with great suspicion by the unlikely invitees and would result in social suicide for the host. His ostracism by his elite friends will be complete after this bizarre banquet.

CONCLUSION

The final verse is an ambiguous conclusion, where it is not clear whether the "I" speaking is the host of the parable speaking to all his new guests (in the Greek text "you" is plural) or to Jesus, who is addressing his fellow diners.[22] As a saying of Jesus it has been interpreted as a metaphor for salvation history, with various identifications of the potential guests. For many interpreters the parable has been understood to refer to Israelites (represented by the scholars of the Law and the Pharisees of 14:3), as the ones first invited. The second group, those who were poor and disabled, would be the marginalized within Is-

---

[19] Rohrbaugh, "Pre-Industrial City," 144–45.

[20] Ibid., 145.

[21] Bailey, *Through Peasant Eyes,* 108, cites Luke 24:28-29 (see also Gen 19:3) as a similar example of the expected first refusal of an unexpected invitation. He also suggests that the guests of the lower social class would consider their inability to reciprocate as reason for refusal. But such people would never expect to host someone of the class of the elite man. At most they would become his clients and would render him services for a beneficence. But eating together would be unthinkable.

[22] A similar construction with *legō hymin,* "I tell you," is found at the conclusion of the parables of the found sheep (15:7) and coin (15:10). Another parable in which it is not clear if the last verse (16:8) is spoken by Jesus or the master of the parable is that of the steward who rewrites the debts.

rael. The third group from the highways and hedgerows are thought to be the Gentiles, outsiders to the promises of Israel. This coheres with Luke's theological construction of salvation offered first to Jews and then to Gentiles (Acts 3:26; 13:46; 18:6; 28:23-38). It is possible, however, to understand the parable as one which takes place entirely within a Jewish world.[23] The contrasts are not about degrees of observance of the Law, but rather have to do with crossing social boundaries between rich and poor. The parable portrays in vivid form the many sayings in Luke about the obstacles that riches pose. The rich people invited to the banquet are too preoccupied with their possessions and relationships to respond to the invitation of the host. The host, having been rejected by his elite peers, turns to those outside his relational circle. What looks like social suicide for him becomes an icon of salvation for all the outcasts. For the rich of Luke's community the parable addresses difficult questions of whether one can be a Christian and still maintain elite social networks. How can one be part of the believing community and at the same time avoid association with poor Christians?[24]

In the context of the gospel Jesus, the host who offers food for a hungry world, experiences rejection from his dining companions of the religious elite. His turning to people who are poor and marginalized, however is not his second recourse, as in the parable, but is the very reason for his being shunned in the first place by the religious leaders of his day. Those who refuse his invitation in the present incomplete incarnation of the reign of God will not taste the future eschatological banquet of God's rule in its full expression. In narrative terms this is the last dinner scene in which Jesus eats with Pharisees, as they increasingly reject him as the journeying prophet.[25]

---

[23] As in the interpretation of Rohrbaugh, "Pre-Industrial City," 125–49.

[24] Rohrbaugh, "Pre-Industrial City," 142. Similarly Robert J. Karris, *Luke: Artist and Theologian* (New York: Paulist, 1978); Willi Braun, *Feasting and Social Rhetoric in Luke 14* (SNTSMS 85; Cambridge: Cambridge University Press, 1995).

[25] David P. Moessner, *Lord of the Banquet: The Literary and Theological Significance of the Lukan Travel Narrative* (Minneapolis: Fortress, 1989) 158.

PREACHING POSSIBILITIES

One theme that the parable opens is that the invitation to discipleship and, ultimately, to the fullness of God's realm, symbolized by the banquet, can be refused. Initial acceptance of the invitation to discipleship does not assure that one is prepared to recline at table when the banquet is ready. Preoccupations with possessions or with other relationships can become obstacles to Jesus' invitation.

There is also, once again, an opportunity to address inclusivity. If our eucharistic celebrations are a foretaste of the eschatological banquet, do they resemble the banquet in the parable? Who is missing? What steps must be taken to welcome those who would not seek to cross our boundaries on their own? What gates and walls (metaphorical or real) bar access? To whom? What social risks are there in taking steps toward greater inclusivity? From the perspective of those who have been made poor or have been exploited by dominant others, what is needed to be able to eat together at table? In Year I, when the parable is linked with the first reading from Romans 12:5-16a, the message of the indispensability of all the members, working in tandem with one another, stands out. Paul's advice about exercising hospitality and associating with the lowly coheres well with the parable. In Year II the first reading (Phil 2:5-11) again speaks the same message in different terms, where Paul admonishes the Philippians to have the same attitude as Christ who willingly relinquished his former godly status to take on human flesh, even accepting death. Such efforts at establishing a table in the present at which all sit together as brothers and sisters equally redeemed give a foretaste of the end-time banquet.

The preacher should be wary of interpretations that are anti-Jewish, that equate the invitees who refuse to come to the banquet with the Jewish people as a whole. As Jesus told the story it took place entirely within a Jewish world. The second and third set of guests were marginalized Jews. Luke's community may have seen an allusion to their Gentile members in the figure of those who were outsiders, along the highway and the hedgerows, but this would have been an unlikely reference on the lips of Jesus.

CHAPTER TWENTY-SEVEN

Making More
(Luke 19:11-28)

Wednesday of the Thirty-third Week of Ordinary Time

¹¹ *While they were listening to him speak,*
  [Jesus] proceeded to tell a parable because he was near Jerusalem
  and they thought that the kingdom of God would appear there immediately.
¹² *So he said,*
  "A nobleman went off to a distant country
  to obtain the kingship for himself and then to return.
¹³ *He called ten of his servants*
  and gave them ten gold coins and told them,
  'Engage in trade with these until I return.'
¹⁴ *His fellow citizens, however, despised him*
  and sent a delegation after him to announce,
  'We do not want this man to be our king.'
¹⁵ *But when he returned after obtaining the kingship,*
  he had the servants called,
  to whom he had given the money,
  to learn what they had gained by trading.
¹⁶ *The first came forward and said,*
  'Sir, your gold coin has earned ten additional ones.'
¹⁷ *He replied,*
  'Well done, good servant!
  You have been faithful in this very small matter;
    take charge of ten cities.'
¹⁸ *Then the second came and reported,*
  'Your gold coin, sir, has earned five more.'
¹⁹ *And to this servant too he said,*
  'You, take charge of five cities.'
²⁰ *Then the other servant came and said,*
  'Sir, here is your gold coin;

> *I kept it stored away in a handkerchief,*
> [21] *for I was afraid of you,*
>   *because you are a demanding person;*
>   *you take up what you did not lay down*
>   *and you harvest what you did not plant.'*
> [22] *He said to him,*
>   *'With your own words I shall condemn you, you wicked servant.*
>   *You knew I was a demanding person,*
>   *taking up what I did not lay down and harvesting what I did not plant;*
>   [23] *why did you not put my money in a bank?*
>   *Then on my return I would have collected it with interest.'*
> [24] *And to those standing by he said,*
>   *'Take the gold coin from him and give it to the servant who has ten.'*
> [25] *But they said to him,*
>   *'Sir, he has ten gold coins.'*
> [26] *'I tell you, to everyone who has, more will be given,*
>   *but from the one who has not, even what he has will be taken away.*
> [27] *Now as for those enemies of mine who did not want me as their king,*
>   *bring them here and slay them before me.' "*
> [28] *After he had said this, he proceeded on his journey up to Jerusalem.*

LUKAN LITERARY CONTEXT

There is a similar parable to Luke 19:11-28 in Matthew 25:14-30, but the differences between the two have left scholars puzzled about the relationship between them. Some postulate that they were originally independent parables of Jesus that had superficial similarities. Others advance that Matthew and Luke each redacted differently a parable from Q. Still others decide that the Lukan version has been composed entirely by the evangelist.[1] A further complication in Luke's version is that there seem to be two distinct parables interwoven. Verses 12, 14, 24a, and 27 introduce an aspect that is not part of Matthew's rendition: that of a journeying and returning king and his dealing with his opponents.

However the parable came to be in its present form, one thing that is notable is the way in which it interrelates with two

---

[1] See Joseph A. Fitzmyer, *The Gospel According to Luke* (AB28A; Garden City, N.Y.: Doubleday, 1985) 1228–39; Bernard B. Scott, *Hear Then the Parable: A Commentary on the Parables of Jesus* (Minneapolis: Fortress, 1989) 217–35.

themes in the Lukan narrative. Coming immediately after the story of Zacchaeus, the rich toll collector who is exemplary in his hospitality and in his almsgiving (19:1-10), this is another parable that addresses the use of money. A traditional interpretation has been that the parable advocates prudent use of the talents entrusted to a person in the time between Jesus' departure from earth and his second coming. It is not entirely clear, however, that this would be understood by the first hearers of the parable.

Attending to the literary artistry of Luke, it is notable that this is the last episode of the great journey narrative that began in Luke 9:51. The theme of God's reign has been prominent in this section.[2] As Jesus is about to enter Jerusalem, the theme of his kingship becomes even more pronounced. Immediately after this parable Jesus is acclaimed as king (19:38). He promises his disciples he will confer on them a kingdom such as his father has conferred on him (22:29). He will be charged with presenting himself as messianic king (23:2) and will be taunted as "King of the Jews" by the soldiers crucifying him (23:37) and by the inscription placed on the cross (23:38). One of those crucified with him will ask for a place in his kingdom (23:42). Thus, the parable can be read as Luke's way of helping his readers interpret how the story of Jesus is unfolding in his narrative. Jesus is the nobleman in quest of kingship and the faithful servants are his disciples. The citizens who oppose his claim are the religious leaders and other Jews who reject his mission and who find themselves irrevocably cut off from life with God.[3]

ESCHATOLOGICAL DELAY

The parable has traditionally been thought to address the question of the delay in the parousia,[4] or to combat a notion of

---

[2] The word *basileia*, "kingdom," usually modified with *tou theou*, "of God," occurs in 9:60, 62; 10:9, 11; 11:2, 17, 18, 20; 12:31, 32; 13:18, 20, 28, 29; 14:15; 16:16; 17:20, 21; 18:16, 17, 24, 25, 29. See above, pp. 306–07, on "kingdom of God."

[3] Luke T. Johnson, *The Gospel of Luke.* Sacra Pagina 3 (Collegeville: The Liturgical Press, 1991) 293.

[4] Fitzmyer, *Luke,* 1229.

overrealized eschatology.[5] Like the query of the disciples to the risen Christ in Acts 1:6, and that of the Pharisees in Luke 17:20, it poses the question of the timing of the coming of the kingdom in its fullness.[6] The leaving and returning of the nobleman in quest of kingship in 19:12-15 is thought to be a metaphor for Jesus' departure and second coming. The use of the verb *dokeō* ("thought") in the introductory verse often designates erroneous perceptions in Luke.[7]

Some scholars have thought that a historical incident underlies the references to a nobleman going away to obtain kingship. Josephus recounts how in 40 B.C.E. Herod the Great had to acquire his kingdom, which had been an ethnarchy under Hyrcanus II. After Herod's death, his son Archelaus inherited half his kingdom (Judea, Samaria, and Idumea) and had to travel to Rome to obtain the title of king (*Ant.* 17.9, 1–3 §208–222; *J.W.* 2.2, 2 §18). A delegation of fifty Palestinians, composed of both Jews and Samaritans, were sent to oppose his kingship.[8] Of Archelaus' two brothers who also went to Rome, Philip supported his plea before Augustus, while Antipas opposed him. In the end he came away with the title of ethnarch, not king.[9] Whether or not Jesus had in mind these specific incidents, what we can say is that the imagery in the parable is familiar to Jesus' audience against the historical circumstances of their day.[10]

INVESTMENT

The parable proceeds with the nobleman entrusting a gold coin *(mnas)* to each of ten servants. This unit of money, *mna*, is

[5] Charles H. Talbert, *Reading Luke: A Literary and Theological Commentary on the Third Gospel* (New York: Crossroad, 1988) 177–78.

[6] See above, pp. 36–37, on Lukan eschatology.

[7] Luke 8:18; 12:40, 51; 13:2-4; Acts 12:9; 17:18, as noted by Johnson, *Luke*, 289.

[8] Josephus, *Ant.* 17.11, 1-2 § 299-314; *J.W.* 2.6,1-2 §80–92.

[9] Fitzmyer, *Luke*, 1235. See Frank Weinart, "The Parable of the Throne Claimant (Luke 19:12, 14-15a, 27) Reconsidered," *CBQ* 39 (1977) 505–14.

[10] F. W. Danker, *Jesus and the New Age: A Commentary on St. Luke's Gospel* (Philadelphia: Fortress) 307–08, notes that Xenophon records that Hiero of Syracuse told the Greek poet Simonides that "a tyrant cannot feel at ease about taking a leave of absence, for he can have no assurance that the property he entrusts to others for safekeeping will be secure" (*Hieron,* 12).

mentioned only here in the New Testament.[11] In Matthew's version of this parable, the money given to the servants is in talents, *talanta*. A *mna* is a small amount of money, one sixtieth of a talent, equivalent to a hundred Attic drachmas, approximately twenty-five dollars.[12] The slaves are told to do business *(pragmateuomai)* with the money until the master's return.

Although ten slaves are given money, a typical parable has three characters, and builds up to the climactic third. The first invested the money and returns ten-fold to the master. For this he is praised as a good and faithful servant and given authority over ten towns, part of the kingdom the master just obtained. The second slave reports a five-fold increase and is given the commensurate authority over five towns. The third kept the gold coin in a handkerchief, fearful of the austere master, and returns it to him as it was given.[13]

The third slave elaborates on the master's severity with a mixed metaphor, one from the banking world and the other from agriculture: the master takes up what he does not lay down, and reaps what he does not plant (v. 21). The result is condemnation of this slave as wicked. The master interrogates him as to why he was disobedient. If he knew that the master was so demanding, why did he not bank the money, and at least collect interest?[14]

The parable ends with the master telling his royal retinue to take the gold coin away from the last and give it to the first. When the other servants object the master replies[15] with a proverb, equivalent to our modern-day saying that the rich get

[11] As noted by Fitzmyer, *Luke*, 1235, *mnas* are mentioned in the LXX in 1 Kings 10:17; Ezra 2:69; Nehemiah 7:71; 1 Maccabees 14:24, as well as classical and Hellenistic Greek literature and in Egyptian papyri.

[12] Fitzmyer, *Luke*, 1235.

[13] In Matthew 25:25 the third servant buried the talent, which was thought to be the safest manner of keeping money.

[14] The phrase *ouk edōkas mou to argyrion epi trapezan*, is literally, "why did you not give my silver on a table," i.e., the moneylenders' table. For the money-changers' tables in the Temple see Matthew 21:12; John 2:15.

[15] It is ambiguous whether the one speaking in v. 26 is the king of the parable or Jesus. A similar difficulty is found in the conclusion of the parable of the banquet (14:24) and of the steward who rewrites the debts (16:8).

richer while the poor get poorer.[16] Contrary to Matthew's account, there is no punishment of the last slave, only a stripping of his responsibility for care and investment of the coin. The deadly punishment instead is meted out to those enemies of the master who opposed his kingship.

In a traditional reading of this parable, it is presumed that the master is a sympathetic character who is in the right for wanting his slaves to invest his money wisely. Conventional interpretations see this story as one that advocates prudent use of the gifts given to a person, monetary or otherwise, during one's lifetime. From a post-resurrection perspective, if we see the king as Jesus, the parable is thought to be aimed at the disciples who are now entrusted with care of the kingdom until his return. Vigilant, active discipleship is required. One who is lazy and does not increase what is given is judged harshly.[17]

Congruent with this approach, but highlighting the detail in v. 21 of what the slave says of the master is an interpretation that focuses on the mistaken estimation by the slave of the master's harshness. His fatal flaw is not his inability to make a good return on his master's money, but to think his master harsh, when he has actually been given a generous gift and opportunity.[18] His downfall for his unwarranted timidity is a warning to disciples not to see God as a harsh judge, but as a generous giver who entrusts to us all that we need to prosper.

A TALE OF TERROR

The above interpretations have recently been challenged by scholars who use insights from social science criticism.[19]

---

[16] Similarly Luke 8:18; also Matthew 25:29 and 13:12; Mark 4:25.

[17] Sharon Ringe, *Luke*. Westminster Bible Companion (Louisville: Westminster/John Knox, 1995) 235; Fitzmyer, *Luke,* 1229.

[18] John Donahue, *The Gospel in Parable: Metaphor, Narrative, and Theology in the Synoptic Gospels* (Philadelphia: Fortress, 1988) 105–08; Lane McGaughy, "The Fear of Yahweh and the Mission of Judaism: A Postexilic Maxim and Its Early Christian Expansion in the Parable of the Talents," *JBL* 94 (1975) 235–45.

[19] Richard Rohrbaugh, "A Peasant Reading of the Parable of the Talents/ Pounds: A Text of Terror?" *BTB* 23 (1993) 32–39; B. Malina and R. Rohrbaugh, *Social Science Commentary on the Synoptic Gospels* (Minneapolis: Fortress,

Taking the stance of a peasant, and placing our sympathies with the third slave, not with the master, yields a very different story. In contrast to capitalist mores, which view wealth as something that can be increased by hard work or investment, the world of the parable is, rather, one of limited good. In such a culture it is thought that there is only so much wealth; any increase to one person takes away from another. The aim of a peasant was to satisfy the needs of his family, not to amass unlimited wealth. From this perspective, the nobleman is the wicked one, who is unfettered in his greed.[20] Moreover, he is not observant of the Torah, as is evident in v. 23. Usury was forbidden by Exodus 22:25; Leviticus 25:36-37; Deuteronomy 23:29.[21]

The third servant, then, is not wicked, except in the eyes of those who are greedy acquisitors or who are co-opted by them, as are the first two servants. The third slave is the one who acted honorably by blowing the whistle on the wickedness of the king. The estimation of the master as demanding is correct, as is the observation that he acquires money he does not earn (v. 21). He exploits the labor of others who do the planting; and he knows how to manipulate money exchanges to his advantage. Verse 26 may be taken as Jesus' interpretive comment, denouncing the injustice visible in such practices whereby the rich continually get richer while the poor keep losing even the little they have. The parable, a warning to the rich to stop exploiting the poor, is one that encourages poor people to take measures that expose such greed for the sin that it is. Verse 27 is a sobering, realistic note of what can happen to

---

1992) 149–50; W. R. Herzog, *Parables as Subversive Speech: Jesus as Pedagogue of the Oppressed* (Louisville: Westminster/John Knox, 1994) 150–68.

[20] Commenting on Matthew's version, which does not have the Lukan details about the nobleman's quest for kingship, Herzog envisions the master's travel for the purpose of increasing his investments and initiating new business schemes. He is building new patron-client relations and is currying favor with imperial overlords (*Subversive Speech*, 157).

[21] Some commentators (e.g., Johnson, *Luke*, 291; Fitzmyer, *Luke*, 1237) try to maintain the master as a good person by envisioning the transactions being with non-Jews. The Mishnah attests to more liberal regulations regarding relations with Gentiles (*m. Bab.M.* 5:1-6).

those who oppose the rich and powerful. But v. 28 is a reminder that Jesus' journey in which he has been doing precisely that, denouncing exploitation and domination and frees those bound by such, will end in Jerusalem. His death there does not end his mission, however, but liberates God's people for new life in a realm that will ultimately be free of all domination and exploitation.

This line of interpretation has confirmation from a third version of the parable from the Gospel of the Nazoreans, which is known to us only from quotations of it and allusions to it in the Church Fathers. Eusebius preserves and comments on another variation of the parable:

> But since the gospel [written] in Hebrew characters which has come into our hands enters the threat not against the man who had hid [the talent], but against him who had lived dissolutely—
> For he [the master] had three servants:
>   A one who squandered his master's substance with harlots
>   and flute-girls,
>   B one who multiplied the gain,
>   C and one who hid the talent
>   and accordingly . . .
>   C' one was accepted (with joy),
>   B' another merely rebuked,
>   A' and another cast into prison
> —I wonder whether in Matthew the threat which is uttered after the word against the man who did nothing may refer not to him, but by epanalepsis to the first who had feasted and drunk with the drunken.[22]

What is evident from Eusebius' comment is that he cannot understand how the first servant is approved, and so proposes epanalepsis (as outlined with A corresponding to A', etc.) as the means by which to find the one who hid the talent as the accepted one. This evidence would confirm that the more appropriate reading of the parable is one in which the slave who held on to the money is the one who acted commendably.

---

[22] Eusebius, *Theophania*, 22, as quoted by R. L. Rohrbaugh, "A Peasant Reading of the Parable of the Talents/Pounds: A Text of Terror?" *BTB* 23 (1993) 36.

PREACHING POSSIBILITIES

In light of the interpretation offered by social science critics, the parable should not be preached as an admonition to use one's God-given talents well. While this is a biblical value, it does not seem to be the meaning advanced by this parable. Moreover, in the Lukan version of the parable, the word "talent" (which can be more easily understood as gifts other than monetary) is not used for the denomination of money involved. The parable would seem, rather, to challenge notions of unfettered increase of monetary gain. While we may not share the same perception of the world as a first-century audience in terms of limited good, we are today becoming more and more aware of the interconnectedness of peoples' lives globally. We see, for example, rich people becoming increasingly rich in the machinations of international corporations that make huge profits from exploited and underpaid workers in sweatshops. This parable could serve as a vehicle to address what Christian response is called for in the light of such global realities. In the same vein it can pose a challenge to believers to be wary of greed in all its forms.

If the parable is preached from the perspective of how it advances the literary theme of Jesus' kingship in the gospel, it is important to highlight the image of Jesus as crucified king. The monarchical image of Jesus and God has too often been evoked in Christian history to justify domination and exploitation of others. In the gospel the reign of God that Jesus inaugurates is a realm that includes all, in which he particularly seeks out the lost, and in which he unmasks injustice for what it is. For this he is willing to go to his death in Jerusalem.

CHAPTER TWENTY-EIGHT

Futuristic Figs
(Luke 21:29-33)

Friday of the Thirty-fourth Week of Ordinary Time

[29] [Jesus] taught [his disciples] a lesson.
   "Consider the fig tree and all the other trees.
   [30] When their buds burst open,
   you see for yourselves and know that summer is now near;
[31] in the same way,
   when you see these things happening,
   know that the kingdom of God is near.
[32] Amen, I say to you, this generation will not pass away
   until all these things have taken place.
[33] Heaven and earth will pass away, but my words will not pass away.

LUKAN LECTIONARY CONTEXT

This final parable is part of the eschatological discourse (21:5-36) in which Jesus speaks about the fate of the Temple (which is already destroyed at the time of Luke's writing), about further signs of the end times, and of coming persecution for the disciples. It is likely that what is presented in the gospel as one long discourse at the end of Jesus' life, were originally isolated sayings spoken by Jesus at different times, that have been constructed by the evangelist into a continuous address of Jesus to his disciples. The Lukan discourse derives mainly from Mark (13:5-37), but also has some specifically Lukan material. There are also verses that echo sayings found in Luke 17, derived from Q.[1] Luke's version makes a clearer separation between

---

[1] Joseph A. Fitzmyer, *The Gospel According to Luke* (AB28A; Garden City, N.Y.: Doubleday, 1985) 1351–54.

what refers to the destruction of Jerusalem and what refers to the eschaton. Both are signs of God's judgment. Luke redacts the Markan material to show that the first is already fulfilled (vv. 20, 24), while the second is yet awaited. In the verses that follow this parable (21:34-36) Luke has sharpened the exhortation to vigilance in the face of the coming end.

The parable is a short comparison (vv. 29-30) with an application introduced with *houtōs*, "just so" (v. 31).[2] To this are added two sayings (vv. 32, 33) which were probably independent sayings uttered in another context.[3]

A FIG IN LEAF

There is a tension in Luke and Acts between sayings and parables that highlight the delay in the parousia. Others point to its imminent coming.[4] This parable is one that emphasizes the nearness of the end time. The point is readily apparent. The fig tree, different from other trees in Palestine,[5] sheds all its leaves in winter. Its budding is a sign of the coming of summer.[6] Just so, the signs of the end, described in the previous verses (vv. 5-28), point toward the nearness of the Human One.

The appended sayings in vv. 32-33 stand in tension with the parable about the timing of the end. The parable and its application (vv. 29-31) imply certitude that the end can be expected imminently. The saying in vv. 32-33 seems to contradict this with the assertion that the present generation[7] will not pass

---

[2] Other parables that make a comparison with *houtōs* are Luke 12:21, 38, 43; 14:33; 15:7, 10; 17:10.

[3] Fitzmyer, *Luke*, 1352.

[4] See above, pp. 36–37 on Lukan eschatology.

[5] Most trees in Palestine are evergreens.

[6] There are only two seasons in Palestine: summer, which is dry and hot, and winter, the rainy season. There is a brief interchange period between the two, but no autumn or spring per se.

[7] On Luke's use of *genea*, "generation," see above, pp. 273–74. Scholars are divided over whether "this generation" in 21:32 refers to Jesus' own contemporary generation, the Jewish people, human beings in general, or the generation of the end-signs. While the first is possible at the first stage of the gospel tradition, i.e., in the saying uttered by Jesus, the last is like Luke's intent. See Fitzmyer, *Luke*, 1353.

away until all has taken place. Both poles of Lukan sayings about the end are joined in this passage.

The parable cuts two ways: for those who are discouraged about the delay in the coming of the parousia it gives encouragement about its nearness. For those who interpret present disasters, wars, and persecution as signs that the end has already come, it corrects their mistaken notion and exhorts them to continue steadfast into the future. The reader of the gospel may also recall the other parable of a fig tree in Luke 13:6-9,[8] where the fruitless fig is about to be cut down when the owner finds it barren three years running. If the gardener in that parable was able to win one more year of grace, this parable warns that the time is near.

The final verse (v. 33) asserts the absolute reliability of Jesus' message. The solemn oath formula, "Amen, I say to you" (v. 32) sets the tone. The function of an oath is to show that the one pronouncing it is honorable and to make clear what may appear ambiguous or incredible about that person's claims. The oath in vv. 32-33 rests on the understanding that from an Israelite point of view, God's creation is good and belongs to God and will forever. The force of Jesus' saying is that it is just as impossible for his words to pass away as it is for God's creation to pass away.[9]

PREACHING POSSIBILITIES

While some early Christians lived in imminent expectation of the end times (e.g., Paul in 1 Thess 4:15), others, such as Luke's community, were trying to interpret their lives and Jesus' message in light of the delay. Most believers today do not anticipate the parousia in their lifetime, much less give it all that much thought. After 2000 years the edge of expectation has diminished and all but select groups of apocalyptically-oriented Christians have settled into day-to-day efforts at long-term Christian living. Nonetheless, this gospel passage can still offer hope in the face of persecution, struggles, and discouragement in the between-times.

[8] See above, chap. 4.
[9] B. Malina and R. Rohrbaugh, *Social Science Commentary on the Synoptic Gospels* (Minneapolis: Fortress, 1992) 263.

In the context of the last week of the liturgical year, the Lectionary pairs this gospel with two different apocalyptic passages: Daniel 7:2-14 in Year I and Revelation 20:1-4, 11-21 in Year II. In these readings and in the verses that precede the parable in Luke 21:7-28 are vivid descriptions of end-time signs. One should resist trying to interpret these happenings literally. Cataclysmic events of every age have been mistakenly thought to be signs of the end. Rather, it is important to recognize that the evangelist is using stock apocalyptic symbols. Cosmic portents of judgment are common in apocalyptic and late prophetic literature.[10]

A more fruitful reflection on such texts is to understand how apocalyptic writing functioned and to relate it to contemporary situations. This genre aimed to give hope to people who were under duress, whether from internal strife or external threats. It can function the same way today. One way in which such texts can be preached is to counter passivity or hopelessness in the face of suffering. The gospel emphasizes that although one cannot know the precise timing, there *is* an end to the present distress. God's ultimate victory in Christ gives hope that suffering and even death itself have been overcome. The fig tree symbol conveys the message that even out of the appearance of death (as a leafless fig in winter) can blossom forth new life. Even wars, natural disasters, and famines can be labor pains that precede new creation.

Finally, one caution about apocalyptic genre. The preacher should be aware of and denounce the kind of apocalyptic thinking that is based on a dualistic mentality that divides people into "us" and "them," as forces of absolute good against absolute evil. While such a construction of reality is understandable as a way to cope with persecution, it is very dangerous to think that through some combination of right belief and behavior one can be aligned absolutely with the good. Such thinking underlies sectarian divisions drawn by racial, ethnic, and religious lines and fuels campaigns of mass destruction of the "enemy." Apocalypticists applaud violence directed against

---

[10] E.g., *1 Enoch* 80:4-7; 4 Ezra 5:4; Isaiah 13:10; Ezekiel 32:7-8; Amos 8:9; Joel 2:10.

"enemies" as evidence of God's punishment, while violence against themselves is interpreted as persecution of the righteous. They see both as signs of the end-times that anticipate their own near deliverance. From such a stance the wellsprings of compassion are shut off toward those with whom one does not identify. Such believers may even oppose efforts to relieve poverty or prevent war, thinking that such will delay God's final intervention.[11]

---

[11] Rosemary Radford Ruether, *Gaia and God* (HarperSanFrancisco, 1992) 81–84.

Conclusion

The Gospel of Luke has more parables than any other gospel. All but one appear in the Lectionary, and many are assigned more than once. Our aim has been not to give an exhaustive summary or analysis of all the work that has been done on the parables in Luke. Rather, our intent has been to sketch some of the new directions of Lukan parables research so as to aid the preacher in her or his understanding of the text. Our hope has been that this exploration of new possibilities of meaning will spark the creativity of preachers as they break open the word for other believers. We have suggested ways in which the homilist may direct the parables, but ultimately the difficult task of discerning which is the word their congregation needs at a particular time and place rests with the preacher. While many points are possible and valid in parable interpretation, the effective homilist will do well to develop only one on any given occasion. Each time that a parable appears in the Lectionary, the task of wrestling with the text begins again. There are no "one size fits all" interpretations.

In the Gospel of Luke the term "parable" applies to many varied kinds of figurative speech. Some parables are vivid stories, others are wisdom sayings, still others are extended similes. Their function is varied. At times they comfort; at other times they instruct and exhort; at still others they challenge. They are directed to both Jesus' disciples and to his opponents. They invite adversaries to a change of heart and they instruct disciples on how to follow Jesus on the journey. Disciples in Luke do understand to some degree and they remain with Jesus to the end.[1] As the disciples on the road to Emmaus came to

---

[1] This is different from the Gospel of Mark, where the disciples are portrayed more consistently as misunderstanding or even opposing Jesus, and ultimately

fuller understanding of the Scriptures (Luke 24:27) and recognized Jesus in the breaking of the bread (24:31), so the parables proclaimed and preached at our eucharistic gatherings can open our eyes and can make our hearts burn within us (24:31-32) as we walk with the risen Christ in our journey of faith.

---

abandoning him. Contrast Luke 24:49, where all Jesus' acquaintances are found at the cross, whereas in Mark 14:50 all flee at his arrest and only the Galilean women witness the crucifixion (Mark 15:40).

Bibliography

Achtemeier, P. J., ed. *Harper's Bible Dictionary*. San Francisco: Harper & Row, 1985.

_____, ed. *SBL 1979 Seminar Papers*. Missoula, Mont.: Scholars Press, 1979.

Anderson, H., D. S. Browning, I. S. Evison, and M. S. van Leeuwen, eds. *The Family Handbook*. The Family, Religion, and Culture. Louisville: Westminster/John Knox, 1998.

Anderson, J. C., and S. D. Moore, eds. *Mark and Method: New Approaches in Biblical Studies*. Minneapolis: Fortress, 1992.

Appelbaum, S. "The Economic Life in Palestine," *The Jewish People in the First Century: Historical Geography, Political History, Social, Cultural and Religious Life and Institutions*. Ed. S. Safrai and M. Stern. Assen/Amersterdam: Van Gorcum, 1976. 2:631–700.

Aune, D. *The New Testament in its Literary Environment*. Library of Early Christianity. Philadelphia: Westminster, 1987.

Bailey, K. E. *Finding the Lost: Cultural Keys to Luke 15*. Concordia Scholarship Today. St. Louis: Concordia, 1992.

_____. *Poet and Peasant: A Literary-Cultural Approach to the Parables in Luke*. Grand Rapids, Mich.: Eerdmans, 1976.

_____. *Poet and Peasant* and *Through Peasant Eyes*, combined ed. Grand Rapids, Mich.: Eerdmans, 1984.

_____. "Psalm 23 and Luke 15: A Vision Expanded," *IBS* 12 (1990) 54–71.

Bailey, R., ed., *Hermeneutics for Preaching: Approaches to Contemporary Interpretations of Scripture*. Nashville: Broadman, 1992.

Barr, J. "ʾ*Abba* and the Familiarity of Jesus' Speech," *Theology* 91 (1988) 173–79.

_____. "ʾ*Abba* Isn't Daddy," *JTS* 39 (1988) 28–47.

Batey, R. A. "Jesus and the Theatre," *NTS* 30 (1984) 564–65.

Bauckham, R. "The Scrupulous Priest and the Good Samaritan: Jesus' Parabolic Interpretation of the Law of Moses," *NTS* 44 (1998) 475–89.

Bauer, W., W. F. Arndt, F. W. Gingrich, and F. W. Danker. *A Greek Lexicon of the New Testament and Other Early Christian Literature*, 2nd ed. Chicago/London: University of Chicago Press, 1979.

Beavis, M. A. "Ancient Slavery as an Interpretive Context for the New Testament Servant Parables with Special Reference to the Unjust Steward (Luke 16:1-8)," *JBL* 111 (1992) 37–54.

_____. "The Foolish Landowner (Luke 12:16b-20)," *Jesus and His Parables: Interpreting the Parables of Jesus Today*. Ed. V. G. Shillington. Edinburgh: T. & T. Clark, 1997. 55–68.

_____. *Mark's Audience: The Literary and Social Setting of Mark 4.11-12*. *JSNT*Sup 33. Sheffield: JSOT Press, 1989.

Benjamin, D. C. "The Persistent Widow," *TBT* 28 (1990) 212–19.

Bergant, D. *Preaching the New Lectionary*. 3 vols. Collegeville: The Liturgical Press, 1999, 2000, 2001.

Blomberg, C. *Interpreting the Parables*. Downers Grove, Ill.: InterVarsity Press, 1990.

Boff, C., and J. Pixley. *The Bible, the Church, and the Poor*. Theology and Liberation Series. Maryknoll, N.Y.: Orbis, 1989.

Bonneau, N. *The Sunday Lectionary: Ritual Word, Paschal Shape*. Collegeville: The Liturgical Press, 1998.

Borges, J. L. *Ficciones*. New York: Grove, 1962.

Boucher, M. *The Parables*. NTMS 7. Wilmington: Glazier, 1981.

Bouwman, G. "La pécheresse hospitalière (Lc. vii, 36-50)," *ETL* 45 (1969) 172–79.

Bowker, J. W. "Mystery and Parable: Mark 4:1-20," *JTS* 25 (1974) 300–17.

Braun, W. *Feasting and Social Rhetoric in Luke 14*. SNTSMS 85. Cambridge: Cambridge University Press, 1995.

Brooten, B. *Women Leaders in the Ancient Synagogue: Inscriptural Evidence and Background Issues*. Brown Judaic Studies 36. Chico, Calif.: Scholars Press, 1982.

Brown, R. E. *The Gospel According to John I–XII*. AB29. Garden City, N.Y.: Doubleday, 1966.

_____. *An Introduction to the New Testament*. ABRL. New York: Doubleday, 1997.

_____. "Jesus and Elisha," *Perspective* 12 (1971) 84–104.

Brown, R. E., J. A. Fitzmyer, and R. E. Murphy. *The New Jerome Biblical Commentary*. Englewood Cliffs, N.J.: Prentice Hall, 1990.

Bultmann, R. K. *The History of the Synoptic Tradition*, rev. ed. Trans. J. Marsh. New York: Harper & Row, 1968.

Burghardt, W. J. *Preaching the Just Word*. New Haven: Yale University Press, 1996.

Burrus, V. *Chastity as Autonomy: Women in the Stories of the Apocryphal Acts.* Lewiston, N.Y.: Edwin Mellen, 1987.

Cadbury, H. J. "A Proper Name for Dives," *JBL* 81 (1962) 300–402.

_____. *The Style and Literary Method of Luke.* HTS 6/1. Cambridge: Harvard University Press, 1920.

Cadoux, A. T. *The Parables of Jesus, Their Art and Use.* London: James Clarke, 1931.

Carroll, J. T. "Luke's Portrayal of the Pharisees," *CBQ* 50 (1988) 604–21.

Coakley, J. "The Anointing at Bethany and the Priority of John," *JBL* 107 (1988) 241–56.

Collins, J. N. *DIAKONIA: Re-Interpreting the Ancient Resources.* New York: Oxford University Press, 1990.

Collins, R. F. *Preaching the Epistles.* New York: Paulist, 1996.

Conzelmann, H. *The Theology of St. Luke.* Trans. G. Buswell. Philadelphia: Fortress, 1961.

Corley, K. E. *Private Women, Public Meals: Social Conflict in the Synoptic Tradition.* Peabody, Mass.: Hendrickson, 1993.

Cotter, W. J. "The Parable of the Children in the Market-Place, Q(Lk) 7:31-35: An Examination of the Parable's Image and Significance," *NovT* 29/4 (1987) 289–304.

Crossan, J. D. *Cliffs of Fall: Paradox and Polyvalence in the Parables of Jesus.* New York: Seabury, 1980.

_____. *The Dark Interval: Towards a Theology of Story.* Niles, Ill.: Argus Communications, 1975.

_____. *In Parables: The Challenge of the Historical Jesus.* New York: Harper & Row, 1973.

Culbertson, P. L. *A Word Fitly Spoken: Context, Transmission, and Adoption of the Parables of Jesus.* Albany: State University of New York Press, 1995.

Culpepper, A. "Seeing the Kingdom of God: The Metaphor of Sight in the Gospel of Luke," *CurTM* 21 (1994) 434–43.

Dalman, G. *Die Worte Jesu. Mit Berücksichtigung des nachkanonischen jüdischen Schrifttums und der aramäischen Sprache erötert,* 2nd ed. Darmstadt: Wissenschaftliche Buchgesellschaft, 1965.

D'Angelo, M. R. "*ABBA* and 'Father': Imperial Theology and the Jesus Traditions," *JBL* 111/4 (1992) 611–30.

_____. "(Re)Presentations of Women in the Gospel of Matthew and Luke-Acts," *Women and Christian Origins.* Eds. R. S. Kraemer and M. R. D'Angelo. New York: Oxford University Press, 1999. 171–95.

_____. "Women in Luke-Acts: A Redactional View," *JBL* 109 (1990) 441–61.

Danker, F. W. *Jesus and the New Age: A Commentary on St. Luke's Gospel,* rev. ed. Philadelphia: Fortress, 1988.

Darr, J. A. *On Character Building: The Rhetoric of Characterization in Luke-Acts.* Literary Currents in Biblical Interpretation. Louisville: Westminster/John Knox, 1992.

Daube, D. *The New Testament and Rabbinic Judaism.* New York: Arno Press, 1973.

DeBoer, E. *Mary Magdalene: Beyond the Myth.* Trans. J. Bowden. Harrisburg, Penn.: Trinity Press International, 1997.

Delobel, J. "Encore la pécheresse. Quelques réflexions critiques," *ETL* 45 (1969) 180–83.

de Mello, A. *The Song of the Bird.* Garden City, N.Y.: Doubleday, 1984.

Derrett, J.D.M. "Figtrees in the New Testament," *HeyJ* 14 (1973) 249–65.

_____. *Law in the New Testament.* London: Darton, Longman & Todd, 1970.

_____. "Law in the New Testament: Fresh Light on the Parable of the Good Samaritan," *NTS* 10 (1964–65) 22–37.

_____. "Law in the New Testament: the Parable of the Prodigal Son (Luke 15:11-32)," *NTS* 14 (1967) 56–74.

_____. "The Parable of the Unjust Steward," *NTS* 7 (1960–61) 198–219.

Dodd, C. H. *The Parables of the Kingdom,* rev. ed. London: Collins, 1961.

Donahue, J. R. *The Gospel in Parable: Metaphor, Narrative, and Theology in the Synoptic Gospels.* Philadelphia: Fortress, 1988.

_____. "Jesus as the Parable of God in the Gospel of Mark," *Int* 32 (1978) 369–86.

_____. "Tax Collectors and Sinners: An Attempt at Identification," *CBQ* 33 (1971) 39–61.

Downing, F. G. "The Ambiguity of 'The Pharisee and the Toll-Collector' (Luke 18:9-14) in the Greco-Roman World of Late Antiquity," *CBQ* 54 (1992) 80–99.

Drury, J. *Tradition and Design in Luke's Gospel: A Study of Early Christian Historiography.* London: Darton, Longman, and Todd, 1976.

Durber, S. "The Female Reader of the Parables of the Lost," *JSNT* 45 (1992) 59–78.

Edwards, R. *A Theology of Q: Eschatology, Prophecy and Wisdom.* Philadelphia: Fortress, 1976.

Evans, C. A. "A Note on the Function of Isaiah 6:9-10 in Mark 4," *RB* 99 (1981) 234–35.

Farmer, W. R. *The Synoptic Problem: A Critical Analysis.* New York: Macmillan, 1964.

Farris, M. "A Tale of Two Taxations (Luke 18:10-14b)," *Jesus and His Parables: Interpreting the Parables of Jesus Today.* Ed. V. G. Shillington. Edinburgh: T. & T. Clark, 1997.

Fitzmyer, J. A. *Essays on the Semitic Background of the New Testament.* Sources for Biblical Study 5. Atlanta: Scholars Press, 1974.

_____. *The Gospel According to Luke.* 2 vols. AB28-28A. Garden City, N.Y.: Doubleday, 1981, 1985.

_____. "Luke," *The New Jerome Biblical Commentary.* Eds. R. E. Brown, J. A. Fitzmyer, and R. E. Murphy. Englewood Cliffs, N.J.: Prentice Hall, 1990. 675–721.

_____. *Luke the Theologian: Aspects of His Teaching.* New York/ Mahwah: Paulist Press, 1989.

_____. *To Advance the Gospel: New Testament Studies.* New York: Crossroad, 1981.

_____. *A Wandering Aramean: Collected Aramaic Essays.* Missoula, Mont.: Scholars Press, 1979.

Flusser, D. *Die rabbinischen Gleichnisse und der Gleichniserzähler Jesus 1.* Teil: *Das Wesen der Gleichnisse.* Bern: Peter Lang, 1981.

Foley, E. *Preaching Basics: A Model and A Method.* Chicago: Liturgy Training Publications, 1998.

Ford, J. M. *Redeemer Friend and Mother: Salvation in Antiquity and in the Gospel of John.* Minneapolis: Fortress, 1997.

Freedman, D. N., ed. *The Anchor Bible Dictionary.* 6 vols. New York: Doubleday, 1992.

Fuller, R. H. "Son of Man," *Harper's Bible Dictionary.* Ed. P. J. Achtemeier. San Francisco: Harper & Row, 1985. 981.

Funk, R. W. "Beyond Criticism in Quest of Literacy: The Parable of the Leaven," *Int* 25 (1971) 149–70.

_____. "The Good Samaritan as Metaphor," *Semeia* 2 (1974) 74–81.

_____. *Language, Hermeneutic, and Word of God: The Problem of Language in the New Testament and Contemporary Theology.* New York: Harper & Row, 1966.

_____. "The Looking Glass Tree is for the Birds," *Int* 27 (1973) 3–9.

_____. *Parables and Presence: Forms of the New Testament Tradition.* Philadelphia: Fortress, 1982.

Gardner, J. F. *Women in Roman Law and Society.* Bloomington/Indianapolis: Indiana University, 1986.

Gerhardsson, B. "The Parable of the Sower and Its Interpretation," *NTS* 14 (1968) 165–93.

Gillingham, M. J. "The Parables as Attitude Change," *ExpTim* 109 (1998) 297–300.

Gillman, J. *Possessions and the Life of Faith: A Reading of Luke-Acts.* Zacchaeus Studies: New Testament. Collegeville: The Liturgical Press, 1991.

Goulder, M. D. *Luke: A New Paradigm.* JSNTSup20. Sheffield: JSOT, 1989.

Green, B. *Like a Tree Planted: An Exploration of Psalms and Parables Through Metaphor.* Collegeville: The Liturgical Press, 1997.

Greinacher, N., and N. Mette, eds. *Diakonia: Church for the Others.* Concilium 198. Edinburgh: T. & T. Clark, 1988.

Hamm, D. "What the Samaritan Leper Sees: The Narrative Christology of Luke 17:11-19," *CBQ* 56 (1994) 273–87.

Harrill, J. A. "The Indentured Labor of the Prodigal Son (Luke 15:15)," *JBL* 115 (1996) 714–17.

Harrington, D. "Sheol," *The Collegeville Pastoral Dictionary of Biblical Theology.* Ed. C. Stuhlmueller. Collegeville: The Liturgical Press, 1996. 904–05.

Hedrick, C. W. "Prolegomena to Reading Parables: Luke 13:6-9 as a Test Case," *RevExp* 94 (1997) 179–97.

Heil, J. P. "Reader Response and Narrative Context of the Parables about Growing Seed in Mark 4:1-34," *CBQ* 54 (1992) 271–86.

Hendrickx, H. *The Parables of Jesus,* rev. ed. San Francisco: Harper & Row, 1986.

Hengel, M. *Crucifixion in the Ancient World and the Folly of the Message of the Cross.* Philadelphia: Fortress, 1977.

Herzog, W. R. *Parables as Subversive Speech: Jesus as Pedagogue of the Oppressed.* Louisville: Westminster/John Knox, 1994.

Hock, R. F. "Lazarus and Micyllus: The Greco-Roman Backgrounds to Luke 16:29-31," *JBL* 106 (1987) 447–63.

Hoppe, L. J. *Being Poor: A Biblical Study.* GNS 20. Wilmington, Del.: Glazier, 1987.

The Inclusive-Language Lectionary Committee, Division of Education and Ministry, National Council of the Churches of Christ in the U.S.A., ed. *An Inclusive Language Lectionary.* Atlanta: John Knox, 1984.

Jeremias, J. *Jerusalem in the Time of Jesus: An Investigation into Economic and Social Conditions During the New Testament Period.* Philadelphia: Fortress, 1969.

_____. *The Parables of Jesus,* rev. ed. New York: Scribner's, 1963.

_____. *The Parables of Jesus,* 2nd rev. ed. New York: Scribner's, 1972.

_____. *Rediscovering the Parables.* New York: Scribner's, 1966.

Jervell, J. *Luke and the People of God: A New Look at Luke-Acts.* Minneapolis: Augsburg, 1972.

Johnson, A. "Assurance for Man: The Fallacy of Translating *anaideia* by 'Persistence' in Luke 11:5-8," *JEvThSoc* 22 (1979) 123–31.

Johnson, E. *Friends of God and Prophets: A Feminist Theological Reading of the Communion of Saints.* New York: Continuum, 1998.

_____. "Jesus the Wisdom of God: A Biblical Basis for Non-Androcentric Christology," *ETL* 61 (1985) 261–94.

_____. *She Who Is: The Mystery of God in Feminist Theological Discourse.* New York: Crossroad, 1992.

Johnson, L. T. *The Gospel of Luke.* Sacra Pagina 3. Collegeville: The Liturgical Press, 1991.

_____. *The Literary Function of Possessions in Luke-Acts.* SBLDS 39. Missoula, Mont.: Scholars Press, 1977.

_____. "On Finding the Lukan Community: A Cautionary Essay," *SBL Seminar 1979 Papers,* vol. 1. Ed. P. J. Achtemeier. Missoula, Mont.: Scholars Press, 1979. 87–100.

Jülicher, A. *Die Gleichnisreden Jesu.* 2 vols. Tübingen: Mohr [Siebeck] 1888, 1899.

Karris, R. J. *Luke: Artist and Theologian.* New York: Paulist, 1978.

_____. "Missionary Communities: A New Paradigm for the Study of Luke-Acts," *CBQ* 41 (1979) 80–97.

_____. "Women and Discipleship in Luke," *CBQ* 56 (1994) 1–20.

Kilgallen, J. J. "What Kind of Servants Are We? (Luke 17,10)," *Bib* 63 (1982) 549–51.

Kim, C. H. "The Papyrus Invitation," *JBL* 94 (1975) 391–402.

King, U., ed. *Women in the World's Religions: Past and Present.* God in the Contemporary Discussion Series. New York: Paragon House, 1987.

Kloppenborg, J. "The Dishonoured Master (Luke 16,1-8a)," *Bib* 70 (1989) 478–79.

_____. *The Formation of Q: Trajectories in Ancient Wisdom Collections.* Studies in Antiquity and Christianity. Philadelphia: Fortress, 1987.

Knowles, M. P. "Abram and the Birds in *Jubilees* 11: A Subtext for the Parable of the Sower?" *NTS* 41 (1995) 145–51.

Kraemer, R. S. "Women's Authorship of Jewish and Christian Literature in the Greco-Roman Period," *"Women Like This": New Perspectives on Jewish Women in the Greco-Roman World.* Ed. A. J. Levine. SBLEJL 1. Atlanta: Scholars Press, 1991. 221–42.

Kraemer, R. S., and M. R. D'Angelo, ed. *Women and Christian Origins.* New York: Oxford University Press, 1999.

Krentz, E. *The Historical-Critical Method.* Guides to Biblical Scholarship. Philadelphia: Fortress, 1975.

LaHurd, C. S. "Rediscovering the Lost Women in Luke 15," *BTB* 24 (1994) 66–76.

LaVerdiere, E. *Dining in the Kingdom of God: The Origins of the Eucharist According to Luke.* Chicago: Liturgy Training Publications, 1994.

_____. *Luke.* NTMS 5. Wilmington, Del.: Glazier, 1980.

_____. "Teaching in Parables," *Emmanuel* 94 (1988) 438–45, 453.

Legault, A. "An Application of the Form-Critique Method to the Anointings in Galilee (Lk. 7.37-50) and Bethany (Mt. 26.6-13; Mk. 4.3-9; John 12.1-8)," *CBQ* 16 (1954) 131–45.

Levine, A. J., ed. *"Women Like This": New Perspectives on Jewish Women in the Greco-Roman World.* SBLEJL 1. Atlanta: Scholars Press, 1991.

Linnemann, E. *Jesus of the Parables: Introduction and Exposition.* New York: Harper & Row, 1966.

Loader, W. "Jesus and the Rogue in Luke 16, 1-8A. The Parable of the Unjust Steward," *RB* 96 (1989) 518–32.

MacDonald, D. "Virgins, Widows, and Paul in Second Century Asia Minor," *SBL 1979 Seminar Papers.* Ed. P. Achtemeier. Missoula, Mont.: Scholars Press, 1979. 169–84.

MacMullen, R. *Roman Social Relations 50 B.C. to A.D. 284.* New Haven: Yale University Press, 1974.

Maddox, R. L. *The Purpose of Luke-Acts.* SNTW. Edinburgh: T. & T. Clark, 1985.

Maier, J. "Self-Definition, Prestige, and Status of Priests Towards the End of the Second Temple Period," *BTB* 23 (1993) 139–51.

Maisch, I. *Mary Magdalene: The Image of a Woman through the Centuries.* Trans. L. Maloney. Collegeville: The Liturgical Press, 1998.

Malina, B. J. *The New Testament World: Insights from Cultural Anthropology,* rev. ed. Louisville: Westminster/John Knox, 1993.

Malina, B. J., and J. H. Neyrey, "First-Century Personality: Dyadic, Not Individual," *The Social World of Luke-Acts: Models for Interpretation.* Ed. J. H. Neyrey. Peabody, Mass.: Hendrickson, 1991. 67–96.

Malina, B. J., and R. L. Rohrbaugh. *Social Science Commentary on the Synoptic Gospels.* Minneapolis: Fortress, 1992.

Marcus, J. "Blanks and Gaps in the Markan Parable of the Sower," *BibInt* 5 (1997) 247–62.

Marshall, I. H. *The Gospel of Luke: A Commentary on the Greek Text.* NIGTC. Grand Rapids: Eerdmans, 1978.

McCreesh, T. P. "Heart," *The Collegeville Pastoral Dictionary of Biblical Theology.* Ed. C. Stuhlmueller. Collegeville: The Liturgical Press, 1996. 422–24.

McDonald, J. I. H. "Alien Grace," *Jesus and His Parables: Interpreting the Parables of Jesus Today.* Ed. V. G. Shillington. Edinburgh: T. & T. Clark, 1997. 35–51.

McFague, S. *Models of God: Theology for an Ecological, Nuclear Age.* Philadelphia: Fortress, 1987.

McGaughy, L. "The Fear of Yahweh and the Mission of Judaism: A Postexilic Maxim and Its Early Christian Expansion in the Parable of the Talents," *JBL* 94 (1975) 235–45.

McGinn, S. E. "The Acts of Thecla," *Searching the Scriptures: A Feminist Commentary*, vol. 2. Ed. E. Schüssler Fiorenza. New York: Crossroad, 1994. 800–28.

Meier, J. P. *A Marginal Jew: Rethinking the Historical Jesus.* ABRL. 2 vols. Garden City, N.Y.: Doubleday, 1991, 1994.

Mesters, C. *Defenseless Flower: A New Reading of the Bible.* Maryknoll, N.Y.: Orbis, 1989.

Metzger, B. *A Textual Commentary on the Greek New Testament,* 3rd. ed. New York: United Bible Societies, 1971.

Meyer, M. *The Gospel of Thomas: The Hidden Sayings of Jesus.* San Francisco: Harper, 1992.

Moessner, D. P. *Lord of the Banquet: The Literary and Theological Significance of the Lukan Travel Narrative.* Minneapolis: Fortress, 1989.

_____. ed. *Luke and the Heritage of Israel: Luke's Narrative Claim upon Israel's Legacy.* Luke the Interpreter of Israel. Harrisburg, Penn.: Trinity Press International, 1999.

Muddiman, J. "Fast, Fasting," *The Anchor Bible Dictionary.* Ed. D. N. Freedman. New York: Doubleday, 1997. 2.773–76.

Murphy-O'Connor, J. *St. Paul's Corinth: Texts and Archaeology,* rev. ed. GNS 6. Collegeville: The Liturgical Press, 1985.

Myers, C. *Binding the Strong Man:. A Political Reading of Mark's Story of Jesus.* Maryknoll, N.Y.: Orbis, 1988.

Navone, J. *Themes of St. Luke.* Rome: Gregorian University Press, 1970.

Neale, D. A. *None But the Sinners: Religious Categories in the Gospel of Luke.* JSNTSup 58. Sheffield: JSOT, 1991.

Neusner, J. *Judaism in the Beginning of Christianity.* Philadelphia: Fortress, 1984.

Newsom, C. A. and S. H. Ringe, ed. *The Women's Bible Commentary,* rev. ed. Louisville: Westminster/John Knox, 1998.

Neyrey, J. H. "Ceremonies in Luke-Acts: The Case of Meals and Table Fellowship," *The Social World of Luke-Acts: Models for Interpretation.* Ed. J. H. Neyrey. Peabody, Mass.: Hendrickson, 1991. 361–88.

_____. *The Passion According to Luke: A Redaction Study of Luke's Soteriology.* Theological Inquiries. New York: Paulist, 1985.

_____. ed. *The Social World of Luke-Acts: Models for Interpretation.* Peabody, Mass.: Hendrickson, 1991.

Nowell, I. *Sing a New Song: The Psalms in the Sunday Lectionary.* Collegeville: The Liturgical Press, 1993.

Oakman, D. E. "The Countryside in Luke-Acts," *The Social World of Luke-Acts: Models for Interpretation.* Ed. J. H. Neyrey. Peabody, Mass.: Hendrickson, 1991.

_____. *Jesus and the Economic Question of His Day.* SBEC 8. Lewiston/Queenston: Edwin Mellen, 1986.

_____. "Was Jesus a Peasant? Implications for Reading the Samaritan Story (Luke 10:30-35)," *BTB* 22 (1992) 117–25.

Osiek, C. "Literal Meaning and Allegory," *TBT* 29/5 (1991) 261–66.

_____. *What Are They Saying About the Social Setting of the New Testament?* 2nd ed. New York: Paulist, 1992.

O'Toole, R. "The Parallels Between Jesus and Moses," *BTB* 20 (1990) 22–29.

_____. "Reflections on Luke's Treatment of Jews in Luke-Acts," *Bib* 74 (1993) 529–55.

_____. *The Unity of Luke's Theology: An Analysis of Luke-Acts.* GNS 9. Wilmington, Del.: Glazier, 1984.

Parker, A. *Painfully Clear: The Parables of Jesus.* Biblical Seminar 37. Sheffield: Sheffield Academic Press, 1996.

Parsons, M. C., and R. I. Pervo. *Rethinking the Unity of Luke and Acts.* Minneapolis: Fortress, 1993.

Parvey, C. F. "The Theology and Leadership of Women in the New Testament," *Religion and Sexism. Images of Woman in the Jewish and Christian Traditions.* Ed. R. R. Reuther. New York: Simon & Schuster, 1974. 139–46.

Patte, D. *What Is Structural Exegesis?* Guides to Biblical Scholarship. Philadelphia: Fortress, 1976.

Pazdan, M. M. "Hermeneutics and Proclaiming the Sunday Readings," *In the Company of Preachers.* Ed. R. Siegfried and E. Ruane. Collegeville: The Liturgical Press, 1993. 26–37.

Perelmuter, H. G. *Siblings: Rabbinic Judaism and Early Christianity at Their Beginnings.* New York: Paulist, 1989.

Pervo, R. I. *Profit with Delight: The Literary Genre of the Acts of the Apostles.* Philadelphia: Fortress, 1987.

Pilch, J. J. *The Cultural Dictionary of the Bible.* Collegeville: The Liturgical Press, 1999.

_____. *The Cultural World of Jesus: Sunday by Sunday, Cycle A.* Collegeville: The Liturgical Press, 1995.

_____. *The Cultural World of Jesus: Sunday by Sunday, Cycle C.* Collegeville: The Liturgical Press, 1997.

Pilgrim, W. E. *Good News to the Poor: Wealth and Poverty in Luke-Acts.* Minneapolis: Augsburg, 1981.

Plummer, A. *The Gospel According to S. Luke,* 5th ed. ICC. Edinburgh: T. & T. Clark, 1981.

Pomeroy, S. *Goddesses, Whores, Wives, and Slaves: Women in Classical Antiquity.* New York: Dorset, 1975.

Powell, M. A. *What Are They Saying About Luke?* New York/Mahwah: Paulist Press, 1989.

_____. *What Is Narrative Criticism?* Guides to Biblical Scholarship. Philadelphia: Fortress, 1990.

Praeder, S. M. "Acts 17:1–28:16: Sea Voyages in Ancient Literature and the Theology of Luke-Acts," *CBQ* 46 (1984) 683–706.

_____. *The Word in Women's Worlds: Four Parables.* Zacchaeus Studies, New Testament. Wilmington, Del.: Glazier, 1988.

Price, R. *The Widow Traditions in Luke-Acts: A Feminist-Critical Scrutiny.* SBLDS 155. Atlanta: Scholars, 1997.

Race, M., and L. Brink. *In This Place: Reflections on the Land of the Gospels for the Liturgical Cycles.* Collegeville: The Liturgical Press, 1998.

Ramoroson, L. "'Parole-semence' ou 'Peuple-semence' dans la parabole du Semeur?" *ScEs* 40 (1988) 91–101.

Ramshaw, G. *God Beyond Gender: Feminist Christian God-Language.* Minneapolis: Fortress, 1995.

Reid, B. E. *Choosing the Better Part? Women in the Gospel of Luke.* Collegeville: The Liturgical Press, 1996.

_____. "The Gospel of Luke and the Lectionary," *Liturgy* 90 (1994) 4–8.

_____. "Lost: Two Rebellious Sons—Who Will Find? (Luke 15:11-32)," *The Family Handbook.* Ed. H. Anderson, D. S. Browning, I. S. Evison, and M. S. van Leeuwen. The Family, Religion, and Culture. Louisville: Westminster/John Knox, 1998. 238–41.

_____. "Luke's Mixed Message for Women," *Chicago Studies* 38/3 (1999) 283–97.

_____. "Once Upon a Time . . . Parable and Allegory in the Gospels," *TBT* 29/5 (1991) 267–72.

_____. *Parables for Preachers: Year B.* Collegeville: The Liturgical Press, 1999.

_____. "Preaching Justice Parabolically," *Emmanuel* 102/6 (1996) 342–47.

Rengstorf, K. "*hamartōlos,*" *TDNT* 1 (1964) 325–28.

Rhoads, D. "Social Criticism: Crossing Boundaries," *Mark and Method: New Approaches in Biblical Studies.* Ed. J. C. Anderson and S. D. Moore. Minneapolis: Fortress, 1992. 135–61.

Ricci, C. *Mary Magdalene and Many Others: Women Who Followed Jesus.* Trans. P. Burns. Minneapolis: Fortress, 1994.

Richard, E. "Luke: Author and Thinker," *New Views on Luke and Acts.* Ed. E. Richard. Collegeville: The Liturgical Press, 1990. 15–32.

_____. *New Views on Luke and Acts*. Collegeville: The Liturgical Press, 1990.

Richter, I. "El Poder de una Protagonista. La oración de las personas excluidas (Lk 18, 1-8)," *Ribla* 25 (1997) 59–68.

Ringe, S. H. *Jesus, Liberation, and the Biblical Jubilee: Images for Ethics and Christology*. OBT 19. Philadelphia: Fortress, 1985. 54–60.

_____. *Luke*. Westminster Bible Companion. Louisville: Westminster/John Knox, 1995.

Robbins, V. K. "By Land and Sea: The We-Passages and Ancient Sea Voyages," *Perspectives on Luke-Acts*. Ed. C. H. Talbert. Danville, Va.: Association of Baptist Professors of Religion, 1978. 215–42.

Robinson, J. A. T. "Elijah, John and Jesus: An Essay in Detection," *NTS* 4 (1957–58) 263–81.

Rohrbaugh, R. L. "A Dysfunctional Family and Its Neighbors (Luke 15:11b-32)," *Jesus and His Parables: Interpreting the Parables of Jesus Today*. Ed. V. G. Shillington. Edinburgh: T. & T. Clark, 1997. 141–64.

_____. "A Peasant Reading of the Parable of the Talents/ Pounds: A Text of Terror?" *BTB* 23 (1993) 32–39.

_____. "The Pre-Industrial City in Luke-Acts: Urban Social Relations," *The Social World of Luke-Acts: Models for Interpretation*. Ed. J. H. Neyrey. Peabody, Mass.: Hendrickson, 1991. 125–50.

Rowland, C., and M. Corner. *Liberating Exegesis: The Challenge of Liberation Theology to Biblical Studies*. Louisville: Westminster/John Knox, 1989.

Ruether, R. R. *Gaia and God: An EcoFeminist Theology of Earth Healing*. San Francisco: Harper, 1992.

_____, ed. *Religion and Sexism: Images of Woman in the Jewish and Christian Traditions*. New York: Simon & Schuster, 1974.

_____. *Sexism and God-Talk: Toward a Feminist Theology*. Boston: Beacon, 1983.

Safrai, S., and M. Stern, eds. *The Jewish People in the First Century: Historical Geography, Political History, Social, Cultural and Religious Life and Institutions*. 2 vols. Assen/Amsterdam: Van Gorcum, 1976.

Saldarini, A. J. *Pharisees, Scribes and Sadducees in Palestinian Society: A Sociological Approach*. Wilmington, Del.: Glazier, 1988.

Sanders, E. P. *Jesus and Judaism*, 2nd ed. Philadelphia: Fortress, 1985.

_____. "Sin, Sinners," *The Anchor Bible Dictionary*. Ed. D. N. Freedman. New York: Doubleday, 1997. 6.31–47.

Sanders, J. T. *The Jews in Luke-Acts*. Philadelphia: Fortress, 1987.

Schaberg, J. "How Mary Magdalene Became a Whore," *BibRev* 8 (1992) 30–37, 51–52.

_____. "Luke," *The Women's Bible Commentary*. Ed. C. A. Newsom and S. H. Ringe, rev. ed. Louisville: Westminster/John Knox, 1998. 363–80.

_____. "Thinking Back Through the Magdalene," *Continuum* 2 (1991) 71–90.

Schneiders, S. "God Is More than Two Men and a Bird," *U. S. Catholic* (May 1990) 20–27.

_____. *Women and the Word: The Gender of God in the New Testament and the Spirituality of Women*. New York: Paulist, 1986.

Schottroff, L. *Let the Oppressed Go Free: Feminist Perspectives on the New Testament*. Gender and the Biblical Tradition. Trans. A. S. Kidder. Louisville: Westminster/John Knox, 1991.

Schottroff, L., and W. Stegemann. *Jesus and the Hope of the Poor*. Trans. M. J. O'Connell. Maryknoll: Orbis, 1986.

Schüssler Fiorenza, E. *In Memory of Her: A Feminist Theological Reconstruction of Christian Origins*. New York: Crossroad, 1983.

_____. *Jesus: Miriam's Child, Sophia's Prophet. Critical Issues in Feminist Christology*. New York: Continuum, 1994.

_____, ed. *Searching the Scriptures: A Feminist Commentary*. 2 vols. New York: Crossroad, 1993, 1994.

_____. *Sharing Her Word: Feminist Biblical Interpretation*. Boston: Beacon, 1998.

_____. "'Waiting at Table': A Critical Feminist Theological Reflection on Diakonia," *Diakonia: Church for the Others*. Ed. N. Greinacher and N. Mette. Concilium 198. Edinburgh: T. & T. Clark, 1988. 84–94.

Scott, B. B. *Hear Then the Parable. A Commentary on the Parables of Jesus*. Minneapolis: Fortress, 1989.

Scott, J. C. *The Moral Economy of the Peasant: Rebellion and Subsistence in Southeast Asia*. New Haven: Yale University Press, 1976.

Scott, M. *Sophia and the Johannine Jesus*. JSNTSup 71. Sheffield: JSOT, 1992.

Seccombe, D. P. *Possessions and the Poor in Luke-Acts*. Studien zum Neuen Testament und Seiner Umwelt. Series B, vol. 6. Louvain: Peeters, 1982.

Segal, A. F. *Rebecca's Children: Judaism and Christianity in the Roman World*. Cambridge: Harvard University Press, 1987.

Seim, T. K. *The Double Message: Patterns of Gender in Luke-Acts*. Nashville: Abingdon, 1994.

Sellew, P. "Interior Monologue as a Narrative Device in the Parables of Luke," *JBL* 111 (1992) 239–53.

Shillington, V. G., ed. *Jesus and His Parables: Interpreting the Parables of Jesus Today*. Edinburgh: T. & T. Clark, 1997.

Shirock, R. J. "The Growth of the Kingdom in Light of Israel's Rejection of Jesus: Structure and Theology in Luke 13:1-35," *NovT* 35 (1993) 15–29.

Siegfried, R., and E. Ruane, eds. *In the Company of Preachers.* Collegeville: The Liturgical Press, 1993.

Sim, D. C. "The Women Followers of Jesus: The Implications of Luke 8:1-3," *HeyJ* 30 (1989) 51–62.

Soards, M. L. "The Historical and Cultural Setting of Luke-Acts," *New Views on Luke and Acts.* Ed. E. Richard. Collegeville: The Liturgical Press, 1990. 33–47.

Stegemann, W. *The Gospel and the Poor.* Philadelphia: Fortress, 1984.

Stock, A. "Jesus, Hypocrites, and Herodians," *BTB* 16 (1986) 3–7.

Strack, H., and P. Billerbeck, *Kommentar zum Neuen Testament aus Talmud und Midrasch.* 6 vols. Munich: Beck, 1922–61.

Stuhlmueller, C., ed. *The Collegeville Pastoral Dictionary of Biblical Theology.* Collegeville: The Liturgical Press, 1996.

Swaeles, R. "Jésus, nouvel Elie, dans saint Luc," *AsSeign* 69 (1964) 41–66.

Swartley, W. M. "Unexpected Banquet People (Luke 14:16-24)," *Jesus and His Parables: Interpreting the Parables of Jesus Today.* Ed. V. G. Shillington. Edinburgh: T. & T. Clark, 1997. 177–90.

Talbert, C. H. *Literary Patterns, Theological Themes and the Genre of Luke-Acts.* SBLMS 20. Missoula, Mont.: Scholars Press, 1974.

_____. *Perspectives on Luke-Acts.* Danville, Va.: Association of Baptist Professors of Religion, 1978.

_____. *Reading Luke: A Literary and Theological Commentary on the Third Gospel.* New York: Crossroad, 1988.

Theissen, G. *The Social Setting of Pauline Christianity: Essays on Corinth.* Philadelphia: Fortress, 1982.

Thibeaux, E. "'Known to Be a Sinner': The Narrative Rhetoric of Luke 7:36-50," *BTB* 23/4 (1993) 151–60.

Thurston, B. B. *The Widows: A Women's Ministry in the Early Church.* Minneapolis: Fortress, 1989.

Tolbert, M. A. *Perspectives on the Parables: An Approach to Multiple Interpretations.* Philadelphia: Fortress, 1979.

Topel, L. J. "On the Injustice of the Unjust Steward: Luke 16:1-13," *CBQ* 37 (1975) 216–27.

Trudinger, P. "Exposing the Death of Oppression (Luke 16:1b-8a)," *Jesus and His Parables: Interpreting the Parables of Jesus Today.* Ed. V. G. Shillington. Edinburgh: T. & T. Clark, 1997. 121–37.

Tyson, J., ed., *Luke-Acts and the Jewish People: Eight Critical Perspectives.* Minneapolis: Augsburg, 1988.

van Merrienboer, E. J. "Preaching the Social Gospel," *In the Company of Preachers*. Ed. R. Siegfried and E. Ruane. Collegeville: The Liturgical Press, 1993. 176–90.

Via, D. O. *The Parables: Their Literary and Existential Dimension.* Philadelphia: Fortress, 1967.

Via, E. J. "Women in the Gospel of Luke," *Women in the World's Religions: Past and Present.* Ed. U. King. God in the Contemporary Discussion Series. New York: Paragon House, 1987. 38–55.

Walker, W. O. "Acts and the Pauline Corpus Reconsidered," *JSNT* 24 (1985) 3–23.

Waller, E. "The Parable of the Leaven: A Sectarian Teaching and the Inclusion of Women," *USQR* 35 (1979–80) 99–109.

Weinart, F. "The Parable of the Throne Claimant (Luke 19:12, 14-15a, 27) Reconsidered," *CBQ* 39 (1977) 505–14.

West, F. *Scripture and Memory: The Ecumenical Hermeneutic of the Three-Year Lectionaries.* Collegeville: The Liturgical Press, 1997.

Wiesel, E. *The Gates of the Forest.* Trans. F. Frenaye. New York: Holt, Rinehart and Winston, 1966.

Wilder, A. N. *The Language of the Gospel: Early Christian Rhetoric.* New York: Harper & Row, 1964.

_____. *Jesus' Parables and the War of Myths: Essays on Imagination in the Scripture.* Philadelphia: Fortress, 1982.

Young, B. H. *Jesus and His Jewish Parables: Jewish Tradition and Christian Interpretation.* Peabody, Mass.: Hendrickson, 1988.

_____. *The Parables: Jewish Tradition and Christian Interpretation.* Peabody, Mass.: Hedrickson, 1998.

Zerwick, M. *Biblical Greek: Illustrated by Examples.* Scripta Pontificii Instituti Biblici 114. Rome: Biblical Institute, 1963.